D1636278

10-20

Valley of Democracy

Valley of Democracy

The Frontier versus the Plantation
in the Ohio Valley, 1775-1818

by JOHN D. BARNHART

UNIVERSITY OF NEBRASKA PRESS · LINCOLN

Copyright, 1953, by Indiana University Press
International Standard Book Number 0–8032–5701–5
Library of Congress Catalog Card Number 53–10020
Manufactured in the United States of America

First Bison Book printing: September 1970

977
B262v-p

*Bison Book edition published by arrangement
with Indiana University Press*

IN TRIBUTE

TO

THE AMERICAN UNIVERSITIES

THAT HAVE MADE POSSIBLE STUDY

WITH SUCH SCHOLARS

AS

| Frederick J. Turner | Charles H. Haskins | Clarence W. Alvord |
| Solon J. Buck | Roger B. Merriman | Charles H. McIlwain |

58004

Introduction and Acknowledgments

A NEW and thoroughly American interpretation of the history of the United States took form immediately after the four-hundredth anniversary of the discovery of the New World. In 1892 a young and comparatively unknown professor of history at the University of Wisconsin, Frederick Jackson Turner, called attention to the influence of "free" land in the growth of democracy in the United States.[1] A year later he published a remarkable essay called "The Significance of the Frontier in American History."[2] From time to time he wrote other articles and in 1906 published *The Rise of the New West*. Recognition of the originality and importance of his interpretation came quickly, and in 1910 he joined the history faculty of Harvard University. Ten years later a volume of his articles was published as *The Frontier in American History*. Until his death in 1932 his views were widely accepted and became the basis for rewriting the history of the United States. Much of the latter was the work of his students, many of whom were the products of his classes and seminars at Wisconsin and Harvard. After his death two other volumes of his writings were published.

The newness of Turner's interpretation was due largely to his emphasis on the influence of the American environment. Historical development in this country differed from that in Europe because of geographical features, the unoccupied character of the land, and the continual adaptation of customs and institutions to the primitive conditions which existed on the frontier. This experience of the people on the frontier where they found unoccupied land and the continual recession of the frontier as the settled area expanded was to Turner the most important influence in the history of the United States previous to 1890. From this experience developed the composite nationality of the United States, the particular type of democracy which has become an article of faith with the American people, and the intellectual traits which have differentiated them from the peoples of Europe. Turner did not deny the significance of European influences but did insist upon the greater importance of American factors.

Among those who looked with favor upon this re-evaluation of the American experience was John H. Finley, a university president, editor, and author, who referred to the "Valley of the New Democracy" in his history, *The French in the Heart of North America.* This remark caught the eye of Meredith Nicholson, who produced a volume called *The Valley of Democracy,* in which he dealt generally with the Middle West. Both men were correct; the great basin of the Father of Waters was the home of the new American democracy which Turner said owed its unique character to its experience on the frontier.[3]

But after Turner's death other historians began to question the accuracy of his work. Some critics who contrasted the richness and maturity of European culture with the newness and rawness of American frontier civilization doubted the correctness of the emphasis upon the frontier, while eastern Americans also rejected the implication that the West was more important than the older sections of the nation. Others rejected the idea that American democracy was the product of the frontier.

Students and followers of Turner, who arose to his defense, asserted their confidence in his fundamental conclusions. The discussion has not settled any issues between the two groups but has become largely an exchange of opinions which has generated more heat than light. The question requires a better foundation in historical fact, a testing of the Turner interpretation by an application to a specific area and time.

These considerations were brought together in this study. The Ohio Valley was chosen rather than the Mississippi because the Ohio came first in frontier expansion and because its smaller size and the shorter time involved in its frontier period made such a study more feasible. The history of the development of democracy in the Ohio Valley is first considered at length in order to provide an adequate factual basis. The writings of Turner and his critics are then reviewed in order to learn which adhered more closely to actual events. Quite generally the history of the Valley supports the writings of Turner, and one must conclude that his work adheres quite closely to the facts. His critics produced valuable works which were far more detailed than Turner's articles and which added much to our understanding of the history of the Ohio Valley, but their interpretation, particularly when it deviated from Turner, was not so dependable nor so accurate as his. One and possibly two of them contradict their own statements. In addition to greater detail, these writers have demonstrated the greater importance of certain factors which were not adequately developed by Turner. Among these factors were land speculation and the plantation. Consequently, the Turner interpretation does not come off unscathed.

The greater opportunity for historians, it seems to me, lies in supplementing and completing Turner's work rather than in trying to refute it. For instance, when did the frontier period in each section of the country come to an end? What was the nature of the economic organization that took the place of the frontier? What different influences came to bear upon the people when the frontier had been replaced by the plantation or by a commercial or industrial type of society? To answer these and other questions will be far more useful than to find an error or a misemphasis in the work of Turner.

A simple statement of my debts to historians and librarians would be too long to publish in this place. Among the historians, I should begin with Frederick J. Turner, Clarence W. Alvord, and Solon J. Buck, who awakened my love for the history of the West. Tom Clark helped to secure photostats of the early conventions of Kentucky. Paul Angle and the late Theodore C. Pease aided in acquiring published materials and photostats of early newspapers of Illinois. Stanley J. Folmsbee located information about some of the members of the Tennessee Constitutional Convention. Wendell H. Stephenson encouraged the work by publishing several early papers in the *Journal of Southern History*. Unfortunately, I failed to preserve the names of many librarians who made available the materials of their respective institutions. Such institutions range from Washington, D.C., and Williamsburg in the east to St. Louis in the west; from Cleveland, Chicago, and Madison, Wisconsin, in the north to New Orleans in the south. Occasionally a small municipal library like the one at Chillicothe, Ohio, or a small college library like the Transylvania Library at Lexington, Kentucky, possessed important newspaper collections. Almost without exception the librarians rendered every assistance possible. The various collections are listed in the bibliography. Dr. Albert L. Kohlmeier, Dr. Leonard Lundin, and Dean O. O. Winther, my colleagues at Indiana University, were kind enough to read this manuscript and to offer their suggestions.

Contents

Valley of Democracy

I

Planters Versus Yeomen

*H*OWEVER indebted the United States may be for the governmental forms and the liberal influences which the colonists brought to the New World, American democracy was not imported from Europe. From England came the common law, local government, and legislative and judicial organization, to name only a few of the significant contributions from the British Isles. From France came the philosophy and the example of the French Revolution, which gave a tremendous stimulus to Americans who were debating the policies and establishing the precedents which were to determine the character of their own nation for at least a century. From the Protestant Revolution came the right of the individual to determine for himself the most important questions in the world: the nature of God, the methods of worship, and the means of salvation. Political rights could hardly be denied after these spiritual privileges had been granted. But in addition to the benefits which these influences may have contributed to the development of democracy, something else was added in the New World.

American democracy was the result of a long struggle in which a number of significant victories were won in the Ohio Valley. The frontiersmen strove to achieve freedom from the states of the Atlantic coast, white manhood suffrage, equal representation according to numbers, and the right to seek elective office without meeting property qualifications. As a result of the control they hoped to gain by the adoption of these reforms, they would be able to establish freedom and equality of opportunity and to eliminate the discriminations under which they labored. Their faith in the worth of the common man led them to demand these reforms and to believe that—once they had accomplished them—the people could solve their own problems. These ideas constituted their conception of democracy.

3

Whatever aided them in destroying the aristocracy inherited from colonial days, whatever helped them to increase the control of the majority, these changes were democratic advances.

The contest may be traced back, for present purposes, to the South Atlantic States and to Pennsylvania at the time the Declaration of Independence was adopted. On one side of the controversy were the unenfranchised and those who were unequally represented in the state legislatures. Arrayed against them were those who doubted the wisdom of granting to all freemen an equal voice in government. The yeomen or farmers sought to make their states representative and responsive to their needs and aspirations, to abolish minority control and other aristocratic features which had been brought from Europe. West of the Appalachian Mountains, impatient frontiersmen who were not protected by existing governments and whose needs were not understood by Eastern officials endeavored to set up their own organizations. Naturally, the governments they founded were less aristocratic than those of the Atlantic seaboard, but to achieve permanence for their work, freedom had to be obtained from the older states. As they conquered the wilderness and marked the trails over the mountains, they found in their midst men who desired to transfer to the Ohio Valley the minority control which the planters and other wealthy groups had established along the coast; therefore, the struggle between planters and yeomen continued, especially south of the Ohio River. Only north of the Ohio were the forces working for democracy strong enough to check the advance of the planter. A realization of the continuity of the struggle is essential to an understanding of the democracy of the frontier.

The life of the English country gentleman was the ideal of the Tidewater planters of the eighteenth and nineteenth centuries. Emulation was more usual than achievement, but the ideal ruled this most picturesque of American societies.[1] Gentlemen managed their plantations and slaves, manipulated government and politics, and with the aid of their ladies dominated society. Although there were many small farmers, the determination of affairs, throughout the Tidewater from Maryland to Georgia, was largely in the hands of the planters.

Economically, this society was characterized by the predominance of an agricultural system based upon servile labor and large-scale production of staple crops for distant markets. Geographically, it stretched along the seacoast and extended westward, generally to the Piedmont. The success of tobacco culture in the Tidewater of Maryland and Virginia and of rice and indigo along the coast of South Carolina and Georgia created two centers of plantation life. Politically, this social order was an aristocracy of the wealthy and the well-born, some of whom showed a sincere attachment to and ability in the public service. Among them, however, were many who were only slightly concerned about the public welfare, and others whose speculations and peculations stained the records of this significant group. Religiously, the planters were generally identified with deism and the Anglican church, which was not entirely tolerant of less "respectable" faiths. Socially, they formed an order of ladies and gentlemen whose wealth and servants made possible the cultivation of the art of leisure, extensive and even lavish entertainment, and a genuine appreciation of all that constituted good living. Their aristocratic way of life was reflected in balls, dances, horse races, and fox hunts. Established families passed on prominent names, large estates, plantation homes, and pride of lineage. It was an attractive and highly developed American social order.

Beyond this domain of the planter lay a vast area of great beauty and marked variety, an area which has played an important role in the development of the American nation. This mountainous region reached from Pennsylvania on the north through Georgia to the south and from the western edge of the Tidewater to the glaciated plains of the Old Northwest and to the Gulf Coastal Plains of the southwest. The rivers were not broad arms of the sea as in the Chesapeake region, but sometimes were dashing mountain streams and sometimes were quietly moving ribbons of placid water winding between gently rolling hills. The landscape varied from the red and yellow hills of the undulating Piedmont to the awe-inspiring view of forested mountains enveloped in blue and gray haze. As the frontiersman looked about him from the top of the Blue Ridge, the Allegheny Front, or the Cumberland Mountains, he beheld a land of indescribable beauty, a land of lovely mountains and graceful valleys. This wide area included the Piedmont, the Blue Ridge, the Great Valley, and the Appalachian Plateau.

Into these hills and mountains and valleys came the pioneers in as great variety as the region they occupied. Exploration began in the seventeenth century when a few of the bolder Virginians entered the Piedmont in search of trade or adventure. Many factors soon caused others to follow the trails of the first pioneers. Primarily the lack of unoccupied land that was suitably located and low in price induced many farmers and many indentured servants who had finished their term of service, to seek land farther west. Secondly the rise of the plantation system, the increasing number of Negro slaves, the expansion of the area of tobacco culture, and the restrictions by Great Britain on the tobacco market produced falling prices and harsher competition. Many of the smaller farmers, who were affected most adversely, sold out to their more opulent neighbors and departed for the West. Some men of wealth obtained large grants of land in the western region on condition that they settle a certain number of persons on the grant.[2] This condition they could meet and still keep considerable tracts of land for themselves. Planters and farmers labored together to develop a new section, but the yeomen farmers were the more numerous.

A great horde of pioneers came from Pennsylvania, where Scotch-Irish and German emigrants were entering the New World in search of privileges withheld in the Old. Thousands of them were moving south and southwestward along the limestone valleys of Pennsylvania to the Maryland Piedmont and the fertile Hagerstown Valley, both of which were largely unoccupied when this migration began. Others crossed the Potomac to the Virginia Piedmont and the Shenandoah Valley. As additional settlers required more land, the migration continued along the western side of the Blue Ridge until the Roanoke River Gap was reached, where many poured southeastward into the Virginia Piedmont and on into the Carolinas and Georgia.

The Virginia Piedmont was not an isolated region, for it was easily accessible from the Tidewater along the river valleys. Settled by a westward movement of people from the lowland as well as by Germans and Scotch-Irish from north of the Potomac, it was therefore less English than the Tidewater and less German and Scotch-Irish than the Valley of Virginia. The western border of the Piedmont was the Blue Ridge Mountains, a low, narrow range which extended in a northeasterly-southwesterly direction but became wider and higher toward the southwest. At several passes near Winchester and at the Roanoke in Virginia the Blue Ridge was comparatively easy to cross. As the Piedmont was occupied, and as the plantation system crowded out the pioneer farmers, a considerable number of the latter joined the migration already progressing west of the mountains.

The Piedmont was less accessible in Carolina than in Virginia, for it was farther removed from the large ports of entry and from the densely settled areas and because the Pine Barrens and Sand Hills along the Fall Line discouraged the movement of planters from the Tidwater. The lateness of settlement and the small number of indentured servants in the Carolinas had delayed the accumulation of a surplus population. For these reasons the Piedmont was settled first by an overflow from Virginia and by the migration coming through the Blue Ridge from the Great Valley. The latter was composed chiefly of Scotch-Irish and Germans who cultivated small farms with free labor or with the aid of a few slaves. A distinctive element in the overflow from Virginia was the Quakers, who became very important in the north-central portion of North Carolina.

But not all of the migration progressing along the west side of the Virginia Blue Ridge passed into Carolina. A portion of it moved into southwestern Virginia and into the valleys which form the headwaters of the Tennessee, where the famous Watauga settlement was founded in 1769. Hardy hands reached the Kentucky Bluegrass just as the Revolution was beginning, and, before the conflict ended, others moved to the French Lick or Nashville region on the Cumberland River. In this manner a vast peninsula had been thrust into the South along both sides of the Blue Ridge Mountains. Its outposts were in Georgia and the Bluegrass basins of what became Kentucky and Tennessee. Altogether it formed the southern part of Frederick J. Turner's Old West and its extension into the Ohio Valley.[3]

The society founded by these pioneers of the back country, rather than the civilization of the planters, was characteristic of the nation they were building. Many racial and national strains contributed to this new society, the larger elements of which were the Scotch-Irish, Germans, and English, the smaller the Welsh, Irish, and French.[4] The religious life was also something of a mosaic. English, Welsh, and German Quakers, together with German Lutherans, Pietists, Dunkers, and Mennonites were intermixed and scattered along with the Scotch-Irish Presbyterians and other faiths. The small number of Anglicans or Episcopalians afforded another significant contrast to the lowland. The Scotch-Irish were Presbyterians and their church broke the path to the interior for other sects. The Baptists and Methodists, coming a little later, found here a productive field for recruiting both members and ministers. Although many of these people were very devoted to their own church and hostile toward other beliefs, the diversity of sects made tolerance a necessary policy for government.

Engaged in forming a democratic and individualistic society, a considerable element among the pioneers supported majority rule in politics, the extension of suffrage to all adult white males without regard to property, equal representation in the legislature, and the protection of civil rights. The economic basis for this democratic society was the small farm which was so typical of the region. It was tilled by the owner with the aid of the members of his family or perhaps a slave or two. Cereals and livestock were the important products. In contrast to the waste and extravagance of the planters, who raised staples on an extensive scale, the back-country farmers were thrifty and cultivated the land intensively. Artisans, too, were comparatively more important in the West than in the Tidewater.[5] Plantations were to be found here and there, especially in the Valley of Virginia and along the river valleys of the Piedmont, where conditions eventually came to approximate those of the Tidewater; but they represented the invasion of the planter society rather than the predominant culture of the Appalachian region. The planters were also somewhat counterbalanced in the back country by men in hunting shirts and coonskin caps who depended upon their long rifles and hunting knives for much of their living.

Social and cultural activity was also different. Work on the farm and in the home limited the leisure of the yeomen class. Social gatherings, such as weddings, funerals, house raisings, harvest festivals, and court days, tended to center about the church and the events of everyday life. Many were strongly opposed to slavery because it tended to degrade labor, to lower living standards, and to induce grave social problems. In the main, a self-sufficient, individualistic, and democratic society of white men and women opposed planter domination of state governments, while many of them were unhappy about the movement of slavery and the plantation system to their section of the country.

Among the settlers in the Valley of the Appalachians were those who kept in touch with events in Pennsylvania, where many of them had begun their trek to the frontier. Antagonism between the exposed frontiersmen of Pennsylvania and the peace-loving Quakers had arisen during the French and Indian War. To maintain control of the colonial assembly the aristocracy refused the franchise to the laboring people of Philadelphia and equal representation in the legislature to the frontiersmen of the western counties.[6]

In Pennsylvania the colonial aristocracy was composed of wealthy farmers, merchants, and bankers, most of whom were Quakers. Located chiefly in the city of Philadelphia and the near-by counties of Philadelphia, Chester, and Bucks, they were generally supported by the German Pietists, such as the Moravians, Mennonites, and Dunkers, who were quite numerous in Lancaster, Berks, and North-hampton counties. Frontiersmen in the western counties of York, Cumberland, Bedford, Northumberland, and Westmoreland, together with the laborers of Philadelphia, were not in sympathy with the aristocracy.[7]

In the agitation preceding the Revolution, the aristocracy, which took the colonial side, utilized the constitutional argument about representation and taxation without realizing that it applied almost as well to the disenfranchised of Philadelphia and the inadequately represented frontiersmen as it did to the colonies in the British empire. When, however, the resistance to England began to develop into a war for independence, many Quakers held back and in time became Tories. But the lower classes of Philadelphia and the frontiersmen organized committees of safety and military associations, overthrew the colonial administration, called a constitutional convention, and organized a new government based on the authority of the people.[8]

The constitution gave to the freemen the right to elect the members of the unicameral legislative assembly.[9] Elections were to be held annually, and the voters were not required to meet a property qualification. Representation in the legislature was distributed on the basis of taxable inhabitants and was to be reapportioned every seven years. This popularly elected legislature was the most powerful branch of the government; the executive was weak, but the judiciary was relatively independent. The bill of rights granted freedom of religion and speech, trial by jury, and other civil rights, and declared that it was not to be violated on any pretense whatever. These developments ended the control of the colonial aristocracy in Pennsylvania.

This democratic victory was in sharp contrast to the limited successes of the popular forces on both sides of the southern mountains. The men of the West tried to pattern their political institutions in part after those of the great state at the northern end of the highway which connected the Piedmont of North Carolina and the Valley of East Tennessee with Philadelphia. It will be interesting to note a little later that the more liberal forces of the state of Franklin and the radicals of Kentucky showed preference for parts of the Pennsylvania government.

In the older settled areas the colonists began the contest for independence from England. The rebels organized states to take the place of colonial governments. To make the new commonwealths democratic and representative rather than aristocratic, the pioneers of the back country of the South struggled with the planters.

In Maryland and South Carolina the proprietary governments had left a heritage of feudalism and an aristocratic class firmly intrenched. Although Virginia was not a proprietary colony, its aristocratic leaders were more influential and powerful than those of its neighbors. In Georgia the planter class was newest and weakest, but nevertheless it managed to protect itself. The land system of the Southern colonies, which was feudal in character, had been utilized to build up an aristocracy by means of discrimination in favor of the wealthy.

Control in South Carolina was obviously in the hands of the rice and indigo planters who led the social order of the Tidewater. They feared the Scotch-Irish and German farmers of the back country, "part of the rolling piedmont frontier, which stretched away southwestwardly from Pennsylvania to Georgia." [10] These two societies were separated by the middle country, a sandy, hilly area covered with pine forests which lay between the coastal region and the Piedmont. Being unsuited to the staples of the colonial lowland, it was at first more like the back country. Failure of the colony to extend local government to the interior led to lawlessness and to the formation of groups of border ruffians, as well as the organization of bands of regulators to hold them in check. The legal settlement of some disputes on the frontier required a long journey to Charleston. Because of the concentration there of the homes of the planters and because of property qualifications upon office holding and voting and inequality of representation, the control of the state was held by the city. Reluctant to surrender its exclusive privileges, the aristocracy exacted the maintenance of the established church as the price for the grant of local government and representation in the colonial legislature, although that church was unpopular on the frontier. The people of the Upland were regarded as intruders, and any possibility of their controlling the government and using its powers to the prejudice of the planter class was vigorously opposed. Consequently, in the organization of state government representation was not based upon population. It has been said, "Apparently no principle had ever been followed, unless it was that of giving the low country a good, safe majority." [11] Even the functions of local government were placed largely in the hands of commissions appointed by the legislature, thus giving the planter element considerable influence throughout the state.

South Carolina was the first Southern colony to draw up a state constitution. On March 26, 1776, preceded only by New Hampshire, its provincial congress adopted a temporary plan which gave 126 members in the general assembly to the low country and only 76 to the middle and up country. The right of voting was restricted to freeholders of 100 acres or of property valued at £60, or to persons who paid a tax of 10 shillings. Civil rights were all but ignored.[12]

Virginia's remarkable group of statesmen soon made notable contributions to American independence and self-government. George Mason produced the Virginia bill of rights, which has been followed directly or indirectly by all who have prepared an American bill of rights. Thomas Jefferson penned the Declaration of Independence, another significant expression of revolutionary philosophy. But Virginia's new constitution, adopted June 29, 1776, was more conservative than these documents. It created an all-powerful legislature, the members of which were not fairly apportioned; it made no change in the franchise, which was limited to freeholders; and it perpetuated the oligarchy of rich Tidewater planters.[13]

That the first constitution of Maryland possessed undemocratic features is not strange since an aristocracy was in control at the end of the colonial period. There were high property qualifications for office holding. Members of the lower house of the assembly were required to own property evaluated at £500, while senators and members of the governor's council were to hold at least twice that amount. The franchise was restricted to freemen who possessed 50 acres of land or property of £30 value. Members of the senate were indirectly elected by an electoral college from the state at large, nine from the western shore and six from the eastern.[14] Economic and social elements of dissent were aggravated by an unequal distribution of representation. Large counties were formed in the Piedmont and western parts of the state, where the settlers were largely German and Scotch-Irish, and where climatic and geographic forces discouraged the plantation system. Although the inhabitants, especially the freemen, were greater in number than in the small eastern counties, the same number of representatives was assigned to each.

In North Carolina the antagonism between Tidewater and Upland was even more pronounced than in Virginia. "A long period of pre-Revolutionary mismanagement had destroyed the faith of the frontier settlers in the wisdom and justice of the rule of the older, more populous, and wealthier seaboard." [15] Because government had been inefficient and corrupt, one of the most tragic and severe conflicts between the Piedmont and the Lowland took place in this colony. Local officials, who were appointed by the governor and council, charged excessive fees, administered tax laws to the injury of the western farmers, and foreclosed on their farms in such manner that wealthy members of the ruling class acquired the property at very low figures. When the courts failed them and the governor dissolved the assembly, the oppressed turned to armed resistance. The defeat of the popular party at the Alamance River and the execution of seven of its leaders stimulated migration and left much bitterness among those who remained in North Carolina.[16]

Because the radical forces were fairly strong in 1776, the state's first constitution has been classified as radical; nevertheless several conservative features were inserted in it. Property and religious qualifications for office holding and property requirements for voting for state senators were stipulated. Representation was not based upon population. The arrangement by which each county was to elect one senator and two members of the House of Commons may not have been particularly unfair in 1776, but the growth of population in the large western counties soon created inequalities which perpetuated Eastern domination after that region had become a minority section.[17]

Georgia's first constitution is considered one of the more democratic of the Revolutionary period, because it provided for a unicameral legislature and contained liberal provisions for voting. The apportionment of representation, however, was so unequal as to be inversely proportioned to population. It enabled the planters to retain control and actually to make the next constitution less democratic.[18]

The first constitutions of the Southern states left much to be desired. Although the bills of rights recognized the radical philosophy of the Revolutionary movement and the governments were republican in form, they were not democratic, nor were they intended to be. In them the planter class preserved its dominant position and inscribed its victory in constitutional law. Representation was based not upon white population or upon the total population, not upon wealth or the payment of taxes, but upon the assumption that planter control was necessary. The early capitals were located in the Tidewater and therefore far from the homes of the western legislators; distance was likely to reduce the attendance of representatives from the counties already inadequately represented. Property and religious qualifications for office holding and voting excluded large numbers of people, especially in the western districts. Some of the soldiers who fought for independence were not eligible to vote when they returned home. Because they were called upon to pay taxes and serve in the militia, they felt that the bills of rights justified their demand for the franchise.

The struggle for democracy and equal representation, which had only begun, continued in periods of varying intensity until it was interrupted by the Civil War. During the remainder of the eighteenth century much criticism of the first constitutions was expressed, and various efforts were made to democratize government in the Southern states. The drafting and adoption of the federal constitution stimulated interest in political science and created a need for revision of state governmental machinery to bring it into harmony with the new constitutional law of the nation. Consequently reformers were active during the later part of the century, and new state constitutions were modeled directly or indirectly upon the federal instrument. The second decade of the nineteenth century was also a period of intense criticism and activity in the South Atlantic states. During this period the forces of reform were generally defeated, although some advance was registered through amendments. During the thirties still another wave of reform swept over these states, this time resulting in the calling of constitutional conventions; but again success was limited. It is not possible to

state what relationship may have existed between these reform
epochs and migration to the West, but it is interesting to note that
they occurred contemporaneously with periods of large emigration
to the interior. The second decade of the century was the period of
the Great Migration, 1814–1819, and the decade of the thirties saw
the Jacksonian Migration, 1828–1837.

During the later years of the eighteenth century, primogeniture
and entails were abolished in Maryland, but the conservative senate
defeated most other reform efforts.[19] Thus began the long fight of
the slave interests against change, in which they defeated, for
seventy-five years, every effort to obtain a new constitution.

The western representatives in Virginia, under the leadership of
Thomas Jefferson and James Madison, initiated a reform movement to eliminate the abuses of the old order. Entails and primogeniture were abolished, religious freedom was granted, and finally
the Anglican church was disestablished. Agitation against slavery
and for a statewide system of education was not successful. During
the Revolution, the capital was moved westward from Williamsburg to Richmond, but even the latter was a long distance from
southwestern Virginia, and especially Kentucky. These concessions
were secured by legislative enactment and not by constitutional
reform. In 1783 and again in 1794 efforts were made to secure constitutional revision, but both were defeated by the conservative
Tidewater region.[20]

The planters of the South Carolina Tidewater skillfully met the
demands for reform in their state. Growth of population and
wealth made concessions almost inevitable, but the concessions did
not endanger planter control. Although democratic reforms were
adopted, the government did not become democratic. Only with
difficulty did the popular party force the adoption of the permanent constitution of 1778, and in it they won only a few of their
demands. Since the Revolution had weakened the Anglican church,
the new constitution placed all Protestant churches in an equal
position, except that the Episcopal church retained its property.
The religious branch of the aristocracy lost strength by this change.
Property qualifications for voting were reduced, but, in return, the
property qualifications for holding office were increased. Apportionment of representation was the real point at issue: "the up
country had 11 senators and 58 representatives, while the tidewater,
with far less population, was given 19 senators and 144 represent-

atives. Thus the system of government was left in the control of the rich, aristocratic tidewater region." [21]

The concessions of 1778 did not long quiet the demand for reform. An act of 1785 granted the written ballot in place of vivavoce voting and other acts created two new counties, thus giving the up country two more senators and six more representatives. When the adoption of the federal constitution seemed to require changes in the state constitution, a convention was called, but the planters exacted the same representation as in the legislature. In other words, they would not permit a convention unless they were assured control. When the convention met, in 1790, the aristocrats again exacted an apportionment that enabled them to retain control of the new legislature. Property qualifications for officeholders were reduced but not eliminated, and requirements for voters were liberalized by the removal of the religious restriction. The capital was removed to Columbia, but much of the state's business remained in Charleston. Freedom of religion was granted, and the legislature was charged to abolish primogeniture and entails as "soon as may be convenient." The changes were not insignificant, but white manhood suffrage and a truly representative government were not secured.

Although Georgia was the youngest of the colonies and the most restricted in its early development, conditions conformed to the general pattern of the other South Atlantic states. After the admission of slavery in 1751 the narrow coastal district developed into a plantation region comparable to the Tidewater of South Carolina. Just above this center of aristocratic society were the Pine Barrens, into which many poor people moved after the expiration of their indenture contracts or after selling their holdings to the rising planter class. Beyond this area stretched the upper Coastal Plain and still higher the Piedmont. Pioneers moving from the north settled the last of these regions. During the Revolution the rice and indigo planters suffered considerably, and officials found it impossible to keep the state government functioning.

The convention called to ratify the federal constitution decided to frame a new state constitution, which was amended by a second convention and adopted by a third. A bicameral legislature was substituted for the unicameral body, qualifications for office holding were increased, and inequality in representation was continued. Although more white people lived in the up country than in the low and although the total populations of the two regions were nearly equal, the counties below the Fall Line elected more than two thirds of the members of the legislature.

Six years later a third constitution was adopted, the chief issue before the convention having been the apportionment of representation. The counties below the Fall Line retained forty-two members out of a total of seventy-one in both houses; the state capital, however, was removed to Louisville, which was near the Fall Line.

A fourth attempt to secure a fair apportionment of representation was made in 1798. The constitution of that year professed to base membership in the lower house upon the federal ratio, "free white persons and . . . three-fifths of all the people of color," but made that profession meaningless by limitations. Regardless of population, each county was to have one member; a county having three thousand persons according to the federal ratio was to have two members; a county having seven thousand persons, three members; and one having twelve thousand persons, four, which was the largest representation. Obviously, this gave an advantage to counties with small populations and was not actually based on the federal ratio. Every county was also to have one senator, regardless of population, and there were fourteen counties in the low country and ten in the up country. Since measures had to be adopted by the senate as well as the house, it appears that little had been surrendered. The century drew to a close without a state government that was truly representative of its people.[22]

But the struggle for democratic and representative government in the Southern states did not come to an end with the turn of the century. As growth and prosperity came to the western counties, their people felt even more important. The plantation system and slavery gradually spread westward under the stimulus of the possibilities produced by the cotton gin and the increased demand for Southern staples. Naturally these developments changed the sectional alignment, but they did not satisfy the desires of the West. During the first twenty years of the nineteenth century efforts were made in each of the states to revise the existing constitutions.

Liberals in Virginia, bolstered by Jefferson's support, presented their demands to the legislature at every session for a decade, 1806–1816. The only tangible result was reapportionment of representation in the senate, a meaningless victory.[23]

The growth of the western counties of North Carolina created inequalities which occasioned a movement for constitutional revision. According to an estimate made in 1816, 37 counties with a white population of 150,000 elected 111 members of the House of Commons, while 25 counties with a white population of 230,000 elected only 75. Had representation been based upon white population the number of representatives apportioned to the two groups would have almost exactly reversed these figures. Resolutions were introduced in the legislature on three occasions (1808, 1811, and 1816) to call a constitutional convention, and the legislature in 1819–1820 was chiefly concerned with this question, but all of these efforts came to naught.[24]

Although reform seemed hopeless, Maryland in 1810 amended her constitution of 1776 to establish white manhood suffrage and voting by ballot, and to abolish property qualifications and plural voting, but unequal representation kept the government in the hands of the men of the low country.[25] South Carolina rearranged its representation in proportion to white population and taxes and adopted white manhood suffrage.[26] Georgia made additional officials elective, but none of these states was willing to call a convention or attack seriously the problem of representation.[27]

Evasion of the question was not to continue, for the decade of the thirties witnessed conventions in Virginia, North Carolina, and Georgia, together with a marked revision of Maryland's constitution by a series of amendments. Six years of agitation resulted in the call of the Virginia convention of 1829–1830. Here again the conservative Easterners refused thoroughgoing concessions, although the radicals struggled bitterly. Suffrage was extended to taxpayers and representation was reapportioned, but not upon a definite principle. The reformers were disappointed and the men of the Trans-Allegheny voted five to one to reject the constitution, which was adopted in spite of their opposition because of the support of the other parts of the state.[28] In Georgia after considerable agitation and the threat of an "extralegal convention" the legislature called a convention in 1833. The reapportionment of representation which it proposed was regarded as unsatisfactory and was rejected by the voters. Approximately the same procedure was followed in respect to a convention in 1839. The sectional alignment had changed considerably since Revolutionary days, and the opposition to reapportionment came from counties with small populations whether rich or poor. But the planters of the Tidewater were still unwilling to give Georgia a democratic and representative government.[29] In North Carolina agitation, which was more or less continuous during the twenties, reached a climax in 1833 and 1834. The legislature submitted the question of a convention to the people, who approved the meeting of such an assembly. The new constitution based representation in the senate upon taxes and in the house of representatives upon the federal ratio. In addition to other less important changes, the governor was made elective by the people. The revision was popular in the western counties and was ratified by a small majority.[30]

Maryland also joined the reform movement, but only after conditions had reached such a state that popular revolt was a possibility. Perhaps the acme of reaction was reached in the appointment of a committee of the legislature "to inquire into the expediency of reporting a bill making it a high crime and misdemeanor for citizens to conspire against the constitution of the state." At this time the legislature would not call a constitutional convention to express the wishes of the people, and the constitution perpetuated an unrepresentative government. The committee reported that sufficient protection against rebellion existed in the power of the governor to call out the militia and to summon a special session of the legislature, in the law of conspiracy, which was a part of the common law, and in the statute law which provided penalties for resisting the government. It did not suggest the reapportionment of representation, which was at the heart of the trouble. The legislature, which preferred to adopt amendments rather than to call a convention, provided that the governor and senators were to be popularly elected. The latter were apportioned one to each county and one to Baltimore City; the lower house according to the federal ratio in a manner reasonably fair to all except Baltimore.[31]

Further crises occurred and continued concessions were made in the different states, but none adopted a permanently fair representation. The ruling class continued to protect slavery, both from hostile legislation and equal taxation, and to prevent western counties from securing internal improvements equally with the eastern counties and from adopting systems of public education.[32]

Qualifications for voting and office holding, the apportionment of representation, and the development of democratic government were not abstract and debatable theories concerning the wisdom of placing government in the control of the wealthy, the well-educated, and the well-born, in place of majority rule and manhood suffrage. These nondemocratic restrictions made possible an imperialistic attempt to control the West as far as the Mississippi and a series of efforts to seize the western lands for personal speculation regardless of the welfare of the settlers.[33] Planter control was partly responsible for the fact that frontier homes were unprotected from the ravages of Indian warfare—warfare which was often caused by frontier aggression. The minority granted special privileges to the plantation system in its contest with the small farms of the yeomen, protected slave property from equal taxation, and also denied the western counties equal expenditures for internal improvements. Such antagonism was created that western Virginia, although it was forced to bide its time until the Civil War, finally formed the separate state of West Virginia. All these things resulted from the aristocratic and undemocratic government of the wealthy, the educated, and the well-born. It is not surprising that the democratic masses, too independent to tolerate the injustice inherent in planter control, should have migrated in considerable numbers to new territories and new states where opportunities existed to establish a more democratic social, political, and economic order.

Not slavery alone, not lack of the franchise, not property qualifications, unequal representation, and unjust taxation, but something larger than these was at stake. The basic issue was the right of the people to establish a democratic society. The contest was between a democratic society and an aristocratic society, and the aristocrats not only refused to surrender a control secured in the colonial period, but they continued to use that control to maintain special advantages which democracy would most certainly have destroyed.[34]

2

The Highways of Frontier Expansion

THE APPALACHIAN Mountains tended to restrict the cultures that had developed along the Atlantic coast and gave opportunity for the formation of a new sectional culture in the interior, even though the political boundaries of the Atlantic states often ignored the dividing line. The mountain ridges, the valleys, and the passes, which determined the course of the roads, influenced the migration of the pioneers who founded the states of the Ohio Valley and thus affected the development of the interior.

The mountains extended from the northeast, where they lie only a short distance from the sea, to the southwest, where their peaks are three hundred miles from the coast. The Appalachian Valley is open to the east in the vicinity of Philadelphia because the Blue Ridge does not extend north of the Potomac River and such ridges as exist are neither continuous nor formidable. As far to the southwestward as the Roanoke River the Valley is drained by rivers that empty into the Atlantic Ocean, and each of them affords a means of access to the Valley. The Blue Ridge from the Potomac to the Roanoke is neither high nor wide and may be crossed at several points besides the river gaps. The Valley is bounded on the west by the sharp escarpment known as the Allegheny Front, and beyond is the vast plateau, which is mountainous near the Valley and wider in the north than in the south.

The Valley was the natural route for the migrations that first left the Philadelphia area and later Maryland and northern Virginia. A road was soon evident from Philadelphia to Lancaster and York, which the German and Scotch-Irish immigrants soon extended into the Hagerstown Valley of Maryland and the Valley of Virginia as they pushed toward the unoccupied land on the frontier. This route, which was much easier than the trails across the mountains

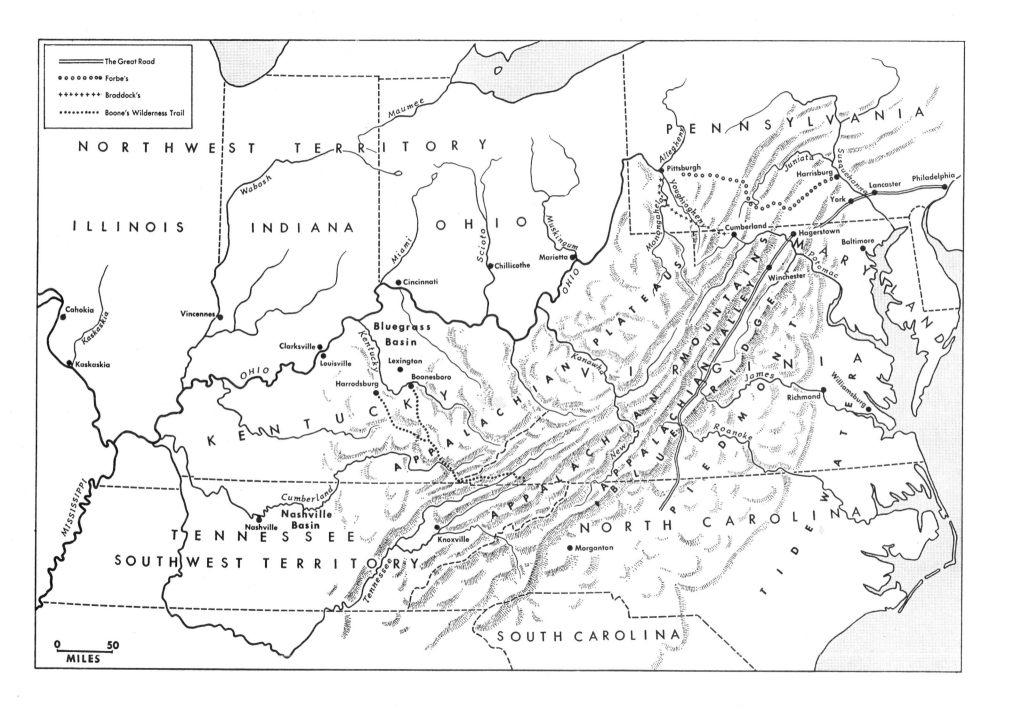

NORTHWEST · **TERRITORY**

PENNSYLVANIA

ILLINOIS · **INDIANA** · **OHIO**

MARYLAND

VIRGINIA

APPALACHIAN PLATEAUS

APPALACHIAN RIDGE AND VALLEYS

BLUE RIDGE MOUNTAINS

APPALACHIAN MOUNTAINS

PIEDMONT

KENTUCKY

TENNESSEE

NORTH CAROLINA

SOUTHWEST TERRITORY

SOUTH CAROLINA

TIDEWATER

Legend:
- ──── The Great Road
- ooooooo Forbe's
- +++++++ Braddock's
- ⋯⋯⋯ Boone's Wilderness Trail

Rivers and places:
Maumee, Wabash, Miami, Scioto, Muskingum, Ohio, Allegheny, Monongahela, Youghiogheny, Juniata, Susquehanna, Potomac, Kanawha, New, James, Roanoke, Cumberland, Tennessee, Kentucky, Mississippi, Kaskaskia

Cities: Pittsburgh, Harrisburg, Lancaster, Philadelphia, York, Cumberland, Hagerstown, Baltimore, Winchester, Williamsburg, Richmond, Marietta, Chillicothe, Cincinnati, Vincennes, Cahokia, Kaskaskia, Clarksville, Louisville, Harrodsburg, Lexington, Boonesboro, Nashville, Knoxville, Morganton

Regions: Bluegrass Basin, Nashville Basin

0 — 50 MILES

to the west, became the highway of the Old West, the first great road of frontier expansion.

On the map drawn in 1751, by Joshua Fry and Peter Jefferson it was called "The Great Road from the Yadkin River thro Virginia to Philadelphia." [1] More appropriate would have been "The Great Road from Philadelphia thro Virginia to the Yadkin River." Into the Shenandoah Valley from the north, it led the settlers through Martinsburg and Winchester, along the North Fork of the Shenandoah River through Strasburg, Woodstock, and New Market to Staunton. It made its way over the low divide to Lexington on the headwaters of the James River, and along these streams and across another low divide to the tributaries of the Roanoke. When the Fry and Jefferson map was drawn, the road turned to the southeast through the Roanoke Gap, and the immigrants following its path turned with it to the Yadkin country in the Carolina Piedmont. The road thus reveals the destination of the thousands who trudged along its way in the middle of the century. Governor William Tryon, of North Carolina, confirmed this fact when he wrote (August 2, 1766), "I am of opinion this province is settling faster than any on the continent, last autumn and winter, upwards of one thousand wagons passed thro' Salisbury with families from the northward, to settle in this province chiefly. . . ." [2]

Before this date, however, other settlers began to push through the Valley of Virginia beyond the Roanoke Gap toward the headwaters of the Tennessee. Dr. Thomas Walker in 1750 passed over New River at Inglis'; apparently the ferry had not yet been started, since he wrote, "we were obliged to swim our Horses over." [3] He mentioned a few scattered settlers beyond New River. In 1758 Colonel John Chiswell opened the lead mines near New River, and soon a road passed Inglis', Chiswells, Stalnakers, Wolf Hills (Abingdon), and gradually advanced along the Middle Fork of the Holston. Three years later a military road was constructed to Long Island, in the south branch of the Holston River, where Fort Robinson was built.[4] A cabin was reported in February, 1769, "on every spot where the range was good" along this route.[5]

Access to this highway from the east and north was easiest near its beginning at Philadelphia, but roads joined it from Baltimore and Alexandria. Through the Buford Gap near the Roanoke came a road from Richmond on the edge of the Tidewater. It joined the "great road, running north and south behind the Blue Mountains," at the site of Salem. By this route Virginians from east of the Blue Ridge could join the migration to the southwest. Walker wrote in 1750, "The Ascent and Descent [over the Blue Ridge] is so easie a Stranger would not know when he crossed the Ridge." [6]

To the south the passes were in the heights of the Blue Ridge Mountains and the trails led across a wide stretch of mountainous territory before the Valley was attained. The Roanoke Gap must have been used in passing to and from North Carolina and the upper Tennessee Valley, for the people of Franklin protested in 1787 that it was necessary to "travel from one to two hundred & more miles through some other State 'ere we can reach your government." [7] Less indirect for the Carolinians but still somewhat roundabout was the route through Wood's Gap or Flower Gap near the point where the Blue Ridge crosses the Virginia-North Carolina boundary. These passes led to the New River, thence across to Reed Creek, which brought the traveler to the Valley road near Chiswells. When Christopher Gist returned from his long exploratory tour for the Ohio Company in 1750, he went to his home on the Yadkin by following New River and by passing through Wood's Gap. [8] Bishop Francis Asbury used this route, but the best description of it came from a traveler in 1819, who wrote of the "impending rocks, stupendous cliffs, and tumbling roaring cascades," and of "valleys . . . that seemed in many places to be threatened with overwhelming destruction. . . ." [9]

Other trails through the North Carolina mountains were known and followed at an early date, but they were even more difficult. One of these was used by Daniel Boone when he went from his home on the Yadkin to the Kentucky country. [10] He followed the Yadkin River to Buffalo Creek, crossed the Blue Ridge at Watauga or Day's Gap, and traveled northwestward over the highland between the tributaries of the New River to the north and of the Watauga to the south. The plateau was said to be almost level. Passing the sites of the future towns of Boone and Zionsville, he penetrated an easy pass through the Stone Mountains to the lower Watauga River. The gap was "so low that one is not conscious of passing over the top of a huge mountain range." This route, however, does not seem to have been used much at any time, although it was as direct and short as any. Perhaps what seemed easy to Boone was difficult to others.

Since Bright's Trace was chosen by the men of the Valley as their route to King's Mountain, they no doubt knew the path at that time.[11] From the Piedmont the road ran westward along the Catawba, over the Linville Mountains, which were declared to be steeper than the Blue Ridge, and coming to North Cove on the North Fork of the Catawba, turned westward and scaled the Blue Ridge through Gillespie Gap at an altitude of 2,900 feet, where it found and followed Grassy Creek to the North Toe River. Along the North Toe it passed the landmarks called Cathey's, Bright's, and Davenport's, then followed Roaring Creek, and passed over the summit of the Unaka Mountains between the peaks of Yellow and Roan mountains. Coming down the westward slope it passed Miller's on the Big Doe River, crossed this stream and went on to the Little Doe and Gap Creek to the Watauga area at the Sycamore Shoals.

André Michaux traveled over this route in 1795. He followed the Doe River but complained of the danger from flooding and of the number of times he crossed it (twenty-seven in twenty miles).[12] Bishop Asbury, who traveled this way in 1796 and 1797, called this process "worming the stream." He experienced much trouble from floodwaters in the latter year.[13] François Michaux, following his father's footsteps in 1802, seemed to find the route less used and harder to follow than had the earlier travelers.[14]

Bishop Asbury also took a still different route from the John's River to the head of the Watauga River, probably through Grandmother's Pass. He followed the Watauga River somewhat south of Boone's route and north of Bright's Trace. He seems to have traveled along its winding and mountainous way in 1788, 1790, 1793, and 1795, after which he tried Bright's Trace.[15]

That few pioneers of the Ohio Valley came from Georgia and South Carolina was in part caused by the difficulty of travel through Saluda Gap or other near-by passes and along the valley of the French Broad. One of the longest and most difficult routes followed the French Broad River. Travelers reached it from any of a number of passes, such as Jones Gap or Saluda, if coming from Georgia or South Carolina, Reedy Patch Gap or Hickory Nut Gap if coming from Rutherfordton, North Carolina, or Swannanoa Gap from Morgantown farther to the north. The river rose near the North Carolina-South Carolina boundary and flowed northward in a great semicircle. In its upper valley its course was fairly smooth, but after the mouth of Swannanoa Creek was passed it ran fifty miles through a deep narrow gorge in which it dashed over huge boulders and fell over rock ledges where the mountain slopes came down into its bed. Finally, near Paint Rock it escaped from its mountain fastness into the broad valley where it joined the Holston to form the Tennessee. Having scaled the wall of the Blue Ridge at any one of the gaps, the traveler found comparatively little difficulty, except in fording the various tributary streams, until the river entered the gorge. The trail followed in a general way this wild and beautiful stream, running occasionally in the bed of the splashing waters, or along its edge on sloping rocks that sometimes wrecked the wagons which attempted to pass over them, or detouring up a tributary in order to cross at a more propitious place. Bishop Asbury, who came this way several times in the first years of the nineteenth century, complained about the roughness of the road and gave up trying to take his chaise through the mountains. "This means of conveyance by no means suits the roads of this wilderness; we are obliged to keep behind the carriage with a strap to hold by and prevent accidents almost continually. . . ." Near Paint Rock his carriage was overturned, but his self-pity was quickly ended when he saw a poor family's wagon load of furniture and bed clothing that had been upset in the stream. He frequently exclaimed about the difficulty of scaling the ridges, the necessary slowness of pace, and the unavoidable danger. He wrote: "O the rocks! the rocks," and "O, the mountain—height after height, and five miles over." His experience on a part of the road in 1802 led him to write: "We laboured over the Ridge and the Paint Mountains; I held on awhile, but grew afraid and dismounted, and with the help of a pine sapling, worked my way down the steepest and roughest part. . . ." Two years later he chose to walk part of the way again. In 1806 he became lost, although he had followed the route five times in the previous six years. He wrote of this experience, "I have gone over rough roads, and a wild country, rocks, ruts, and sidelong difficult ways, sometimes much obscured." Three years later he bestowed the name "Alps" on these mountains.[16]

Not until the decade of the 1790's could the Carolinians follow a route through the mountains that was neither a long, roundabout road through Virginia nor a winding, mountainous pack trail.[17] Not so many people traveled over these early trails as used the much better road through the Valley of Virginia. The extension of this great road to the Tennessee Valley and the outbreak of the War of the Regulators tended increasingly to deflect the migration from passing southeastward through the Roanoke Pass and to send it southwestward to the Watauga. The settlement of the Tennessee Valley in the early years was therefore largely a continuation of the migration through the Valley of Virginia.[18]

Here at the Long Island in the South Branch of the Holston, just before it joins the North Branch, there developed an area of great importance in the settlement of the Ohio Valley. A few miles to the southeast the Watauga River enters the South Branch of the Holston after making its way from the slopes of Grandfather Mountain near the eastern edge of the Blue Ridge in North Carolina. Here the first pioneers began to locate as early as 1769. Four fairly distinct settlements existed by 1772: the area north of the South Branch of the Holston, the banks of the Watauga, the Nolichucky Valley to the south, and, finally, Carter's Valley on the northwestern side of the Holston River southward from Long Island. "A flood of Virginia humanity flowed . . . into the Watauga Valley in the years 1771–1772. . . . [and] newcomers pressed forward to the Tennessee Country in swelling numbers in the years 1773–1775," wrote Samuel C. Williams.[19] Later they learned that they had moved beyond the Indian line as fixed by the Treaty of Lochaber and that they were beyond the jurisdiction of Virginia. Consequently they were not protected by the laws and government of Virginia nor eligible to receive land as a settlement right. The British Indian agent ordered the settlers to depart from Indian territory, but they remained, organized their own government, and adjusted matters with the Indians.

Three hundred miles to the north of the settlements along the Watauga and Holston rivers a second important highway of frontier expansion had developed. When the pioneers of the Valley of Virginia had been crossing the New River only a few years, a grave international crisis led to the building of a roadway from the Potomac to the Monongahela. In an effort to wrest the Forks of the Ohio from the French, the British sent General Edward Braddock to America in 1755. He decided to follow and improve the trail which the Indian Nemacolin, Thomas Cresap, and Christopher Gist had made for the Ohio Company in 1752 and over which the young George Washington had journeyed twice on his way to the Monongahela Valley. It extended from the Ohio Company's warehouse at the juncture of Wills Creek with the Potomac River to

the point where Red Stone Creek flows into the Monongahela
River, or from the modern city of Cumberland, Maryland, to
Brownsville, Pennsylvania.[20]

It was at best a poor trail for pack horses, but Braddock widened
and improved it for his supply wagons. At the very beginning a
difficult ascent was made through Wills Mountain along Wills
Creek and over Dans Mountain, which is more than 2,600 feet in
height. Obstructing the way at a short distance was Savage Mountain and a little farther rose Meadow Mountain, both of which
were 300 feet higher than Dans. Beyond Meadow Mountain was
Little Meadows at a distance of 24 miles from the mouth of Wills
Creek, 24 miles which Braddock's army took 10 days to travel.[21] In
scaling Meadow Mountain, the army ascended the steep Allegheny
Front, and at Little Meadows it was on the Allegheny Plateau.
Here, the first branch of the Youghiogheny River was forded at
Little Crossing.

Soon came the laborious climb over Negro Mountain. The
modern road passes over its summit at a height of 2,906 feet. The
upper Youghiogheny River was passed at the Great Crossing, not
far beyond. Laurel Hill—or Briery Mountain, as it is now known,
to the south of the road—and Chestnut Ridge, the last of the big
hills, were crossed before General Braddock gained the lower
Youghiogheny and moved on the Monongahela and the scene of
his defeat. Between Laurel and Chestnut mountains lie the Great
Meadows, where Washington had built Fort Necessity. A little farther beyond, the path of Nemacolin, which the National Road was
later to follow, turned off to the west and ran along Red Stone
Creek to the Monongahela.

After the defeat of Braddock, General John Forbes led a second
expedition, which resulted in the British gaining possession of the
Forks of the Ohio. With his Highlanders, provincial troops, and
supply wagons he moved slowly through Pennsylvania rather than
follow the route of his ill-fated predecessor. He started from Harris'
Ferry (Harrisburg) and moved through Carlisle southwestward in
the Cumberland Valley to the site of Chambersburg and westward
over Cove Mountain, which was over 2,000 feet above sea level. He
proceeded by way of Forts Loudon and Littleton, which had been
built for the protection of Pennsylvania after the defeat of Braddock. He crossed Sideling Hill and Rays Hill, both of which were
as high as Cove Mountain, and reached the Juniata River, which

he followed through Warrior Ridge and Tussey, Evitts, and Wills mountains. The stream was on a level of 1,000 feet, but the mountains towered from 800 to 1,000 feet higher. He built Fort Bedford as his base of supplies before climbing the steep ascent of the Allegheny Front, which reached heights of more than 2,700 feet. Beyond was the plateau of the same name, and even here Laurel and Chestnut ridges barred his way to the Forks of the Ohio. Between the two was built Fort Ligonier, approximately fifty miles from Fort Duquesne.[22]

Braddock's and Forbes's roads were so close together that they may be thought of as a single route between the Valley of the Appalachians and the Forks of the Ohio. Travel over them in the early days was much more difficult than it was along the Valley of Virginia. Most of the people who moved to the frontier followed the latter. A few, however, took up land in the Valley until its western limit was reached, and a few came over the mountains to the banks of the Monongahela and the Ohio. With one trace leading from the Potomac and another from eastern Pennsylvania, the mixture of people was probably much the same as that moving down the Valley of Virginia. The claims of the Old Dominion to southwestern Pennsylvania served to encourage Virginians to migrate over Braddock's Road to this area, and during the early years they may have been as numerous as the Pennsylvanians. They were likely, however, to have come largely from western Virginia and therefore not to have differed much from the Pennsylvania settlers. After the Revolution, the disputes over the claims to the region were settled, Indian warfare declined, the number of people using these roads multiplied, and the settlements grew larger.

The area which these frontiersmen settled was roughly triangular in shape and was bounded by the Ohio and Youghiogheny rivers, with its apex at the Forks of the Ohio and its base along the Mason and Dixon line. Through the center, flowing from south to north, was the Monongahela River. Before the Seven Years' War began, the Ohio Company had planned to locate settlers as well as trading centers in this area; and log cabins were to be found in the coves, meadows, and bottom lands of the Monongahela Valley. Important events in the struggle between the French and English for possession of the Mississippi Valley took place here. The war, which was precipitated by Washington's campaign, and Pontiac's Rebellion, which followed the war, drove all or nearly all of the frontiersmen back to the older settlements. Peace with both the French and the Indians brought a resumption of settlement, and over the roads of Braddock and Forbes toiled the pioneers of southwestern Pennsylvania and of present-day northern West Virginia. In 1770, when Washington was returning from the Kanawha River, he noticed that the best lands along the Ohio had been taken as far as the mouth of the Little Kanawha and that settlers were coming into the Monongahela Valley and along the Ohio.[23] To Wheeling came the throngs of pioneers who followed Braddock's route, and to Pittsburgh by way of Forbes's Road came many others. Among those who were clearing land along the Ohio was George Rogers Clark, who like others followed the frontier to Kentucky.[24] By the outbreak of the Revolution this frontier, like the region around the Long Island of the Holston, was well enough occupied to act as a springboard for early immigrants to Kentucky.

A new expansion of the frontier began just before the outbreak of the American Revolution, as a result of which each of these two areas, the Holston-Watauga and the Monongahela-Ohio, was soon connected with Kentucky. At Sycamore Shoals in the Watauga area Judge Richard Henderson negotiated in 1775 a treaty with the Cherokee, who granted him the territory between the Ohio, Kentucky, and Cumberland rivers. He formed the Transylvania Company to found a proprietary colony in the new purchase, and Daniel Boone was employed to mark a trace from Watauga to the Kentucky Bluegrass early in 1775. This route came to be known as the Wilderness Road, although at this time it was a trace and not a road. It began at the Block House, a little to the north of the Long Island in the Holston, turned westward from the Valley of Virginia through Moccasin Gap of Clinch Mountain, followed along Little Moccasin Creek, and passed over an easy divide to the Clinch River. The ford was not particularly difficult unless the river was higher than usual. It then turned almost due northward to Kane's Gap in Powell Mountain, making a hard ascent before proceeding southwestward and crossing Wallen Ridge to Powell Valley.

William Brown, who went over this route in 1782 from Virginia to Kentucky, described the trail from the Block House to Powell Valley, some thirty-five miles long, as generally bad, "some part very much so," and the country as "very mountainous." [25] He did not exaggerate the difficulty of crossing Purchase Ridge and Powell

Mountain, and the name of Troublesome Creek may be regarded as descriptive of some of the more level stretches. John Lipscomb in 1784 referred to Powell Mountain as "very Bad and long and stony 15 miles over." [26]

The next part of the route was through Powell Valley from Wallen Ridge to Cumberland Gap, a distance of fifty miles. Brown thought that this portion of Boone's Trace was "pretty good." The country was rolling and hilly but not mountainous. In its midst was Martin's Station, where the early travelers found the last habitation of white folks. "As you travel along the valley, Cumberland Mountain appears to be a very high ridge of white rocks, inaccessible in most places to either man or beast, and affords a wild, romantic prospect." [27]

The ascent to the Gap was steep, winding, and awesome, for Pinnacle Mountain just to the north towered some nine hundred feet higher, but Brown thought that it was not very difficult. Since its early use was by pack-horse train, he may have been correct; but the modern visitor is likely to wonder how it was managed when wagons were used.

At the Gap the Wilderness Road entered and followed a portion of the Warriors' Path, which connected the Tennessee Valley and the Great Lakes by way of the Kentucky mountains and the Scioto Valley north of the Ohio River. The two routes ran along Yellow Creek to the Cumberland River and passed through Pine Mountain, where the Cumberland has carved Pine Mountain Gap. Boone's Wilderness Road crossed the Cumberland just beyond this Gap and, leaving the Warriors' Path, moved northwestward past Flat Lick. It crossed mountains and valleys to Richland Creek, the Hazel Patch, and the Rockcastle River. The trail to Boonesboro branched off before the Hazel Patch, and from that point a variant route called Scagg's Trail followed a different course to the head of Dick's River. From Dick's River, where the two routes again became one, the trail passed on to the Crab Orchard, where the mountains were left behind; at last the traveler emerged into the Bluegrass, the promised land that had led him to persevere in face of all obstacles. The Kentucky part of the Wilderness Road was not only more difficult, but it was longer than the distance from the Block House to Cumberland Gap. From the Gap to the Crab Orchard the route was over a hundred miles in length. Brown found very little good road until the Rockcastle River was crossed, and he characterized the region as mountainous—a conclusion which the modern traveler may easily confirm. John Lipscomb in 1784 wrote that the route along the Little Rockcastle was "very stoney & knobby." [28] From the Rockcastle to the Crab Orchard "the way [is] tolerable good." [29]

Although Peter Cartwright himself could hardly have remembered his family's journey over this route shortly after the Revolution, he no doubt did remember his parent's description. Allowing for some exaggeration, his account is a fairly accurate picture of travel conditions. "It was an almost unbroken wilderness from Virginia to Kentucky, . . . [which] was filled with thousands of hostile Indians, and many thousands of the emigrants . . . lost their lives by these savages. There were no roads for carriages . . . and although the emigrants moved by thousands, they had to move on packhorses. Many adventurous young men went to this new country. The fall my father moved . . . [two hundred] families . . . joined together for mutual safety. . . . One hundred young men, well armed, . . . agreed to guard these families through, and . . . they were to be supported for their services. . . . We rarely traveled a day but we passed some white persons, murdered and scalped by the Indians. . . ." A night's camp was also described. "The captain of our young men's company placed his men as sentinels all round the encampment. The stock and the women and children were placed in the center. . . . Most of the men that were heads of families, were placed around outside of the women and children. Those who were not placed in this position were ordered to take their stand outside still, in the edge of the brush." [30]

The Ohio, which furnished a route from the Monongahela Valley to the Kentucky, was used as early as Boone's Trace, for the Harrod brothers and party came this way in 1775. During the Revolution, Indian warfare against the frontiers of Pennsylvania, Virginia, and Kentucky made the use of the Ohio very dangerous; but nevertheless, when George Rogers Clark came down the river on his way to the Illinois Country in 1778, he was accompanied by twenty families to the Falls of the Ohio. With the construction of Fort Nelson at the Falls and the arrival of three hundred boatloads of emigrants, an important settlement grew on the banks of the river.[31] Although Colonel Daniel Brodhead wrote on September 23, 1780, "The emigrations from this new country to Kentucky are incredible . . . ," [32] the population of the Bluegrass region grew slowly until after the Revolution. The experience of Spencer Record at the mouth of Limestone Creek in 1783 indicated that few had come to central Kentucky by way of the Ohio, for a trace had not been marked from the river to the settlements.[33] But the next year Limestone, or Maysville, was founded and quickly became an important place of entry for newcomers to the Bluegrass region, where the older communities were located. Travel continued to be dangerous, but the river became a commonly accepted route of immigration.

Travel on the Ohio was generally seasonal, for better conditions prevailed in the spring and in the autumn, when rainfall and melting snow supplied adequate water for boats.[34] The winter season was always dangerous because of the cold weather and the possibility that the river might freeze or that a thaw might bring a rush of ice from a tributary or from the upper river.[35] Low water in the summer often made navigation dangerous or impossible.[36]

By the late 1780's immigration down the Ohio by flatboats had led to the establishment of boat yards along the Monongahela from Pittsburgh to Brownsville, where the travelers could buy boats for their journey.[37] Many were abandoned at Limestone, Kentucky, but Fort Washington was built of lumber obtained from these boats.

The dangers of Indian attack were probably more terrifying than those of nature. During the Revolution the use of the Ohio was highly dangerous, but from 1784 to 1788 peace brought a respite. By the latter year, however, the expansion of the frontier, the survey of land north and west of the Ohio, and the questionable Indian policy of the government brought about a resumption of frontier warfare, during which time boats on the Ohio were attacked with increasing frequency.[38]

The movement of people along the mountain roads to the Ohio Valley, like the earlier migration across the ocean, sifted the population. The advantages of the West could be gained only after dangerous passes had been crossed and long and tortuous trails had been followed, for the mountain region is some two hundred miles in width. Those who were not discontented with their lot in the East, who were not intent upon reaching the West, and who lacked strength of heart and brawn of muscle were not likely to brave these dangers. Only those who were driven onward by religious faith, by determination to achieve individual freedom and self-government, by ambition to escape the economic limitations of the eastern society, or by a desperation born of poverty were likely to make the crossing. When one or more of these aspirations possessed a man like a consuming fire, the dangers were merely obstacles to be surmounted on the way to the land of promise. Not all were urged onward by such desires, but there were always enough to keep up the ferment from which reforms spring.

The highways by which the crossing was made not only served to sift the people who entered the Ohio Valley but to create a mixed population, composed of different national strains, varied religious faiths, and various economic groups. Much of the Ohio Valley is in the South, but its pioneer people possessed many of the characteristics of the population of the Old West and fewer of those of the Tidewater region. All along the Valley of Virginia and in East Tennessee, in the Bluegrass of Kentucky and in the Nashville Basin of Tennessee were families that came from Pennsylvania. As the plantation system developed in Kentucky and Tennessee, various individuals became planters although they had not come from the Tidewater but had migrated through the Valley of Virginia. Since these various types of people came from areas of differing institutions and customs, the prestige of the plantation social order did not appeal with equal force to all of them.

The plantation system invaded the Ohio Valley at an early date although hindered by many forces. The planters were likely to be contented where they were. The dangerous journey to the West, the lack of adequate transportation to market, differences of soil, temperature, and topography, and frontier conditions tended to discourage many of them. The slave was a costly investment to expose to the insecurity of the frontier. But the governments of Virginia and North Carolina, which were controlled by the planters, protected the institution of slavery and aided the wealthy to gain possession of large quantities of land, particularly in the southern half of the Ohio Valley.

The Appalachian Mountain region has had much influence on the formation of the people of the Ohio Valley. The roads passing through these highlands have directed to the valley of the "Beautiful River" the people who were leaving the older states, especially those from Pennsylvania to the Carolinas. The expansion of the American frontier in this area first followed the Valley of the Appalachians from Pennsylvania to the Carolina Piedmont, mixing together the various types of people who came from the Keystone State with other types moving westward from the Southern Tidewater. This migration was then turned to the headwaters of the Tennessee, where the Valley people were blended with additional elements from east of the Blue Ridge. Meanwhile, a transmontane expansion by way of Forbes's and Braddock's roads peopled the Monongahela-Ohio area with frontiersmen from Pennsylvania and Virginia. From the headwaters of the Ohio and the Tennessee two different groups of people moved on Kentucky. The characteristics of the two groups were not very different; perhaps there was a larger Pennsylvania contribution from the northern area after the Revolution and a larger Southern element from the Watauga-Holston area in the later years. When they reached Kentucky, there was a new fusion, but in the frontier period the planter element, although aided by the mother states, was at a disadvantage. The frontiersmen were the more numerous—frontiersmen who were in the main men of the Old West who carried with them the ideals, the prejudices, and the memories of their former homes.

3

O'er the Mountains

Cheer up, brothers, as we go
O'er the mountains, westward ho,
Where herds of deer and buffalo
Furnish the fare.

Then o'er the hills in legions, boys,
Fair freedom's star
Points to the sunset regions, boys,
Ha, ha, ha-ha!

When we've wood and prairie land,
Won by our toil,
We'll reign like kings in fairy land,
Lords of the soil! [1]

*T*HE PRELIMINARIES for the settlement of the Ohio Valley were completed by 1776. An outpost had been thrust southwestward from Pennsylvania along the Great Road through the Valley of Virginia to the Watauga-Holston region, which was connected with the Piedmont of Virginia and the Carolinas by traces through the mountain passes and with Kentucky by way of Boone's Wilderness Road. Another outpost had been established at the Forks of the Ohio, which was connected with the more densely settled East by the roads constructed by Generals Braddock and Forbes and with Kentucky by the Ohio River. In Kentucky there were four little settlements where the people sought to protect themselves in crude fortifications. The movement of migration into Trans-Appalachia continued although the beginning of the Revolution with its attendant Indian warfare created very unfavorable conditions. Nevertheless, within fifteen years the southern half of the Ohio Valley was ready for separation from Virginia and North Carolina.

The advance guards of the pioneers moved on Kentucky at the very outbreak of the Revolution. Slowly at first and in small numbers they came. They often left their families in the older settlements; but as they fought off their Indian and English foes they gained confidence, and after the Revolution the little streams of people became an overwhelming flood. The movement of population to Kentucky during these years may be divided into four periods: the small migration in the early years of the Revolution, a larger increment in 1780, smaller ones in 1781 and 1782, and the much larger movement after the Revolution.

The initial migration, which resulted in the founding of the four stations in Transylvania, as Kentucky was then called, was diminished by the beginning of the war. At one time Indian raids seem to have closed temporarily all but two of these settlements, in which only one hundred fighting men were said to have remained. But the movement was not checked for long. By 1778 it was resumed, for twenty families accompanied George Rogers Clark to the Falls of the Ohio and eighty men came to Boonesboro from the Holston. People were moving into Kentucky in considerable numbers the following year. Indian attacks were no longer sufficiently strong to stop travel on the Wilderness Trail, and Virginia made provision for its improvement.[2]

The success of George Rogers Clark in the Illinois and Wabash country and the opening of a land office in the neighborhood of Harrodsburg combined to make the attractions of Kentucky brighter. A large number of settlers and speculators came to Kentucky in 1780. It was stated that 1,600,000 acres of land were entered at the land office on the first day of registry.[3] According to one observer, people talked as though half of Virginia intended to go to Kentucky,[4] while another feared the depopulation of the Monongahela Valley.[5] New stations were founded and the population of older ones increased. Migration was not restricted to the Wilderness Road, for the Ohio began to be used increasingly as a highway. In recognition of the growing population, Kentucky was divided into three counties.[6] One thousand men, if the Virginia soldiers at Fort Nelson be included, could be put in the field in August.[7] One estimate placed the population at twenty thousand.[8]

One source of immigrants was the Monongahela Country of southwestern Pennsylvania, where events had disappointed many settlers, especially those who had come from Virginia and Mary-

land. From colonel days Virginia had believed that this region
was within her boundaries, and great stretches of unoccupied and
mountainous land between the Monongahela and eastern Pennsylvania obscured the probable location of the dividing line. Cabins
were built around Ligonier, Pittsburgh, Redstone, the forks of the
Youghiogheny, the mouth of the Cheat, Stewart's Crossing, and
generally along the Monongahela and the Ohio. In addition to the
settlers from the South, many Pennsylvanians claimed the region as
their own. Dunmore's War and Indian raids and massacres during
the Revolution kept the settlers in turmoil. To add to the confusion, all but armed conflict broke out between the officials and
militias of the rival colonies.[9] There was much uncertainty as to
which land titles were valid, what laws were in force, and what
official was to be obeyed.

On August 31, 1779, representatives of Virginia and Pennsylvania
reached an agreement which was ratified by Virginia on the following June 23 and by Pennsylvania on September 23. A temporary
boundary between the two states was run by November, 1782, and
the permanent one was surveyed in 1784 and 1785. Disputed land
was to be awarded to "the elder or prior right which ever of the
said states the same shall have been acquired under. . . ." [10]

Whether the disorders before 1780 or the settlement of the dispute at that time proved to be the greater stimulant to emigration
would be impossible to determine.[11] The land laws of Virginia,
which were more liberal than those of Pennsylvania, ceased to
operate in the disputed area after 1780, and many landless settlers
may have seen in the agreement the extinction of their hope of
acquiring settlement or bounty claims in this region. The prohibition of slavery at this time probably affected more Virginians than
Pennsylvanians. The change from the laws and constitution of
Virginia to those of Pennsylvania may have been an additional cause
of unrest. Where all government was not trusted, a strange government would be the subject of greater suspicion.[12] The collection
of taxes followed the location of the boundary. Taxes were to be
paid in cash, of which the frontier possessed very little, and that
little would soon be drained off if they were paid. A local historian
suggested that "many of our early settlers . . . had an ineradicable
aversion to the burdens of government," which means that they
did not want to pay any taxes.[13] The efforts to prevent the survey
of the boundary line and to organize a new state were also due in

part to a desire to delay the imposition of taxes.[14] The Reverend James Finley wrote in 1783, "those Settlements are nearly destitute of cash," and suggested the use of produce in place of specie.[15] Thomas Scott wrote to President Reed in 1781, "Our condition is realy deplorable, for Gods sake, dear sir Interest yourself in having some thing done that may put an end to the present destractions of this country." [16] Pennsylvania, however, passed an act, December 3, 1782, which declared: "That if any person . . . shall . . . form, or shall endeavour to . . . form, any new and independent government, within the boundaries of this commonwealth . . . such person . . . being . . . legally convicted . . . shall be adjudged guilty of high treason." [17] Thus did the Quaker State fail to realize the causes of the difficulties and resort to force in place of humanitarian action.

The difficulties of the Kentuckians may not have seemed as threatening as those of the settlers in the disputed corner of Pennsylvania. Emigration, at least, offered an exchange of perils. Colonel Daniel Brodhead said at this time that the migrations from this country to Kentucky were unbelievable.[18] William Irvine wrote to George Washington, April 20, 1782, "Emigrations and new states are much talked of." [19] That it was not all talk is demonstrated by the contemporary records of persons settling across the Ohio River and by the growth of Kentucky's population.

From 1781 through 1783, however, immigration to Kentucky seems not to have continued so rapidly. Conditions there were not particularly encouraging. Dissatisfaction arose over the Land Act of 1779 and the consequent rush of speculators to obtain the choice locations. The vast majority of the people were poor frontiersmen who expected to secure land on a settlement right or a military warrant, and the speculators lessened their opportunity. The Revolution with its raids and counterraids made living conditions all but unbearable. Clarks' last effort, in 1781, to take Detroit and check the Indians failed to get started. The year 1782 has been called "The Year of Sorrows," [20] for this was the year in which the murder of the Christian Delaware Indians enabled the British to turn the fury of Indian vengeance upon the frontier. Consequently Kentuckians in every part of the country were attacked. The disaster at Blue Licks was the most severe blow which Kentucky received during the Revolution. Daniel Boone and eight others in a petition to the governor of Virginia declared: "Our number of militia decreases. Our widows & orphans are numerous, our

officers and worthiest men fall a sacrifice. . . . Our settlement . . .
seems to decline, & if something is not speedily done, we doubt will
wholly be depopulated. . . ." [21]

The Revolution, however, finally came to an end, the Indian
attacks declined, and migration again increased. The Ohio River
became a route of migration as travel on its waters became less
dangerous, but it was not immediately as important as the Wilderness Trail. Immigration to Kentucky, except possibly in the area
about the Falls, continued to come largely by way of Cumberland
Gap.[22]

A visitor wrote in 1785: "The population of the country of
Kentucky will amaze you; in June, 1779, the whole number of
inhabitants amounted to 176 only, and they now exceed 30,000. I
have now been 39 days at this post [Fort Finney], and there have
passed 34 boats for the falls; and not more than one third the
boats which come to this country with settlers, go as far down as
this place: it is a moderate computation to number 10 to a boat,
this gives an addition of 1000 at least in the last 40 days, and I
am informed more than one half of the settlers come through the
wilderness from Virginia. . . ." [23] The figure which he gave for
1779 was quite likely inaccurate and the number for 1785 was
obviously an estimate, but a population of approximately this size
must have existed and have been supplemented by a continued
heavy immigration for the following five years to reach the total
which the census takers found in 1790. With Indian troubles again
becoming acute near the end of the period, it is possible that the
movement down the Ohio declined. By any possible computation,
however, it was a remarkable migration that settled Kentucky between the years 1775 and 1790.

This extensive immigration could hardly have come over the
Wilderness Road. The Ohio River was an additional and eventually
a more important route. The early settlers of the Bluegrass region
came largely by Boone's road, but with the building of Fort Nelson
the use of the Ohio increased and the occupation of Kentucky was
hastened. A number of witnesses have left accounts of the traffic
on the "Beautiful River" from the Monongahela Valley to the land
of Kentucky. One statement from the West declared that the Adju-
tant at Fort Harmar in 215 days from October 10, 1786, to May 12,
1787, had counted 177 boats containing 2,689 persons and that
some vessels had passed in the night. The boats were said to be

bound for Limestone and the Falls.[24] This same spring a report from Fort Pitt stated that in 48 days beginning March 1, upwards of 50 boats had left Pittsburgh for Kentucky, and that some of them had three or four families with fifteen or twenty children on board. In April another observer described 2,000 persons waiting for the water in the Ohio to rise that they might go to Kentucky.[25] "You cant form an idea, of the Emigration, to this Western Country. . . ." wrote still another.[26] Lieutenant Colonel Josiah Harmar stated that 146 boats with 3,196 persons on board passed Fort Harmar in 183 days beginning on June 1, 1787.[27] Soon after this period, navigation was closed and not until March, 1788, did it again open. In the spring the Pittsburgh *Gazette* commented: "Since the opening of navigation of the Monongahela and Ohio Rivers, which has been closed since last December, until within these few days, a number of boats have passed this place for Kentucky, containing from 20 to 30 persons each." [28]

The experience of Dr. Antoine Saugrain in 1788 illustrates the danger of traveling on the Ohio. With three companions he started down the Ohio from Pittsburgh on March 18. Five days later the party was attacked by Indians, one of the men being killed and Saugrain wounded. Another boat brought him to Louisville, near which he spent six weeks recuperating from his wound. Before leaving he wrote in his journal: "The number of boats that come down here is considerable; here comes the seventeenth and a great number of them will continue to come; the number, however, is not so great as at Limestone, where a prodigious number comes continuously." Above Limestone on his return, he met seven Kentucky boats in one day and four in another.[29]

The Pittsburgh *Gazette* presented the statistics of traffic on the Ohio for two years, October, 1786, to December, 1788, from the register kept at Fort Harmar. The number of boats totaled 857 and the passengers 16,203.[30] An earlier report stated, "Accounts from the city of Marietta say, that within twelve months past, more than 10,000 emigrants have passed that place to Kentucke and other parts of the Ohio and Mississippi rivers." [31]

The dangers of Indian attack were greater than ever near the end of the 1780's. In negotiating the Treaty of Paris in 1783, the British temporarily deserted the Indians, but the United States inaugurated a policy of trying to divide them and to force them to retire north and west from the Ohio. The Iroquois were separated

MIGRATION ON THE OHIO [32]

From	To	No. of Months	Total Boats	Total Souls	Monthly Average Boats	Average Monthly Souls
Oct. 10, 1786	May 12, 1787	7	177	2,689	25	384
June 1, 1787	Dec. 9, 1787	6 +	146	3,196	24	533 −
Dec. 9, 1787	June 15, 1788	6 +	308	6,320	51	1,053
June 15, 1788	Dec. 4, 1788	6 −	203	3,405	34	567
Dec. 4, 1788	May 8, 1789	5	185	3,151	37	630
		30	1,019	18,761	34	625
Aug. 1, 1786	Dec. 7, 1789	40	1,264	23,618	31	590

from the Indian confederacy and in 1784 surrendered their claims to land beyond the Ohio; the Delaware and other tribes agreed at Fort McIntosh the following year to give up much of their lands. In 1786 the government tried to induce the other tribes to enter negotiations at Fort Finney but continued pressure tended to strengthen the Indian confederacy under British auspices and to produce a resumption of border warfare. Boats on the Ohio were attacked in 1788, and the attacks soon became more frequent.[33]

Meanwhile, after government surveyors had begun to mark off the Seven Ranges just west of the upper Ohio under the Land Act of 1785, Indians, resentful of their activity, interrupted and delayed the work.[34] Squatters who had occupied desirable tracts of land along the Ohio and its tributaries also irritated the Indians and threatened the new land policy with pre-emption or settlers' rights. Since a proclamation in 1783 against this occupation produced no withdrawal, on January 24, 1785, Lieutenant Colonel Josiah Harmar was ordered to use troops in driving off the squatters.[35] Harmar was also ordered to establish himself with troops on the Indian side of the Ohio in order to check the occupation of the land by the squatters and to protect the surveyors on the Seven Ranges from the Indians.[36] On two occasions in 1787 the squatters were driven away, cabins burned, and crops destroyed, but some of the squatters returned as soon as the troops departed. Congress resolved on October 3 to locate 700 soldiers on the frontier "to protect the settlers on the public lands from the depredations of the Indians; to facilitate the surveying and selling of the said lands in Order to . . . prevent all unwarrantable intrusions thereon." [37] The Ohio was soon protected by a line of forts: Franklin, Pitt, McIntosh, Steuben, Harmar, and Vincennes. To these was added Fort Washington at Cincinnati in 1789.

A report to the British government in 1789 described Kentucky. Louisville and Lexington were towns of 200 houses, Danville of 150, Boonesboro of 120, and Harrodsburg and Leestown of 100 each. Limestone was described as the general landing place on the Ohio. It declared that there were 62,000 persons in Kentucky in 1788.[38] In 1790 the first census of the United States gave the population of Kentucky as 73,677. Nearly all of these persons had come there in a twelve-year period. During some of the years the migration must indeed have been prodigious.

Through these years when the migration on the Ohio River to Kentucky was growing in volume, the pioneers also continued to pass in growing numbers over the Wilderness Road. In addition, another emigration still farther to the southward joined forces with the Kentuckians along the Wilderness Road. When the first settlers of the French Lick region on the Cumberland River departed from the communities along the Watauga and Holston rivers under the leadership of James Robertson in the fall of 1779, they followed Boone's road well into Kentucky. They left the trace after reaching Dick's River at Whitley's Station and turned west and southwest to the Green River, which they crossed above the Little Barren River. Then they traveled westward, some distance south of the Green River, crossed the Little and Big Barren rivers, passed Blue Spring, and turned southward along Drake's Creek, the Red River, and Mansco's Creek to French Lick.[39] A crop of corn was planted and harvested in preparation for a settlement, and on New Year's Day, 1780, Robertson was back again with a band of settlers. Although his route continued to be used particularly for travel between Kentucky and Nashville, it was a difficult and roundabout way between two points in the Tennessee Country.

Another party, which contained many of the families of the men who had gone with Robertson, set out on December 22, 1779, from Fort Patrick Henry near Long Island to go down the Holston and Tennessee and up the Ohio and Cumberland rivers to French Lick. Some thirty vessels under the direction of John Donelson were in the flotilla. The "Journal of a Voyage . . . in the good boat Adventure," which tells of their harrowing experiences and hardships, vividly pictures an epic in the annals of the West. The tricky attacks of the Chickamauga Indians, the loss of the Stuart

family, the narrow escape of the Jennings family, the thrilling
voyage through Muscle Shoals, the division of the company when
the mouth of the Tennessee was reached, the long hard pull up the
current of the Ohio and the Cumberland, the inadequacy of food,
and the cold winter were happily ended for the survivors by the
joyful reunion of the families when the French Lick was reached.
It was one of the more unusual voyages in American history.[40]

The Cumberland settlement was all but destroyed by extraordi-
narily severe Indian attacks during which its local government
ceased to function. Not until the end of the Revolution and the
arrival of new settlers was relief assured. The government was revived for a short time until North Carolina created the county of
Davidson to give the area an officially recognized government. By
1790 the population was estimated at 7,000.

Other parties had used the Tennessee before, and many were to
use it after the Donelson flotilla, but its dangers increased for a
time. The opportunity for robbery and plunder encouraged the
worst of the Indians to congregate in towns along the banks of
the river below Chickamauga, from which vantage points they
preyed upon the boats descending the Tennessee, and from which
they sent marauding expeditions upon the Cumberland settlements.
Indian attacks made immigration dangerous and threatened the
existence of these outlying settlements.[41]

Finally in 1788 a new road, known as Avery's Trace, was cut by
troops provided by the North Carolina legislature. Beginning near
the site of Knoxville at the end of Clinch Mountain, it crossed the
Clinch River in a westerly direction, ascended the Cumberland
Mountains through Emory Gap, and passed through the wilderness
by Crab Orchard and Flat Rock to Fort Blount, where it crossed
the Cumberland River. On the north side of the river, the road
continued by way of Bledsoe's Lick or Gallatin and recrossed the
Cumberland to Nashville. Although a military guard was furnished
for emigrants at periodic intervals and the road was supposed to be
usable for wagons, it continued to be difficult and unsafe without
the guard.[42]

At the same time the older frontier region through which the
roads to Kentucky and the Cumberland Basin passed also expanded
and grew in population. The Tennessee Valley, lying a little to the
south of the Virginia boundary, was just off the main highway to
Kentucky. Boone's Wilderness Road tended to shunt the immigrants

from the Valley of Virginia westward to Kentucky or to the Cumberland region rather than to eastern Tennessee. The early settlers had come before 1775 when the trace was marked. By that time newcomers were moving beyond the first settlements north of the South Branch of the Holston, along the Watauga, in Carter's Valley, and along the Nolichucky. The increase in population during the Revolution does not appear to have been large. The Tennessee flowed close to the villages of the Cherokee, Creek, and Chickamauga Indians, particularly the Cherokee, and the attacks of the Indians were severe. Settlement advanced to the lower French Broad, however, and shortly after the Revolution North Carolina granted land still farther to the south.

The State of Franklin on May 31, 1785, negotiated the Treaty of Dumplin Creek with the Cherokee, by which the Indians agreed to white occupation south of the French Broad and north of the watershed between the Little River and the Little Tennessee. This agreement brought the settlers southeast of the site of Knoxville, which was founded in 1796. Settlement hugged the edge of the mountains and was slow to move west of the main Holston except in the north. It seems that fewer persons made their homes in the Valley of East Tennessee before 1790 than passed through it on their way to Kentucky and the Cumberland settlements. The number given by the federal census of that year was in excess of 28,000. They formed, however, only the spearhead of the frontier which had been advancing southwestwardly through the Appalachian Valley. The number would be more comparable to the population of the Monongahela-Ohio region if the people in southwestern Virginia beyond the watershed were added. The two widely separated Tennessee settlements, the Cumberland region and the upper Tennessee, were organized in 1790 as the new federal territory south of the Ohio River.

The Monongahela-Ohio region was no longer separated from the older settlements by vast stretches of unoccupied land but had become a peninsula of settlement reaching along the roads built by Braddock and Forbes to the head of the Ohio River. There were nearly 100,000 persons west of the Allegheny Front in this region.

This first great wave of frontier migration beyond the mountains was one of the important achievements of the generation that fought the War of Independence. The little settlements that existed in 1776 in the Monongahela-Ohio region had grown until they contained approximately 100,000 persons, while the Watauga-Holston area beyond the boundary of Virginia had increased in population until some 28,000 people made it their home. From these earlier outposts new colonies were established in the Bluegrass of Kentucky and the Nashville Basin of Tennessee. By 1790 the former was the home of a prospective state with 73,000 inhabitants. Not far to the southwest was another colony where some 7,000 were living by the end of this period. All together some 250,000 people had found homes west of the Appalachian watershed by 1790.[43]

4

An Epidemic of State Making

THE LARGE migration which followed the close of the
American Revolution put a tremendous strain upon the political
and economic organizations of the new nation. An expanding frontier meant new roads, new migrations, new forts, new lands, and
new communities. It made imperative new policies of land disposal,
of Indian removal, and of foreign relations. It also required expanding governmental services or the creation of new governments
for those settlers who moved beyond the effective range of government and beyond the realm of established economic activity.
Furthermore, postwar problems created distress which neither state
nor nation was prepared to alleviate. Some of the soldiers of the
Revolution had given the years of their youth to their country
while others had sacrificed property or business; now they expected
government to render some assistance as they sought to find new
homes on the frontier. And in the West the government had to deal
with men who were accustomed to greater freedom and with a
society made up of various elements each acquainted with customs
and institutions that differed from those of others. The Revolutionary philosophy of the day found ready welcome, and the fluid
condition of society in a new region permitted and even encouraged
change.

Three different conditions stimulated attempts to found new
governments. The first and least complicated occurred when the
frontiersmen pushed beyond the effective jurisdiction of existing
governments. A new agency was then created, not primarily because
of discontent but because some authority was needed, and this
government was sometimes expressive of the simple wishes and
ideals of the frontiersmen. The second circumstance involved the

operation of a government which was more or less ineffective because of distance and which was under the control of a non-frontier
group of people, unacquainted with frontier conditions and chiefly
concerned with their own interests. This condition led to inequality
and injustice, and the efforts to form a new government give some
measure of the depth and breadth of dissatisfaction. There is some
similarity between these attempts and the third parties of a later
period.

The third factor was that the frontier gave opportunity for men
of wealth and boldness to engage in land speculation. The Virginia
Land Act of June 22, 1779, gave rights to the few settlers who had
come before the act was passed, but it also granted a remarkable
opportunity to the state's wealthy citizens to acquire vast quantities
of land for speculative purposes. Professor Thomas P. Abernethy
called it a colossal mistake and stated that "the growth of the
country was retarded, the resident population forced to protect the
property of those who took no part in its defense, and the great
public domain was exploited by a few individuals for their private
gain." North Carolina, also, before ceding her western claims,
threw nearly all of her trans-Appalachian lands on the market in
1783 at "no more than five dollars in specie [per hundred acres],
and the speculators reaped a rich harvest during the seven months
that elapsed before the act was repealed." [1] "Nearly four million
choice acres were entered. . . . yielding handsome fortunes to those
who were in a position to profit by it." [2] Such opportunities for
profit furnished stimulus enough to induce the speculators to create
or attempt to form new governments that would be useful in securing title to other quantities of land. The rash of state making that
broke out in the last quarter of the eighteenth century indicates the
need for new governments, the energy and boldness of the speculators, and the widespread dissatisfaction of frontiersmen with the
inefficiency, injustice, and inequality of older governments which
refused to grant them self-determination.

Very often all of these conditions affected a given area, and it is
impossible to distinguish which was more important. Watauga
would seem to have been of the first type. Westsylvania may have
been of the second, but the factor of speculation was present. Transylvania was clearly the work of the land speculators. One should
not, however, overlook the reality of the factors producing discontent on the frontier after the Revolution.

The first of these governments was the Watauga Compact, which the settlers along the Holston and Watauga rivers formed when they learned that they were beyond the jurisdiction of Virginia and beyond the Indian line. They adopted the laws of Virginia and chose judges to settle disputes. It was an effort to supply political authority for an area to which neither the British Empire nor the individual colonies had given much thought. It did not stem from dissatisfaction; it was a simple expression of the wishes of the people and was based upon the popular will.

Their own words describe briefly their activities and their reasons for forming a government. "Finding ourselves on the Frontiers, and being apprehensive that, for the want of a proper legislature, we might become a shelter for such as endeavoured to defraud their creditors; considering also the necessity of recording Deeds, Wills, and doing other public business; we, by consent of the people, formed a court for the purposes above mentioned, taking (by desire of our constituents) the Virginia laws for our guide, so near as the situation of affairs would admit; this was . . . done by the consent of every individual. . . ." [3]

Some three years after the formation of the Watauga government and at the time when the thirteen colonies were taking their first steps towards independence, the people also set up a committee of safety. "Alarmed by the reports of the present unhappy differences between Great Britain and America . . . (taking the now united colonies for our guide,) we proceeded to choose a committee, which was done unanimously by consent of the people. This committee (willing to become a party in the present unhappy contest) resolved, (which is now on our records,) to adhere strictly to the rules and orders of the Continental Congress, and in open committee acknowledged themselves indebted to the united colonies their full proportion of the Continental expense." [4] The petition from which these words were taken was addressed in 1776 to the North Carolina Council of Safety, which superseded the colonial government, requesting it to take Watauga under its protection and to organize a county government for them. Since their petition was received favorably by North Carolina, the Watauga experiment came to an end after functioning for four years. Delegates from the new county, which was named Washington, were present in the Provincial Congress that formed the first constitution of the "Old North State." The people supported the cause of independence, and their troops at King's Mountain proved their loyalty to the new state and the new nation with their blood and lives.[5] This simple government which expressed the wishes of the frontier was in marked contrast with the governments of the Tidewater.

The second effort at state making on the frontier was the adoption of a petition by the people of the Monongahela-Ohio area in 1776 in which they asked to be organized as the "fourteenth Province of the American Confederacy" and invested with the rights and privileges of the other provinces.[6] This action was expressive of discontent. Authority was not only exercised from afar but was divided between Virginia and Pennsylvania because each claimed the area. The people not only differed in allegiance but were separated into Loyalists and Patriots by the Revolution. Speculation complicated the problem of securing title to land, Indian warfare made life itself insecure and dangerous, and isolation and distance from the older settlements interfered with economic development. For the solution of these difficulties the parent states seemed incapable of rendering effective assistance.

Pennsylvania claimed the region and regarded it as a part of Cumberland County with its county seat at Carlisle, almost at the eastern end of Forbes's Road. Attendance at court would have involved a journey of 150 miles or more over mountainous roads. In 1771 Bedford became the seat of Bedford County, which reduced the distance by one half but still did not remove the necessity of a journey over Laurel and Chestnut mountains and down the Allegheny Front to reach the county court which exercised jurisdiction over all western Pennsylvania. Finally, in 1773 Hannastown, on Forbes's Road, thirty miles east of Pittsburgh, became the site of local government of Westmoreland County, which included southwestern Pennsylvania. Probably no one was farther than seventy-five miles from the county officials.

On the other hand, Virginia claimed this area west of Laurel Ridge, which included the Forks of the Ohio, on the basis of her charter of 1609. By means of the District of West Augusta, she extended government to Pittsburgh by 1775, and a year later the three counties of Ohio, Monongalia, and Yohogania were organized by Virginia to be partially or entirely in what is now southwestern Pennsylvania.[7] This action of Virginia, bringing confusion in government, taxes, and land titles, certainly did not improve the situation for the settlers of this frontier. Pennsylvania did not resist effectively, perhaps because of the uncertain definition of her boundaries and her desire for peace.

With the beginning of the Revolution a new element of division came into being. The majority of the settlers seem to have become Patriots, but among them were Loyalists. The Patriots organized a committee of correspondence at Pittsburgh on May 24, 1775, and an Association of Westmoreland established a militia.[8]

Land speculators, including the Indiana and Vandalia companies, had claims upon considerable quantities of land, which claims of course clouded titles of others until adjudicated. Under Virginia laws the acquisition of land was easier than under the laws of Pennsylvania. In the disputed area for a time, land might have been secured from a speculator, from Pennsylvania, or from Virginia. The unlearned frontiersman would not know where to apply to secure a good title.

Indian hostility harassed this area at the time of Pontiac's Rebellion, in Dunmore's War, and during much of the American Revolution. The Indian warfare directed by Lieutenant-Governor Henry Hamilton of Detroit and his successors almost destroyed the settlements in the neighborhood of Wheeling. Virginia took over Fort Pitt in 1774 and held it until Edward Hand with Congress troops took command on June 1, 1777, but, during much of the Revolution, the commander at Fort Pitt was almost powerless to prevent Indian depredations, and raids and attacks were the order of the time.[9]

Economic development of the area was slow because of the long, difficult, and dangerous roads over which communication and trade with the East were conducted. The importance of the Ohio River was early realized, but the rise of inland water transportation had to await the subjugation of the Indians and the acquisition of the mouth of the Mississippi River by the power holding the Forks of the Ohio. That much of the West's future interest would not be identical with that of the Eastern states was also understood.

Despairing of the solution of their problems by the Eastern states and anxious to try their own hands, the people of southwestern Pennsylvania petitioned Congress to permit them to form a state government and come into the Union as the fourteenth state. This action has been explained as the work of "land-jobbers" who were trying to secure the recognition of the claims of the Indiana and Vandalia speculators, a recognition which it was thought was more likely to be granted by Virginia or the Confederation than by Pennsylvania.[10] Another possible source of the movement was the Virginia settlers who had depended upon Virginia laws to secure the land upon which they had settled. It is also possible that it was a movement of the people and that speculation had little to do with it. Similar agitation was the normal reaction of American frontiersmen when existing governments did not give them ample protection and when their various problems stirred them to action. Regardless of the origin, a discussion of democratic principles resulted.

Making allowances for exaggeration and fine writing, which are characteristic of such documents, it is probable that the petition expressed with reasonable accuracy and honesty the wishes of its signers.[11] It began "That whereas the province of Pennsylvania and Virginia have set up Claims to this large & extensive Country which for a considerable time past have been productive . . . of discordant and contending jurisdiction, innumerable Frauds, Impositions, [and] Violences, to the utter Subversion of all Laws, human & divine, of Justice, Order, Regularity & in a great Measure even of Liberty itself & must unless a timely and Speedy Stop be put to them in all Probability terminate in a Civil War, which . . . may effect the Union of the Colonies. . . ." Fears were expressed for further aggravation because of "fraudulent Impositions of Land Jobbers, Pretended Officers & Partisans, the great imminent & manifest danger of involving the Country in a Bloody, ruinous, and destructive War with the Indians, [and] private or other claims to Lands within the limits of this Country equally embarrassing & perplexing. . . ." The claim that they "through almost insuperable Difficulties, . . . & Dangers at the most imminent Risque of their lives, . . . and everything that was dear and valuable to them, were endeavoring to secure an Asylum & a Safe Retreat from threatening Penury for their tender numerous families with which they had removed from the lower Provinces and settled themselves . . . agreeable to the usual Mode of Colonization & an Ancient Equitable & long established Custom & Usage of the Colonies, the Right of Pre-Emption. . . . , now unhappily find themselves in a worse & more deplorable Situation than whilst living on the poor, barren rented Lands in their various respective Provinces below. . . ."

They complained of the "uncertainty of every kind of Property" and of lack of "Regular Administration of Justice & of a due and proper Executive and . . . of a system of Laws . . . adapted to their peculiar Necessities. . . ." They described themselves as a "rational and Social People . . . from almost every Province of America, [who] having imbibed the highest and most extensive Ideas of Liberty, will with Difficulty Submit to, the being annexed to or Subjugated by . . . any one of those provinces much less the being partitioned or parcelled out among them, or to be prevailed on to entail a state of Vassalage & Dependence on their Posterity, or Suffer themselves . . . to be Enslaved by any set of Proprietary or other claimants, or arbitrarily deprived & robbed of those lands . . . to which by the Laws of Nature & of Nations they are entitled as first Occupants. . . ."

They asked to be organized as "The Province & Government of Westsylvania . . . and . . . invested with every other Power, Right, Privilege & Immunity, vested or to be vested in the other American Colonies" and to be the "fourteenth Province of the American Confederacy. . . ." [12]

By resolution of October 10, 1780, Congress pledged itself to carry out those principles (equality of the states and membership in the Union) which the Westsylvanians had requested in 1776.[13] Virginia incorporated them as provisos in her second offer of cession of December 10, 1783; [14] they were reiterated in Jefferson's "Report of Government for the Western Territory" of April 23, 1784; [15] and, finally, they became a part of the Northwest Ordinance.[16]

In Kentucky, Judge Richard Henderson and party, who followed Boone over the trace which he had marked, found the men who had accompanied the Harrods and Clark. On May 23, 1775, delegates from the four stations which these groups had founded met in convention. A constitution or compact was finished in five days.[17] It is significant to note how far the leaders in this land speculation went in promising democratic government in order to secure the support of the settlers. In speaking to the convention, Henderson said, "All power is originally in the people," and "we have a right to make such laws [for the regulation of our conduct] without giving offence to Great Britain, or any of the American Colonies. . . ." The convention in its reply to Henderson stated: "That we have an absolute right, as a political body, without giving umbrage to Great Britain or any of the Colonies, to frame rules for the government of our little society, cannot be doubted by any sensible, unbiased mind. . . ." [18]

The work of the convention resulted in a compact between the proprietors and the representatives of the people, thus offering recognition of popular sovereignty. It provided for the annual election of delegates but not for any scheme of representation based upon population. It declared in favor of "perfect religious freedom and general toleration." Judges of the superior courts were to be appointed by the proprietors but were to be answerable to the people for their malconduct. It also provided: "That the legislative authority, after the strength and maturity of the Colony will permit, consist of three branches, to-wit: The Delegates, or Representatives, chosen by the people; a Council, not exceeding twelve men, possessed of landed estate, who reside in the Colony; and the Proprietors." [19] Presumably this latter provision would have given the proprietors a veto over the actions of the other houses of the legislature. The government which the compact provided was democratic in form but not in reality.

The significance of this governmental experiment lies in its failure. Many factors contributed to its lack of success, among which may be mentioned the outbreak of the Revolution and the hostility of Virginia and North Carolina. Very important, also, was the decision of the proprietors to retain title to the land and to collect quitrents according to English law. The inhabitants of Kentucky who opposed Henderson referred in their petition to Virginia not only to the exorbitant price of the land, but to a policy which did not harmonize with that of the United Colonies and "whose principles are inimical to American Freedom." [20] A land policy and government, both illiberal, were not the kind of inducements to persuade men to make the long, hard journey over mountain and valley to an insecure home in the "dark and bloody ground" of Kentucky. Henderson gave up Translyvania after failing to secure the help of Congress and after receiving a sizable allotment of land from Virginia as a reward for his trouble and expense.

The action of the opposition is equally interesting. Present in Transylvania when Henderson came was a group of men at Harrodsburg, led by the Harrod brothers and George Rogers Clark. These men appealed to Virginia to assert her authority and to extend her protection. Clark claimed that he called a general meeting to elect deputies to treat with Virginia respecting the country. "If valuable Conditions was procured," he proposed "to declare our selvès Citizens of the State otherways Establish an Independent Government." [21] A general meeting was held, delegates, not deputies, were chosen and sent to Virginia with a petition requesting that they be admitted to the convention and that Kentucky be taken under the jurisdiction and protection of Virginia. No evidence has been found that anyone was authorized to call this meeting or hold an election. This procedure, like that of the people of Watauga, of Westsylvania, and of Transylvania, was not the result of any regularly constituted authority, except the sovereignty of the people. Virginia, however, created Kentucky County as her agent,[22] and the people of Kentucky continued their political activity by organizing a committee of safety to give support to the movement for national independence.[23]

Judge Henderson, the former leader of Transylvania, was the inspiration of another colonizing venture, this time at the bend of the Cumberland River in central Tennessee to which James Robertson and John Donelson had led groups of colonists. The men of Nashborough assembled on May 1, 1780, and signed a compact which was written by Henderson. In this second effort, he did not seek to establish the archaic land system of Transylvania with its quitrents, or its undemocratic government. He did not claim independence from the Eastern states. The Cumberland government, like that, at Watauga, was similar to a county court, having judicial and administrative duties but little or no legislative power, for the laws of North Carolina were adopted. The freemen were to elect twelve "conscientious and [deserving] persons" who were to serve as judges and who could be removed by the voters if their conduct as officials was not satisfactory. "As often as the people in general are dissatisfied with the doings of the Judges or Triers . . . they may call a new election . . . and elect others in their stead. . . ." The compact did not make such verbose professions of popular sovereignty as the Watauga petition, but it stated: "That as this settlement is in its infancy, unknown to government, and not included within any county within North Carolina, the State to which it belongs, so as to derive the advantages of those wholesome and salutary laws for the protection and benefit of its citizens, *we find ourselves* constrained from necessity to adopt this temporary method of restraining the licentious, and supplying, by unanimous consent, the blessings flowing from a just and equitable government. . . ." [24] It gave ample evidence that Henderson had learned not only not to oppose the claims of the Eastern states to extend their authority to the Mississippi, but also not to attempt to establish a feudalistic land system and an arbitrary government on the frontier.

The beginning of a separatist movement of Kentuckians, although based upon many fundamental causes, seems to have been touched off by Virginia's Land Act of 1779. A petition was signed in that year protesting the heavy losses which the inhabitants suffered at the hands of the Indians, the inability of many of them to secure land under the new law, and "the disagreeable necessity of . . . becoming tennants to private gentlemen. . . ." unless they were to escape these eventualities by going down the Mississippi to Spanish territory.[25] Apparently, others expressed themselves more vigorously for George Morgan wrote: "We have distressing news from *Kentucke* which is entirely oewing to a Set of Nabobs in Virginia, taking all the Lands there. . . . Hundred of Families are ruin'd by it. . . . It is a Truth that the People there publicly say it—Let the great Men, . . . who the Land belongs to, come & defend it, for we will not lift up a Gun in Defence of it.' "[26] John Floyd confirmed this statement when he wrote: "Most of the people who have no families in the Country are flying to the Settlement, and others who cannot go declare against defending the country because they have no land."[27]

Of a similar character was the petition of May 15, 1780, of the "Inhabitants of Illinois, Kaskaskias and Kentucky," to which 640 names were attached. It protested the "several acts of the general assembly of Virginia for granting large Grants for waist and unapropriated lands" in the West, the necessity of paying taxes while serving in garrisons and suffering from Indian attacks, and the inadequacy of a distant government which was unable to preserve order. The signers asked that they be formed "into a Separate State." The petition interestingly reveals the confusion as to which government allegiance was due and something of the grievances endured:

The Petition and Prayr. of the people of that Part of Contry [sic] now Claim'd. by the State of Virginia in the Countys of Kaintuckey and Ilinois Humbly Sheweth—That we the leige Subjects of the United States Labour under many Greivences on account of not being formd. into a Separate State or the Mind and Will of Congress more fully known respecting us. . . . We remain uncertain whether the unbounded Claim of This Extencive Contry Ought of right to belong to the United States or the State of Virginia, They have by another late act required of us to Sware alegince to the State of Vir-

ginia in Particular Notwithstanding we have aredy taken the Oath of ale-
gance to the united States. These are Greivences too Heavy to be born, and
we do Humbly Pray that the Continental Congress will Take Proper Methods to form us into a Seperate State or grant us Such Rules and regulations
as they in their Wisdom shall think most Proper. . . .[28]

George Rogers Clark insisted that the movement was due to the
non-Virginian settlers, that their motives were questionable, and
that their actions were dangerous to the Revolutionary efforts in
the West. He wrote that he was again being solicited to head the
"partizans" who favored a new government, but that his duty
obliged him to suppress all such proceedings.[29] It must have been
difficult to maintain the authority of the Old Dominion, because
Virginia failed to renew her government of the County of Illinois,
and Congress on October 10, 1780, adopted resolutions promising
that western lands ceded to the federal government by the states
should be used for the common benefit and formed into republican
states.

As a result of the separatist movement, Kentuckians were divided
into factions. The "partizans," as Clark called them, included poor
pioneers who had difficulty securing land, the wealthy speculators
of the Northern states who preferred federal control, and the non-
Virginians generally. This group became critical of Clark's fortifica-
tion of the lower Ohio, which left the more densely settled part of
Kentucky without adequate defenses, and of Virginia's land laws.
Virginia's inability or unwillingness to give effective aid against
the enemy and efficient government to Kentucky were difficult
points to justify. It may be that the suffering caused by the war led
some to question the value of the War of Independence. On the
other hand, the Virginians expected to profit from the land laws
of Virginia and they generally supported Clark's efforts to win and
to hold the Illinois Country.[30]

Although the movement died down in 1781, events were taking
place which were to produce a revival of separatism. On January
2, 1781, the Virginia Assembly adopted resolutions favoring the
cession of its claims northwest of the Ohio River, but Congress
refused to accept the terms of the proffered cession. The land companies renewed their activties to secure a cession of all land west of
the Allegheny Mountains. These events increased the confusion in
the West, lessened Virginia's interest in the transmontane region,

encouraged the land companies, and stimulated the exponents of new states beyond the mountains.[31]

In the spring of 1782 John Donelson called a meeting at Harrodsburg in Fayette County, in compliance with a suggestion of Arthur Campbell, to attend which the people chose selectmen. Although their activity was interrupted by a Major McGarry and some Virginia troops, a petition was prepared and sent to Congress by a Mr. Rees.[32] Another petition was sent to Virginia requesting the mother state to grant separation and to recommend to Congress that Kentucky be admitted to the Union.

The petition to Congress stated that

the petitioners had, at the risk of their lives, settled a tract of country westward of the Allegheny Mountains on the waters falling into the Ohio, that the State of Virginia had lately granted large tracts of land within that district without any condition of settlements, that she had undertaken to form them into Counties and claimed jurisdiction there, that being removed above 800 miles from the seat of Government, it could not be exercised with justice & energy; that they were in danger of losing their rights, if they must go to Richmond where the Supreme Court sat & there contend with the last Grantees; that they have taken an Oath of Allegiance & considered themselves subjects of the United States & not of Virginia, that the Charter under which Virginia claimed that Country, had been disolved; that in consequence of the dissolution the Country belonged to the Crown of G. Britain & that by the revolution the rights of the Crown was devolved on the United States, and therefore praying Congress to erect them into a separate and independent State and admit them into the federal Union.[33]

The other petition, which was sent to Virginia, first called attention to the hardships of the settlers, then to the opening of the land office, and to the law which permitted the purchase of land without the necessity of cultivating it. This last act they regarded as specially injurious. What they preferred was the sale of land to actual settlers rather than to speculators. Because this was not done there had been a diminution of the number of fighting men. They also claimed that the relief act of 1781 was ineffectual and requested that they be permitted to take out land in other areas. Finally, they asked that Virginia grant them better government or "a Separation with your Intercession with the Honourable the Continental Congress for their Incorporation with them. . . ."[34]

Clark continued to oppose the new-state movement. He wrote vaguely of his efforts to suppress it and "to reduce the people to subordination." He also stated: "I believe in a short time it will be dangerous for a man to speak of new Government in this Quarter, except among a small party of black guards. . . ." [35] This statement is partly explained by another remark that he regarded the new-state group as " a powerfull party indeavouring to subvert the government. . . ." [36] He and some seventy others of the party loyal to Virginia admitted the reality of the grievances by adopting a petition calling attention to a previous request for better government which remained unsatisfied, to the difficulty of those in poorer circumstances maintaining their just right in lands because of the distance of the capital, and to the action of Congress which questioned Virginia's right to land west of the mountains. Rather lamely they suggested that the land belonged to themselves if not to Virginia, and that they were not subject to Congress until they applied for admission as a new state. What they wanted was to continue as a part of the Old Dominion but to persuade Virginia to redress their grievances.[37]

Another phase of this early movement seems to have occurred in Jefferson County in 1783. A number of petitions were circulated, secretly at first and then openly, addressed to Congress as the immediate sovereign of the signers. The attorney for the commonwealth, Walker Daniel, prosecuted the leaders before the District Court as divulgers of false news under an "old law" passed at the time of the English Restoration. The attorney later confessed: "I was for a considerable time almost at a loss to know under what Law he [one of the leaders] should be punished. To prosecute him for high crimes & misdemeanors, was unprecedented . . . [and] his crime did not amount to Treason. . . ." Apparently, Daniel, like Clark, was chiefly interested in reducing "the people to subordination." One of the leaders, who was named Pomeroy, was fined two thousand pounds of tobacco, the extent of the law, and was put under bond for good behavior. "The other members of the party are two [sic] inconsiderable to dread any Danger from . . . ," he observed.[38] After the movement was temporarily suppressed, Virginia refused any substantial reform of the land law and the Confederation Congress was unable to act contrary to the wishes of Virginia. Consequently, the movement disappeared until revived under new leadership a year later.

At the same time that the Kentuckians were considering the possibility of separate statehood, the question was raised again in the

Monongahela-Ohio area, where in 1776 a petition had been signed requesting the establishment of a state with the name of Westsylvania. During the Revolution, the settlers had been kept in confusion by the boundary dispute between Virginia and Pennsylvania. An agreement, reached on August 31, 1779, proved disappointing to the Virginians and to the Croghan-Indiana-Vandalia speculators who combined all of the speculative claims since 1749. The speculators furnished the leadership of the statehood movement, but intolerable conditions gave them their opportunity and stimulated the settlers to act.

That conditions were bad may be seen from letters of various leaders.[39] Some of the settlers who had failed to complete their land titles had been satisfied with pre-emption claims or mere occupancy. Now the establishment of Pennsylvania's authority ended their opportunity to secure title to the land and necessitated service in the armies and the payment of taxes in specie. The abolition of slavery may also have been a cause of discontent to a few. In the midst of war the frontiersmen were scarcely able to meet the responsibilities of regular government imposed by Pennsylvania, although the end of confusion was certainly much to be desired. The agitation over the cession of western land claims to the national government tended to increase the uncertainty, particularly since it was thought possible that all land west of the mountains might be ceded. That the movement for statehood was continued in order to increase this possibility is entirely reasonable. The inefficiency of government, state and national, not only permitted agitation but actually stimulated it. Virginians felt that Virginia had abandoned them. Pennsylvania authority was scarcely established for a year after the organization of Washington County in 1781, and the national government was, at times, unable to keep or supply an adequate garrison at Fort Pitt, much less to defend the area.

Before the middle of 1780 petitions were signed in support of a new state, meetings were held, and excitement swept the region. One of the petitions after referring to that Freedom and Independence "due to all Freeborn Sons of Liberty" and the hardship and grief of pioneer life requested that Congress organize the people west of the Alleghenies in a distinct and separate state. It claimed that the mountains between them and the Eastern states, which kept their produce out of Eastern markets, created a different interest and made impossible the payment of taxes in specie. Were they a separate state, trade would develop on the western waters, and they would be able to bear their share in the Revolution. "The people have a right to emigrate from one State to another, and form New States. . . . Whenever they Can thereby promote their own Ease & Safety," the petition asserted.[40]

Agitation continued through 1781 and 1782. A proposal to emigrate into the Indian country and to establish a government for themselves was discussed.[41] This was the plan of desperate men. Pennsylvania was sufficiently disturbed to pass an act, already referred to, declaring it to be treason to attempt to form a new government within the boundaries of the state. [42] Congress, too, recognized the situation by issuing a proclamation on September 22, 1783, prohibiting "all persons from making settlements on lands inhabited or claimed by Indians, without the limits or jurisdiction of any particular State, and from purchasing or receiving any gift or cession of such lands or claims without the express authority and directions of the United states. . . ." [43] The congressional proclamation gives a clue to what may have happened to many of the new-state people. A considerable number may have carried out the plan of migrating to the Indian country northwest of the Ohio and of forming their own government.

The people of western Virginia sent in 1783 to the Virginia Assembly an interesting petition requesting that the territory west of the mountains be erected into a separate state. It breathed loyalty to the Union and pride for the part taken in the Revolution, at the same time that it warned of the dangers of despotic government and of one state's exerting an undue influence over others. It contains the passage which Frederick J. Turner enjoyed quoting: "Some of our fellow citizens may think we are not yet able to conduct our affairs, and consult our interest; but if our society is rude, much wisdom is not necessary to supply our wants, and a fool can sometimes put on his clothes better than a wise man can do it for him. . . . If indeed our inexperience should disqualify us from the management of ourselves, there is not a right with which our constitution indulges us, but might be taken from us upon the same principles. . . ." [44]

The situation in the Illinois Country was such that complaints and a petition were sent to Virginia and to Congress. François Carbonneaux talked with Walker Daniel on February 3, 1783, and complained that the Illinois Country was without government, that crimes went unpunished, and that great purchases of land were being made and settled by "men wholly subservient" to the purchasers. He asked that an executive officer be sent with troops to keep order, that civil officers be appointed to reside in each village, and that they might be permitted to enjoy their own laws and customs.[45] When this and other efforts proved fruitless, appeals were sent to Congress. One of these was carried east by Dorsey Pentecost, formerly engaged in the new-state activities in the Monongahela Valley. After noting the aid they had rendered to George Rogers Clark, the losses and suffering during the Revolution, and the nonpayment of the petitioners' claims by Virginia, the petition requested the formation of a new state and aid in framing a constitution.[46]

Washington County, Virginia, was the most distant from the state capital except Kentucky and Illinois. Like them, it was also the scene of dissatisfaction and the residence of a man who became a persistent leader of the discontented. Arthur Campbell laid plans for separation from Virginia, suggesting the election of delegates to form a new state in what is now southwestern Virginia and northeastern Tennessee. The apportionment of representation was to be based upon "the number of farmers above eighteen years of age." [47]

When Congress adopted Jefferson's Ordinance of 1784, when North Carolina passed its first cession act, and when the people just south of the Virginia boundary began to discuss statehood, Campbell could not restrain himself. "A Memorial" was sent to Congress requesting the formation of a mountain state between the Great Smokies and the Cumberland Mountains to extend from the New River in southwestern Virginia to the great bend of the Tennessee. With this petition he forwarded articles of association which had been drawn up resolving, among other things, "that the lands 'cultivated by individuals belong strictly to them, and not to the government, otherwise every citizen would be a tenant and not a landlord, a vassal and not a freeman; and every government would be a usurpation, not an instrumental device for public good.' " [48]

Because of his activity looking to the separation from Virginia of its southwestern counties, the government deprived Campbell of his offices in the militia and the county court and adopted a law which declared it to be high treason to erect an independent government within the state. He gave up his agitation and was quickly restored to favor. Perhaps his most important work was in encouraging the separatist movement in the Kentucky and Tennessee areas.

Seemingly the desire for new state governments was widespread west of the mountains, but in the Valley of the Tennessee the desire was to find embodiment in the State of Franklin. Settlers following the headwaters of the Tennessee had advanced from the Watauga along the Holston to the Nolichucky and the French Broad. The valley lying between the Blue Ridge and the Cumberland Mountains formed an area divided from the states to the east and separated from the unoccupied lands to the west. It was a natural area for a distinctive community, a "castle for a Commonwealth." [49]

Fundamental causes contributed to this effort to obtain a new government. The most important factors were the burden of self-defense, the difficulty and cost of a journey over the mountains to attend the legislature or the higher courts, the inability of a distant government to understand the needs of the westerners, the drainage of specie in the payment of taxes and in the purchase of necessities in the East, the impossibility of exporting surplus products because of distance and the intervening mountains, the presence in the population of many who were not North Carolinians, the normal desire of the people to form their own government, and the provision in the constitution of North Carolina for a western state. More immediate than these were the promise of Congress to form new states in the West, the offer of North Carolina to cede her western lands, and the uncomplimentary remarks by North Carolina legislators about the desirability of being rid of the people over the mountains.[50]

Before the news reached them that North Carolina had repealed its acts of cession, militia companies had elected delegates to meetings in each of the three western counties; they in turn had chosen members of a convention which assembled at Jonesboro on December 14, 1784, to form the state of Franklin. The constitution of North Carolina, with slight changes, was tentatively adopted. The property qualification for representatives was abolished; for senators and the governor, it was reduced by two thirds and three fourths, respectively. Another convention was called to adopt a permanent constitution in the following year.

When this convention met in November, 1785, a committee introduced a new constitution, which is often called the "Houston Constitution." Although the committee stated that the North Carolina constitution had been taken as the basis of its work, approximately one third of its sections had been copied from the Pennsylvania constitution of 1776; another third differed from those of any other existing state constitution, but the remaining third resembled sections of the North Carolina constitution. Several of the latter were also to be found in the Pennsylvania document. The declaration of rights had been copied from the North Carolina bill of rights. Obviously, the committee had not adhered closely to its avowed basis, nor had it produced an original constitution, although it possessed some new and unusual features.

The members of its proposed unicameral legislature were to be required to meet property, religious, and moral qualifications. They were to own one hundred acres of land, which was the same as the requirement for senators in the temporary constitution. They were to believe in a future state of rewards and punishments, in the divine inspiration of the Scriptures, and in the Trinity. They were not to be guilty of "such flagrant enormities as drunkenness, gaming, profane swearing, lewdness, Sabbath breaking, and such like. . . ." [51] The legislature was to establish and endow a university and "if experience shall make it appear useful to the interest of learning" a grammar school in each county. State and local officers were to be elected by free manhood suffrage. A system of meetings in districts of a hundred freemen, directed by registrars, for purposes of petition or remonstrance was to provide a scheme of popular agitation very similar to the Pennsylvania associations or the New England town meeting. The attitude of its supporters is revealed in the protest signed by them when their work was rejected. They said it was intended to secure "the poor and the ruled from being trampled on by the rich and the rulers; also their property and money from being taken from them to support the extravagance of the great men—and that it is full of that which tends to free them from prevailing enormous wickedness, and to make the citizens virtuous, also, that it is well calculated to open the eyes of the people to . . . know and judge for themselves when their rights and privileges are enjoyned or infringed; and therefore suitable to remove ignorance from the country, which is . . . beneficial to men who wish to live upon the people. . . ." [52]

Its rejection by the convention may have been from one point of view a defeat of democracy in the wilderness, but clean-cut victories or defeats are rare. Human history proceeds from one compromise to another. It may have been "a sincere attempt to put the reins of power . . . into the hands of the people, and to provide an enlightened administration," [53] but it also smacks of clerical influence and of the rule of the righteous. The people of the Southern colonies had experienced an aristocracy built upon wealth, family, and religion, and in the early state constitutions were often found provisions excluding ministers from holding office. What percentage of the people would have been excluded from office by the provision that officers must not be guilty of "such flagrant enormities as drunkedness, gaming, profane swearing, lewdness, Sabbath breaking, and such like . . ." is not ascertainable; but it could not have been small, for these offenses were common. If put into effect, it might have established an undemocratic theocracy that would have rivaled Massachusetts Bay under the original charter. Furthermore, its property qualification for members of the legislature was as high as that for senators in the constitution later adopted. For anyone not owning a hundred acres of land the chance of being a legislator was theoretically greater as a result of the defeat of the Houston constitution. It would, therefore, seem far too simple a statement to identify democracy with this defeated constitution. It seems to have been a mixture of Pennsylvania's radical democracy, Presbyterian theocracy, and conservatism.

The temporary constitution, which was a slightly modified form of the North Carolina constitution, was adopted in its place. This action in reality merely followed the Ordinance of 1784, which provided that the constitution and laws of one of the original states should be adopted. In addition to the debatable provisions of the Houston constitution another factor had arisen in the need of persuading North Carolinians to agree to the independence of Franklin, which might be furthered by the adoption of a constitution so similar to their own. Independence would mean freedom from the aristocracy of the Tidewater, which would have been in itself a marked advance in democracy, irrespective of minor details.

That land speculation was involved in the fate of the State of Franklin cannot be denied. It does not seem to account for the fundamental causes of the movement, although it may have been influential in providing the immediate occasion for the revolt. More plausible, however, is the contention that its defeat was caused by the anxiety of the speculators to protect their ill-gotten claims before the Westerners should be allowed to govern themselves. The conflict was not a simple or an edifying struggle, but the self-seeking of the few does not obscure the desire of the many for the chance to free themselves from the Tidewater aristocrats and to establish their own government. The conduct of the Old North State, under the control of a group of land speculators, is the best possible justification of the Westerners' request for independence.

Gradually, the strength of North Carolina wore down the young state, whose leader, John Sevier, may have been untrue to his trust. But another attempt was made to persuade the mother state to let them go. In December, 1787, a petition was again presented to the General Assembly of North Carolina, explaining their conduct. It eloquently pleaded for freedom from North Carolina.

The Inhabitants of the Western Country Humbly Sheweth—That it is with sincere concern we lament the unhappy dispute that have long subsisted between us, and our Brethren on the Eastern Side of the Mountains, respecting the Erecting a new Government. We beg leave to represent to your Honourable body, that from Acts passed in June, 1784, ceding to Congress your Western territory with the reservations and Conditions therein contained. Also from a clause in your Wise and Mild Constitution, setting forth that there might be a State, or States, erected in the West whenever your Legislature should give consent for the same, and from our local situation numberless advantages, bountifully given to us by nature, to propagate & promote a Government with us. Being influenced by your Acts and Constitution, and at the same time considering that it is our undeniable right to obtain for ourselves and posterity a proportionable and adequate share of the blessings, rights, privileges and Immunities allotted with the rest of mankind, have thought that the Erecting a new Government would greatly contribute to our welfare and convenience and that the same could not militate against your interest and future welfare as a Government. Hoping that mutual & reciprocal advantages would attend each party & that cordiality and unanimity would permanently subsist between us ever after. We earnestly request that an impartial view of our remoteness might be taken into consideration. The great inconveniency attending your seat of Government, and also the great difficulty in ruling well & giving protection to so remote a people. To say nothing of the almost impassable mountains, Nature has placed between us, which renders it impracticable for us to furnish ourselves with a bare load of the necessaries of life, except we in the first instance travel from one to two hundred & more miles through some other State 'ere we can reach your government. Every tax paid you from this county would render us that sum the poorer, . . . and by these means our property would gradually diminish and we at last reduced to mere poverty and want by not being able equally, to participate with the benefits and advantages of your government. We hope that having settled west of the Apalachian Mountains ought not to deprive us of the natural advantages designed by the bountiful hand of Providence for the conveniency & comfort of all those who have Spirit and sagacity enough to seek after them. When we reflect on our past & indefatigable Struggles, both with savages and our other Enemies during our late war, and the great difficulty we had to obtain and withhold this Country from those Enemies at the expence of the lives and fortunes of many of our dearest friends and relations, and the happy conclusion of peace have arrived, North Carolina has derived great advantages from our alertness in taking & securing a Country from which she has been able to draw into her Treasury immense sums of money, and thereby become enabled to pay off, if not wholly, yet a great part and sink her national debt. We therefore humbly conceive you will liberally think that it will be nothing more than paying a debt in full to us for only to grant what God, Nature & our Locality entitles us to receive. Trusting that your magnanimity and justice will not consider it a crime in any people to pray their just rites and privileges, we call the world to testify our conduct and exertion in behalf of American Independency, and the same to judge whither we ask more than free people ought to claim agreeable to Republican principles, the grand foundation whereon our American fabric now stands. . . . Lastly, we hope to be enabled by the concurrence of your State to participate of the fruits of the Revolution; and enjoy the essential benefits of Civil Society under a form of Government which ourselves alone, can only calculate for such a purpose.[54]

North Carolina, however, refused to be persuaded. She tried to win back the rebels by forgiving unpaid taxes and by accepting their representatives as members of the state legislature and of the convention which ratified the federal constitution. Although the government of Franklin functioned until 1788, success seemed out of the question; the easiest way to escape their dilemma was to return to their allegiance to North Carolina. Franklin came to an end, but fundamental causes soon led others to draw a state boundary line in part where the Franklinites had tried to draw it.

The constitution of Franklin, therefore, represented only a slight constitutional advance toward greater democracy. The real defeat of liberal development was the refusal of independence and, in the main, this was due to the Tidewater aristocracy, which denied democratic government to the people of North Carolina as well as of Franklin.

5

Independence From the Tidewater: Kentucky

A GREAT trans-Appalachian migration, between 1775 and 1790, peopled Kentucky with a mixed population. Settlers had come by way of Boone's Wilderness Road from the Watauga-Holston area, where the stream of frontiersmen from the Valley of Virginia had received tributary streams from the Carolinas. Another important movement came on the waters of the Ohio River, bringing frontiersmen from the Monongahela-Ohio region, where Pennsylvanians, Marylanders, and Virginians had already intermingled. The different frontier people who traveled these routes generally had enough experiences in common to work together. Boone's Trace was undoubtedly preferred by Carolinians and probably by a majority of Virginians from the southern counties.

Not only were the Kentuckians from various Eastern states, but they represented different social classes and economic interests. Even the Virginians must not be considered as forming a single group. The early Kentuckians recognized the difference between the Tuckahoes, or eastern Virginians, and the Cohees, or the Virginians who lived west of the Blue Ridge.[1] The latter were often Scotch-Irish and Germans who entered the Valley from Maryland and Pennsylvania. Included also were poor frontiersmen who hoped to obtain small farms, yeoman farmers who could buy small pieces of land, and rich planters who brought a few slaves to Kentucky. Some of the farmers preferred the yeoman way of life, but others were able to acquire enough land to lift themselves into the planter class. At the top were the representatives of wealth who secured large family estates or who speculated in thousands and even hundreds of thousands of acres. Possibly influenced by their economic position were radicals who strove to change existing conditions, moderates who saw little need for extreme changes, and conservatives who sought to establish west of the mountains the aristocratic political, social, and economic order of the Tidewater, and who regarded the radicals as dangerous to eminently satisfactory institutions and customs. The wealthy planters were not numerous; but their family connections, training, ability, and wealth often enabled them to exert influence disproportionate to their numbers.

The settlement of Kentucky and other areas west of the Appalachian watershed had created grave governmental and economic problems which had produced various separatist movements in the different regions.[2] Virginia had received ample warning that discontent was widespread on her far-flung frontier. Some of her responsibilities had been shifted by the cession to Congress of her claims to lands northwest of the Ohio and by the settlement of her boundary dispute with Pennsylvania. But she failed to understand the needs of her Kentucky frontier, or, if she understood, to satisfy those needs until she had exploited the choicest of Kentucky lands, a policy which gave great advantage to rich speculators at the expense of poor settlers. It may be pleaded that Virginia was hard pressed during the Revolution and that from time to time she undertook to remedy some of Kentucky's grievances. But she did little better after the Revolution, and the aristocratic features of her philosophy prevented a realization of fundamental conditions on the frontier or a recognition of the ideals of the frontiersmen. Virginia was not alone in this failure, for the national government often acted in a similar manner. Only the organization of territorial and state governments gave an opportunity for persons well acquainted with the problem of the frontier to initiate measures for their solution.

The government at Richmond, controlled by Virginia planters, did not understand or appreciate the needs of the frontier sufficiently to provide for adequate government and defense. The distant state government regulated the militia of the frontier counties and thus determined the methods of defense.[3] The location of forts, the distribution of the troops, and the procedure to be followed by the militia were sometimes determined by men who knew relatively little about actual conditions or held aims other than those of the settlers. Kentucky's militia was ordered to remain within their own borders and to act on the defensive in Indian warfare, although Westerners well knew that the best defense was a vigorous and swift offense. Finally, when the national government scattered a few troops along the northwest bank of the Ohio, Virginia required that permission be sought in Richmond before the Kentucky militia could co-operate and finally ordered the dismissal of the scouts and rangers on the assumption that the scattered garrisons filled the need.[4] By the time a messenger traveled to Richmond and back, Indians could easily lose themselves in the Canadian woods. The testimony of informed and intelligent men that Virginia's policy was inadequate seems unanimous.[5] But the policy was continued, and the real cost in property, blood, and lives was paid by Kentuckians.

Connection with Virginia involved other disadvantages. Representation in the legislature, appeals to the superior court, petitions or protests to state officials involved a long, costly, and dangerous journey to Richmond. The distance to the capital worked to the advantage of the wealthy. The purchase price for land went to Virginia, and taxes tended to drain away the slender supply of specie which the frontier possessed. Even a portion of the surveyor's fee went to William and Mary College. The mountains to the east and Spanish closure of the Mississippi River prevented the export to distant markets of surplus products which might have met expenses like taxes, the cost of land, and necessary imports. To her credit, Virginia recognized the significance of the navigation of the Mississippi and cannot be held responsible for the intervening mountains; but land and governmental policies were hers, and their continuance in the face of discontent could lead only to a demand for separation. Various individuals acquired princely domains which were defended by the poorer frontiersmen: John May was granted by Virginia prior to statehood 369,813 acres; Thomas Shore, 254,763; and James Reynolds, 254,340. Altogether eight individuals received more than 200,000 acres each.[6] Some of the wealthy were absentee landowners, but some of the men who defended Kentucky failed to secure even a small farm. Furthermore, when Kentuckians saw the colonies win their rights to independence and self-government and themselves experienced inefficient government and inadequate defense, it was only natural that they should aspire to autonomy and self-determination in local affairs.[7]

At the supreme [district] court in November 1784, Col. Benjamin Logan called together at Danville a large number of the Inhabitants from all parts of this District who were attending there on business, and informed them that he had lately been to the Cherokee Nation to enquire about certain hostilities that had lately been committeed on this Country; and from the information he gave of the mischiefs that had been done, and the then hostile intention of the Savages, it was thought necessary immediately to carry an expedition against them. The meeting adjourned until the next day, when a large number met to devise ways and means for carrying on the said expedition; But finding there was no law to call out Militia or procure provisions, they were obliged to decline it.

Alarmed at this situation, every one present saw the absolute necessity of calling together the wisdom of the District in a general Council to take into consideration the then state of our detached and distressed Country; and they directed that every Captains company should elect a man for that purpose.[8]

"A Real Friend to the People" implied that this statement about the calling of the meeting was not complete, but he did not offer specific information. A recent writer has emphasized the falseness of the Indian alarm. It seems, however, unwise to minimize the danger of Indian attack, the lack of wisdom concerning the restraints placed upon the militia by Virginia, or the failure of Virginia to be more co-operative in defense. Kentucky had come into existence and had lived only in the midst of Indian warfare. It is hardly in accord with the character of Westerners and particularly Kentuckians that they should bear these disadvantages indefinitely and remain quiescent.[9]

In May, Virginia had passed an act levying a tax of five shillings per hundred acres on all land grants in excess of fourteen hundred acres.[10] It has been suggested that this was the real reason why prominent Virginians, who had formerly opposed separation, began and supported a new independence movement, and that the meeting called by Colonel Logan was initiated by land speculators rather than by persons aroused chiefly by other grievances.[11] This interpretation seems to exaggerate the importance not only of land speculation, however prevalent it may have been, but particularly of this taxation measure. It would have been far easier to secure its repeal directly, rather than to go to the trouble of forming a new state to accomplish the purpose indirectly. As a matter of fact, the act was repealed at the October, 1785, session of the Virginia legislature,[12] and its revocation had little effect upon the statehood movement. It should also be borne in mind that fundamental causes of long standing had produced a separatist movement more widespread than the boundaries of Kentucky, and that the new movement in Kentucky differed from the older in being supported by more Virginians and more prominent Kentuckians. Was it not possible that an accumulation of grievances, of which the land tax was one, finally convinced former Virginians of a situation which others had seen first?

The assembled leaders discussed the situation for two days and recommended that each militia company elect one representative and that these representatives meet on December 27 to consider the desirability of requesting separation from Virginia.

"The measure thus recommended was adopted. Elections were held; and the persons elected convened at the time and place appointed; and after deliberating on the state of the country for about ten days, resolved, that many inconveniences under which they laboured might be removed by the legislature of Virginia. But that the great and substantial evils to which they were subjected, arose from causes beyond the power or control of that government, viz. from their remote and detached situation, and could never be redressed until the district had a government of its own." [13] Thus commented William Littell, who wrote one of the earliest accounts of Kentucky's efforts to secure statehood. The statement was later copied by John Bradford in his *Notes on Kentucky*.

During the sessions of the convention, various resolutions were adopted. The first group called attention to a number of defects of existing laws, and, although quite mild, may have served to convince the delegates that their meeting was justified.[14] A second group which was adopted five days later demonstrated considerable feeling because of Eastern discrimination against the West.[15] The protest against the tax recently imposed upon large land grants in Kentucky was the only one upon which a roll call was recorded, and the defeated opposition apparently demanded and got a resolution against large land grants as subversive of republican principles and conducive to speculation and other evils. The third set of resolutions declared that many grievances stemming from the remoteness of Kentucky could not be remedied by Virginia.[16] The delegates recommended that a convention be called to consider the expediency of separation from Virginia and that representation in it be arranged on the basis of equal numbers.[17]

As suggested by the first convention a second met in Danville, May 23, 1785. Virginia was requested to establish Kentucky as "a separate and independent state" and to recommend to Congress that it be "taken into union with the United States of America, to enjoy equal privileges in common with them." The convention declared "that the remote situation of the district from the seat of government, together with sundry other inconveniences, subjects the good people thereof to a number of grievances too pressing to be longer borne, and which cannot be remedied whilst the district continues a part of the state of Virginia. . . ." Asserting in a mild form the right of revolution, the convention listed the grievances which justified its action. Although separation was requested, a third convention was called to give further consideration to the question.[18]

In explanation of this latter action, "A Farmer" wrote: "But as we had no press in the Country, and fearing the good people in general had not sufficient notice, and would not be fully satisfied with the measure, they resolved to publish their resolutions in writing as well as they could at the Court-houses and elsewhere; and ordered a new Election, recommending it to the people (as before) seriously to consider of the expediency of the measure proposed." [19]

Accordingly, a third convention, which assembled on August 8, 1785, adopted a new series of resolutions affirming those of the previous convention and adding additional details. Among them is a vigorous protest against the tax imposed upon large holdings of land. The resolutions do not refer to membership in the Union, but the appeal to Virginia describes it as the consummation of their desires.[20]

In response to the petition, Virginia authorized the calling of a convention to accept the terms of separation. The proposed state must assume a share of Virginia's indebtedness, guarantee that land rights were to remain unchanged, and that resident and non-resident landholders were to be taxed equally. If Congress agreed to admit the new state, a constitution was to be prepared under which Kentucky could become a state in the American nation.[21]

Normally, Kentucky would soon have become a state, but a combination of circumstances interrupted the process. Indian warfare, which had been less prevalent since the close of the Revolution, again broke forth. In September, 1786, at the time set for the meeting of the fourth convention, which was to accept or reject the terms of separation, many of the members were absent with George Rogers Clark in the Wabash Valley or with Benjamin Logan in the Scioto Valley on expeditions against the Indians. "On the 26th day of September the members present formed themselves into a committee, prepared a memorial to the legislature of Virginia, stating the reason why the convention could not proceed to business, & requesting that some alterations might be made in the act of separation. . . ." [22] John Marshall was the messenger who carried the memorial to Richmond. A quorum was not present until January, when a resolution was adopted favoring separation.

Whether "A Farmer" referred to the work of this committee and to John Marshall or to another group is not entirely clear. He charged "A Real Friend to the People" (was he John Marshall?) with preparing a petition, securing about seventy signatures, and carrying it to Richmond, where he caused the legislature to doubt the popularity of the separation movement in Kentucky. An act was passed requiring the election of another convention which was to restate Kentucky's desire in respect to separation. The bearer of the petition returned with a copy of the new act, just as the fourth convention resolved in favor of separation. Fearing that further proceedings might be illegal, the convention adjourned.[23]

Kentuckians must have been very much discouraged during the winter of 1786–1787. First came the news of the failure of Clark's expedition. Then came the action of Virginia in respect to statehood, which meant a year's delay. In fact, it eventually caused a much longer delay, for it gave time for other events to intervene. In March came word that John Jay was about to surrender the navigation of the Mississippi River to Spain in return for concessions advantageous to Eastern commercial interests. Finally, in the spring, Indian relations reached a new crisis. It is not surprising that the statehood movement ceased to move along as smoothly as before.

In the columns of the Kentucky *Gazette*, which was founded before the next convention was scheduled to meet, opponents and supporters of separation appealed to the public. A letter "To the Good People of Kentucke" set forth in some detail the argument that the need of adequate military defense was the strongest reason for separation.[24] "A Virginian" replied in three communications in which he opposed this solution, minimized the grievances upon which the separationists based their case, and denied that Kentuckians had a real case against Virginia in respect to defense.[25] "An Inhabitant of Kentucke" also opposed independence, claiming that taxes would be too heavy if a state government were established and asserting that Virginia's aid was needed in defense against the Indians and against Spain, whether the contest was diplomatic or military.[26] "A Kentuckean," in answer to "A Virginian," repeated the contention that Kentuckians could not defend themselves as long as they were subject to the restrictions which Virginia had imposed.[27] "A Native of Virginia" attacked "A Virginian" without adding very much to the discussion.[28] Perhaps more radical ideas than these circulated by word of mouth or by handbills, for Littell asserted that some of the leaders favored a declaration of independence without waiting longer for Virginia.[29] More conservative counsel prevailed, however, and the delegates who were elected to the fifth convention were not greatly different from their predecessors.

This new representative assemblage, meeting on September 17, 1787, again resolved in favor of separation and sent to Congress a request to be admitted to the Union. Provision was also made for the election of a convention, which was to meet in July of the next year to frame a constitution for the proposed state.[30]

Individuals offered suggestions about the constitution which they expected to be prepared. "Republicus" preferred a legislature of only one house and regretted that the new constitution for the United States contained a provision which prevented the prohibition of the slave trade at that time.[31] "Mancipium," who claimed to be a Negro, wanted a scheme of gradual emancipation adopted.[32] "A Citizen of Kentucky" favored representation by numbers rather than by counties, as well as a unicameral legislature, but opposed high salaries for officials.[33] A letter copied from the Maryland *Journal* represented an extreme viewpoint, for it sought to arouse the people everywhere against the aristocrats who were in control of government.[34] One might ask what were the opinions of the editor who copied such a letter?

The expectation indicated by these suggestions was not to be fulfilled immediately, for the Congress of the Confederation refused to admit Kentucky before the new national constitution took effect.[35] When the Kentucky convention met to prepare a constitution, the delegates were confronted with the disappointing news. Kentuckians who had repeatedly experienced the failure of Virginia to defend them and a more recent but similar failure on the part of Congress, now learned that the navigation of the Mississippi was in danger of surrender to a foreign power and that they were not to be permitted the right of defending their interests on the floor of Congress.

In the face of this second defeat of their expectations, the delegates organized and recommended that a new convention, the seventh, be elected and that it be given power to take the necessary measures to secure admission to the Union, the navigation of the Mississippi, and the preparation of a constitution.[36] These were broader powers than had been granted to any previous convention, and they seem to indicate the possibility of more radical procedure.

Stimulated, perhaps, by the fear of what a convention might do when granted such broad powers, the antiseparationists, in spite of much opposition, made a concerted effort to persuade the public that the connection with Virginia was preferable. "Cornplanter," who was utterly opposed to separation from Virginia and independence from Congress, denied the contentions that separation would help solve the problem of defense or secure the navigation of the Mississippi River. Believing that the movement for statehood was not favored by the majority of Kentuckians,[37] he made a second plea for the postponement of separation and called attention to the repeal by Virginia of laws that bore heavily on Kentucky.[38] "A Fellow Citizen," who criticized the views of "Cornplanter," asserted that the conventions had repeatedly indicated the people's wish for separation.[39] A petition of "Real Cornplanters" requested that "Cornplanter" be silenced as he was bringing disgrace upon them.[40] "Poplicola" came to the defense of "Cornplanter" but differed with him in respect to the advisability of separation.[41] "A Farmer" traced briefly the statehood movement from the beginning, defending it as both desirable and popular. Maintaining that the laws were executed with favoritism for the rich,[42] he criticized existing conditions as very severe on the poor. George Muter, the only writer to sign his own name, was willing to secure separation only in a constitutional manner and with the consent of Virginia, but not as the result of revolutionary action. He also opposed any activity to secure the navigation of the Mississippi River except with the aid of Congress or Virginia.[43] "Brutus," in the same issue of the *Gazette,* assured the public that, although there were considerable differences about giving the convention such broad powers, these differences had been sensibly compromised, and denied the existence of treason or danger of passing under the control of Spain.[44] "An Inhabitant of Kentucke" expressed a deep-seated fear of separation, indicating that he thought the separationists might endeavor to set Kentucky free of Congress as well as Virginia. He warned them that the law of treason would apply and demanded some system other than a convention to ascertain the wishes of the people.[45] "Valerius" also wrote against separation, assuring his readers that additional taxes and political offices would be the only results of the change.[46]

Just what passed by word of mouth or by handbill of which no record is preserved today, one can only guess. Littell wrote that sharp differences of opinion appeared in the elections and among the delegates.[47] Some of the delegates may have preferred an immediate declaration of independence from Virginia and the formation of a constitution, leaving the relation with the national government to be determined later and possibly in connection with the navigation of the Mississippi River. Even this more radical procedure did not necessarily imply disloyalty to the United States, for it was followed by Vermont under somewhat different conditions with the result that Vermont was admitted to the Union two years ahead of Kentucky, which followed more conservative and constitutional methods.

Because the journal is meager and because the activity of James Wilkinson, soldier, merchant, and conspirator, then resident in Kentucky, serves to arouse ideas of disloyalty in the mind of the reader, it is difficult to reconstruct developments in the convention which met November 3–10, 1788. The opinions held about Wilkinson have, no doubt, determined the attitude many have taken about the convention. A resolution to draw up a decent and respectful address to Virginia requesting independence and another resolution stating that the people wished to be separated from Virginia and erected into an "Independent member of the Federal Union" were laid on the table. Wilkinson then introduced a resolution which stated that "the discordant opinions which at present divide the good people . . . renders it doubtfull whether they can, adopte any plan, which will . . . secure the support of a majority . . . [and therefore the convention should] draft an address, to the good people . . . [requesting] instruction." The convention seemed to be badly divided, with Wilkinson endeavoring to secure further delay. At this point Sunday intervened, and on Monday the delegates reassembled and acted without apparent confusion. Wilkinson reported a petition to Congress on the navigation of the Mississippi and an address to Virginia requesting separation. He may have written both documents, since they were inflated or even bombastic in style; [48] both, however, were conservative. At some time during the convention Wilkinson reported upon his recent journey to New Orleans, and the delegates by resolution approved the address and thanked him for it. If he planned either to defeat the movement or to secure radical action, his efforts resulted in failure. He may, however, have merely desired to appear prominent, and in this effort he succeeded.

Virginia responded promptly but less generously, requiring Kentucky to assume a part of the domestic as well as the public indebtedness of Virginia and reserving to herself a right to unappropriated lands in Kentucky for a short time after separation had been granted.[49] The Kentucky *Gazette* contains little evidence that the people were excited about the coming convention. "A Real Friend to the People," who replied to the earlier communication of "A Farmer," denied that the separation movement was favored by a majority of the people, charged that it was cleverly manipulated, and implied that its supporters were the aristocratic party.[50] Returning to the attack, "Valerius" asserted that the arguments for independence were based on ignorance and that taxes would not be lowered or the laws more wholesome if independence were achieved.[51]

The convention regarded the new terms as unacceptable and as injurious to the people of the district.[52] Virginia was asked to restore the terms that had been previously offered, and she replied by passing a fourth act, which repealed the objectionable terms and called a ninth convention to express again the will of Kentucky in respect to separation.[53] Again the period passed with little comment in the Kentucky *Gazette,* a fact which may indicate that nearly everyone regarded the issue as settled. In a disjointed and absurd letter, perhaps written that way to give support to the claim that he was a mechanic, "A Real Friend to the People" tried again to persuade the people against separation. He asked: "Is there not a decided majority of our inhabitants without even a claim to land in this district?" Ignoring the fact that this condition had developed under the laws of Virginia, he suggested that separation would result in a monopoly of trade by the Spanish and an ecclesiastical establishment and therefore recommended instructing the delegates against separation.[54]

Again Kentuckians went to the polls to elect delegates to a convention to decide that it was expedient to establish a new state. Apparently Virginia experienced some difficulty in believing that Kentuckians actually wanted to govern themselves. The ninth convention met on July 26, 1790, accepted the new terms, provided for the election of a constitutional convention, and set June 1, 1792, as the date when the state of Kentucky should come into being. It also petitioned the President and Congress of the United States to admit "into the federal Union the people of Kentucky by the name of the State of Kentucky." [55] Congress answered this petition favorably on February 4, 1791. Elections were held in December and the convention met in April, 1792.

An analysis of the membership of the conventions reveals interesting information about the separation movement. Lists of the membership of eight of the ten conventions have been preserved; 287 delegates were chosen to attend these assemblies. Because several individuals were elected to more than one convention, only 143 different persons were in attendance. Of these, twenty were delegated as members of four or more of the eight conventions. Generally, they were former residents and often natives of Virginia, who received moderate grants of land from that state. They do not seem to have been the great land speculators, nor had they been residents of other states. Among them were Samuel McDowell, Caleb Wallace, Isaac Shelby, and Benjamin Logan, men from the Valley of Virginia who had struggled to liberalize the government of that state. They were of non-English extraction—Scotch-Irish and Welsh—and their families had been part of the migration from Pennsylvania into the Appalachian Valley.

Among the twenty a few in all probability were not in agreement, either because they were more radical or more conservative, but in each convention were other moderates who belonged to less than four conventions. Generally, the individuals of this group of twenty formed from one third to one half of each of the eight conventions. With the help of a few others of like principles, they seem to have controlled each convention, although the seventh, in November, 1788, seems to have given them considerable trouble. Since the actions of the conventions remained within the limits of constitutional procedure, following a moderate course between the conservatives who opposed separation from Virginia and the extremists who wished to act without the approval of Virginia or Congress, the group which piloted Kentucky through this difficult period must be regarded as moderates. Since they were not the great land owners, but were men of moderate means, land speculation hardly seems to explain their actions. In all probability, a long list of reasons led them to conclude that Kentucky needed a state government of her own and that the need was great enough to keep them active in the movement for eight years and through ten conventions.

Kentuckians had traveled a long and tortuous road during the years 1784–1792, a road which rivaled the Wilderness Road in its windings and discouragements. At last they drew near to the promised land: separation from Virginia, a state government of their own, and membership in the federal Union. Their patience and peaceful perseverance should be recognized as proof of their devotion to constitutional government, their loyalty to the nation, and their determination to govern themselves.

The victory of the separationists should also be regarded as a defeat of the most conservative group in Kentucky. Regardless of the personal beliefs of individuals within the group about the application of democratic principles in state government, attachment to Virginia obstructed self-government in Kentucky. Antiseparationists preferred the political, social, and economic order which had developed in the Old Dominion and its extension to the West. Individuals who had received thousands of acres of land or political preference from Virginia would most likely take this atitude. Their communications to the Kentucky *Gazette* offered no remedies for existing problems. Perhaps a recognition of the reality of the grievances of which the separationists complained and an effort to remove the most glaring inequalities might have saved them from defeat, but like true conservatives nothing alarmed them so much as change. With their defeat Kentucky was ready to try to solve her own problems. The influence of the frontiersmen pulled in one direction, while the beneficiaries of political, social, and economic inequalities pulled in another.

The separation of Kentucky was of national importance. The Northwest Ordinance had provided for the admission of new states "to a share in the federal councils on an equal footing with the original States," and the state of Vermont had been so admitted.

Kentucky, however, belonged to Virginia and not the federal government. With her admission as an equal state the precedent might well be regarded as firmly established. A mother state of superior power was not to control a subordinate area. Whatever exploitation had taken place or might be developed in the United States in the future, it was not to be that of the seventeenth- and eighteenth-century colonial imperialism. The United States was to contain states of equal powers, and this was to give opportunity in the future for Western states to determine the character of the national government.

6

Radicalism in Pioneer Kentucky

*W*HEN IT was apparent that the separation movement would succeed and especially when the time approached for the election of delegates to the constitutional convention, an agitation burst forth which indicated a deep-seated hostility between the classes. It is not possible to differentiate sharply the various classes or to identify the various writers or the views of the different groups with exactitude; but it is possible to get a clear general picture.

From time to time, bits of evidence appeared which give some details about the hostility between the different groups within Kentucky. The statements of George Morgan and John Floyd of 1780 about the landless settlers refusing to fight in defense of the possessions of absentee speculators, which have been previously quoted, are early examples.[1] The convention of 1784–1785 resolved against large grants of land as "subversive of the fundamental Principles of a free republican Government" and as opening the door to "speculation by which innumerable evils may ensue to the less opulent."[2] According to the convention of August, 1785, the expense of suits in the Court of Appeals at Richmond put the poor in the power of the rich.[3] "Our battles have been hitherto fought and our frontiers defended by the poor Militia, the most of whom have little or no property. . . . ," wrote "A Farmer" in 1788.[4] "A Real Friend to the People" asked, as previously noted: "Is there not a decided majority of our inhabitants without even a claim to land in this district?"[5]

These comments indicate the presence at least of a wealthy group which owned most of the land and a poor group which owned little but was expected to do most of the fighting. For convenience they may be referred to as planters and frontiersmen: planters who desired to establish for themselves a social, political, and economic order resembling that of Virginia; and frontiersmen who hoped to establish a somewhat more democratic order having fewer inequalities and injustices. Frontier society was generally very fluid, and a frontiersman might in a few years become a planter.

The frontiersmen of Kentucky, who had come largely from the back country of the older states, had been subjected to unfair distinctions at the hands of the planter class, who lived in the main in the eastern counties. These discriminations included unequal representation, property qualifications for office holding and voting, an established church, inequalities in taxation, and the failure of the government to provide adequate defense for the frontiers. Probably the majority did not own land but were squatters or tenants. They were hunter-farmers or farmers who worked in the fields and who owned few, if any, slaves. Among them were also many small landowners. But they were generally poor, individualistic, and democratic. They were opposed to the aristocracy of the Tidewater. Some objected to competition with slave labor and to the social problems attendant upon slavery. Clergymen of the churches on the frontier, who were likely to have been shocked at the deism and the worldly ways of the wealthy, were sometimes leaders of the frontiersmen.

It is necessary not to idealize the frontiersmen as so many have done, for they were rough, uncultured, uneducated, undisciplined, and hard to lead. Many may not have been informed about or interested in political questions. Society, however, had to depend upon them for the conquest of the wilderness and the Indians. In other instances they could be aroused by unjust treatment or by skillful leaders. Since coming to Kentucky they had witnessed the imperialism of the Tidewater aristocracy, the seizure of land by the few for personal speculation without regard to the interests of the settlers, and repeated failures to provide adequate defense or to permit the frontier to act efficiently in its own defense.

Planters, lawyers, government officials, and land speculators, who had received offices and large land grants from Virginia, or whose wealth enabled them to invest in western land, formed a conservative or upper class. The campaign of the radicals threatened each of these groups at some vital point. Separation from Virginia would end the offices of the official group, and dislike of slavery threatened the plantation structure. Lawyers were classed with pickpockets and were criticized even more bitterly than the others by

the writers in the Kentucky *Gazette*. Control by Virginia, as has
been seen, was surrendered with great reluctance by many. Having lost on this point, they favored a social and political order patterned on Virginia at least in its general features. The conservatives did not resort to the newspaper to advance their cause, and
only the broadest outlines of their position may be seen. They favored the continuance of the plantation system and slavery, which
was probably accepted by all but the most radical. In order to continue control of politics by the landed aristocracy, they favored
retention of some of the devices which the South Atlantic states had
found so useful—representation based upon geographical areas
rather than numbers of people, property qualifications for office
holding, and a restricted franchise. Above all, they had to defeat
the efforts to place government in the hands of the squatter class.[6]

Between the frontiersmen on the one hand and the planter and
official class on the other hand was a middle or moderate group,
made up of persons of medium wealth and those who utilized the
opportunities of the frontier to secure land and to improve their
social standing. Many of them had experienced the inequalities
of which the frontiersmen complained but had succeeded in escap-
ing some of the worst of them. They did not always surrender the
attitudes and prejudices which they acquired as frontiersmen, and
some of the smaller and more liberal planters were moderates rather
than conservatives.

The demands of the writers whose letters appeared in the Kentucky *Gazette* are more important than the classification of the authors into conservative, moderate, or radical groups. Since they applied various appellations to each other, and since they were not
always consistent, it is difficult to place them accurately. Perhaps
the desire to use the term "aristocratic" as derogatory is significant.[7]

The controversy over the features of the proposed government
for Kentucky began before the success of the separation movement
was assured. In contrast to their opponents, the separationists proposed specific features for the new government. As has been seen,
"Republicus" advocated a unicameral legislature, "Mancipium"
a plan of gradual emancipation, and "A Citizen of Kentucky"
representation according to numbers in a legislature having only
one house. The last also opposed high salaries for officers.[8] "Philo-
patria," who revealed a strong religious leaning and an interest in
education, offered a long bill of rights as material for a constitu-

tion and suggested representation according to numbers.[9] "Theologues" objected to granting religious freedom to any but Protesant Christians.[10] "A Stranger" called attention to the serious prejudice against lawyers and important persons and to the extravagant disposition displayed by the wealthy. "Would to God that this extravagant disposition had never obtained a Pass port through the Allegany Mountains," he wrote. Beyond this letter, however, his radicalism was confined to a suggestion that official salaries should be limited by law.[11]

After the ninth convention accepted the terms offered by Virginia, attention could be devoted entirely to the character of the new state. Two writers seem to have opened the discussion with a series of letters in which they endeavored to instruct the public in the proper principles of political science. "The disinterested Citizen" wrote numerous letters revealing his great interest in establishing a conservative state government. He opposed following Virginia's constitution in permitting the legislature to assume whatever power it pleased, but favored a bill of rights, a bicameral legislature, and a system of checks and balances. In order that it might judge whether the representatives of the people had acted wisely, the upper house of the legislature should not be directly representative of the people. He also opposed manhood suffrage.[12] "A.B.C." was more of a moderate, since he defended the statehood movement but opposed the activities of the radicals. He favored a system of checks and balances and the election of the ablest men to form the constitution.[13]

Meanwhile the radicals began the formation of local and county committees to secure the election of delegates favorable to their views and to prepare instructions to inform them of what the people expected them to do in the convention. Each militia company was to choose a local committee, and each local body was to send two members to a county committee. The latter was to appoint two persons to belong to a general committee for all of Kentucky.

The radicals soon outlined a program and a set of principles. Supreme power was declared to be in the hands of the people, whose wishes could be ascertained in two ways. Annual elections of officials was one of the two, but they noted that elections had been corrupted by flattery and "grog." Because of this corruption they preferred their system of committees. A unicameral legislature, the exclusion of immoral men from office, the choice of civil and militia officers by the people, elections by ballot, the formation of a simple and concise code of laws rather than the reception of English law, and the taxation of all lands and property were features of the radical program. An "Address to the freemen" contained an appeal: "let us . . . be wise enough now, not in any measure to be wheedled out of our just rights, by flattery, grog, or the wag of a ruffled hand." [14] Another communication requested a general committee meeting to form a bill of rights and a constitution that would be suitable.[15]

Because of the emphasis by "A.B.C." upon electing great men to the convention, a proposition which would normally be accepted by everyone, the radicals were placed at a disadvantage.[16] Great men were likely to be planters, land speculators, officers, or lawyers, all probably aristocrats. This situation led "Will Wisp" to reply, "I plainly see that he is not for the good of the country, and therefore he must be a great man. . . . Does he not try to prove that all the common people are fools . . . ? I have long been of opinion, that the business of government is a cheat. . . . Is it not to get good salaries, and to keep the common people in subjection? . . . He deserves great credit, who first raised the cry against great men in this country. . . . There was no other way to manage them, and prevent them from running away with every advantage as they do in other countries. . . . What if they were all hanged, as I hope will shortly be the case? . . . All great men are designing men, . . . let everyone who is for the good of the country keep up the cry against Judges, Lawyers, Generals, Colonels, and all other designing men, and the day will be our own; but my life for it, if we condescend to consider and reason upon the case, we shall remain clod-hoppers forever." [17]

"Felte Firebrand," who proved to be little less than a Tory and far from an arsonist, attacked the committees as disorderly and unauthorized by law and as constituting a violent attempt of the few to rule the many. He claimed that the committees of the Revolution assumed unlimited powers and committed many acts of tyranny and injustice which would have disgraced a Spanish Inquisition. Men of talents, he insisted, would be unwilling to serve under such conditions.[18]

The controversy was now joined by "The Medlar," who claimed to be a woman. Attacking the conservative writers, she stated: "Much learning hath made them mad, for they seem to allow that

riches and learning gives wisdom. . . . I find most solid wisdom
among those who live above poverty and yet below affluence. . . .
A.B.C. seems to allow they [farmers and mechanics] have no time
to spare for improvement, and the citizen ["The disinterested Citizen"] endeavours to prove that farmers and mechanics at best can
be nothing more than good ignorant men. . . . But I would wish
these gentlemen to recollect how the greater part of the wealthy
and learned spend their time. . . . Are not a number of our legislative and executive officers . . . covetous, extortioners, profane
swearers, sabath breakers, drunkards, gamblers and even boasting
of their scenes of brutality.

"Now how can you think a pure stream of government can flow
from so corrupt a fountain?" [19]

"Philip Philips," who pretended to be an unlearned son of a
learned Irishman and a recent arrival in Kentucky, commented:
"I never was a frend to larned men for I see it is those sort of
fokes who always no how to butter thare own bred and care not
for others. I always thought it was not rite they shude go to convention or to the legislater." [20] He was very much opposed to slavery and advocated gradual emancipation. He wanted a committee
in every county to watch the lawyers and learned men who were
to go to the convention or to the legislature.[21]

At this stage in the discussion, "H.S.B.M." began his series of
communications which ably presented the radical point of view. He
objected strenuously to the past conduct of elections which the rich
carried by viva-voce voting, to the limitation of voting places to
one for each county, and to the use of liquor. "Those who are
most liberal with their grog generally carries the election. . . . The
Rich is always able to produce the greatest quantity of Spirituous
Liquors . . . and by this means be elected." Annual elections he
considered an "inestimable privilege." "But I lament to see it so
amazingly corrupted; [22] and I think it dangerous . . . to risque our
liberty and that of our posterity upon this rotten pillar only. I
think it calculated to cast us into an Aristocratic government . . . in
the hands of a few wealthy men. . . . I would wish to see a clause
in our Constitution, providing that county committees duly elected
by the people, might have a power of passing a negative upon bills
passed by the Assembly (which was to have a single chamber); and
would not this be a more reasonable check in order to prevent
hasty, unjust, and oppressive measures, than having the power of

a negative invested in the hands of a few great men." Other suggestions of "H.S.B.M." included the submission of the constitution to the committees for ratification prior to adoption, a bill of rights, consistency between the constitution and the bill of rights,[23] supervision of elections by the committees, and the subdivision of counties, with a polling place in each subdivision.[24]

Later he recommended the reading of Paine's *Common Sense*, but wrote against a government of lawyers and entangled laws, against extravagance, and in favor of the payment of taxes in produce. "Lawyers and designing men . . . artfully led us into a considerable degree of aristocracy [since the Revolution]." Noting that a large part of the land in the district was in dispute, he stated that "artful lawyers can make the law say almost any thing . . . so that he who has the heaviest purse will generally gain the cause," and that "the labouring man's property will become a prey to the few monied men that may be amongst us." [25]

Three conservative writers came forward with attacks upon the committees and their radical exponents. "A Citizen" objected to the secrecy of the committees and the fact that many were not included in their councils. He reiterated the demand that men of ability and integrity should be sent to the convention.[26] "Little Brutus" defended slavery and denied the right of government to deprive him of legally acquired property.[27] "X.Y.Z." argued against the radicals' claim to instruct the delegates. In his first letter he admitted the rights of assembly, petition, and remonstrance, all of which he considered as not binding upon the convention, but the doctrine of instruction he declared to be absurd.[28] In his second letter he referred to "paupers, new comers, women, and others, who ought not to have a vote," which opinion seems to establish his opposition to manhood suffrage.[29] Both his letters were quite critical of the radicals.

Meanwhile other radical writers managed to get their communications published. "Salamander" commented that "the fewer Lawyers and Pick pockets there are in a country, the better chance honest people have to keep their own; and then what will become of these pretended wise men, who would fain persuade us that men of common abilities and common honesty, ought not to be trusted with Legislative powers. . . ." He also observed that the committees "have only made a declaration of the common rights of mankind, with their reasons for publishing them at this time. . . ." [30]

"Rob the Thrasher" wrote sarcastically of the aristocrats; like other radicals, he favored a unicameral legislature, but unlike them he declared that a bill of rights was unnecessary.[31] "H.S.B.M." had insisted that a bill of rights that was not upheld by the constitution was of little value,[32] but otherwise the radicals accepted this part of a constitution as very desirable. "Torismond," who defended the committees as "the voice of the people," [33] regarded "A.B.C." as an aristocrat. "Brutus" attacked "Little Brutus" for his defense of slavery, reminded him of the evils of the slave trade as contrary to the spirit of Christ, asked him whether it was a greater injustice to deprive a man of his legally acquired slave property or the slave of his liberty, and asserted that emancipation "will invite thousands of honest industrious citizens; while it will shut out only a few who wish to live at the expence of others. . . ." [34] John Boyd, of the Bourbon County committee, published a plan of government which included in each subdistrict in each county three registers who were to keep a roll of the freemen of the district, to call them together to consider matters of public interest, and to conduct elections. It was in reality the committee system, including instruction of representatives, petition, remonstrance, and manhood suffrage for freemen. The statement served as a summary of the radical position.[35]

Near the end of the discussion, "Philanthropos" contributed a scheme of education. This name was used later by the Reverend David Rice when he published his pamphlet, *Slavery, Inconsistent with Justice and Good Policy.*[36] Whether Rice wrote the article in the Kentucky *Gazette* is not clear. At any rate, "Philanthropos" said that his scheme was considered in Virginia (the former home of Rice) when its laws were revised. Each county was to be divided into hundreds, about the size of townships, and in each hundred a school was to be established for instruction in reading, writing, and arithmetic. The teacher was to be supported by the government. Every person could send his children for three years gratis and longer by paying for the additional time. The most capable boy whose parents were too poor to send him longer was to be sent to one of the grammar schools, of which there were to be seven or eight in the state; in them Greek, Latin, geography, and the higher branches of arithmetic were to be taught. After a year the most capable boy was to be chosen and continued for six years. At the end of this period, half were to be discontinued. From among these the teachers of the grammar schools could be chosen. The remainder were to be sent to the university for three years. It was claimed that the scheme would give the poor an equal chance with the rich. The spirit behind the plan may have been indicated in part by the remark: "the poor in almost every age and nation have been rubbed [robbed?], mangled and emaciated by a set of vile rascals and unprincipled despots. . . ." [37]

Rice's views in regard to slavery were not inconsistent with this educational scheme. "A man, who has no Slaves," he declared, "cannot live easy and contented in the midst of those, who possess them in numbers. He is treated with neglect, and often with contempt . . . his children are looked upon and treated by theirs as underlings. . . . When he sees an open way to remove from this situation, . . . he will not long abide in it. . . . His place is filled up with Slaves. Thus this country will spew out its white inhabitants; and be peopled with Slave-holders, their Slaves, and a few [Overseers]. . . . Therefore . . . , the first thing to be done is, *to resolve unconditionally to put an end to slavery in this state.*" [38]

The newspaper comments of the radicals and the formation of county committees indicated that they looked back to the philosophy and methods of agitation employed by the patriots during the American Revolution, and particularly to the radicals of Pennsylvania.[39] There is also some resemblance to the Houston constitution in the state of Franklin, which included a unicameral legislature, a system of committees, and a proscription of men whose shortcomings appeared to Presbyterian clergymen as reasons to exclude them from office.[40] The committee system was also being called into use in western Pennsylvania at this time to express dissatisfaction with the whisky tax.

The radical program included a unicameral legislature, popular election of civil and military officials, elections by ballot, taxation of all land and other property, gradual elimination of slavery, manhood suffrage for freemen, representation based upon population, a polling place in each precinct, and the committee system. The last was to serve in the conduct of elections, by informing the convention and later legislatures what the people wanted and by ratifying or rejecting the work of the legislative bodies. It is not clear how many were united in support of a particular feature of the program or whether the educational program suggested by "Philanthropos" should be included. A bill of rights was criticized by one writer as unnecessary, and another maintained that it must be consistent with the constitution; but this criticism does not mean that the radicals were opposed to a bill of rights.[41] The weight of the evidence indicates that they accepted it as a part of the constitution. A strong moral tone in the radical communications was indicated by the complaints that the laws had been laxly enforced, pernicious vices encouraged, and that elections had been corrupted by the use of liquor.

The moderates and conservatives appeared to be on the defensive in the newspaper campaign after the discussion started, but it may be that their lack of aggressiveness was the better strategy. The more extreme conservatives had opposed separation and had suffered defeat, but the moderates had controlled the statehood movement and had kept it within constitutional limits. In so doing, it had been necessary to defeat the antiseparationists, and to avoid too close an alliance with any extreme group. In the campaign to choose delegates to the convention and to influence its work, the radicals quickly assumed leadership. Because it was natural for the moderates and conservatives to join forces, it is impossible to differentiate their programs completely. The conservatives, defeated in their efforts to keep Kentucky a part of Virginia, would most likely want to reproduce Virginia's system in Kentucky; but the moderates, on the contrary, would wish to eliminate some of the least justifiable features of Virginia's government.

The nonradical program began with the demand that men of recognized ability, wisdom, and integrity be elected to the convention. They criticized the activities of the committees as an attempt of the few to control secretly and in an unauthorized manner the votes of the many and particularly to dominate the convention by instructing the delegates. They preferred a bicameral legislature and a system of checks and balances. The more conservative, at least, supported a limited franchise, property qualifications, and the continuation of slavery. It is probable that the moderates may have been opposed to some of these more conservative features. Along with most of the radicals, both favored a bill of rights.

Although it is not possible to classify the communications to the Kentucky *Gazette* with complete accuracy, it is far more difficult to classify the delegates to the constitutional convention. There was no publication of the names of the candidates, or of those elected, which gave information about their views or groupings. The journal of the convention contains only one vote on which the "Yeas" and "Nays" were recorded, the vote on slavery; this roll call is helpful as far as it goes, but it is hardly an adequate basis for classification. The campaign of the radicals, which has been described, was an attack upon men of wealth, owners of slaves, and persons of social and political prominence—an attack upon aristocracy. It was only natural for the planters, lawyers, governmental officials, land speculators, slaveholders, and a few of the wealthy farmers to oppose them. It has generally been assumed that the election was a defeat of the radicals.[42] Some of the main features of their program were not incorporated in the constitution, but this omission may have resulted from the action of the convention rather than the election. An analysis of the delegates chosen in the different counties and a comparison of them with the personnel of the previous conventions throws some doubt upon·the defeat of the radicals in the election.[43] The conservatives were probably the smallest of the three groups. The moderates may have held a majority, but the conduct of affairs in the convention, as seen in the next chapter, leads to the conclusion that their control was based not upon numbers but upon the experience, ability, knowledge, and eloquence of George Nicholas.

At any rate, the campaign of the radicals demonstrates that freedom of the press existed in Kentucky, and that the political control of the planters was under attack by the democratic forces of the frontier. Where else in the United States in 1792 could such a campaign have been conducted? The Kentucky frontier with its inequitable distribution of land, the protection of slavery, and the presence of a planter class produced an unusually radical form of democracy.

7

The Contest in the Convention

THE KENTUCKY constitutional convention, which assembled April 2, 1792, was representative of early Kentucky. It contained a few wealthy men, some lawyers, a number of preachers, and a few who left very meager records. Among the delegates were Irish, Germans, Scotch-Irish, Welsh, or their descendants, as well as persons of English origin. Among them were pioneers who had come with the earliest to the "dark and bloody ground," but newcomers were there also. The landless or squatter element was not represented in proportion to its numbers, if at all.

Included in the membership of the convention were a number of planters, among whom were Alexander S. Bullitt, John Edwards, Richard Taylor, Matthew Walton, and Robert Johnson. Bullitt, the master of Oxmoor, near Louisville, and Edwards were born near the western border of the Tidewater in northern Virginia, while the others were from the Virginia Piedmont. Johnson had participated in the life of the frontier as a military leader and a surveyor. As a speculator, he secured grants for an acreage in excess of 100,000. To the youthful minds of his children, however, as they gathered about the family table or at the fireside when the toils of the day were ended, he unfolded the free spirit of democracy and the principles of civil and religious liberty.[1]

Land speculation was a prominent activity of Kentuckians and nearly one third of the delegates were among the largest recipients of land grants from Virginia before 1792. Robert Johnson, one of the planters just noted, was one of twenty-nine Kentuckians each of whom received more than 100,000 acres.[2] George Lewis and Matthew Walton, two other delegates, were in a group of thirty-six who received more than 50,000 and less than 100,000, the former receiving over 88,000 and the latter over 68,000 acres. Thomas

Lewis, Hubbard Taylor, Richard Young, John Campbell, and James Garrard were recipients of more than 25,000 acres and were among eight members of the convention who received from 10,000 to 50,000 acres. There were 212 in Kentucky who had been as fortunate. From less than one per cent of the population of the state, therefore, came thirteen of the forty-five delegates. Much has been made of the influence of land speculation upon the statehood movement as an effort of speculators to escape Virginia's control, but the biggest speculators in the convention had been well treated by the mother state.[3]

Three prominent lawyers, who came from eastern Virginia, were members of the convention. They were George Nicholas, Benjamin Sebastian, and Harry Innes. Nicholas, the most prominent member of the convention, was born in Williamsburg, the colonial capital, where his father had served for a time as treasurer of the colony. A student at William and Mary and a soldier in the armies of the Revolution before moving to western Virginia, George became a friend of Thomas Jefferson and James Madison as well as a participant in the struggle for religious liberty. A member of the Virginia ratification convention, he was an ardent advocate of the new federal constitution. After moving to Kentucky in 1790, he became a member of its constitutional convention and took an important part in preparing the Kentucky Resolutions of 1798.[4]

From these planters, land speculators, and lawyers must have come the few conservatives who belonged to the convention. But it must be obvious that they were less aristocratic than similar individuals in the older states. With the biggest landowner in the convention a man who taught his children the principles of democracy and of civil and religious liberty, and the greatest lawyer in the convention a personal friend and supporter of Jefferson, one would not expect a reactionary constitution to be produced. As a matter of fact, the records of the convention indicate that Nicholas was not a conservative, but a moderate.

The chief opponents of the conservatives were the radicals whose campaign in the newspapers and whose formation of county committees indicated that they looked back to the philosophy and methods of agitation employed by the Patriots during the American Revolution, particularly in Pennsylvania. Squatters, tenants, or small landowners, who owned few if any slaves, they were not learned in the law and were generally not members of the official class; many were natives of western Virginia, a few of Pennsylvania. The clergy may have furnished much of the leadership of the radicals, since their communications were often characterized by a strong moral tone[5] and since a number of ministers were elected to the convention, where they were recorded as opposed to slavery.

Nine of the delegates to the convention, or one fifth of the membership, either were or had been Protestant clergymen. Two of these, however, had ceased to exercise the office and had given some evidence of departing from its ideals.[6] David Rice, one of the two delegates who were Presbyterian ministers, was regarded as among the more able members of the convention. The son of a poor but respected Virginia farmer, he served twenty years as a clergyman in the Old Dominion, during which time he participated in the struggle for religious freedom. Moving to Kentucky, he came to be recognized as the father of the Presbyterian church in his adopted state. Like his family before him, he was opposed to slavery, and on the eve of the convention wrote a pamphlet setting forth his views under the pen name of "Philanthropos." He attacked slavery from the political, economic, and religious points of view. He obviously was opposed to the plantation system because it was based upon slavery and aristocracy. His remedy was to stop the introduction of slaves into Kentucky and gradually emancipate those already there.[7]

That the leadership of the democratic masses of the Kentucky frontier should have included in addition to Rice, the Presbyterian, three Baptist preachers,[8] a German Reformed minister,[9] and a Methodist local preacher,[10] was entirely fitting, for such a mixture was characteristic of the Upland South. The attitude of the Baptists may have been determined by the struggle within the Elkhorn Association on the subject of slavery where a memorial to the convention in respect to religious freedom and perpetual slavery was first approved and then rejected.[11] All of the active ministers except Rice, who had resigned, voted against slavery in the convention.[12]

Radical opposition to the conservative class was indicated by eight other delegates who voted against slavery. Each one of these had received comparatively small grants of land from Virginia, and there is little evidence that they held office in the government. One was said to be of Scotch descent,[13] one came from northern Ireland,[14] two had German names, [15] two others were from the Valley of Virginia,[16] and one had lived on the Pennsylvania frontier.[17] The eighth was described as a Virginian, a slaveowner, but a farmer who opposed slavery.[18] James Smith, the Pennsylvanian who had been born on the frontier and who was captured by Indians, among whom he lived several years, had served in the defense of the frontier. Before moving to Kentucky, which he had visited on an early exploring trip, he aided in forming Pennsylvania's radical constitution of 1776. He participated in the statehood movement and later became a member of the Kentucky assembly. His last days were spent as a missionary to the Indians and in writing about his travels, captivity, and religious work. These men were not the kind of which aristocracies were formed.

Very little has been recorded about nine other members of the convention. Because of what is known about them as well as what is not known, they seem more likely to have been frontiersmen than planters. Some of them came to Kentucky in the very early days and so knew personally the struggles of the people to settle, defend, and develop the region. None of them had received large land grants. Probably they did not hold office or more would have been recorded about them. Two had lived in the fort at Boonesboro,[19] one was said to have been of Scotch-Irish stock,[20] one came from Maryland,[21] and another probably was a Pennsylvanian.[22]

Probably most of the clergymen and the opponents of slavery in the convention, as well as the delegates about whom little is known, were radicals. Altogether they numbered twenty-six of the forty-five members of the convention. Even if one subtracts the two inactive ministers, the radicals had a slight majority. They did not, however, control the convention.

Since the conservatives were too few, and since the radical plan was not adopted by the convention, as will be seen, there must have been a group of delegates who were moderates. They were numerous enough to be quite influential. Their control of events, however, seems to have been based upon reason and ability rather than numbers. They were delegates whose economic and social position was neither that of the landless squatter nor the wealthy owner of many thousands of acres.

It is possible only to estimate the personnel of the moderates. Some of the delegates had been connected with the statehood movement since 1784, and it would seem that they were most likely to belong to the dominant group. Samuel McDowell, for instance, had been chosen president of a majority of the conventions. Also among the delegates were men from the Valley of Virginia who had struggled against the planter domination of that state but who seem in Kentucky to have adopted some of the ideals of their former opponents. It is probable that the liberalism of their younger days was not entirely surrendered when they became successful and prominent citizens of the District of Kentucky. Among these men may have been, in addition to McDowell, Benjamin Logan, Caleb Wallace, Isaac Shelby, and Robert Breckinridge.

McDowell, Breckinridge, Logan, and Wallace were of Scotch-Irish extraction, and Shelby was Welsh. Their families had settled first in Pennsylvania before moving into Virginia and then to Kentucky. Before locating in the Holston Valley, the Shelbys lived for many years in western Maryland.[23] The McDowells, Breckinridges, and Logans were residents of the Valley of Virginia,[24] where they participated in the Revolution as Patriots and where Wallace and McDowell, at least, struggled to make Virginia more democratic. The latter rejected the idea of primogeniture and divided his father's estate equally with his brother and sister. Wallace participated in the contest for religious freedom, secured a law confirming and authorizing marriages in the remote parts of Virginia not performed by Anglican clergymen, and aided in founding Presbyterian educational institutions.[25] The land grants given to these men before 1792 were for less than ten thousand acres each. All but Breckinridge were members of the convention of 1784, where they voted against the resolution protesting the Virginia land tax, which act was at least an indication that they were not then considering matters as speculators. Shelby and Logan were foremost among the frontiersmen in their younger days, and it is doubtful that they ever ceased to be frontiersmen. The views of Nicholas as expressed in his papers indicate that he was not the conservative he is usually pictured has having been. He favored slavery and opposed a number of the demands of the radicals, but he favored a house of representatives popularly elected, manhood suffrage, and a bill of rights. It was probably his ability, information, and experience rather than the number of the moderates that enabled them to dominate the convention.

Moderates and conservatives worked together in the Danville, Kentucky, Political Club from 1786 to 1790. Its records indicate that the members were not radicals. On the other hand, they favored separation from Virginia, representation proportioned according to numbers rather than to counties, biennial elections, a bicameral legislature, and the choice of the members of the upper house by an electoral college. They opposed the clause in the United States Constitution, which denied to Congress the right to prohibit the slave trade before 1808 and declared that the culture of tobacco would not be beneficial to Kentucky. These resolutions do not read like the platform of conservatives, although some of the members were probably of that group. A committee was appointed to prepare a bill of rights and a constitution which would be suitable for the proposed state, and the members of the club discussed at length the constitution of the United States. Among the members of this interesting organization were Samuel McDowell, who became president of the constitutional convention; Christopher Greenup, who became its secretary; and three delegates, Benjamin Sebastian, Matthew Walton, and Harry Innes.[26]

The election of Samuel McDowell as president of the convention on the first day of its meeting may have indicated that the same group of moderates that had controlled the preceding nine conventions were also in control of the tenth. Only a few things which happened in the convention can be learned from the journal of its proceedings, which recorded decisions rather than debates or discussions.[27] The Kentucky *Gazette* did not enlighten its readers about the activities of the convention during its sessions. But a general picture and some of the details may be secured by patching together the little bits of evidence which still exist.

For ten days the delegates met in committee of the whole. The journal does not indicate what was discussed or what decisions were reached until the end of the period, when the committee reported a series of resolutions which outlined a scheme of government. In the George Nicholas Papers,[28] however, are extensive notes for speeches or discussions probably delivered in the convention on various topics which correspond roughly to these resolutions. There is also a copy of the resolutions, in Nicholas' handwriting, which may have been a preliminary copy of the committee's report to the convention.

These days seem to have been days of intense activity, divided between the important work for which they had met and a serious contest between Rice and Nicholas. Since these men were leaders among the radicals and moderates respectively, the contest was probably between the two groups rather than between the two leaders. On the sixth day of the convention, Saturday, Nicholas resigned. A quorum was not present on the following Monday, which could have been by agreement. Nicholas again appeared on Tuesday, having been re-elected a delegate. How an election could have been arranged and held with such speed is not clear. Certainly two days constituted insufficient time to notify the voters of an entire county. Rice resigned the day after Nicholas returned. Full information about these events would help explain the entire action of the convention, but such information is lacking. Tradition has it that Nicholas resigned on the issue of the original jurisdiction of the supreme court in respect to land titles, and that Rice resigned because he was defeated on the slavery issue.[29] It may be, however, that these actions were a part of the continued effort of the radicals to control the convention and that the moderate and conservative delegates had to resort to unusual methods to win the contest. Rice was not re-elected and Nicholas was left in possession of the field.

On the opening day of the convention, Nicholas probably spoke in a conciliatory manner on the necessity of mutual forbearance and confidence, of the importance of the work to be done, and of the impossibility of perfection. The objects of government, he said, are the public happiness, national prosperity, and the protection of the natural rights of the individual.[30]

It seems probable that Nicholas spoke to the convention as each new division of its work was undertaken and that the "Resolutions," which were adopted on the second Friday, give a rough indication of the order in which they were considered. If so, Nicholas may have discussed the separation of powers in his next speech.[31] He thought that it was necessary to give the government adequate powers, but to divide them among the three branches of government so that power would be confronted with power and its abuse prevented.

The legislative division of the government seems to have received the attention of the delegates. Here Nicholas differed from the radical position because he favored a bicameral legislature, arguing that a single house did not give a sufficient degree of responsibility and that Georgia and Pennsylvania had found their unicameral legislative bodies inadequate. In discussing the house of representatives, he sketched the rise of the English House of Commons and made several references to the experience of other nations. In every government, he said, a few strive to govern the rest of the people, and they possess an advantage in the unity and consistency of their actions. This trait could be counteracted only by delegating the power of the people to a few representatives, who would be animated by the greatness of the trust imposed on them. A short term of office and the identity of interest with their constituents would prevent the abuse of their power. The lower house should be chosen annually, but the senators should serve for longer terms. A senate was necessary to guard against the unanimity of a single legislative body, and its members should be chosen from the state at large to avoid localism. He recommended the Maryland electoral college as the preferable method to select the most able men who would be concerned with the interests of the state at large. This mode of election he considered consistent with liberty and republican principles.[32]

If Nicholas disappointed the radicals with respect to the legislature, he probably proved more satisfactory on the subject of the suffrage. The right of voting, he maintained, could be more safely exercised in America by the people at large than in any other country in the world. The American yeomanry possessed great information, for in no other country was education so general. In no other country had the people such knowledge of the rights of men and the principles of government. The idea of a property qualification had been taken from Europeans whose situation had never been similar to that of Americans. If landed property were made a necessary qualification, why not require the preposterous distinctions of blood and rank? The representative should be so connected with the mass of the community by a society of interests and passions that the will of the people when it was determined and permanent would always prevail. Every subject of the state should enjoy the privilege of choosing representatives.[33]

The earlier state constitutions had made the governor little more than a figurehead and had often created an executive council with such powers as to form a plural executive. Nicholas spoke in behalf of a popularly elected governor, unrestricted by an executive council, and possessing length of term, independence of salary, and a qualified veto. Nicholas feared a weak government more than a powerful government, which would be prevented from abusing its powers by a system of checks and balances and a dependence upon the will of the people.[34]

In respect to the courts, Nicholas probably faced his most difficult task. With the exception of the defense of frontier districts, government probably failed to adapt itself to the needs of the mass of the people in the judicial division more than in any other branch. Courts, especially the higher courts, were separated from the people by considerable distance, by misunderstanding, and by costly procedure. The radicals in Kentucky were more antagonistic to the lawyers than to any other group. They offered little criticism of the land speculators, who may have been the real culprits, for they were generally also speculators in heart if not in fact, but the lawyers who helped in questionable and unscrupulous court procedures were thoroughly despised. The radicals had also insisted upon a simple law that could be readily understood by the common people.[35] It is entirely likely that Nicholas' speech on this part of the constitution was his greatest effort.

The judiciary ought to be considered, he stated, as the guardian of the constitution and the bill of rights. No government could exist without courts, which were necessary to preserve the peace of society. They should be sufficiently numerous, and their sessions sufficiently frequent, to carry justice as far as is practicable to every man's door, and to establish a speedy, uniform, and equal administration of justice. It was indispensably necessary that there should be one supreme tribunal before which cases might be brought by way of appeal from all the other courts.

The judges, he continued, should be appointed by the governor to hold their offices during good behavior and should receive competent but fixed salaries. The House of Representatives should have the power of impeachment; and the governor, on the address of two thirds of each house of the legislature, should have the power of removal in order to secure the responsibility of the judges.

It had been contended that if the people wished to become really free, he argued, the laws by which they were governed must be *few* in *number* and *simple* in their *nature*. But, whenever there was a *right* which was not *protected*, or a *wrong* which was not *prohibited*, there was one law too few.[36] The more numerous the laws, the greater the degree of liberty. The convention should adopt the laws of Virginia, which included the acts of Assembly, the ordinances of convention, and the common law of England; the latter could not immediately be replaced by statute law.

The number of inferior courts should be determined by the

legislature as it should, from time to time, think proper. The courts should be at all times open to the citizens and the law be duly administered, freely without sale, fully without denial, and speedily without delay.

The subject was further complicated by the inadequate land system which Virginia had established and the complicated court procedure for the adjudication of disputed titles. This situation Nicholas endeavored to remedy by an unusual procedure. In this he apparently met vigorous opposition and, according to tradition, it was on this issue that he resigned. It is, of course, possible that his opponents may have regarded this point as the best one at which to attack his program.

The land laws of Virginia, he contended, had been so framed as to lay the foundation of an infinite number of suits. Those disputes were of such a nature as to render a decision of them under the present system impracticable, either in a moderate time, or at such an expense as would not be ruinous to the country. The present regulations of the courts prevented proper and effectual steps from being taken to insure justice to the parties, even at a remote period, and then only after the most ruinous expenses had been incurred. All this might be remedied by granting the Court of Appeals original and final jurisdiction as to land disputes.[37]

Perhaps the bill of rights was considered next in order to allay the feelings of radicals after the court question occasioned such a rupture. Nicholas asserted that the want of a bill of rights would endanger the loss of those rights and privileges which government was instituted to preserve, without which there could be no liberty, and over which it was not necessary for government to have control. Liberty consists not only in the security of these rights but also in the opinion each citizen had of the sufficiency of that security. Having recourse to the contract theory of the origin of government, which was basic to his entire political philosophy, Nicholas reminded the convention that a bill of rights was necessary to secure that residuum of human rights which was not given up to society and of natural liberty which was not sacrificed to public convenience. Without a bill of rights, either the legislature would have authority to take away any of these rights or the courts must have the power to define them and to declare which actions infringe them, either of which eventualities would be destructive of those rights.[38]

Another explosive situation developed over the demand of the radicals that the convention adopt a plan of gradual emancipation of slaves. Nicholas' speech on this question was probably his poorest on any major subject, for he could see only the rights of the slave-owners, not of the slaves, while his remarks resemble those of the demagogue rather than those of a great political philosopher. If the convention had the power to destroy property in slaves, he insisted that all property was insecure. The owners had a right in the Negroes "too sacred to be sported with." If free, they should have political rights. Since he considered the right of the Indians to the land to be as good as the right of the Negroes to freedom, he advised the delegates to disband without forming a government, to recommend to their constituents to abandon the country to the Indians, and to advise the Negroes to form alliances with the true proprietors of the soil. If emancipation were adopted, the owners of slaves would move away and immigration would be discouraged.[39] On this occasion Rice is reputed to have resigned.

Provision for amendment was yet to be adopted, and Nicholas seems to have pointed out the advantages of adapting the government to existing conditions and of providing for new constitutional conventions at definite intervals to secure adjustments to changed conditions. He stated that it was the transcendent and precious right of the people to abolish or alter their government in such a way as to them might seem most likely to effect their safety and happiness. Such procedure would encourage immigration, he said, and would not be dangerous in a free country.[40]

The committee of the whole reported on April 13, after deliberation in which Nicholas probably took a leading part, a series of resolutions which represent in brief form the views of Nicholas on the one hand and an outline of the future constitution on the other. A committee was then appointed to draft a constitution following these resolutions as a guide.[41] Nicholas was the first delegate named on this committee, which reported a constitution four days later. It was amended on April 18 to exclude ministers from membership in the legislature, a change which has been interpreted as expressing disapproval of their political activity and of their opposition to slavery. If so, it was an ungenerous move on the part of the victors, for time has probably dealt more kindly with the views of the ministers, in respect to slavery at least, than with those of their opponents. On the same day, the radicals made their final and unsuccessful effort to eliminate the provision in the constitution which denied the legislature the authority to emancipate slaves without the owner's consent and without compensation.[42] On the next day the convention finished its labors and adjourned.

The constitution which the convention prepared [43] resembled very much the resolutions which the committee of the whole reported and the speeches which Nicholas probably made in the convention. The separation of powers was provided in the first article. The legislature was to be composed of a senate and a house of representatives. The representatives were to be elected annually by free manhood suffrage and apportioned every four years according to the number of eligible voters. The senators were to be chosen from the state at large for terms of four years by an electoral college the members of which were popularly elected in the several counties. The governor was to be selected by the electoral college for a four-year term. Nicholas had recommended direct popular choice, and the resolutions of the committee of the whole had so directed; but the committee to draft a constitution had evidently made this change. The constitution provided for a supreme court and such inferior courts as the legislature might establish. The judges were to be appointed by the governor and senate for good behavior. The supreme court was to have original and final jurisdiction in all cases respecting land titles under the land laws of Virginia. Local governmental and militia officers were to be popularly elected. The legislature was denied the power to emancipate slaves without first paying for them and securing the owner's consent. The bill of rights denied to the government the authority to violate the natural rights of its citizens, such as the freedom of religion.

Although this narrative of developments brings out in greater detail and certainty the influence of Nicholas, another factor must be noted. A careful comparison of the constitution with earlier constitutions makes it possible to identify the sources from which it was drawn. Neither the constitution of Virginia nor that of the United States served as a model.[44] Almost three fourths of its sections were taken from the Pennsylvania constitution of 1790, many having been copied verbatim and others with only the change of a few words necessary to adapt them to the new state. Twenty-seven of the twenty-eight sections of the bill of rights, fourteen of the seventeen sections of Article II describing the executive branch,

and eighteen of the twenty-nine sections of Article I, which
established the general assembly, were drawn from Pennsylvania's
constitution. Articles III and IV were also derived from the same
source. Seventy-five of the 107 sections were so similar to corresponding sections of the Pennsylvania document as to justify the
conclusion that it was used as a model. If Nicholas was the author
of Kentucky's first constitution,[45] one may be certain that the
Pennsylvania document lay before him when he wrote seventy-five
per cent of Kentucky's constitutional law.

The following table will give the necessary details: [46]

Article	Subject Matter	No. of Sections	No. of Sections like Pa. 1790	No. of Original Sections	No. of Sections like Other Constitutions
Preamble		1			1 S. C. 1790
I.	Legislature	29	18	4	5 Md.
II.	Executive	17	14	2	1 N. C.
III.	Elections	3	3		
IV.	Impeachment	3	3		
V.	Judiciary	7	3	2	2 U. S.
VI.	Local matters	7	4	3	
VII.	Oath of office	1	1		
VIII.	Miscellaneous	7	2	4	1 U. S.
IX.	Slavery	1		1	
X.	Location of capital	2		2	
XI.	Amendments	1		1	
XII.	Bill of rights	28	27	1	
	Total	107	75	20	10

The choice of a model is significant. It involved a departure
from the government of the mother state, which the conservatives
had favored. The radical program was very similar to the first
Pennsylvania constitution, and one of the Kentucky radicals had
belonged to the convention which adopted it.[47] After the ratification of the federal constitution, Pennsylvania revised its own in the
light of its previous experience and the work of the federal convention. The new constitution of Pennsylvania offered to Kentucky
the most modern and up-to-date state government available. It was
less radical, but it preserved the democratic spirit of the earlier
one.[48] It awarded the franchise to free adult males who paid taxes,
provided no property qualifications for office holding, and apportioned representation to taxable inhabitants. The influence of

Pennsylvania upon Kentucky's constitution made it more democratic than other Southern constitutions. The chief deviation from this model was the electoral college, which was adopted from Maryland. This provision has generally been regarded as a conservative feature of the Kentucky constitution, lessening popular control; but the electors were popularly chosen, and voters were not limited by property qualifications. It tended to delay rather than defeat the popular will. It was, however, unsatisfactory in other respects and was soon eliminated.

Few as these facts are, it is possible to suggest certain conclusions about the convention, several of which have not been recognized. The radicals were a strong party numerically in the convention, so numerous that one may question whether or not they were defeated in the elections as has been suggested. The most influential delegate in the convention, as has been recognized, was George Nicholas. His papers indicate, however, that he was not the conservative that some have thought, but that he was a Jeffersonian of moderately liberal principles. He seems to have been less liberal than Jefferson, but his notes and speeches were clearly not those of the Eastern or Southern conservative. If he were a conservative, he was a Western conservative, who believed in a democratic and representative government of all the people rather than a government in the hands of a favored class. Like Jefferson, he expected the people to have the good sense to choose able men, like himself, to represent them. He did not betray the fear of the people so characteristic of Alexander Hamilton, or the distrust of the people which was written into the constitutions of many of the Southern states.

The constitution was obviously the result of compromise. It was neither so liberal as the radicals desired nor so aristocratic as the conservatives wished, but in comparison with other constitutions of that day it was very democratic. The principles which the back country and the lowland had fought over in the older Southern states were in Kentucky decided according to the wishes of the more liberal forces. The constitution embodied popular control of government, freedom of religion, suffrage for free men, and representation apportioned to free men. The democratic forces in the South Atlantic states were to continue to struggle for some of these principles until slavery and secession distracted their attention. The control of the Tidewater aristocracy in the older states was based upon property qualifications, inequality of representation, an established church, large landholdings, and slavery. Only the last two, large landholdings and slavery, crossed the mountains into Kentucky; the others failed to make the crossing. The frontiersmen, including the radicals and the moderates, had won a substantial victory. The limitations of this victory were chiefly social and economic, and the American people were hardly ready to use their political democracy to secure social and economic democracy.

This victory was important in itself, but, viewed in the long range of historical development, the significance is increased. The Kentucky constitution in turn served as a model either directly or indirectly for other constitutions of neighboring states. The convention of 1799 in Kentucky made but few changes in the older document, and states from Ohio, Indiana, and Illinois on the north, to Missouri and Arkansas on the west, and Mississippi and Louisiana on the south preferred to follow many of the provisions of the Kentucky constitution in forming their own fundamental law.[49] As the Kentuckians had done before them, they chose many of the parts of their constitutions from earlier documents, and gradually these new constitutions showed progress toward a more complete and workable democracy.

The contest in Kentucky was one in which Southern and Western influences clashed. Superficially, the result may appear to have been a Southern victory. Virginia's influence in establishing a highly inequitable land system and in contributing so many planters to Kentucky's social order was too great to be destroyed by the democratic influence of the frontier. But north of the Ohio a fairer land system was being developed, and slavery was prohibited. There many of the common people of the South found their opportunity to aid in building a more democratic social, economic, and political order. But even in Kentucky after the emigration of these frontiersmen and the passage of two generations of plantation development, the devotion of the Bluegrass state to the South was not sufficient to make the Ohio River the northern border of the Confederacy.

8

The Frontier in the Formation of Tennessee

THE FRONTIERSMEN of Tennessee had recorded in deeds a notable and significant history before they formed a self-governing commonwealth of their own. They had participated in the formation of the famous Watauga association, in some of the early steps of the Transylvania enterprise, in the Cumberland compact at French Lick, in the King's Mountain and other Revolutionary campaigns, and in the almost continuous warfare by which they were gradually winning the Valley of the Tennessee from the southern Indians. They had attempted to establish the state of Franklin and thus achieve local self-government. Defeated in this effort, they were organized as the "Territory of the United States, south of the river Ohio," commonly called the Southwest Territory.[1] Its government, inaugurated by Governor William Blount on October 23, 1790, was like that under the Northwest Ordinance, except for the provision in respect to slavery.[2] Although organized later than the Northwest Territory, it nevertheless became a state first.

Three forces, at least, hindered the democratic influence of the frontier in this area: the unequal distribution of land, slavery, and the importance of military activity. Before North Carolina ceded her claim to western territory, much of the land had been transferred to private hands in such a manner that a few had acquired very large holdings. When North Carolina surrendered her claim, it was stipulated that "no regulations made or to be made by Congress shall tend to emancipate Slaves." This condition was observed by Congress in the "Act for the Government of the territory south of the river Ohio," which made an exception of the antislavery provision of the Northwest Ordinance. The state's responsibility for the inequality of land distribution is direct. What Southern frontiersmen would have done if left to themselves cannot be guessed, but North Carolina's hostility to the state of Franklin, her protection of slavery, and her encouragement of the land speculators were certainly not conducive to the development of democracy.

The settlements of the Southwest Territory had been wrested from the Indians at the cost of almost constant fighting. The treaties which were made with the tribesmen did not purchase new lands for settlement, but readjusted the boundary between the frontiersmen and the Indians in the light of the latest frontier encroachment. Generally, the treaty lines failed to keep pace with expansion. Settlement could advance only as the Indians retreated from their lands, and intrusion of the pioneers caused bitter Indian resentment. The Cumberland region, which was especially exposed and busy with defense, showed little dissatisfaction with the territorial government except to urge more military activity against the Indians. Settlers fighting for their existence had little time to debate about the forms or principles of government.

The significance of this point is emphasized by reference to the exposed character of the frontier, which was divided into two widely separated areas. The Holston Valley was an extension of the Valley of Virginia; settlement extended in 1791 as far as fifteen miles south of Knoxville and included the land between the Holston-Tennessee and the Carolina boundary. More than 28,000 persons lived in four counties and in territory not yet supplied with local government, although for judicial and military purposes they were organized into the two districts of Washington and Hamilton. The area was a "very exposed Frontier of upwards of two hundred miles, upon almost every part of which the Indians have killed & robbed. . . ." [3]

The Nashville Basin in the Cumberland Valley was an isolated island of settlement more than 150 miles from the Holston Valley. Its 7,000 persons were organized in three counties, which formed Miro District. Possibly because of its weakness and isolation, Indian resentment over the encroachment of the frontier led to severe attacks on this distant settlement. In reality the ten years since its founding had been a cruel and harsh struggle for existence which only hardened and experienced frontiersmen could endure. Population had increased at the rate of 700 each year, while Kentucky had had an average annual increase since 1776 of 5,000 per year.

According to Governor Blount, the settlement in this district extended along the Cumberland River for a distance of eighty-five miles with a width generally of thirteen miles but never exceeding twenty-five. A heavy stand of large timber with dense undergrowth where the land was not covered with thick, high cane concealed the Indians before an attack. The frontier around the settlement was at least two hundred miles in length.[4] Much of the time the inhabitants were forced to live in their little forts and stations and to raise their crops between Indian raids and campaigns. Andrew Pickens stated in 1792: "I found that Country particularly Cumberland, in a most pitiable and distressed situation almost continually harrassed by the Creeks and the four lower Towns of the Cherokees on the Tenessee [sic]. . . ."[5]

During the years in which the Southwest Territory existed, the population grew rapidly but not evenly over the entire area. The increase in the Valley of East Tennessee from 1790 to 1795 was 128 per cent, while the increase in the Cumberland region was 69 per cent, and in the entire territory 124 per cent. That the westward-moving pioneers were not migrating to the Cumberland in these years as rapidly as in the latter half of the decade is revealed by a comparison of these statistics with those of the first and second federal census. During the ten years from 1790 to 1800 the growth in numbers for the eastern portion was 156 per cent, and in the Cumberland settlements 357 per cent, while the entire state grew 196 per cent.[6] Seemingly Indian warfare affected adversely the more distant region until the middle of the nineties.

Governor Blount seems to have been a successful and popular executive. He was so much concerned about defense that the federal administration was worried about the expense and the possibility that he would involve the country in a general Indian war with the southern tribes. The secretary of war reminded him early in 1792 that "The militia must not be called out excepting in cases of real danger. . . ." Near the end of the year he was more urgent and specific. "The number of Militia which you appear to have called into service might probably at the moment of danger have appeared to be necessary and justifiable by the occasion—But Sir it is of the highest importance that they should not have been retained in service any longer than circumstances rendered indispensible. . . . This is a point to which I am directed to request your serious attention." In 1795 he wrote a long critical letter in which he observed: "I cannot refrain from saying that the complexion of some of the Transactions in the South western territory appears unfavourable to the public interests." When David Campbell eulogized the governor's conduct, the secretary of war stated: "He [Campbell] aims at the poetic stile; and perhaps very properly; as poets deal in fiction." [7] But the situation was so critical that the governor's zealousness in providing defense could serve only to increase his popularity in the territory, regardless of the possible relations between his land investments and Indian policy. Undoubtedly he favored war upon the Creek and Cherokee Indians and did not check the encroachment of the frontiersmen upon Indian land, but this policy was also a virtue in the eyes of the people, whatever the federal administration might think.

Although the governor worried the federal administration with his Indian policy, the people were dissatisfied because the federal government was so inattentive to their needs and seemingly more concerned about protecting the Indians than the whites. William Cocke tried to arouse the people in 1792, and John Tipton threatened to lead an expedition against the Cherokee towns the following year.[8] Captain John Beard with fifty men pursued Indians who murdered a white family, and at the Hanging Maw's town killed some nine to twelve Indians, among whom were important chiefs called together by the President's order for purposes of negotiations.[9] Immediate war was feared and court-martial proceedings were undertaken against Beard. But he was not punished and in a short time was preparing another campaign. In the meantime, Samuel Wear led about sixty men to Tellassee, where some sixteen Indians were killed.[10] Later in the same year Colonel Doherty led a larger group beyond the Tennessee destroying Indian towns and killing some fifteen Indians.[11] John Sevier indicated his restlessness by requesting permission to go on an exploring expedition. Perhaps fearing that he might go without authorization, Secretary Daniel Smith ordered him to proceed.[12] This expedition resulted in the Etowah campaign in the Coosa and Estinaula valleys. Obviously Sevier was finding the peace policy of the territorial and federal governments hard to endure.

The election of the territorial house of representatives may have been a further expression of dissatisfaction, for the petition requesting a legislature criticized the Indian policy of the federal government, and the men who were elected included the leaders of the unauthorized Indian campaigns and several others who did not co-operate later with the governor's friends in the constitutional convention. At one time Blount privately opposed a legislative assembly.[13] When representatives met, on February 24, 1794, they demanded a declaration of war against the Cherokee and Creek Indians.[14]

Both houses of the legislature, which assembled on August 25, 1794, repeated the demand for more adequate defense. "If the people of this Territory have borne with outrages which stretch human patience to its utmost," the members asserted, "it has been through our veneration for the head of the Federal Government [Washington], and through the hopes we entertain that his influence will finally extend, to procure for this injured part of the Union, that justice, which nothing but retaliating on an unrelenting enemy, can afford." [15]

The governor may not actually have been opposed to such expressions personally, but he could hardly have been pleased with the tax bill which the assembly passed. The lower house wanted a higher tax on land while the upper house insisted upon a lower tax. The representatives refused to yield, apparently representing the poorer people, and the council finally agreed.[16] Although defense was the first concern, this action indicates that the people were both able and willing to use the democratic features of their government in their own interest.

A further advance toward self-government was taken when the governor called the territorial legislature into special session, on June 29, 1795, and inquired whether the people desired statehood. The legislators replied, "The great body of our constituents are sensible of the many defects of our present . . . government, and of the great and permanent advantages to be derived from a change and speedy representation in Congress. . . ." [17] The census indicated a population of 77,262, which total was considered to be sufficient for a state government. When the census was taken, more than six thousand voters expressed a desire to make the change.[18]

The statehood movement, however, was not caused by widespread dissatisfaction with the territorial administration such as existed in the Northwest Territory under St. Clair.[19] Discontent over the Indian policy existed along with hope that representation in Congress would enable the state to secure better treatment. But only a few held Blount responsible, for the legislators, when statehood was achieved, unanimously chose him to be a member of the

United States Senate, which honor they declared to be the highest proof of their confidence in his integrity and ability to serve them.[20] On the other hand, 2,500 voters and one member of the territorial legislature opposed the change. Most of them lived in the District of Miro, where the territorial government was popular. No one offered any serious opposition. Satisfaction with the territorial administration and fear of higher taxes were probably responsible for such disagreement as existed.[21] The governor, therefore, called for the election of delegates on December 18 and 19, and the meeting of the convention on January 11, 1796.

Most of the delegates who were elected to the convention had been born along the immigrant trails by which the pioneers came to Tennessee. The places of their nativity and former residence, as well as their previous experience, indicate not only their character but also that of the early Tennesseans. Sometimes it is not possible now to learn in which state the birth occurred, but the various possibilities mark the path along which the family moved. From Pennsylvania on the north came eight delegates, their birthplaces strewn along the road from Philadelphia to the Cumberland Valley, except that one may have been born in Ireland, a second in southwestern Pennsylvania, and a third in North Carolina.[22] Two other delegates were born in the Hagerstown Valley and one in the Piedmont of Maryland. All of these Marylanders lived for a time in the Valley of Virginia before going to Tennessee.[23]

Among the Virginians elected to the convention—and these formed the largest group of delegates—where six natives of the Valley, nine of the Piedmont, and only two who were born near the Fall Line, possibly in the Tidewater region.[24] One of the natives of the Tidewater lived for a time in the Valley, and three of the Piedmonters seem to have moved to North Carolina before crossing the mountains. In addition to these, there was Landon Carter, who had moved with his father from Virginia to the Watauga settlement when he was about ten years of age.

Before turning to the Carolinians, it is interesting to note that the convention included three natives of Ireland and one of England.[25] Three of the four came by way of the valley route from Pennsylvania or Maryland, and only one came by way of South Carolina.

Even the Carolinians in the convention gave some evidence of having been a part of the migration from Pennsylvania by way of the Valley of Virginia. One of the North Carolinians was born in Rowan County of Irish parents; of another it was said that he was born in Scotland or North Carolina; and a third may have been born in Pennsylvania, Virginia, or North Carolina.[26] Another came from the state without leaving any available record of his birthplace.[27] Three, however, were born in the Tidewater region.[28] All of the four South Carolinians came from the frontier, three from the Spartanburg District, and one from the Waxhaw settlement.[29] A record of the nativity of eleven of the fifty-five delegates has not been found.[30]

The convention, therefore, was formed by delegates who were generally the products of the frontier which Frederick J. Turner called the "Old West." The number that came from the Tidewater was surprisingly small, and such origin did not seem to have made planters or conservatives of all of them. It is interesting that those who are known to have come from the Carolinas constituted only one fifth of the convention. A few others may have lived in North Carolina before moving west of the mountains, but it seems that a majority came from north of the southern boundary of Virginia. In fact, three fifths of the convention came from abroad or from Pennsylvania, Maryland, and Virginia, in contrast to the one eighth that came from the mother state.

The deliberations of the convention were marked by great moderation and unusual harmony, according to information secured by historian James G. Ramsey from Richard Mitchell, the last surviving member of the convention.[31] Perhaps this information has been generally accepted too readily and without adequate investigation of the political alignment that existed within the convention. The practice of great moderation, singular courtesy, good feeling, and liberality quite generally, and, in respect to the main goal of statehood, unusual harmony does not eliminate the possibility of important differences or disprove that the Blount group sought to replace its control of the territorial government with domination of the new state.

The alignment is now quite obscure and it may not have been very precise or exact at the time. Blount and his friends were not hesitant or modest when there was anything to be gained, and the state government offered various offices worth filling. As large property holders, they were interested in the adoption of the proper policies by the new state. In addition, friendships, loyalties, enmities, and prejudices were not easily forgotten.

The same group endeavored to control the politics of the new state as soon as the convention finished its work. Blount, as has been seen, was elected to the United States Senate, and Andrew Jackson was elected a congressman. But Sevier and Cocke broke away and were elected governor and United States senator, respectively. The Blount organization lasted for many years, surviving the Blount conspiracy with little difficulty.[32] Since this group was active before and after the constitutional convention, it hardly seems reasonable to assume that it was not functioning during the convention. It also possessed motives for attempting to continue its activities in the convention.

When the delegates assembled, it was obvious that many of the territorial officials had been elected to the convention. Among the fifty-five men who represented the eleven counties were William Blount, the territorial governor; Daniel Smith, the territorial secretary; Joseph Anderson and John McNairy, territorial judges; and eight of the territorial legislators, as well as others who were or had been local officials. The official group tended to follow Governor Blount, but most of the legislators seem to have had other connections.

Among the Blount group were found many of the delegates whose wealth, family connections, ability, and ideals distinguished them from the frontiersmen. Foremost of these was the governor himself, who was descended from an English gentleman and whose brother lived in Blount Hall in the coastal region of North Carolina. The governor held office almost continuously, speculated extensively in western lands, and entertained rather lavishly in his Knoxville home.[33] Another was Daniel Smith, born in Stafford County, Virginia, near the home of George Washington, who had appointed him secretary of the territory. During the Revolution he lived on the frontier of southwestern Virginia. At its close he moved to the Cumberland settlement, acquired a block of valuable land, built a large family home called Rockcastle, and associated with a group of wealthy Virginians who lived near Nashville as country gentlemen. He was associated with Blount in the Spanish conspiracy and in land speculation.[34]

James Robertson, the pre-eminent figure in the Cumberland Valley, was also "a loyal and steadfast supporter of the governor as well as his agent for the landed interests" in the Cumberland Country.[35] A native of southern Virginia, who had been born along the Fall Line, he was a former judge of Watauga, and a leader of the early settlers on the Cumberland. In their wars with the Indians he was the chief reliance of the whites and was appointed brigadier general, probably at Blount's suggestion, February 22, 1791.

Andrew Jackson, John McNairy, and Archibald Roane were young lawyers who were friends and protégés of Governor Blount. Jackson, who as an orphan of fourteen years, lived in Charleston, South Carolina, had managed by 1790 to secure legal training and influential friends. He speculated in land, secured the "Hermitage" tract, and lived the life of a planter after 1795. "From the beginning of his career [he] set himself up to be a 'gentleman.' He was not to the manner born but on the frontier a gentleman was a man who could play the part, and Jackson played the part convincingly." [36] McNairy had been elected judge of the Superior Court of Miro District before he left North Carolina and was later appointed a judge of the Southwest Territory.[37] Roane, a native of Pennsylvania, had lived in southwestern Virginia before coming to the Valley of East Tennessee. As a member of the Blount faction, he rose to the governorship and to the bench of the Superior Court of Tennessee; eventually he came to be recognized as one of the state's most cultured men.[38] Other well-known followers of Governor Blount were Charles McClung,[39] General James White,[40] Landon Carter,[41] William C. C. Claiborne,[42] and possibly John Rhea.[43]

To identify with certainty the less prominent members of Blount's group in the convention is not possible. A majority generally co-operated with his friends, but it was not an organized party. Apparently the control which it exercised was very tolerant, since concessions were made to satisfy those who differed. The leaders and some of the members were more closely identified with the plantation system than were the rest of the delegates, and an aristocratic government was well suited to their purposes. It seems that the delegates from the Carolinas formed a larger percentage of this group than of the rest of the convention.[44]

Another group of delegates seems to have opposed the friends of Governor Blount in the early sessions of the convention. Among its more prominent members were Joseph Anderson, Alexander

Outlaw, and Joseph McMinn. A native of Pennsylvania, Anderson was one of the territorial judges; later he served as United States senator and as the comptroller of the national treasury.[45] Outlaw was his father-in-law, a native of the North Carolina Tidewater, and a man of education and ability. A democrat and an individualist, he favored self-government for the people west of the mountains from the beginning of the Franklin experiment to the accomplishment of statehood.[46] McMinn, like Anderson a native of Pennsylvania, was a man of simple habits and democratic beliefs who later served three terms as governor and learned to co-operate with the Blount faction.[47] Other members of the group included six territorial representatives, two of whom had led unauthorized Indian expeditions when Blount was responsible for the maintenance of peace.[48]

This group furnished the opposition to the Blount faction in the convention. Its members came largely from Pennsylvania rather than from the Carolinas, and several had been close friends of Sevier for many years. As a group, the members possessed the character of frontiersmen rather than that of planters. It was made up of legislative rather than administrative officials and of several individuals who left scanty records of their origin.[49]

The members of a third group, with the exception of John Tipton, were comparatively unknown men who were rather inactive in the convention. They, too, were frontiersmen rather than planters, and most of them came from the northward. On the recorded votes, they acted as often with Blount as against him.[50]

Tipton was much better known and more active in the convention than the men just described. Of a Scotch-Irish family which located near Baltimore, he had lived in the Shenandoah Valley for several years before moving to the Watauga at the close of the Revolution. Opposed to the formation of the state of Franklin and Sevier's most unrelenting enemy, he was nevertheless not favored by Blount with appointments to office but was elected to the territorial house of representatives. In the constitutional convention he probably refused to co-operate either with the friends of Blount or the friends of Sevier.[51]

The election of Governor Blount as president and the choice of other officers served to organize the convention. The delegates from each county designated two of their number to draft a constitution. While the committee was at work, the convention decided that a bill of rights should be prefixed to the constitution. A discussion occurred over one of its provisions which declared that the state should possess the "right of soil." Probably the opposition wanted to terminate North Carolina's right to make additional land grants in Tennessee, while the Blount group wanted to protect grants and pledges already made. The measure that was adopted was a compromise.[52] The convention also began to discuss at this time the structure of the legislature. The earlier motions indicate that the members had not reached definite conclusions. A provision that each member of the law-making body own not less than two hundred acres of land was introduced by Cocke and Jackson and was adopted by the convention.[53] It was quite natural for Jackson to take this action at this time, although it seems inconsistent with his later position as the leader of Western Democrats.

When the committee of the whole at the end of the third week reported the constitution to the convention, it seemed as though Tennessee were about to follow the conservative examples of the older Southern states in respect to the apportionment of representation. Each county was to elect two representatives and one senator regardless of population, and the legislature was not required to apportion representation according to numbers for sixteen years. Whether it could be depended upon at the end of that time to apportion it according to population could only be the subject of speculation. A special committee was appointed, with Anderson as chairman, to redraft the provisions concerning the legislature. This committee's report required that within three years representation was to be apportioned on the basis of taxable inhabitants with reapportionment every seven years. The legislature was to be a bicameral body. It is possible that the opposition secured a compromise in this matter, gaining representation based upon numbers but giving up its insistence upon a unicameral legislature.[54] The hostility of the opposition to an upper house was shown during the convention by an unsuccessful effort to limit the power of the senate.[55] This hostility may also have been the reason for the opposition's effort to reduce the remuneration of legislators lower than the figure adopted by the convention.[56]

Several other interesting actions were taken during the fourth or final week of the convention's sessions. Outlaw and Anderson suggested that the new state should continue as an independent state if Congress should not admit it to the Union.[57] Perhaps this was the method chosen by the opposition to say that it had had enough of territorial government. Specific limitations were placed upon official salaries.[58] The Blount faction was largely responsible for the defeat of a motion to extend the franchise to militiamen. But it also defeated a proposal to substitute viva-voce voting for the written ballot.[59] Voting on this last measure is hard to rationalize because it violated the general attitude of both the official group and the opposition. The constitution as reported to the convention contained a section requiring that all land should be taxed at the same rate, and limiting the taxation upon slaves. The principle had been followed by North Carolina to the comparative advantage of the owners of better land. Tennessee unwisely placed it in her constitution after providing that town lots and slaves could be taxed as high as the amount upon two hundred acres.[60] Apparently the Blount group did not appreciate the political activity of the ministers. The constitution as reported barred them from civil and military office, and the Blount followers defeated an attempt to exclude this section. Finally it was changed to make them ineligible to the legislature only.[61] After adopting a section in the bill of rights prohibiting a religious test, the convention inserted a provision which required officeholders to believe in God and in future rewards and punishments. The voting, although somewhat confused, indicates no serious opposition to the test,[62] but rather reveals the strong religious character of some of the frontiersmen.

Putting together the evidence afforded by these various developments, it appears that the opposition worked out something of a program by the time the constitution was completed. It included a bill of rights, the apportionment of representation according to population, and a provision to continue as a state even if not admitted to the Union. These provisions were incorporated into the constitution. The so-called "right of soil" was rendered innocuous before it was adopted. Other features which the opposition advocated, but which were rejected, included the extension of the franchise to all militiamen; viva-voce voting; and either a unicameral legislature or a reduction in the power of the senate. The failure of the opposition to dominate the convention was probably due to the uncertainty about what it wanted, to its lack of organization, and to the individualism of its members, more than to its lack of numbers.

The advantages possessed by the Blount group, on the other

hand, included the prestige of the territorial offices, the greater experience, and the determination to maintain control even at the price of concessions. It insisted upon the bicameral legislature, the use of the written ballot, the exclusion of ministers from office, and probably the emasculation of the right of soil and the adoption of the principle of taxing all lands alike.

Neither group had a monopoly upon wisdom, or upon democracy. Progress toward a more democratic government resulted partially from the contests between the two. The constitution provided for a popularly elected governor, a bicameral legislature apportioned to taxable inhabitants, a property qualification for members of the legislature and the governor, free manhood suffrage, a judiciary generally chosen by the legislature, elective militia officers, an inclusive bill of rights, and an appointive county government.

A considerable portion of the constitution was copied from other state charters. Although parts of it came from the constitutional law of North Carolina, the influence of that document was not as great as has been assumed. Nine of the twenty-seven sections of the first article, which provided for the legislative assembly, were probably taken from the Pennsylvania constitution of 1790, in contrast to six that seem to have been derived from North Carolina. Two sections of the second article, which created the executive division of the government, were copied from the North Carolina charter, but the other fifteen probably came from Pennsylvania. Almost every word of the fourth article, which established the procedure for impeachment, was taken from the constitution of Pennsylvania.[63] Almost half of the bill of rights was copied from or patterned upon the Pennsylvania bill of rights, as contrasted with a fourth of the sections which were taken from North Carolina. Altogether, 40 per cent of the 116 sections of Tennessee's first constitution were drawn from the constitution of the Keystone State and only 16 per cent from that of North Carolina.

Other portions were patterned upon various constitutions; some were differently expressed, and a few were original.[64] The provisions in Article VII for the militia incorporated the local custom of the Tennessee frontier. Cavalry companies, which had proved very effective in Indian warfare, were included, and the officers were generally elected. But the words and arrangement of the article were so similar to the Massachusetts constitution that it must have been used as a model.

This constitution was more democratic than the older constitutions of the South Atlantic states. The relatively slight influence of the North Carolina constitution may have been occasioned by the presence in the convention of so many frontiersmen, many of whom had been born in Pennsylvania. Generally, the provisions that were copied from North Carolina were conservative, while those taken from Pennsylvania were liberal and likely to show the influence of the federal constitution. Among the democratic features were those granting the franchise to freemen, apportioning representation according to the number of taxable inhabitants, and making the governor a popularly elected official.

The following table gives a comparison of the Tennessee constitution with other constitutions:

Article	Subject Matter	No. of Sections	No. of Sections like Pa.	No. of Original Sections	No. of Sections like N. C.	No. of Sections like Other Constitutions
	Preamble					
	Right of admission	1	½			½ Mass.
I.	Legislature	27	8½	6	5½	5 S. C., 1 Vt., 1 Del.
II.	Executive	17	15		2	
III.	Elections	3	1		1	1 Del.
IV.	Impeachment	4	4			
V.	Judiciary	12	2	5	2	2 S. C., 1 Ky.
VI.	Election of officers	3		3		
VII.	Militia	7		2		5 Mass.
VIII.	Religion	2			1	1 N. Y.
IX.	Miscellaneous	4	1	1	1	1 Vt.
X.	Miscellaneous	4		4		
XI.	Bill of rights	32	15	4	7	1 U. S., 1 Va., 1 Mass., 1 Del., 2 N. H.
	Total	116	47	25	19½	24½

The conservative features included property qualifications for the governor and members of the legislature, the rigid restriction upon taxation, the religious test, and the life tenure of justices of the peace with their power to appoint county officers. The constitution

provided a more democratic government than the people had experienced under the territorial government or the state of North
Carolina. It was an important change to have the government of
the state in their own hands and to escape the control of distant
officials, whether they were located in the federal capital or in North
Carolina. It was not a completely democratic instrument, but it
ended successfully the long struggle for self-government.

It cannot be said that the frontier influence won a complete
victory. The control which North Carolina exerted over this frontier superseded the Watauga association, helped to destroy the state
of Franklin, restored the jurisdiction of a distant government under
the influence of aristocratic planters, established a land system which
was not democratic, and strengthened and protected slavery. Against
these factors, the frontier brought to the Tennessee a race of fear-
less, individualistic, and able representatives of the Old West, im-
petuous and impulsive Irishmen, hard-headed and unquenchable
Scotch-Irish, pacific but resistant Germans, and colonials of all
kinds, the majority of whom had probably not known allegiance
to North Carolina before they entered the Tennessee Valley. Many
had suffered economic, political, and social discrimination at the
hands of the Eastern states. A large majority of the delegates to
the convention were natives of the Great Valley or of the Piedmont.
The strength of the Tidewater influence was not in numbers but in
what its way of life offered to the bold, acquisitive, and able. The
frontier was also too often disturbed by Indian warfare to permit
the frontiersmen to devote their normal attention to political
processes. The aristocratic planters, placed in control during territorial days, were forced to be more democratic than their fellows
who remained in the Tidewater and to compromise with the spirit
of the frontier in order to maintain their control. The frontier
influence was strong enough to force a compromise, a compromise
which was at least a partial victory and not a defeat. The forces
which made Tennessee a part of the Old South and which overthrew much of the frontier influence were economic changes which
developed largely after 1796.

9

A National Frontier: The Old Northwest

TO THE north and west of the Ohio River there developed a new frontier under national law and protection. The earlier frontiers had been subject to colonial or state laws and to policies which had encouraged the establishment of the social, political, and economic order of the mother state. In the southern half of the Ohio Valley state control had favored the expansion of the plantation civilization of the Tidewater region. Its economy of large estates, servile labor, staple agriculture, and aristocratic social and political order interfered with the influence of the frontier toward a more democratic social, political, and economic culture. Across the Ohio, however, state claims to much of the land were ceded to the national government, and the laws by which the land was transferred to individual citizens were national statutes; the Indian policies, which had so much influence in determining whether the frontier enjoyed peace or endured war and whether the settled area expanded rapidly or slowly, were nationally determined policies; and the Ordinance of July 13, 1787, by which the pioneers were governed, was adopted by the Congress of the Confederation and readopted by the federal government under the constitution. Would the nation prove to be a more successful colonizing power than Virginia or North Carolina? Would the influence of the frontier have greater or less opportunity to determine the social order of the states of the Old Northwest? [1]

To a considerable degree the early occupation of the lands in the northern half of the Ohio Valley was a continuation of the expansion of the Old West which had first occurred in the territory to the south and east of the Ohio. Frontiersmen from the Monongahela Valley, from other parts of Pennsylvania, from the Upland South, and emigrants from the Tidewater came north as well as south of the Ohio using the same mountain passes and the same roads. To the north of the "Beautiful River" came also many settlers from Kentucky and Tennessee, some of whom were disappointed in the organization of government or their inability to acquire land.

But there were differences also, for a smaller number of the planter class moved to the northern half of the valley in contrast to the southern half. The Pennsylvania-New Jersey element was more densely settled in the communities directly west of the Pennsylvania border than in the Southern states.[2] And, finally, New England made important contributions to two large areas of the Old Northwest in the early period of settlement, the lands of the Ohio Associates and the Connecticut Western Reserve. The people, because of the broad scope of their origins, were not only representative of all parts of the nation but differed from those in the southern half of the Ohio Valley because of the smaller number of planter families and the larger number of natives of the Middle States and New England.

Important policies which affected the Northwestern frontier were adopted by the national government in the early years of its existence. The decisions led to the creation of a national domain, to the formation of a nation of equal states, to the protection of the settlers and the gradual exclusion of the Indians, to the enactment of a national land policy, to the gradual substitution of greater consideration for the land-hungry but poor pioneer, and to the adoption of a national colonial policy.

The cession of state claims to western lands was fundamental in creating the national character of this frontier and was a necessary antecedent to the land policy and to the Northwest Ordinance. After the cession, the land formed a bond of union between the older states and removed the possibility of numerous quarrels over their conflicting claims. It prevented the existence of an overwhelmingly powerful Virginia and the possible consequent augmentation of her imperialism.[3]

Although New York ceded her shadowy claims without conditions, Virginia and Connecticut required that certain reservations should be recogized by the national government. Connecticut retained both the land and the jurisdiction over some 3,800,000 acres located along the southern shore of Lake Erie and reaching westward from the Pennsylvania boundary for 120 miles.[4] The concentration of so many persons of New England descent in this particular part of the Old Northwest was due in part to this act of cession, for the region was so close to Pennsylvania that its citizens would otherwise have considered it a field for their settlement. The Virginia act of cession also left permanent marks on the territory.[5] The reservation of the Virginia Military District and Clark's Grant were destined to be areas of Virginia influence in the same manner that the Western Reserve was a center of New England influence. Another provision stipulated that the French inhabitants in the ceded lands who had professed themselves citizens of Virginia should have their "possessions and titles" confirmed to them. This provision became a significant weapon in the service of persons anxious to legalize the further introduction of slavery to the north of the Ohio.

In the process of procuring the cession of state claims to the western lands, the national government committed itself to an important policy. When Congress on October 10, 1780, urged the states to cede their claims to the western lands, the principles which the Westsylvania petition of 1776 embodied were reworded and given the sanction of Congress. The resolution provided that the lands ceded to the United States should be "formed into distinct republican states, . . . become members of the federal union, and have the same rights of sovereignty, freedom and independence, as the other states. . . ."[6] These words were repeated in the Virginia cession of March 1, 1784.[7]

This commitment was further strengthened by Congress when Thomas Jefferson presented a report on the subject of government for the West, much of which was enacted into law in the act of April 23, 1784. It required that the states to be formed "shall for ever remain a part of this confederacy," that "their respective governments shall be republican," and that they "shall be admitted . . . into the Congress of the United States, on an equal footing with the said original states. . . ."[8] These principles were to be a compact between the original states and each new state, unalterable except by the consent of Congress and of the particular state wishing to make a change.

This policy was not forgotten or rejected but was written into the Northwest Ordinance in even more exact and complete form than in the Ordinance of 1784. "Whenever any of the said States," referring to the states to be formed in the Northwest, "shall have sixty thousand free Inhabitants therein, such States shall be admitted by its Delegates into the Congress of the United States, on an equal footing with the original States, in all respects whatever; and shall be at liberty to form a permanent constitution and State government, provided the constitution and government so to be formed, shall be republican, and in conformity to the principles contained in these Articles. . . ." [9]

Great was the significance of these words. In the United States colonies were not to be held in continual subjection, incapable of protecting themselves from exploitation through political action because of their inferior status. The American Union was to be a federation of states having equal powers, privileges, and responsibilities. It was not to be a colonial empire, at least not before 1898, with a ruling government and its subordinate territories held in a dependent status. North of the Ohio a state of Franklin was not to be destroyed with the aid of the mother state, nor was there to be a district of Kentucky kept in suspense for years by another mother state reluctant to surrender control.

The national government also aided the development of the Northwestern frontier by protecting its settlements from the Indians. Its Indian policy contained three parts: the negotiations of treaties to release additional land for settlement and to remove the Indians from the vicinity of the settlements; the building of forts to protect the frontier; and the dispatch of military forces to punish hostile Indians. Although the national government was weak and its plans were often inefficiently administered, the frontier northwest of the Ohio was given valuable help.

At the close of the Revolution, the government chose to regard the Indians as having been defeated and to require them to evacuate much of what became the state of Ohio.[10] In resistance, the Indians formed a confederation from which the United States separated the Iroquois by the Treaty of Fort Stanwix in 1784. Continued pressure led to the Treaty of Fort McIntosh early the next year, by which Wyandot, Chippewa, Ottawa, and Delaware chiefs agreed to retire northward and westward from the Ohio. But the Shawnee and Miami remained obdurate. Some of the Shawnee came to Fort Finney, where on January 31, 1786, they signed a treaty by which they, too, agreed to move back from the north bank of the Ohio. Later the tribe insisted that their chiefs had gone to a meeting of the Indian confederacy and that those who attended the negotiation at Fort Finney lacked authority to surrender any of their land.[11]

The irritation of the Indians because of these treaties and the surrender of so much land led to difficulties. The survey of the Seven Ranges was delayed. The Shawnee began to attack boats descending the Ohio as they passed the mouth of the Scioto. The Miami, who raided the Kentucky settlements, drew upon themselves the expeditions of George Rogers Clark along the Wabash and of Benjamin Logan in the Miami Valley.[12]

When Governor Arthur St. Clair arrived in the Northwest Territory, he made arrangements for a new treaty, hoping to conciliate the Indians and to settle peacefully the difficulties between them and the United States. At Fort Harmar he negotiated with the Iroquois a treaty which kept them inclined toward peace and another with the Lake Indians, but he did not pacify the Miami or the Shawnee.[13]

Additional efforts at peaceful settlement of the differences having failed, the governor was authorized to send General Josiah Harmar to try the expedient of military force. In September and October, 1790, Harmar led some eleven hundred Kentucky and Pennsylvania militiamen and three hundred regulars from Fort Washington to the source of the Maumee, where he destroyed the Miami villages but did not inflict any serious punishment. On the contrary, he suffered rather rough treatment at the hands of the Miami.[14] Congress authorized a second expedition, this one under St. Clair, to construct a chain of forts from the Ohio to the Maumee and to force the Indians to agree to a satisfactory boundary line. His poorly trained and badly equipped force was thrown into confusion and thoroughly defeated on November 4, 1791, long before it reached the Maumee.[15]

In addition to the treaties and the expeditions, the government constructed a line of forts westward from Fort Pitt along the Ohio. Fort McIntosh was located at the mouth of Beaver Creek; Fort Harmar was erected in 1786 at the mouth of the Muskingum to protect the public lands from the squatters and the surveyors from the Indians; and Fort Washington was built in 1789 to assist the settlers on Symmes' Purchase. Small garrisons were established at Fort Nelson at the Falls, Fort Knox at Vincennes, Fort Massac on the lower Ohio, and at other posts in the Illinois and Miami countries. Fort Steuben was also maintained for a few months at the site of

Steubenville. Although the troops were few in number and the forts could be by-passed easily, the presence of the troops and the existence of the forts gave the settlers a considerable degree of security and protection.

The failure of St. Clair's expedition was very embarrassing to President George Washington because of its adverse influence upon his efforts to obtain the surrender of the northwestern posts by the British, upon the sale of the Seven Ranges, and upon the pacification of the Indians.[16] He, therefore, determined to send a third military expedition against the Indians, which was to be larger, more adequately equipped, and more efficiently trained. General Anthony Wayne was given command. By the summer of 1792 he began the training of his troops near Pittsburgh; in the following spring he continued the process near Fort Washington; and in the fall he advanced to winter quarters at Greenville. The next year, with a thoroughly prepared and disciplined army, he proceeded to the Maumee and on August 20, 1794, administered a thorough defeat to the confederated Indians. Nearly a year later, on August 3, 1795, he signed with them the Treaty of Greenville after notifying them of the British agreement in the Jay Treaty to surrender the posts. The Indians were required to leave the territory south and east of a line beginning at the mouth of the Cuyahoga River where it flows into Lake Erie, running south to Fort Laurens on the Tuscarawas River, west to the Miami River and Fort Recovery, and thence southwestward to the Ohio River opposite the mouth of the Kentucky. It freed approximately two thirds of the future state of Ohio for settlement, marked a temporary end to British influence over the Northwestern Indians, and removed the Indian menace from the settlements.[17] Perhaps the nation had acted slowly, but it had at last acted effectively.

If the Congress seemed benevolent in providing for republican government for the proposed states, for their admission to the Union on a basis of equality with the original states, for the negotiation of treaties with the Indians, for the construction of forts, and for the expeditions against the hostile tribes, its benevolence did not so obviously influence the national land policy. The foundation of this policy was laid in the Ordinance of May 20, 1785.[18] Especially at the beginning, the government gave little consideration to the poorer citizens who were anxious to secure farm homes in the West. Land was sold by the government in order to reduce the national debt, not to make freeholders of squatters or to enable the poor to improve their economic status. Speculators were actively trying to direct the formation and execution of this policy and to take advantage of every opportunity for personal gain, and it is surprising that they were not more successful.[19]

The Land Act of 1785 provided for the survey and sale of the Seven Ranges which were to be located in the eastern part of the Northwest Territory. They were limited on the east and south by the Ohio River, on the north by a line stretching forty-two miles west from the point where the Ohio crossed the western boundary of Pennsylvania, and on the west by a line drawn south to the Ohio River from the western end of the above line. This area was surveyed into townships six miles square and sections one mile square. The sales were to be held in the East far from the lands to be sold. The minimum amount that could be purchased was the section of 640 acres and the price must equal or exceed $640. The act also provided: "There shall be reserved the lot No. 16, of every township, for the maintenance of public schools, within the said township. . . ." [20] Although this provision applied only to the Seven Ranges and was omitted from the acts of 1796 and 1800, it was revived in 1802. It served to encourage education in the public-land states.

The act of 1785 was not suited to the needs of the numerous poor squatters who were at the time of its passage beginning to occupy the choice lands across the Ohio, including some which were a part of the Seven Ranges. They wanted cheap lands along the Ohio without delay and pre-emption until the sales began. They were offered land only after surveys were completed. The lands placed on sale were mostly in the interior at some distance from the river, and the minimum price was far beyond their means. When the first sales were held in New York City in 1787, fewer than 73,000 acres were purchased. This lack of extensive sales seemed to indicate that the act was not very helpful to the land-hungry and that it would not yield a very large revenue with which to pay the public debt. By providing secure titles and definite boundaries, it eliminated most of the litigation and uncertainty which caused so much trouble in Kentucky. The terms of sale were the same whether the minimum or maximum amount was purchased. It established the basis of a system that was later adapted by successive changes to the needs of the people.[21]

At no point was the land policy of the government to undergo greater modification than in its attitude towards the squatter settlers. Many of them claimed to have been loyal soldiers during the Revolution. They said that they wanted to purchase land but were poor. Congress, however, wished to sell lands in quantity to persons able to buy. Undoubtedly many were discontented, turbulent, and even violent spirits, but instead of adapting its policy to their needs, the government sought to drive them away.

These squatter settlers lived along the outer edge of the frontier in isolated cabins and in scattered and sparsely inhabited settlements. A petition at the close of the Revolution pictured their unfortunate plight. "When the Joyfull sound of Peace had Reached our Ears; we had scarce Enough left us to Support the Crying Distresses of our families Occasioned wholy by being Exposed to the ravages of a Cruel and Savage Enemy; on an Open Frontier where the most of us had Misfortune to Reside through the whole Continuance of the war; where the only Recourse was to Sit Confind; in forts for the Preservation of our lives; by which we ware Reduced allmost to the Lowest Ebb of Poverty; the Greatest part of us having no property in Lands: our stocks Reduced almost to nothing: our Case seemed Desperate. . . ." 22

The number of these people in the Ohio Valley was increased by the failure of the various separatist and statehood movements. The defeat of these efforts left the political control of the East and the state land systems, which were unfavorable to the poor, substantially unchanged. As their aspirations for separation and self-government were disappointed, an unknown number of the early settlers of the Monongahela Valley were dispersed along the Ohio and its tributaries. At the same time, and extending over a longer period, was the failure of the radicals in Kentucky to secure a state government according to their own ideas. The number of landless people in Kentucky at this time is unknown, but estimates indicate that it was large. General Richard Butler estimated the squatter Kentuckians in 1786 as nine tenths of the population. "Thousands are gone to that country expecting to get land on easy terms; in this they are disappointed, and obliged to settle on other persons' lands, on sufference, and only wait the result of a treaty . . . to repass, and cross the Ohio to fix on these lands," he wrote.23 Governor St. Clair reported in 1788 that there were "many Thousands of People" in Kentucky who were without a "foot of Land," and who were unable to obtain any. He thought that they were so numerous that the land between the Mississippi and Wabash rivers should be set aside for them.[24] Meanwhile in Franklin the frontiersmen were unsuccessful in their efforts to establish a new state. If, therefore, the landless in the Monongahela Valley, in Kentucky, and in Tennessee were not ready to accept defeat, to become tenants on the estates of the larger landholders, or to attempt to buy a farm from the speculators, they must hope for success on another frontier. The land beyond the Ohio beckoned them to try again.

As early as 1776 reference was made to "encrouchments on the Indian Territorial Rights . . . on . . . some of the Islands in the Ohio . . . and on the Western side of said River. . . ."[25] Thus wrote the signers of the Westsylvania petition, who may have sought a few years later the same western side of the Ohio. Captain John Clarke in 1779 reported "small improvements all the way from the Muskingum River to Fort McIntosh & thirty miles up some of the Branches."[26]

Two years later, General William Irvine wrote, "There have been sundry meetings of people at different places [in western Pennsylvania], for the purpose of concerting plans to emigrate into the Indian country, there to establish a government for themselves."[27] A few months later, General Irvine wrote that the date was set for the emigration, that a constitution had actually been written, and that the affair was attracting much attention.[28] In the following fall additional emigrants were reported going beyond the Ohio, and an opinion was expressed that their improvements might make a foundation for a legal title to the land, since there was not a law prohibiting their settlements.[29]

Congress recognized the situation by issuing a proclamation in 1783 prohibiting settlements on Indian lands.[30] Little attention was paid to this pronouncement, and squatters seem to have spread farther into the interior.[31] When the surrender of state claims to the western lands increased the responsibility of the national government, the commissioner of Indian Affairs ordered Josiah Harmar to employ his troops to remove the squatters from the national domain.

Advertisements were found calling an election to choose members of a constitutional convention. The advertisement claimed that "all mankind agreeable to every constitution formed in America have an undoubted right to pass into every vacant country, and there to form their constitution, and that from the confederation of the whole United States, Congress is not empowered to forbid them. . . ." [32]

Ensign John Armstrong, who was ordered to dispossess the intruders, reported several groups of settlers as he came down the Ohio toward Wheeling. He ordered them to leave, destroyed a few "sheds," but granted the larger groups a little time. A petition was sent to Congress protesting innocence of wrongdoing and requesting permission to remain in their settlements and to buy their lands from Congress.[33] Armstrong reported that two justices of the peace had been elected, that elections for delegates to a convention were to be held at the mouths of the Miami and Scioto, on the Muskingum, and in the neighborhood of Wheeling, that three hundred families were located on the Hocking and on the Muskingum and fifteen hundred on the Miami and the Scioto, and that new settlers were coming by the forties and fifties.[34] An interesting but unconvincing item in the Pittsburgh *Gazette* indicates the possibility that a government was formed and a governor elected.[35] Armstrong, however, did not visit all the areas on which he reported and the larger numbers were said to be in those parts which he did not visit. The term "governor" which appeared in the Pittsburgh paper may have been a nickname. The squatters, however, were numerous or the government would not have betrayed such concern. The building of Fort Harmar may have defeated plans for a new state northwest of the Ohio River.

Intruders were driven off or warned to leave at other times from 1785 to 1787, and their presence was one of the reasons for building forts along the Ohio.[36] Ensign Ebenezer Denny was sent in the fall of 1785, perhaps to see if the squatters whom Armstrong had permitted to remain had left as they promised. Richard Butler warned them again in October but agreed that they might harvest their crops. A month later, Major John Doughty reported that he had destroyed forty houses, but that he supposed they would be rebuilt because "the poor devils have nowhere to go." Many of the houses which were demolished in the spring were found rebuilt. Captain John F. Hamtramck performed a similar tour in the summer of 1786, and twice in 1787 intruders were driven away.[37] These efforts seem not to have been effective; perhaps the agents of the government were less harsh than the government itself. Judge Rufus Putnam stated that it was well known that individuals took possession of the most valuable land on the Muskingum, Hocking, and other rivers, built cabins, girdled trees, and planted corn.[38] Governor Arthur St. Clair noted the rapid increase of settlement in 1788 and its continuation as late as August, 1789.[39]

From the squatters and other early settlers valuable aid in founding and protecting new communities was gained by the inexperienced and the latecomers. The Ohio Company, Benjamin Stites, the Cincinnati Associates, and John C. Symmes gave land to a limited number who would come and build in their settlements.[40] Occasionally someone recognized the usefulness of these men. Congressman Thomas Scott, of Washington, Pennsylvania, told Congress on July 13, 1789, that settlement

in a wilderness upon the frontiers, between the savages and the least populated of the civilized parts of the United States, requires men of enterprising, violent, nay, discontented and turbulent spirits. Such always are our first settlers in the ruthless and savage wild; they serve as pioneers to clear the way for the more laborious and careful farmer. These characters are already in that country by thousands, and their number is daily increasing. . . .[41]

In marked contrast to the intruders on the public domain were the representatives of the Ohio Company of Associates who came from New England to request a purchase of lands for which they offered to pay one million dollars. Payment was to be made in depreciated Continental currency, but Congress was obligated to honor these promissory notes. The signing of the contract on October 27, 1787, by the Reverend Manasseh Cutler and Winthrop Sargent involved an option to purchase 1,500,000 acres for their own company and 5,000,000 acres for the Scioto Company, a secret partner which the speculators and politicians forced on the veterans. Fortunately, the two companies were not closely tied together, and the failure of the latter did not seriously affect the former.

The contract required that section 16 in every township be reserved for education and section 29 for religion. A half million was paid when the contract was signed, and a second half million was to be paid when the survey of the exterior lines was completed. At this time title for a million acres was to pass to the company. In the meantime, the company was to proceed with its settlement. The work of Cutler, the lobbyist, had been well done.[42]

Influenced by the grant to the Ohio Company, other groups sought to obtain land on the same attractive terms, and Congress was in danger of giving up the land policy it had written into the act of 1785. Only one of the groups, however, succeeded in signing a contract. John Cleves Symmes, a representative of New Jersey in Congress and soon to be one of the judges of the Northwest Territory, headed a group of speculators who secured the option to buy a million acres along the Ohio and Great Miami rivers on substantially the same terms that were granted to the Ohio Company. With this contract, however, Congress ceased to make large sales to companies outside the regular land system.[43]

When the Ohio Company of Associates made its offer to buy land, Congress was ready to read for the third time an ordinance for the government of the territory northwest of the Ohio River. But a quorum was lacking for two months. The ordinance was then referred on July 9 to a new committee, which reported two days later. Changes were made the following day, and the Ordinance was adopted, July 13, 1787.[44] The final product was not the result of these few days. The formation of a government for the West passed through three main stages. The first of these was Jefferson's Report of April 23, 1784, the second was the ordinance which Congress referred to the committee on July 9, 1787, and the third was the Ordinance of July 13.

Jefferson's Report provided that republican states should be organized in the West, that they should forever be a part of the confederacy, and that they should be admitted to Congress with powers equal to those of the original states.[45] The people who were expected to settle the proposed states were authorized to form a temporary government by adopting the constitution and laws of any one of the original states, and to elect a delegate to Congress who could speak but not vote. When twenty thousand inhabitants resided in any one of these states, they were to be permitted to call a constitutional convention and establish a permanent constitution and government. The new state was to be admitted into Congress by its delegates when its population equaled that of the original state having the least population. The new states were to be subject to the acts of Congress and were to assume a share of the national debt. These various conditions were to be formed into a compact between the original states and each of the new states.

The ordinance which Congress referred to a committee on July 9 bore much resemblance to the final ordinance, but it also lacked some very important provisions of the latter. The territory was to be governed by a governor assisted by a secretary and three judges during the early period when the population was small. This act was an improvement over the Ordinance of 1784, which did not provide any government until the people met and adopted the laws and constitution of one of the original states. It also gave the initiative and the responsibility to Congress. After five thousand free male inhabitants of full age were resident in the territory a legislature was to be formed. The members of the lower house were to be popularly elected by freeholders, but the members of the upper house were to be appointed by Congress to hold office during good behavior. The state was to be admitted to Congress whenever its population equaled one-thirteenth part of the people of the nation.[46] This form of the ordinance did not provide for the large number of small states that formed a conspicuous part of Jefferson's Report.

Undoubtedly the men interested in the Ohio Company of Associates stimulated Congress not only to sell them land but to finish the ordinance and provide government for the region in which they wished to locate their lands. To Jefferson's exceedingly important principles and to the less important contributions of various members of Congress [47] which were made while the subject was under consideration between 1784 and 1787, certain significant features were added as a result of the influence of New Englanders. Among these were the bill of rights which protected the civil rights of the settlers, the provision establishing the equal distribution of the property of a person dying intestate, the prohibition of slavery, and the carefully described method of forming a state government. The people were also given greater participation in the choice of members of the legislative council.[48]

The Northwest Ordinance has been so highly evaluated that it is difficult to assess accurately its influence upon the development of democracy in the Ohio Valley. It furnished immediately a government that was altogether unrepresentative and undemocratic. During the first stage the people were governed by a governor, a secretary, and three judges, all of whom were appointed by the national government. The local officials were appointed by the governor. There were no voters and no elections, and the people were governed without their consent or their participation. The royal governor of colonial Virginia ruled with the co-operation of an assembly, the lower house of which was elected, but the governor of the Northwest Territory ruled without an assembly.

The civil rights which the Ordinance protected included freedom of religion, the right of habeas corpus, trial by jury, proportional representation in the legislature when it was established, judicial procedure according to the common law, right of bail, moderate fines and punishments, and protection of property and contracts. This provision might be compared with the first Virginia charter, which promised the colonists "all Liberties, Franchises, and Immunities . . . as if they had been abiding and born, within this our Realm of *England*. . . ." [49] The Northwest Ordinance did not include some of the liberties which had been defined in the English Bill of Rights of December 16, 1689, but it contained others that were not in the former.[50] If the Ordinance of 1787 is compared with the Virginia Bill of Rights of 1776, it is obvious that protection to only a limited number of rights was assured to the settlers of the Northwest Territory.[51]

The people subject to this government in the so-called first stage were not satisfied with their status. As will be noted later, the people of the Northwest Territory, Indiana Territory, and Illinois Territory exhibited dissatisfaction with this type of government and signed many petitions asking to be advanced to the semirepresentative stage.[52]

This change was to take place when five thousand free adult males resided in the territory. The free adult males who owned fifty acres of land or more were then to elect members of a house of representatives. Only persons owning two hundred acres of land or more were eligible to be elected. The members of the lower house assembled first to choose the names of ten men who owned five hundred acres of land or more, from which number the national government chose five to be members of the upper house or legislative council. The two houses were then assembled to function as a legislature. The term of the members of the lower house was two years, and that of the councilors was five years. The legislators were, however, restricted by the governor's power to convene, prorogue, and dissolve the assembly when in his opinion it was expedient; by his absolute veto over their acts; and by the requirement that their laws were not to be repugnant to the principles and articles of the Ordinance. The representatives and councilors were also empowered to elect a delegate to Congress who could speak but could not vote. While this type of government was in operation, the people who owned at least fifty acres of land enjoyed a limited participation in their own government. In the Northwest Territory and in the Indiana Territory, this period was characterized by contests between the governor and the legislature, indicating that the people desired more complete self-government.[53]

Three other provisions exerted an influence that must be noted. The first required that the property of a person dying without a will should be distributed equally among the heirs of equal relationship. This provision was intended to break up estates by division among the children rather than keep them intact as under the law of primogeniture in colonial Virginia. It probably exerted an intangible influence as an ideal which extended beyond the number to whom it applied.

The second of these other provisions was contained in the sixth article, which prohibited slavery. It was a simple statement: "There shall be neither slavery nor involuntary servitude in the said territory, otherwise than in the punishment of crimes whereof the party shall have been duly convicted. . . ." At least one and possibly two other parts of the Ordinance limited this provision. Fugitive slaves were not freed by it but were subject to being reclaimed and conveyed to their owners. This law preceded by two years the first national fugitive slave act of 1789. The second possible limitation was contained in the words excepting the French—permitting them to keep their laws and customs relative to the descent and conveyance of property. This was buttressed by the provision in Virginia's cession of her western claims which stated that the French were to have "their possessions and titles confirmed to them" if they had professed themselves citizens of Virginia. Therefore slavery did exist under the Ordinance, and the governors interpreted the sixth article as not being retroactive even to the extent of not ending existing slavery.[54] They made no effort to enforce the prohibition and apparently winked at its violation. It is also very doubtful whether it was binding beyond the territorial period. It will be interesting to note that the proslavery advocates of a constitutional convention in the state of Illinois claimed that the guarantee of admission to the Union with equal powers gave to the people the authority to legalize slavery and that the prohibition contained in Article VI applied only to the territorial period.[55]

Nevertheless, the prohibition accomplished its purpose. Although violated and circumvented and although slaves lived and labored under its rule, it discouraged slaveowners from migrating north of the Ohio with their slaves lest they be declared free. This influence was strengthened by geographical factors which prevented large-scale production of tobacco and cotton. The conventions which prepared the constitutions of Ohio, Indiana, and Illinois adopted provisions prohibiting slavery, perhaps fearful lest Congress refuse admission to the new states. In these two ways the Ordinance's prohibition of slavery was significant.

Finally, it may seem ironical to praise the Ordinance because it provided a means by which the people who were subject to its provisions might escape from them and establish a more democratic government. And yet, this lack of finality was, perhaps, its strongest feature. The unrepresentative and undemocratic character of the government of the first territorial stage and the very limited nature of the representative portions of the government of the second stage were criticized sharply. But they were not permanent. They were intended to lead the pioneers through those difficult early years when they were too few to bear the costs of more elaborate government and when the task of establishing themselves consumed so much of their energy, and to introduce them to a semi-representative government before they were to assume the responsibilities of statehood and participation in national affairs.[56]

The significance of all these developments is quite clear. Not only large numbers of people from the Upland South, but other immigrants from all parts of the United States and from some parts of Europe came to the Old Northwest. The population was considerably like the people in the southern half of the Ohio Valley, but it was more national in character. The nature of the population movements created sectional settlements; but they tended to counteract each other, and the established customs of any one section were not able to dominate the entire territory. The process of securing the cession of state land claims to the national government committed Congress to the policy of admitting the new states to the Union and of promising them republican governments with powers equal to the old states. The aid given in defending the frontier and in removing the Indians before the westward advance of the people made possible a rapid growth of settlement.

After a faltering beginning, the land policy gave secure titles and equal treatment to large and small purchasers alike. At first the Congress was unfriendly and its land policy unsuited to the poorer people, but efforts were begun almost at once to adapt the later to the needs of the people. Seemingly some quantity of land was acquired by a large portion of the population, a more equitable distribution than that which the Old Southwestern frontier developed, and in time the acquisition of land became easier. And Congress adopted a cautious governmental policy which led the people to statehood, local self-government, and participation in national affairs. Altogether these policies offered a fairly definite program, including a method of acquiring land, aid against the Indians, and a progressive scheme of government. The settlers experienced less of that uncertainty from which springs radical agitation.

Furthermore, the program offered hope for the future. If land could not be acquired immediately, hope existed for future acquisition. If the Indian menace was serious, the growth of population added to government aid would certainly bring victory before long. If government was unsatisfactory, a few years would bring a change and before very long statehood could be achieved. Furthermore, the federal government did not seek to perpetuate the institution of slavery as a basis of an aristocratic social and economic order. When all of these factors were combined with the natural fluidity and the freedom characteristic of new settlements, they gave to the frontier influence an excellent environment in which to work.

A State of the National Frontier: Ohio

*T*HE FIRST significant application of the nation's frontier policies was made in the early settlement of the Northwest Territory, and the result was embodied in the state of Ohio. Although the states exerted considerable influence by means of the provisions which they made when surrendering their claims to western lands, the reservations tended to counteract one another and to prove less powerful than the national policies. Certain areas were settled by sectional migrations, and the majority of the people in the territory resembled the settlers in other parts of the Ohio Valley; nevertheless the pioneers of Ohio were collectively more representative of the nation than were those of the Southern frontier.

The occupation of the Ohio Company's land was begun by an advance guard of forty-eight on April 7, 1788. General Rufus Putnam led them from New England across the mountains of Pennsylvania to the banks of the Youghiogheny, where boats were built, one of which was named the *Mayflower*. After the little party arrived at the mouth of the Muskingum, they founded the village of Marietta across the river from Fort Harmar. Before the end of the year there were 132 men in addition to women and children about the village and its stockade. The arrival of Governor Arthur St. Clair and the other territorial officials gave the settlers a government sanctioned by the nation, and the coming of a minister gave them the services of the church and a school.[1] The second year 152 men arrived, a third of them accompanied by their families. During the third year, 200 men came, 33 of whom brought families. Because expansion was necessary, additional villages were founded: Belpre on the Ohio, Waterford, Plainfield, and Big Bottom on the Muskingum. In 1793 some 430 settlers were estimated to be living in the region.[2] The connection with the Scioto Company, like a skeleton in the closet, led to the arrival of a host of French immigrants for whom a location was provided in the Ohio Company's purchase. The community was called Gallipolis, but the conditions attendant upon its founding were so unfortunate that other groups did not come. Aside from this French village, the area became a little New England in the West with emphasis upon church and school. In it were founded Marietta College and Ohio University. Its people were conservative democrats for other values sometimes seemed to have greater significance than the will of the majority.

In the Symmes Purchase, Benjamin Stites and party founded Columbia just below the mouth of the Little Miami on November 18, 1788. The leaders were from New Jersey, but many of the settlers were from western Pennsylvania and Kentucky. The group which settled Losantiville was also a mixture of people from New Jersey and Kentucky. Symmes founded a third settlement at North Bend early the following spring,[3] and before the end of 1789 Fort Washington was built and garrisoned by national troops. When Governor St. Clair organized the area as Hamilton County early in 1790, he changed the name of Losantiville to Cincinnati. Dunlop's Station and Ludlow's Station marked the expansion to the northward. Daniel Drake thought that the population continued to increase until St. Clair was defeated by the Indians. "Notwithstanding all the perils of an indian war, . . . the stream of emigration after the commencement of the year 1790 was lively. . . ." Cincinnati "increased in population up to the fatal 4th of November," 1791. Apparently, this growth continued to be true of the Miami Valley, for he wrote of 1792, "this year brought a greater increase of inhabitants than the last." "The presence of a large force in the rear of . . . Cincinnati commanded by Wayne inspired great confidence and the town grew with rapidity this year [1793]— The Indians were drawn off from the river above and emigrants of all kinds floated down in numbers. . . ." [4] About 2,400 persons were thought to be in the various settlements in 1793.[5] The Battle of Fallen Timbers on August 20, 1794, and the Treaty of Greenville of August 3, 1795, removed the Indian menace, and migrants poured into the Northwest in still greater numbers. The special census of Hamilton County taken in 1798 indicated a population in excess of 10,000, extending as far north as Dayton and Fairfield.[6]

Although the population was mixed, the Kentucky and Middle States elements were thought to have been quite numerous.[7]

Only a beginning was made in the occupation of the Virginia Military District and the Seven Ranges before the Indian resistance was broken at Fallen Timbers. The founding of Manchester on the Ohio River not far from Limestone, Kentucky, marked the commencement of successful operations in the Virginia Military District. In like manner the accumulation of cabins about the short-lived Fort Steuben was the beginning of a village in the Seven Ranges. During these early years, settlers had been rather closely limited to the vicinity of forts, either those of the national government or others erected by the settlers of a particular locality.[8] Persons lived in or near the fort and farmed their out-lots some distance from the village. But the victory of General Anthony Wayne changed this practice. Settlers could now move into the rural districts and the distinction between in-lots and out-lots lost much of its significance. A large number of new villages came into existence and migration across the Ohio increased many fold.

The founding of Chillicothe in 1796 marked the beginning of settlement in the interior of the Virginia Military District. Only fear of the Indians had prevented Nathaniel Massie from making locations in the Scioto Valley in the vicinity of the mouth of Paint Creek, for Congress had agreed in 1790 to the location of lands in the military district. The crowding of settlers into Kentucky, the confusion of titles, and speculation in lands created a considerable number of potential immigrants for the Northwest.[9]

A regular business in military warrants was developed. Speculators in Virginia bought the certificates from the veterans and sent them to surveyors in the military tract, who located land for the Eastern speculators in return for a share in the land. The surveyors also purchased warrants which they located for themselves. Nathaniel Massie, who founded Manchester and Chillicothe, was the largest of these surveyors and speculators. Born above Richmond on the James River, he moved to Kentucky at the close of the Revolution. There he learned surveying, land speculation, the arts of the backwoodsman, and the methods of frontier commerce, while he successfully accumulated considerable property. About him collected a group of able and unusual men. Duncan McArthur, a native New Yorker who lived for a time on the Pennsylvania and Kentucky frontiers, gained further experience in Massie's service and combined a military career with politics and speculation. Massie was joined in 1797 by Thomas Worthington, a descendant of an English Quaker family that had moved along the Appalachian Valley route and located south of Harper's Ferry. Here he married and acquired by industry and inheritance considerable property. When Worthington moved to the Scioto Valley, he was accompanied by various relatives, including Edward Tiffin, the husband of his sister Mary. Both men had freed their slaves but brought colored servants with them to the Northwest. Both were more successful politically than Massie, but their speculations were not so extensive. These three able and industrious men brought the traditions of Virginia to the Northwestern frontier. They held views that have come to be called Jeffersonian and were soon to take significant roles in the statehood movement.[10]

The beginning of Conneaut, Cleveland, and Youngstown marked the start of the New England and Pennsylvania migrations to the Western Reserve. In 1796 the Connecticut Land Company, of which Moses Cleaveland was a director, sent along the shore of Lake Erie surveyors who founded the first two of these villages. The establishment of Youngstown resulted from the coming of German and Scotch-Irish settlers of western Pennsylvania. Settlement was slow at first, but more than a thousand persons were thought to have come to the reserve by 1800. The quieting of the remaining Indian claims in 1805 and the building of roads removed other obstacles to settlement. After jurisdiction over the area had been surrendered by Connecticut to the United States, July 10, 1800, it was incorporated into the Northwest Territory. It was one of the less populous sections when Ohio became a state.[11]

The development of the Seven Ranges was retarded by the unsatisfactory terms of the land acts of 1785 and 1796 and by the competition of other areas. Four of the Seven Ranges were surveyed in 1786 and 1787, but at sales held in New York City in the latter year only 72,974 acres were bought. Further sales were not held during the years from 1788 to 1795; but the survey was completed and sales were opened in 1796 at Pittsburgh and Philadelphia. Only 48,566 acres were purchased at this time, and sales were interrupted until July, 1800. Fifteen years had passed, and approximately 190 sections, or only five and two-sevenths townships, had been transferred to private ownership. In all probability most of the squatters in the Seven Ranges were still squatters. Bezaleel Wells laid out the city of Steubenville in 1797, but it did not grow so rapidly as Pittsburgh, Wheeling, or Cincinnati.[12]

In 1796 the federal government set aside a considerable tract of land within which the promised bounties for Continental soldiers were to be granted. It was located between the upper parts of the Seven Ranges and the Virginia Military District, south of the Greenville Treaty Line and north of the future National Road. The administration of the act proceeded slowly, and few persons moved into the tract before Ohio became a state.[13]

A land act, superseding the Ordinance of 1785, was enacted on May 18, 1796. It provided for the opening of land offices in Pittsburgh and Cincinnati and for the sales of additional lands beyond the Seven Ranges. Surveyors were to survey the land that was freed of Indian claims by the Treaty of Greenville. The land below the Great Miami was to be sold at Cincinnati; that between the Scioto River and the Ohio Company's purchase, and between the Seven Ranges and the Connecticut Reserve at Pittsburgh; while the portions of the Seven Ranges remaining in government hands were to be sold at Philadelphia and Pittsburgh. This first extension of the territory on sale provided land offices near the lands to be sold. But most of the potential advantages of the act were destroyed or greatly lessened by the terms of sale. The price was raised to two dollars an acre, and the minimum amount that could be bought remained at one section of 640 acres. Few pioneers could raise $1,280, or meet the terms of one-twentieth cash, one half in thirty days, and the remainder in one year. Two years passed before any lands were surveyed under this act, and its influence upon the settlement of the Northwest Territory was very slight.[14]

The Harrison Act of 1800 was fostered by the congressional delegate from the Northwest Territory, William H. Harrison, and was intended to adjust the land system to the views of the frontier. The lands west of the Muskingum River were to be sold in sections and half-sections, and payment could be made in four annual installments with an additional year of grace before forfeiture was to take place. Credit was intended to give the purchaser time to raise crops on the land from which he could make the second, third, and fourth payments. Since the minimum price remained at two dollars an acre and the minimum purchase was reduced to 320 acres, individuals possessing $160 could secure a half-section of land. Three similar payments were to be made by the close of the second, third, and fourth years. Land offices were to be opened in Steubenville, Marietta, Chillicothe, and Cincinnati.[15]

Large sales of the public lands began under this act. Almost 400,000 acres were sold from July, 1800, to the end of 1801, and 340,000 were sold in 1802. Probably the law was a contributing cause of the large migration which justified the statehood movement for Ohio.[16]

When Congress in 1788 prepared to place territorial government in operation, it chose Arthur St. Clair to be the governor. An excellently educated native of Scotland, and a resident on the Pennsylvania frontier, whose service in the Revolution led to a major-generalcy, he was elected to the Confederation Congress and became its president. He was undoubtedly an able, experienced, and distinguished man when he came to his new post in the Ohio Valley.[17] The secretary was Winthrop Sargent, a native of Massachusetts, a graduate of Harvard, and a leader in the formation of the Ohio Company of Associates.[18] Judges Samuel Holden Parsons and James Mitchell Varnum [19] were New Englanders, while the former was also one of the founders of the Ohio Company. The third judge was John Cleves Symmes, who was not connected with the Ohio Company but had a speculation of his own along the Ohio and Great Miami.[20] The offices seem to have been heavily weighted with New Englanders and men who took a Federalist point of view on a frontier where Southerners who were democratic in political philosophy formed a large and important element in the population.

When Governor St. Clair crossed the Muskingum from Fort Harmar to Marietta on July 15, 1788, and proclaimed the beginning of government of the Northwest Territory, the frontiersmen of the Ohio Valley became subject to the nonrepresentative stage of territorial government. They remained under this form of control until the first territorial assembly was opened on September 24, 1799. Eleven years was a long time for frontiersmen to be subjected to arbitrary authority without the opportunity to participate in their own government or to give their consent to laws and taxes of the government.[21]

The inauguration of the territory at the beginning of a period of Indian warfare, which tended to stress the dependence of the people upon both territorial and national administrations in military matters and which delayed rapid settlement, was in part responsible for the acceptance of this type of government for so long. Shortly after the governor's arrival in the territory, he plunged into the negotiations which on January 9, 1789, resulted in the Treaty of Fort Harmar. His long-delayed tour to the Illinois Country was interrupted by the seriousness of the Indian problem. Attacks upon the settlements of the territory and in Kentucky indicated the beginning of hostilities. From an Indian camp at the mouth of the Scioto, assaults were made on the boats of immigrants coming down the Ohio. Punitive expeditions were sent under the command of Generals Harmar, Charles Scott, and James Wilkinson. They were followed by the expedition under St. Clair which resulted in his disastrous defeat of November 4, 1791. If the Indians caused the governor much embarrassment, it is also probable that their activities tended to preserve the unity of the white settlers and to deprive them of the opportunity for serious discussion of political differences.[22]

The governor, with the aid of the lesser officials, also had other important services to perform for the people of the territory, services which the vast extent of the territory made very difficult. From the beginning until after the Treaty of Greenville, the governor, the secretary, and the judges were busy organizing local government, holding courts, and adopting laws. On July 27, 1788, Governor St. Clair organized the territory east of the Scioto as Washington County; on January 2, 1790, Hamilton County between the Miamis; and St. Clair County on April 27, 1790, in the Illinois Country. Secretary Sargent established Knox County in the Wabash Valley on June 20, 1790. Not until the surrender of the Northwestern posts by the British in 1796 was it possible to organize Wayne County, in the Detroit area. Legislative meetings of the governor and judges were held in order to supply laws for the guidance of the officials and the people. The judges were required to hold four sessions of the general territorial court annually, but only one session was to be held in any county. The judges were very lax in holding courts in the distant counties.[23]

Criticism of the government and of the officials was not lacking in this early period. "Manlius," who complained of the high licenses charged traders and tavern keepers, suggested that the great landholders were trying to avoid taxes on their lands. "If we will let the great land-holders go exempt from taxes, they will keep their lands until their avarice is satisfied in the sales of them; on the contrary, if their property be taxed with that of the trader, and poor tavern keeper, they will be obliged to sell their great tracts in small parcels to such people as will make immediate settlements and who will be more terrible to the savage enemies of this country, than all the three dollar soldiers that can be collected. . . ." He also complained that the judges of the general court paid little attention to the country and that the county courts were tyrannical.[24] Although "Plebius" objected to his views on taxation, he wrote: "It is not impossible but the judges of this territory may have been too inattentive to the interests of the public—a thing very common with territorial and colonial officers; who are appointed by, and only accountable to a foreign power. . . ."[25] "Manlius" wrote again, this time asserting that "taking away their money without their consent, was the highest species of oppression," but he revealed an irresponsible character when he stated, "There are occasions in which the hand of an assassin would be very useful."[26] This revolutionary tone was sounded again in the Fourth of July celebration of 1794, in the toast "The Sans Culottes of France and [the] cause of Liberty, triumphant."[27]

The Northwest Ordinance and the government it provided were the subjects of criticisms by "Vitruvius." It was impossible for the inhabitants to enjoy "the rights and liberties of free citizens" under this system he asserted. "In all free republics . . . the people have a right to form their own government." He thought the method of appointing the territorial officials produced tyranny and despotism. The territorial judges violated the Ordinance in their legislative function, and the county judges were acting arbitrarily.[28] The advance to the semirepresentative or second stage of territorial government, he suggested in a second communication, would not end the people's grievances. The governor's veto and other powers over the legislature would prevent so fortunate an event, and the delegate to Congress would not be serviceable. He referred to the Ordinance as "this preposterous constitution."[29] In a third protest he complained of the fees granted the officers in addition to their salaries and suggested that experience under territorial government proved the necessity of separating the three separate departments. The governor, he said, was a much greater man than George III. "Let me now ask the question; are not the people in this territory in a much worse situation, than the United States were, before the late revolution? Are we not obliged to pay taxes without our consent? Are not judges of inferior courts, and others in commission, dependent on the will of the governor for the tenure of their offices? Have we a free legislature in the territory? —Or have we a representative in any legislature?" [30]

Judge Rufus Putnam in his charge to a grand jury on October 7, 1794, took cognizance of these protests although he did not consider the complainant a substantial citizen. "Whilst I despise the anonymous scribler who libels the ordinance for the government of the territory and in a billingsgate dialect abuses the principal officers of it, I glory in the unprejudiced enquiry of a grand jury into . . . any grievance the people labours under." [31] In a reply to Putnam, "Philo Vitruvius" insisted that Vitruvius was correct and that the judge was interested in his position and fees.[32] "Dorastius" joined the discussion by observing that the government of the territory had been established on the same principles the colonies had opposed when the British taxed them without their consent. It was a natural right for the people to appoint their own form of government.[33]

Although another "scribler" suggested that one person was using several pen names, dissatisfaction was not restricted to letter writers. At a Fourth of July celebration at Cincinnati in 1795 toasts were drunk protesting against the "old harlot of aristocracy" and the prostitution of the territory by speculators and land jobbers. Republican government, a universal land tax, and a system of land distribution that would produce equal rights and guard against speculation were requested.[34] Two communications appeared in which the writers gloated over the judges when the national house of representatives disapproved the laws of the territory.[35] Still another wrote, "Though the inhabitants of the North-Western Territory may properly be stiled [sic] the citizens of a free country, yet necessity, supposed necessity or something else has (for the present) placed them under a kind of despotic government." [36]

Objection was also voiced to the cost of judicial procedure and the time required to secure justice. Probably the greatest dissatisfaction in this connection was due to the very limited jurisdiction of individual justices of the peace, a situation which necessitated taking many cases to the courts at the county seats. The liberals favored extending the jurisdiction of the individual justice from cases involving five dollars or less to cases involving as much as fifty dollars. They also suggested the use of smaller juries.[37]

Other difficulties tended to assume a personal character. During St. Clair's frequent absences from the territory, Sargent as acting governor generally proved to be less tactful. In 1790 at Vincennes he vetoed a bill favored by Judges George Turner and Symmes authorizing local officials to exercise considerable power. For the next five years he was engaged in intermittent quarrels with the leaders of Cincinnati. He endeavored to enforce strict conduct on the militia and interfered with the county and territorial judges. His opponents generally succeeded in placing him in an embarrassing position. Throughout the controversy the Cincinnati leaders were determined to manage their community affairs without executive interference.[38]

The desire for representative government expressed in Cincinnati at the celebration on July 4, 1795, was reasserted early the next year in the *Centinel of the North-Western Territory* and in a statement of grievances adopted at a public meeting at Columbia. Among the defects of government which were criticized were the absence of popular control of the governor, the nonparticipation of the people in legislation, the lack of a high court of chancery, and the frequent absences of the governor and judges from the territory. Judge Symmes was criticized as a land jobber and as being interested in most of the cases before his court. The governor, it was said, called the people subjects, not citizens, and seemed "to be so crowded with British princely ideas, that he apparently plumes himself on his being analogous to a king." A series of meetings in Cincinnati late in 1797 resulted in a census being taken in Hamilton County, an appeal for help being made to the republicans of Adams, Washington, and Wayne counties, and a demand being voiced for immediate statehood. In response to the last, St. Clair directed that the free adult males should be counted, but did not wait to learn the results before proclaiming the representative stage of government on October 29, 1798.[39]

The semirepresentative or second stage lasted from the meeting of the first territorial legislature, September 24, 1799, until the meeting of the first general assembly of the state on March 1, 1803. The house of representatives of the territory was composed of men each of whom owned at least two hundred acres and who were elected by free adult men who owned a minimum of fifty acres. The house chose the names of ten men, each of whom owned at least five hundred acres, from which the President of the United States with the advice of the Senate appointed five to form the upper house or the legislative council. This assembly could be summoned, prorogued, or dissolved by the governor whenever he wished and its bills were subject to his power of absolute veto. It, therefore, had little real power and was representative of the landowners but not of the poor people. Nevertheless, the legislature had a significant function to perform. It brought the representatives of the people together and gave them the opportunity to organize and to express their ideas publicly. They possessed the authority to elect to Congress a delegate who could represent the territory before the national government. It served, before long, to place Governor St. Clair before the people of the territory as a conservative and an undemocratic official.

The representatives included a number of individuals who were to become significant leaders in the formation of the new state, Thomas Worthington, Edward Tiffin, and Nathaniel Massie. In the council was Jacob Burnet, a pre-eminent lawyer and Federalist of Cincinnati. William H. Harrison was chosen delegate to Congress, defeating the governor's son for this important position. When the governor vetoed several bills at the end of the first session, his action crystallized the opinions of the liberal leaders into the conviction that escape from arbitrary government could be gained only by leaving the territorial status. Rejection of bills creating new counties because the number of the people was unknown and the simultaneous veto of a bill to take a census were unreasonable and contradictory. Refusal to sign the bill to change the county seat of Adams County antagonized Nathaniel Massie. The message which announced the rejection of these measures placed considerable emphasis upon the prerogatives of the governor while it disregarded the wishes of the people.[40]

The responsibilities and expenses of the second stage of government, however, had not been appreciated by the people in the Illinois and Indiana settlements. They petitioned for a division of the territory so that they might return to a less expensive type of government.[41] The creation of Indiana Territory satisfied the petitioners, but placed the Cincinnatians in a less attractive position. Located in the southwestern corner of what remained as the Northwestern Territory, their city was less likely to become the capital of a state the western boundary of which would be drawn northward from the mouth of the Great Miami. They therefore began to work with St. Clair and the leaders of Marietta for a threefold division of the Old Northwest by means of lines drawn northward from the mouth of the Scioto River and from Clark's Grant. According to this plan, Cincinnati and Marietta would later become the capitals of their respective states. This change in alignment threatened the hopes of the Chillicothe leaders, who wanted the boundary to be drawn northward from the mouth of the Miami. They also thought of Chillicothe as the capital city.

The second session of the first territorial assembly continued the struggle for greater self-government. Although the legislature was controlled by the friends of St. Clair, the territorial delegate was requested to seek a modification of the governor's veto power and the extension of the franchise to all free adult male citizens who paid county or territorial taxes. Following the suggestion of St. Clair, counties were divided into districts in which voting places would be erected on election day and in which voting would be by ballot rather than viva-voce. When the governor announced that he would prorogue the assembly in a few days, his opponents seized the opportunity to launch a vigorous drive for statehood. A committee was appointed to prepare an address asking the people to express their wishes in regard to statehood. It called attention to the advantages of a state government and suggested that the population was probably adequate for the advance. The address was adopted by the representatives and five hundred copies were printed and distributed.[42]

The second legislature which was elected before the second session of the first assembly was held, was also friendly to the governor. During its meeting from November, 1801, to January, 1802, consent was given to alter the territorial boundaries and create three territories rather than two. When this consent was transmitted to Congress, it was accompanied by a minority protest of the house which declared that its purpose was to delay statehood indefinitely.[43]

In support of the movement to secure a state government, Thomas Worthington and Michael Baldwin were sent to Washington. Baldwin was a native of Connecticut, a brilliant young lawyer, and an ally of the Chillicothe group; but he lacked some of the steady habits usually regarded as characteristic of persons from the Nutmeg State. Petitions from supporters of statehood were sent to them with large numbers of signatures. Congress replied by passing an enabling act, approved on April 30, 1802, which authorized the election of delegates to form a state constitution.[44] At last the Republicans were on the road to victory.

The campaign for delegates to the convention was largely but not entirely submerged in the continued and revitalized discussion of the statehood issue. The contest lacked the radicalism of the earlier statehood movements.[45] This was probably occasioned by the acquisition of land by many of the poorer frontiersmen who had not been able to secure it in the older states, the services rendered by the government in defending the territory against the Indians, and the more stable leadership furnished by Massie, Worthington, and Tiffin.

Republican corresponding societies, very similar to but less radical than the committees of Kentucky, were formed to direct public opinion and to secure the election of delegates who favored statehood. Representatives of these societies met in county convention in Hamilton, Ross, and Belmont counties to nominate candidates for the constitutional convention; the Federalists in Washington County held a similar meeting.

The rise of the Republican societies in Hamilton County indicated the lack of appeal of the Federalist program to the people outside Cincinnati. Three lists of candidates were recommended to the voters, two of them by meetings of citizens; the Republican ticket was nominated by representatives of seventeen societies. Questions were put to the candidates and letters were published in the *Western Spy* of Cincinnati.[46]

The campaign in Ross County, where so many Southerners had settled, revealed the conduct and principles of the Chillicothe leaders. The candidates were requested to publish their views in regard to the desirability of statehood, the national administration, the terms offered by the enabling act, and the possible admission of slavery. Tiffin, Worthington, and Baldwin wrote in favor of statehood in accord with the conditions offered by Congress, in favor of the Jeffersonian administration, but in opposition to the admission of slavery. Massie admitted that he thought the acceptance of slavery might be of immediate advantage but, because it would "ultimately prove injurious," should "not be admitted in any shape whatever." James Grubb insisted that the slavery question was raised by the Federalists in an effort to discredit the Republicans. Otherwise the views of Massie and Grubb coincided with those of Worthington, Tiffin, and Baldwin. Other candidates revealed their lack of sympathy with the group directing the statehood movement or with the national administration. Two were not opposed to slavery. Others expressed substantial agreement with the statehood leaders.[47]

In Belmont County nine local committees each sent three representatives to a county convention. One candidate received a majority vote of these representatives and another less than half of the twenty-six votes cast. The latter was James Caldwell, who was vigorously attacked as a former Federalist who had turned Republican to secure political preferment. Perhaps his critic made a tactical mistake when he asserted that Caldwell did not write grammatically.[48]

The Federalists rather than the Republicans held a county convention in Washington County, which included the Ohio Company's purchase. "Some rebellious townships" were reported as refusing to elect delegates. Three of the four nominees were natives of New England. The Jeffersonians also nominated candidates, one of whom was Return J. Meigs, Jr., who had recently deserted the Federalists. This nomination, with the slavery issue, produced a lively campaign.[49]

The position of the Federalists changed considerably by the time the campaign for delegates was started. Originally St. Clair sought to delay statehood. During the early phase of the statehood movement when he joined with the Cincinnatians and the Marietta leaders, he had sought to divide the territory into three divisions in the hope that Marietta and Cincinnati might dominate the state in which each would be located, and that the eastern state, at least, would be Federalist. He was aware that this program would delay statehood. When the desire to escape the territorial status became so general, the Federalists asserted that no delay was involved, or at least not more than a year or two, and that their plan would result in the creation of two states rather than one. They attempted to defend St. Clair and his administration, to minimize or deny the grievances about which the Republicans complained, and to assert the adequacy of the territorial assembly.

When Congress passed the enabling act, the Federalists in Congress and in the territory denied the right of Congress to act and particularly to establish conditions upon which the state would be admitted into the Union. They maintained that the territorial assembly should call the constitutional convention. After the constitution was formed and a state government organized, they said, Congress was to decide whether it was a republican state; if so, it was to be admitted. The conditions in the enabling act were criticized seriously. It was also maintained that unsold lands should become the property of the state as soon as the government was organized. The Federalists insisted that the Jeffersonians intended to introduce slavery, if not openly, at least under the guise of indentured servitude. In the face of the action taken by the territorial legislature and the declarations of the Republican candidates, the Federalists were obviously trying to embarrass their opponents, rather than assert a truth.[50]

In contrast to this position of the Federalists, the Republicans maintained that the issue was the right of self-government. Stating that the absolute veto of the governor denied them this right, they strenuously criticized its arbitrary use, and even attempted to persuade Congress to abolish it. They also sought to prevent his reappointment and finally to secure his removal. Their appeal to Congress they defended on the grounds that the appointment of the members of the upper house prevented the territorial assembly from being representative. The Republicans charged the Federalists with opposition to statehood, with attempting to perpetuate a tyrannical government, with playing politics in the interests of the cities of Marietta and Cincinnati, and with supporting a discredited national administration and an arbitrary governor. They insisted that they had no intention of introducing slavery and that the issue was raised by their opponents only to deceive the voters.[51]

In the election the Republicans won an outstanding victory. Four fifths of the delegates were Jeffersonians and only seven were Federalists. One or two of the Republicans were regarded by their fellow delegates as uncertain, but the control of the convention was not in doubt.[52] The personnel appears to have been affected by the various divisions which had resulted from the cession of state land claims, the development of the land system, and the sectional migrations to these areas.

Eight of the ten delegates from Hamilton County, which included the land bought by Judge Symmes, were nominees of the Corresponding societies and an additional member was a Jeffersonian in favor of statehood but not in good standing with the societies;[53] only one was a Federalist. Three were Virginians and three were

Pennsylvanians. One of the Virginians was Charles W. Byrd, secretary of the territory and a son of Colonel William Byrd of Westover.[54] Three of the delegates had resided on the Monongahela frontiers in southwestern Pennsylvania and five in Kentucky before they moved to Ohio. John Reily, one of the Pennsylvanians, had lived for a time in the Valley of Virginia and in Kentucky.[55] John Paul, another Pennsylvanian and one of Clark's soldiers, had formerly resided in western Pennsylvania, western Virginia, and Kentucky.[56] Only two seem to have come directly from the East without stopping for a time on the way. The records of these delegates indicate the importance of the Monongahela and Kentucky frontiers in the settlement of the Miami Valley.

All of the delegates elected from the counties located in the Virginia Military District were Republicans, and most of them were natives of Southern states. One of the representatives of Clermont County came to Ohio by way of Virginia and the other by way of Kentucky. Both were natives of Maryland.[57] It was to be expected that Adams County on the Ohio River would choose Republican delegates who would follow the leadership of Massie, for he founded its first settlement, quarreled with St. Clair over its county seat, and represented it for a time in the territorial legislature. Two of its delegates were former residents of Kentucky, one a native of the Valley of Virginia and the other of New Jersey.[58] A third member, who was born in Ireland, came west by way of Pennsylvania and Kentucky.[59] Ross County was the home of the Chillicothe Junto, the leaders of the statehood movement. It would have been surprising if Tiffin, Worthington, and Massie had not been elected. In addition to these, Baldwin, a native of Connecticut, and James Grubb were sent to the convention.[60] All were Jeffersonians and three, at least, were from Virginia.

Three counties which were formed from land that was subject to the general land acts of 1785, 1796, and 1800 elected seven Republicans and two Federalists whose previous experiences were less connected with the Kentucky frontier than with those of the Virginia Military District and the Symmes Purchase. Belmont County, located in the Seven Ranges across the Ohio from Wheeling, Virginia, chose two Republicans, one a Virginian who had spent a winter in Kentucky and the second a native of Maryland who had lived for a time at Wheeling.[61] To the north, but also in the Seven Ranges, was Jefferson County, which elected three Republicans and two Federalists. Little has been learned about the Republicans, except that one was said to have been a native of Pennsylvania. One of the Federalists was a Quaker and a native of York, Pennsylvania, who had moved to the Shenandoah Valley but left it because he disliked slavery. The other was a native of Baltimore who had moved to extreme northwestern Virginia, where he became an associate of St. Clair's friend, James Ross.[62] West of the Seven Ranges was Fairfield County, which sent two Republicans to the convention. One had lived in Kentucky,[63] and the other, a native of Lancaster, Pennsylvania, moved to Wheeling and then to Lancaster in the Northwest Territory.[64]

Trumbull County, which included the Connecticut Reserve, chose two Republicans who were New Englanders. One was a native of Massachusetts who had studied at Yale, the other of Connecticut, where he had been opposed politically by the Federalists of that state.[65]

Washington County, which contained the land purchased by the Ohio Company, remained true to its New England leaders and elected four Federalists to the convention. Three were well-known natives of New England: Ephraim Cutler, Benjamin Ives Gilman, and Rufus Putnam.[66] The other delegate, who was from Virginia, generally took sides with the Republicans whenever the racial issue was involved.[67]

The election gave control of the convention not only to Jeffersonians but to men who had lived on the Monongahela and Kentucky frontiers. None of the delegates is known to have been born south of Virginia, but a majority lived for a time in that state as bounded before the separation of Kentucky. In contrast, the delegates from the Connecticut Reserve who moved westward through New York state and the delegates from Washington County who were New Englanders had not previously lived on the frontiers of the Ohio Valley. If the delegates were representative of the people who elected them, the majority of the citizens of the new state apparently had come to Ohio from the older frontiers of the Monongahela Valley and Kentucky.

The officers chosen by the convention were also from the South. Tiffin, an Englishman who had lived and married in Virginia, became president; Thomas Scott, the Methodist preacher who had converted him in Berkeley County, Virginia, was chosen secretary; [68] and Nathaniel Willis, who had formerly edited a paper in the same county, and later published the *Scioto Gazette,* the organ of the statehood movement, was elected printer to the convention.[69]

The majority of the Republicans was so large that it tended to split into divergent groups. Little evidence has been found of organization or discipline. The group in control varied from a plurality of seventeen votes to a majority of twenty-seven votes. On two occasions President Tiffin's deciding vote was necessary to save the Republicans from defeat. A group of seventeen or more delegates voted rather regularly and seem to have held control. Their chief opponents were the seven Federalists. Between the two groups were from eight to eleven Republicans whose voting records show important deviations from the regular Republicans, particularly where questions relating to Negroes were involved. Among them were men whose idealism was marked; some had emancipated their slaves, others had become preachers. They were determined that the plantation system or a system of indentured servitude should not be adopted. The entire group of Jeffersonians voted together with all the Federalists in opposition only once on a recorded vote.

The committees always contained a majority of Republicans, but the ones to prepare the articles for the bill of rights and local government were probably not in control of the regulars. Their dominance of some other committees was probably tenuous.

Governor St. Clair endeavored to participate in the organization of the convention, but this action was prevented. Permitted to address the delegates, he declared the enabling act a nullity and the terms which it stipulated unwise, undesirable, and harmful. He urged the convention to take a new census, call a new convention, form a constitution for the entire territory, and demand admission without any conditions.[70] It appeared that he still hoped to delay statehood and to avoid the division of the territory which would give the Republicans control of the new state. St. Clair's speech was reported to President Jefferson, who thereupon removed him from office.

The answer of the convention was a resolution stating that it was expedient to proceed to form a state government. Only Ephraim Cutler voted against it.[71] Apparently fearful of the territorial legislature, the convention requested the governor to prorogue the session that was scheduled to meet late in November, and he complied with the request.[72] Another move by the Federalist opposition was a resolution to submit the constitution to the people for ratification. On the face of the motion it was a reasonable and democratic request; but, in the light of St. Clair's advice and the views of the Federalists, it is not surprising that the Republicans rejected it by a straight party vote.[73] No doubt they considered that it gave their enemies another opportunity to defeat statehood. The Federalist record on white manhood suffrage does not permit them to claim to have been more democratic than the Republicans. Their most democratic efforts were exerted in behalf of the Negroes, not the poor whites, and this could have been an effort to make the constitution unpalatable to the large number of Southerners in the state. With the rejection of St. Clair's advice, the elimination of the territorial legislature, and the refusal of the referendum, the Republicans must have felt that victory was near.

As the work of the convention proceeded, differences of opinion became evident and contests of some importance developed. One of the first of these was the proposal to limit official salaries. The principle was introduced and adopted, but eight additional recorded votes were taken before the details were determined. The Federalists were generally in the opposition both in respect to the basic principle and the detailed provisions.[74]

When the franchise was being considered, it was proposed to strike out the word "white," which if adopted would have extended the right to vote to all adult males charged with a tax. The Federalists, except McIntire, and eight Republicans cast fourteen votes for this amendment. A motion was then offered to strike out the tax requirement. Not a Federalist and only eight Republicans voted for this proposal.[75] Neither side seemed interested in universal manhood suffrage. It was then proposed that Negroes and mulattoes living in the state at that time should be given the franchise. Six Federalists and thirteen Republicans secured the adoption of this proposal. Another amendment was offered to extend the privilege to the male descendants of the resident Negroes. A total of five Federalists and eleven Republicans was one short of a majority for this measure. Four days later, the provision for Negro suffrage was stricken out, when the president cast a deciding vote; six Federalists opposed its elimination.[76] An effort was made to omit a provision granting the franchise to white men who were forced to work on the roads, regardless of taxes. Seven Federalists and six Republicans favored the motion.[77] Two of the Republicans were from New England, one from New York, one from Ireland, and two from

Virginia. It seems that the Federalists and a few Republicans were more interested in having Negroes vote than poor white men.

While the provision for Negro suffrage was still a part of the proposed constitution, a new section was added making the Negro or mulatto ineligible to hold office, to testify in court against a white person, to serve in the militia, or to pay a poll tax. It was adopted against the opposition of the Federalists and of the Republicans who frequently co-operated with them. After Negro suffrage had been eliminated, the above prohibition was also struck out, by a vote of seventeen to sixteen.[78] Nevertheless, the Negro could take only a negligible part in the activities of the new state, for he was not permitted to vote and was not counted in the apportionment of representation.

The Federalists and irregular Republicans seem to have been responsible also for the judiciary article. Ephraim Cutler wrote that the original form was written by Byrd from the Virginia code and that final appellant jurisdiction was vested in the supreme court which met only at the capital. Its adoption was long delayed; and, when the convention was nearing an end, substitute sections were adopted. The most important change seems to have been the requirement that the supreme court meet each year in each county on the grounds that it would bring justice "as near every man's door as was practicable; to the poor man equally with the rich."[79]

The constitution as adopted was closely related to the charters of Tennessee, Kentucky, and Pennsylvania. Sixteen of the twenty-eight sections of the first article, which provided for the legislature, were largely copied from the Tennessee constitution. Ten of the sixteen sections of the second article, which was concerned with the executive branch of the government, were also copied almost verbatim from the same source. The seven sections of the fifth article regulating the militia were patterned upon but not copied from the similar article adopted by Tennessee. More than one third of the bill of rights was taken from the Tennessee bill of rights, a second third from the Pennsylvania and Kentucky constitutions, and the remaining third was in part different and in part taken from other constitutions.

The third, fourth, and sixth articles, which provided for the judiciary, elections, and state and local officials, respectively, were not modeled upon the fundamental law of Tennessee. Two thirds of the twelve sections of the judiciary article were very similar to the

Pennsylvania and Kentucky constitutions, while the remainder seems to have been unlike any earlier organic law. The article regulating elections was in part original and in part taken from the Kentucky, Tennessee, and Delaware constitutions. The sixth article was one fourth different, one fourth like the Tennessee, and one half like the Kentucky constitution.

Altogether 87 of the 106 sections of the Ohio document show very considerable similarity to the corresponding portions of the constitutions of Tennessee, Kentucky, and Pennsylvania. In contrast, the sections which show the direct influence of New England constitutions were four in number.[80]

The following table gives a comparison of the Ohio constitution with other constitutions:

| Article | Subject Matter | No. of Sections | No. of Original Sections | No. of Sections like Other Constitutions | | | | | | |
				Tenn.	*Pa.*	*Ky.*	*Del.*	*Vt.*	*Md.*	*N.H.*
	Preamble	1	½	½						
I.	Legislature	28		16	8	2	2			
II.	Executive	16		10½	2	1	½			*
III.	Judiciary	12	4⅔			4	2⅓			*
IV.	Elections	5	2			1				*
V.	Militia	7		7						
VI.	Local and state officials	4	1	1		2				
VII.	Miscellaneous	5		5						
VIII.	Bill of Rights	28	3	10	5	1		3	1	1 *
	Total	106	11⅙	50	19	9⅓	2½	3	1	1

* There are 2 sections in Art. II and 4 in VIII that are like similar sections in Pennsylvania, Kentucky, and Tennessee. In Art. IV there are 2 like Delaware, Kentucky, and Tennessee. In Art. III there is one section like Pennsylvania and Kentucky.

The territorial struggle between the legislature and the governor had been in some respects a repetition of the colonial experience of the original states; and, like them, Ohio deprived its governor of any real power. He was popularly elected for a two-year term, but was not given the veto or real power of appointment. The legislative branch of government was the most powerful. Its members were popularly chosen in annual elections, the representatives for one year and the senators for two. Both were apportioned according to the number of white male inhabitants. Property qualifications were not required of any of the officials, and the franchise was extended to white adult males who were charged with a tax or required to work on the roads. Township and county officials were also popularly elected rather than appointed by county courts whose members were in turn appointed for life as in Tennessee. The judiciary was an elective branch of the government, with a definite and short term of service. The bill of rights not only prohibited slavery but also prevented the employment of a system of indenture as a substitute for slavery. It also prohibited any religious test and provided equal opportunities in education and equal treatment of all religious denominations.

The statehood movement in Ohio had many facets. It was in part a contest between a New England group and a Southern group, each of which mistrusted and misunderstood the other. It was a part of the nationwide rivalry between the Federalists and the Jeffersonians, both of whom were anxious to strengthen their uncertain political position. It was in part a struggle between authoritarianism and democracy. It was the striving of a frontier people for self-government, a people impatient with colonial officials who were responsible only to distant authority. It was also a regional contest between the three cities, Cincinnati, Marietta, and Chillicothe, in which each sought to become a state capital. Finally, it was an expression of the desire of a colonial population to be recognized as a part of the nation and to participate in the determination of national policies. It was all of these, and yet, fundamentally, it was a movement of the frontier to govern itself according to individualistic and democratic principles so dear to its heart. To emphasize the limitations upon its democracy is to miss the point. America was striving to achieve democracy, and the Ohio Valley was in the forefront of the strife.

The new state is revealed by the above facts to have been an integral part of the Ohio Valley frontier and not a separate entity in the Valley. Its settlers had come largely from the same general source, the migrating thousands of the Old West or the Appalachian Highland province. They came generally by the routes that connected the Cumberland Valley of Pennsylvania and the Valley of Virginia with the Ohio. Before their arrival many of them had lived on the Monongahela and Kentucky frontiers. The statehood movement was in part a rising of the Ohio Valley frontiersmen against arbitrary governments which denied to them the determination of their own affairs and the expression of their democratic ideals.

Although its points of similarity to other parts of the Valley of the Ohio were fundamental, differences between it and the states south of the Ohio were as significant as the similarities. Frontier influences did not have to struggle against such obstacles as slavery, a planter aristocracy, and state land systems favorable to the existence of large landed estates and speculative holdings. These were parts of the heritage which Kentucky and Tennessee received from Virginia and North Carolina. Although the territorial government was not democratic at first, it permitted the growth of self-government and prevented the widespread introduction of slavery. In general, national control made possible a freer expression of frontier democracy.

The Democratization of Territorial Government: Indiana

Little islands of French settlers, entirely surrounded by a wide sea of green forest, were to be found along the rivers and lakes of Indiana Territory at the beginning of the nineteenth century. Many had come from Canada and a few from France and Louisiana. Among them were descendants of French men and Indian women. Grouped about Catholic missions or churches, military garrisons, and fur-trading posts, they varied from the faithful priest and devout Jesuit to the soldier, the wilder *coureurs de bois,* the women of ill repute whom the government had mistakenly hoped would be transformed by the virtues of the New World into suitable wives for the distant sons of France, and finally to the dark-skinned aborigines of the American forests. Living together in small villages, the French tilled their long, narrow farms which stretched back from the rivers. Although their methods and tools were primitive, they managed to raise more food than they consumed. They carried the surplus crops and the furs from the Indian trade down the Mississippi to exchange for the necessities they could not produce and such luxuries as they could afford. Their houses were usually primitive and characteristically equipped with porches or galleries. Within were sometimes housed highly esteemed furniture, dishes, and clothing which had been imported from France. Usually the amount of wealth acquired was small, and the economic system was not based upon land as in the remainder of the United States.[1]

"Self-sufficient in their traditional isolation," the French were of a gentle and indolent nature, dependent upon authority, devoted to community life, possessed of a taste for some refinements, and possibly more temperate and law-abiding than many of the American frontiersmen, who seemed to them as intruders upon an idyllic past. Disappointed with the passing of French control and the subsequent displacement of French law, the villagers began to emigrate to Louisiana. After 1779 "a trickle of American immigration . . . replaced them and was becoming by 1800 a stream manifestly destined to overflow and fill in the whole of the . . . country." Many of the French were ruined by generous loans to the cause of the Revolution and by the maintenance and pillage of troops. They were neglected for years by Congress and threatened with the loss of their slaves by the Ordinance of 1787. In many instances, the lands which Congress promised them fell into the control of speculators. The character of their records, or their absence, gave great opportunity for corruption and deceit. They were not only confronted with a new political system under American sovereignty but were soon excluded from its offices. It is not surprising that many left the villages of Vincennes, Kaskaskia, and Cahokia for the territory of Spain west of the Mississippi.[2]

The presence of the French affected the character of the civilization that developed on this Middle Western frontier. Their good relations with the Indians, which gave them immunity from attack, made their villages a good place for the earliest Americans to settle. The confused state of their titles and their willingness to part with claims or to make grants freely to the newcomers enabled some of the frontiersmen to secure farms long before the United States placed land on the Indiana market. These conditions offered the kind of opportunities upon which the land jobber thrived. The ownership of slaves and the guarantee of their property rights made it difficult to enforce the prohibition of slavery which the Ordinance of 1787 contained. "Royalist by tradition, Federalists by tendency, content with the paternalistic administration vouchsafed their ancestors, they were equally content with the centralized rule of governor and judges. They . . . resented the burdens and . . . seemed indifferent to the supposed virtues of popular government."[3] Their votes and influence could often be controlled by political adventurers who cultivated their favor. It is not surprising that Governor William H. Harrison, with his Virginia background and with this type of environment in which to formulate his early policies, should have been regarded by some of his people as a Federalist. Eventually the French and their influences

were submerged in the mass of the energetic and numerous frontiersmen, but these early contributions to the rising way of life in
Indiana Territory were significant.

The village of Vincennes, which became the capital of the new
territory, received an early American migration. Apparently the
Piankashaw Indians had granted the French a considerable piece
of land, which became known as the Vincennes Tract. From it the
members of the court granted to themselves and the newcomers
generous portions of land. To every "adventurer" who came to
live among them they gave "a plantation of four hundred acres."
They requested Congress to approve these grants and pointed out
that the amount wanted for themselves and the American frontiersmen would require a tract only 30 miles square. The latter
explained that they were reduced to poverty and misery at the end
of the long and severe Revolutionary War by their participation
and contributions, by the decline of trade, and the neglect of hus-
bandry, and that they had migrated to this distant country in the
hope of obtaining a subsistence by their industry.[4]

By an act of March 3, 1791, Congress granted as much as 400
acres to those who made improvements on the land which the
French had given them and 100 acres to the militiamen who had
not received any other grant.[5] To persons who had located in or
near Vincennes by 1787 were assigned 48,000 acres.[6] Perhaps, therefore, somewhere between 100 and 150 American families lived in
the vicinity by 1787. In that year Colonel Josiah Harmar reported
that Vincennes contained about 900 French and 400 Americans.[7]
It seems likely that the proportion of the latter was larger when a
census was taken in 1801. At that time the town of Vincennes was
reported to contain 714 persons and the neighborhood 819 more.[8]
In 1810 Knox County, which was by then restricted to this part of
the territory, numbered its people at 7,945.[9] Many frontiersmen
had obviously followed in the footsteps of the first adventurers.

On the northern bank of the Ohio River opposite the Falls was
the little village of Clarksville, surrounded by the 150,000 acres
of Clark's Grant, which Virginia had given to the soldiers and
officers of Clark's campaigns. Settlement of this area began in 1784
and by the turn of the century it contained 929 persons, many of
whom were Clark's soldiers.[10] Across the Ohio was Louisville, an
important town for travelers and settlers, located at the Falls and
at the end of an extension of Boone's Wilderness Road. Quite gen-

erally, also, boats coming down the Ohio stopped at Louisville and unloaded at least a portion of their passengers and cargo before running the Falls.[11] Down the Ohio and over the roads through Kentucky came the settlers of Clark's Grant and many who traveled to the northward and westward. The essentially democratic character of the immigrants from the Southern States was to be revealed when this area became one of the anti-Harrison and anti-slavery strongholds in the struggles of the territorial period.[12]

Quite apart from the settlement of Vincennes and Clark's Grant was the occupation of the "Gore," which was added to Indiana Territory in 1802. Freed from Indian claims by the Treaty of Greenville in 1795, it included the land east of the treaty line but west of the boundary adopted by the state of Ohio. Immediately after the treaty its settlement was begun by squatters who located along the northern bank of the Ohio. Governor St. Clair reported that "numbers of People from Kentucky" were making improvements on the public lands in such numbers that "along the River, and a considerable distance inland the Country is covered with Hutts." [13] Secretary Sargent stated that there were a thousand of these intruders west of the Miami.[14] Farther north, in the Whitewater Valley, settlement was in part an expansion from the Miami Valley of which it is a tributary. The entire valley contained many settlers from the Southern states who came from Kentucky or along the Ohio to Cincinnati. In April, 1801, a missionary recorded that on the lower Whitewater a farm had been started almost every mile and that the owners had nearly all moved here from Kentucky.[15] The early immigrants who came by Cincinnati followed roads that led northward to Colerain, Hamilton, and Eaton, Ohio, but an Indian trail along the Whitewater was later turned into a road.[16]

When Indiana Territory was only a few years old, the migration of Quakers to the Whitewater began. Dissatisfied with the spread of slavery into the Piedmont of North Carolina and even among their own people, the Friends carefully considered the incompatibility of the institution with their faith. Large numbers left North Carolina, and the Whitewater country became the destination of so many of them that it developed into one of the leading Quaker strongholds. They concentrated in the upper parts of the valley, to which they generally followed one of three routes. Leaving North Carolina by way of the Yadkin River and Wood's or Flower Gap, they reached the New River; proceeding along this stream until it became the Kanawha, they followed it to the Ohio; and thence they crossed the state of Ohio by way of Gallipolis and Chillicothe to Indiana Territory. This was sometimes referred to as the Quaker route. It was the most direct but was not the easiest. In the earlier years of the migration, it was thought better for those traveling with loaded wagons to leave the New River and to take Boone's Wilderness Road into Kentucky. They then turned northward to Cincinnati and thence moved on to the upper Whitewater. Still others came north through Virginia and turned westward over Braddock's Road.[17] The Quaker migration, which was often undertaken for conscience' sake, brought into the territory a serious and sturdy people with democratic principles and a prejudice against slavery. The settlement of this area was an important political development in the history of the territory.

The three areas—the town and vicinity of Vincennes, Clark's Grant, and the Whitewater Valley—were soon joined by trails through the forests and by the expansion of settlement along the Ohio and the traces which led into the interior. The cessions of land by the Indian tribes facilitated this expansion. The Indians first agreed upon the boundaries of the Vincennes Tract which they had granted to the French. In August, 1804, the land between the Wabash and the Ohio, south of the Vincennes Tract and the Buffalo Trace, was ceded by the Delaware and Piankashaw. Other tribes gave up their claims to this cession a year later, at which time the land lying between Clark's Grant and the Gore was also ceded. The north bank of the Ohio from the Great Miami to the Wabash and the interior for thirty to sixty miles north of the Ohio was thus open to settlement.[18]

The triangle between Clarksville, Vincennes, and the mouth of the Wabash was soon crisscrossed with trails over which settlers moved into this part of the territory. The main routes led to Vincennes from points on the Ohio where they connected with Kentucky roads and with Ohio River traffic. They indicate that the early settlers in this area probably came from or through Kentucky or from points on the Ohio River in Virginia, Pennsylvania, or Ohio.

The most important of these routes was the Buffalo Trace, which ran from Clarksville to Vincennes, where it connected with the trace to the Illinois Country. Over it came many of the settlers of southwestern Indiana. Its various names epitomize its history, for it was called the Old Indian Trail, the Buffalo Trace, the Governor's Road, and the Kentucky Road. It became the approximate northern boundary of the Indian cession of 1804, and as late as May 10, 1807, settlement did not extend beyond it. Along the trace were founded the villages and farms of the early settlers.[19]

Southeastern Indiana, between Clark's Grant and the Gore, was settled somewhat more slowly. Like the Whitewater Valley, it was more closely connected with Cincinnati than with the western portions of the territory. The Ohio River was an important thoroughfare, and along its banks were founded during the territorial period, a series of settlements from Lawrenceburg to Vevay, Madison, and Jeffersonville. Trails and roads also ran between Cincinnati and these communities, particularly to the Falls of the Ohio. The movement of settlers across the Ohio from Kentucky and the roads of that state was, even here, probably the dominant migration.

In 1809 Governor Harrison negotiated the treaties of Fort Wayne, which antagonized the Prophet and Tecumseh. A large extent of land north of the Vincennes Tract between the Wabash River and the East Fork of the White River and a twelve-mile strip along the upper part of the Gore were ceded at this time. Approximately one third of the future state was then open to settlement, and shorter roads were soon marked between Cincinnati and Vincennes.

By 1810 the population of Indiana Territory was approximately twenty-five thousand, but Indian difficulties were to check migration for a short time. The trails as well as the nativities of the early settlers indicate that this population came largely from south of the Ohio River and practically all over trails through Pennsylvania and the Southern states.

The experiences of this pioneer population in establishing its social and political institutions form an interesting and significant chapter in the development of democracy. The forces which handicapped the influence of the frontier in the South were absent or so weak as to be unable to control the formation of government and society. Largely lacking were the numerous planters and their slaves. Undemocratic state governments with their policies which favored land speculation, slavery, and aristocracy were not in control. Climate and other geographic forces did not make possible an agricultural regime based upon staple products such as cotton, rice, indigo, or tobacco.

A few aspired to be country gentlemen in imitation of the planter class; farms were often called plantations; a few colored slaves and workers were held as house servants; and land speculation existed on every hand, but more often was the activity of the small landholder rather than of the rich who dealt in thousands of acres. The little coterie of able men who gathered around Harrison at Vincennes came to be called the Virginia Aristocrats. Some of them held Negro servants. Aristocratic manners, characteristic of the plantation South or of the Old Country, had been carried into this frontier region. General James Dill, a native of Ireland and a Harrison appointee, attended court as a prosecuting attorney in the costume of a gentleman of the Revolutionary period—knee breeches, silver buckles, and cue—"a mild protest against the leveling tendencies of the age" and of the frontier.[20]

But the character of society was not determined by these forces. The large groups of citizens were small landowners and squatters. Until the land was surveyed and placed on sale, nearly all were squatters. When the sales were opened, those who had the money bought small pieces of land. Since the credit system held sway from 1800 to 1820, many a poor man got together enough money to make the first payment and then hoped that industry and good fortune would enable him to meet the succeeding payments before it was too late. The arrears of interest and principal indicate that many had been too optimistic.[21] But the point is that the Indiana frontier was a poor man's home and its development in the formative period was shaped by frontier influences.

The law which created Indiana Territory re-established the same nonrepresentative type of government which existed in the first stage of the Northwest Territory.[22] William Henry Harrison, the governor of the new territory, had gained experience in the former, where he had served for a short period as secretary and delegate to Congress. He avoided many of the arbitrary acts of St. Clair, but his policies and appointments as governor attracted to him many conservative leaders and antagonized a few vigorous men and a growing number of the newer settlers.[23] Although the secretary, John Gibson, spent his life along the frontier from Pittsburgh to Vincennes, he had little influence upon the government, and the judges were not noted for their sympathy with the ways of the frontiersmen. From the beginning, however, much interest was taken by the people in the acts of government, and neither their efforts to make the government more democratic nor the governor's critics were suppressed. An almost immediate and continuous movement was begun not only to make the government responsive to the wishes and needs of the people, but also to place it in their hands.

The causes of this movement included the uncertainty of land titles, the activity of land speculators, the desire of the people for greater self-determination, the lack of self-government in the early territorial period, the political ambitions of various individuals, the efforts to legalize slavery, the difference of opinion as to the best methods of attracting settlers to the country, and the lack of unity in a territory which was composed of remote settlements occupied by people of different origins. Persons of aristocratic tendencies emphasized the importance of securing men of wealth, family, and education. The closest source of such settlers was the planter class of Kentucky and other Southern states. The planters owned slaves, hence the efforts to legalize slavery. On the other hand, the democratic masses from the South, many of whom had there suffered political, social, and economic discriminations, and settlers from the North were not enthusiastic about the pretensions of the aristocrats to superior talents; neither were they willing to pay the price of their coming—the admission of slavery. It was the old contest of a white man's society with democratic features against the planters' social order with its aristocratic characteristics. Often the contest degenerated into petty quarrels in which every act of the governor was attacked and defended with spirit and acrimony, but if one sees only these disputes, the trees have obscured the forest.[24]

The territorial history of Indiana falls rather naturally into five divisions. These were the nonrepresentative stage of territorial government, which lasted four years; the early part of the second stage before the separation of Illinois Territory in 1809; the shorter term between the division of the territory and the resumption of Indian warfare; the three years of warfare from the Tippecanoe campaign in 1811 to the end of Harrison's campaign in 1813; and, finally, the successful struggle for statehood, 1814–1816.

Before the formation of Indiana Territory, petitions for the admission of slavery in the Northwest Territory were sent to Congress from the Illinois Country. Before Harrison arrived another memorial, containing 270 names and requesting a limited type of slavery, was forwarded from the same region. Petitions and letters were sent to Governor Harrison early in 1801, largely from the Illinois counties, advocating an advance to the second or semirepresentative stage of government. This twofold agitation created a problem, and the new governor apparently decided to resist the request for a change in government. He supposedly wrote a letter in opposition, calling attention to the increased costs which the people would have to bear. As a result, this phase of the agitation came to an end.[25]

The next year, 1802, the slavery phase of the movement was resumed, when the governor was requested to call a convention to consider the propriety of repealing the prohibitory article of the Northwest Ordinance. He decided to support this phase of the agitation, professing to believe that a majority of the people favored this procedure. He called an election of delegates, and the convention assembled at Vincennes on December 20, 1802. Formal consent to the suspension for ten years was given on Christmas Day. Three days later a petition to Congress requested suspension on the grounds that desirable settlers were forced to move west of the Mississippi because they could not bring their slaves into Indiana Territory. It was also requested that the slaves that would be brought to the territory during the proposed suspension should not be freed at the end of the ten-year period. The government was also asked to clear the Indian title to the southern part of the territory, to sell land in small quantities and at a lower price, to grant preemption to the squatters who were awaiting the opportunity to buy the farms on which they were living, to hasten the settlement of the claims possessed by the early settlers, and to grant lands to encourage the building of roads and taverns and the establishment of educational institutions. They also petitioned that the fifty-acre property qualification for voters be repealed and that the right of suffrage be extended to free adult male inhabitants. If it is realized that the members of the convention were interested chiefly in developing the territory, their labors are rational even though their support of slavery on the one hand and of democracy on the other was philosophically inconsistent. They sought to attract wealthy settlers by legalizing slavery, and poor people by the opportunity to buy land in small pieces at low prices and to have a potent voice in their own government. Even the meeting of the assembly was a step in the direction of self-government.[26]

Because Congress did not act favorably upon the petition of the Vincennes Convention, the governor and judges of the territory evidently decided to meet the situation in part by an official evasion of the Northwest Ordinance. In their legislative capacity they adopted from the Virginia code a law concerning servants which provided that Negroes and mulattoes had to perform service due their masters and that contracts between master and servants were assignable.[27]

Although the admission of slavery appears to have been the leading issue in this first period of territorial history, it was not the only one. Continuing dissatisfaction with the first stage of government was reflected in petitions to reform the land policy, to add the Illinois counties to Upper Louisiana, to separate Detroit from Indiana Territory, and not to reappoint Harrison for a second term as territorial governor.[28]

The first period of territorial government came to an end when Harrison reversed his position on the advisability of passing into the second or semirepresentative stage of government in 1804. He stated that petitions asking for representative government were presented to him. To ascertain the wishes of the people, he called an election on September 11, at which time the majority of those voting favored the change. The governor thereupon proclaimed the second stage and called an election of representatives for the lower house of the territorial assembly.[29]

Whether or not the change represented the wishes of the majority, a violent newspaper controversy, in which Harrison's critics soon made known their opposition, broke out. "A freeholder of Knox County," who was probably William McIntosh, criticized Harrison's sponsorship of the Vincennes Convention as well as a recent meeting in Vincennes to petition for the second stage. He asserted that the advance should have come spontaneously and not have been forced by the governor.[30] The meeting to which he referred had adopted an address which objected to the limited legislative powers of the governor and judges, to the power of Congress to countermand their action, to the unsuitability of the laws of other states for Indiana Territory, and to a lack of a voice in any act of the territorial or national government. In extravagant language, the address referred to the first stage of territorial government as the most abominable and tyrannical system ever organized for freemen. The second stage was described as imperfect but as an improvement. It also asserted that the expenses would not be too heavy, that a delegate in Congress was needed, and that able men could be found to serve in the legislative assembly.[31] "Gerald," who was probably Benjamin Parke, asserted that the petitions induced a strong belief that a majority of the freeholders wanted the change in government, while "A Citizen," probably McIntosh, denied this contention, and a "Plough Boy" defended the governor.[32] Name calling and heat were soon substituted for reasoning, the writers revealed each other's identity, and Parke obviously tried to provoke McIntosh into challenging him to a duel, but the latter asked Parke if calumny was Harrison's last defense.[33]

For a time, however, Harrison and his supporters kept things well in hand. President Thomas Jefferson requested Harrison to choose for him the five members of the upper house of the legislature and Benjamin Parke, Harrison's close friend, was elected delegate to Congress.[34]

The legislature functioned with reasonable wisdom, thus disproving the allegation that the territory lacked the necessary men of talents. Two of the measures which seem to demonstrate the good sense of its members were the substitution of a single county court for the former complicated system, and the codification of the laws.[35] More important was the gradual assertion and execution of the wishes of the people in a territorial government that was only partially representative.

But harmony was not to continue uninterrupted, for the war of petitions was soon begun. Late in 1805 the inhabitants of Randolph and St. Clair counties prayed the suspension of Article VI of the Northwest Ordinance and the creation of a western territory, referring again with some poignancy to the haste with which the advance to the second stage had been accomplished. About the same time, several members of the territorial legislature petitioned the admission of slavery and the formation of a state government for the entire territory.[36] Early in the fall the legislature passed an act which provided that slaves could be indentured and held to service and that the children of these servants would not be free until they attained the ages of twenty-eight and thirty.[37]

Perhaps the controversy over slavery furnished the leading issue in dividing the people into parties, the administration group being composed of the friends of Harrison and the rising popular party of his opponents. Giving reality to the slavery question was the effect that the existence of the institution would have on the type of people who settled in the territory and the consequent influence

on the social and political order. The popular movement was not
a mere struggle against slavery but a widespread movement to work
out a popular government at the level of the common man, one
that would prevent the development of an aristocratic social and
political system. It sought also to secure a land system advantageous to the common man and unfavorable to speculation and
large holdings. A broader movement than those in Tennessee and
Ohio, it quickly resulted in a two-party political contest. Representatives of the people took over the government even in the face
of the absolute veto of the governor. Petitions were forwarded to
the proper authorities about a variety of subjects: the appointment
of a new territorial judge, popular election of members of the
council and of the delegate to Congress, and broadening of the suffrage; forgiveness of interest, extension of time for making payments on land and for filing claims, pre-emption, and restrictions
on speculators; abolition of indentured servitude; reappointment
and non-reappointment of Governor Harrison; and the division
of the territory. Persons attending a meeting in Clark County asked
that Congress not admit slavery but wait until the territory became
a state and let the people decide.[38]

The territorial legislature soon reflected the sentiment of the
people. The second session of the second general assembly which
began on September 26, 1808, indicated a growing appreciation of
its powers and of the popular will in contrast to the wishes of the
governor and his supporters. The legislative council petitioned
Congress that its members should be popularly elected, and the
lower house requested the division of the territory and the popular
election of the delegate.[39] The representatives may have exceeded
their authority by insisting that a federal officer should not have a
seat in the legislative council.[40] After a number of petitions opposing slavery were received and after General Washington Johnston
delivered a very able report against the admission of slavery, the
representatives voted unanimously to repeal the territorial act concerning the introduction of Negroes and mulattoes into the territory; but the repeal was rejected by the upper house.[41] The lower
house also petitioned that the veto power and other controls over
the legislature be restricted.[42] Jesse B. Thomas was chosen to be the
delegate to Congress after he pledged himself to work for the
division of the territory.[43] The election of Thomas resulted from
a union of the antislavery forces east of the Wabash with the

proslavery forces west of the Wabash in opposition to the Harrison party. From this, Harrison's first serious defeat, stemmed the events which gave the popular party control of the legislature after the division of the territory.[44]

Congress responded to these demonstrations of the will of the people by providing for the popular election of the councilors and the delegate and for the division of the territory by the creation of Illinois Territory.[45] The Harrison group was now face to face with a growing popular party which already included a majority of the people in the new Indiana Territory and which received the opportunity to control the entire legislative branch of the government as well as the delegate to Congress. Harrison remained quite popular, perhaps in part because he was public spirited and above much of the petty politics which accompanied the larger struggle.

In 1809, the changes in the structure of the territorial government caused a long and acrimonious contest which revealed a democratic spirit and procedure in advance of its time. The regular election for members of the legislature had been held on April 3, 1809, before official word was received of the creation of Illinois Territory. Because the division of Indiana necessitated the election of additional members, the new legislators and the delegate to Congress were all chosen on May 22.[46] Throughout the early months of the year, a partisan controversy was waged in the columns of the *Western Sun*, through handbills, and in public meetings. Even after the last election, charges, countercharges, and explanations of what had happened were published in an anticlimactic campaign for and against the reappointment of Governor Harrison. The election had resulted in the choice of Jonathan Jennings as delegate to Congress, in which position he became the leader of the anti-Harrison forces. For the first time the voters had chosen the upper house of the territorial legislature. The protests of the Harrison leaders leave no doubt of the significance of the results.[47]

The wide scope of the discussion and the intelligence and restraint demonstrated in its conduct may prove surprising to those who belittle the frontier. The controversy was initiated by "A Citizen of Vincennes," Doctor Elias M'Namee, when he wrote: "In the United States there are two parties of men, commonly distinguished by the epithets of Republicans, and Federalists. These parties have always existed, in this obscure portion of the Union, but from the trimming disposition of the public officers, they have been jumbled together in chaotic confusion, and perhaps would long have remained so, if a question of vast moral and political importance, had not been started, and which necessarily separated the two parties, and called each into action. I mean the introduction of slavery." [48] M'Namee wrote, philosophically, that the Federalists were aristocrats who distrusted the people and that the Republicans were democrats who had faith in the people. The doctor's analysis seemed inaccurate to many of his contemporaries and very annoying to the aristocrats of Indiana Territory, but there was a large amount of truth in what he wrote. Perhaps, too, his treatment of the slavery issue was correct; that is, it was the issue which crystallized the differences between the two groups and which spurred them to action.

In this pre-election discussion, General W. Johnston suggested that the labor of the poor would be reduced in value by competition with slave labor.[49] "Slim Simon" denied this charge and asserted that the slaveowner could not undersell the farmer. He held that slaves were dangerous only in a few states, that their diffusion would aid them and the Southern states, and that no moral question was involved.[50] M'Namee asked why Indiana should admit into its midst the danger which beset the Southern states.[51] Johnston suggested that plenty of room existed in Southern territories without bringing the slaves into Indiana.[52] "A Farmer" settled the diffusion argument by stating that if Negroes were happy they would multiply proportionally, that the admission of slaves into Indiana would not affect the general condition, and that the only result would be to place Indiana in the same perilous condition as the Southern states. He asked, "How can humanity be enlisted on the side of slavery . . . ?" He also asserted that the adoption of slavery would be a political evil.[53] Jonathan Jennings challenged the constitutionality of the indenture act.[54] M'Namee also followed this idea, holding that its unconstitutionality would deter the slaveowners from coming to Indiana and that the spirit in favor of slavery manifested by the official class would prevent the immigration of those opposed to slavery.

M'Namee further attacked Harrison and Judge Benjamin Parke for interfering in the elections, engaging in intrigues, and writing scurrilous pieces over various signatures for the newspapers. Much criticism was offered because Parke, the first delegate, and Randolph, the Harrison candidate in 1809, held office under Harrison's appointment. The conduct of the land sales was objected to, including the participation of the governor. His veto and appointive powers were attacked. It was denied that a majority of the people ever favored slavery but that Harrison's influence in the elections and among the official class was too strong at first to be resisted.[55] After the election was over "A Friend to Truth" observed that

the experience of nine turbulent years, has taught the peaceful citizens of this territory, who migrated and purchased the government lands under the pledged faith of government that their rights should be protected, and slavery should never be admitted, that while the president continues in office a governor from a Southern state, who in political function or ordinary occupation, violates that faith, they will never enjoy tranquility, nor the territory receive any great accession of population. . . .[56]

The controversy reached a climax in the election of the delegate to Congress. It is possible that Harrison was ready to compromise before it was over. The "Detector," just before the voting, reviewed the slavery controversy in a manner to allay the feeling of all engaged, recognized that the proslavery admissionists were beaten and ready to abandon the idea, and proposed that all "unite . . . upon other schemes to improve our country." He asserted that the opposition did not care about the slaves but were interested only in getting offices.[57] Late in the year the legislature petitioned the reappointment of Harrison,[58] but the defeated Thomas Randolph could not be silenced and peace was not declared.

When the elections for the new legislature were called in 1810, only a slight revival of the contest of the preceding year occurred. Outside of Knox County the popular party was successful, and in Knox General W. Johnston, who was not a Harrisonite, was elected as one of the representatives. This legislature wrote the victory of the popular party into law. New counties were formed, members of the legislature were reapportioned, the date for the election of the congressional delegate was set, the indenture law was repealed, and the law requiring servants of color to fulfill the contracts under which they had entered the territory was also repealed.[59] Nothing is more revealing than Harrison's failure to use his absolute veto upon any of these acts. No longer was his influence dominant. His friends could not browbeat a critic into silence. He was willing to give up the struggle if peace could be restored.

But some of his followers and many of his opponents were unwilling to make peace. The people were unwilling to give up the democratic advances and indeed, wanted to make their government more democratic. The violent storm in the press ceased, however, and something very much like a calm ensued. Jennings endeavored to persuade Congress to declare ineligible for election to the legislature officers appointed by Harrison, to move the territorial capital from Vincennes, to grant manhood suffrage, and to provide for the election of sheriffs in place of appointment by the governor. He even wrote about filing impeachment charges against the governor.[60] Two petitions were sent to Congress late in 1811 complaining of Harrison's interference in elections and asking that officials of the United States be prohibited from interfering improperly in elections.[61] When Harrison vetoed a bill to move the capital from Vincennes, the people of Jefferson County petitioned that the veto power be taken from him.[62]

In response to the wishes of the petitioners, Congress extended the franchise to free white adult males who paid taxes, and made ineligible to seats in the territorial legislature the officials appointed by Harrison except the justices of the peace and the officers of the militia.[63] Jennings was re-elected in April, 1811, again defeating Thomas Randolph; in fact, he served for the remainder of the territorial period. The legislature transferred the conduct of the elections from the sheriffs to the judges of the court of common pleas, provided that polls be opened in each township in contrast to one in each county, and changed the method of voting from viva-voce to written ballots.[64] It is quite possible that the change in the number of polling places enfranchised more persons than the congressional act extending the right of suffrage. The seat of government was soon moved from Vincennes to Corydon, where the governor's political friends were much less numerous. This measure, however, was not so important as the broadening of the franchise and the election law.

The advance to the second territorial stage of semirepresentative government, the division of the territory, the election of delegates who represented the opposition, the winning of control of the territorial legislature, the repeal of the acts which encouraged the violation of the prohibition of slavery, the extension of the franchise, the democratization of the territorial government, and the subduing of Harrison and his more aggressive supporters constituted a democratic victory of significant proportions. In a very real sense the democratic forces won their victory in the territorial period. Only the election of the executive, the escape from Congressional supervision of local government, and full participation in national affairs, all of which came with statehood, remained to be won. Also generally overlooked is the democratizing of the territorial system of the United States, which was involved in the victories of the people of Indiana Territory.

12

Indiana's Ideal: A Democratic State

THE TIPPECANOE campaign and the War of 1812 formed an important interlude in the development of Indiana Territory. When news of the Battle of Tippecanoe arrived in Vincennes the territorial legislature in the third day of its session resolved that its members should wear crape on their left arms in "memory of the departed heroes who fell in the attack made by the Indians." [1] The political contests of previous sessions were forgotten, and controversial questions were largely omitted from the proceedings. When war with England came and the Indians struck swiftly and almost decisively, the settlers were stunned by the blows. The Fort Dearborn Massacre on August 15 and Hull's surrender of Detroit the following day exposed the frontier of Indiana to the fury of Indian warfare. The Pigeon Roost Massacre of twenty-two persons on September 3 brought the war close to the Ohio River and farther south than Cincinnati or Vincennes. It was followed by the attack on Fort Harrison on the following two days and the siege of Fort Wayne from September 6 to 12. "Our former frontiers are now wilds and our inner Settlements have become frontiers," said Acting Governor John Gibson.[2] The defeat at the River Raisin on January 22, 1813, increased the alarm, and the territorial legislature appealed to President James Madison for aid in defending their settlements, stating that "whole townships are precipitately abandoning their homes." [3]

In the face of these attacks, politics were largely forgotten. James Scott, whom Harrison had formerly appointed to office, was chosen speaker of the house of representatives at the session early in the year 1813. When he resigned to become a judge, he was succeeded by James Dill, a former Harrisonian stalwart. The slavery and indenture questions were not permitted to assume great importance, and the recorded votes of the house do not indicate a definite division of the members in two groups. There was one exception, however, in which the danger of war may have been used to accomplish a political end. The house of representatives cited "the hostile disposition of the Indians," "the danger to which the Village of Vincennes is thereby subjected," and the need to protect the "publick acts and records of the Territory in this our perilous situation" as reasons for removing the seat of government from Vincennes.[4] Upon this issue as many as thirteen votes were recorded, and the alignment showed a definite tendency toward a sectional or geographical division.

But if the people were stunned by the war, it was only temporarily. When Harrison carried the war into Canada and defeated the enemy, the danger was soon forgotten and political differences reappeared. The house of representatives in the second session of the fourth general assembly in the winter of 1813–1814 elected James Noble, of Franklin County, to be speaker.[5] The house seemed particularly disturbed about the conduct of administrative officers, including the governor, secretary, auditor, and treasurer, and about the conduct of elections, both of which would indicate that the legislature was expanding its control over the executive division of the territorial government. Unsuccessful efforts were made to move the capital farther east. Although the question of indentured servitude was not important, it was revived. The political alignment was much more definite than in the preceding session, and the sectional tendency was even clearer. It was often the eastern representatives against the western, with Harrison County the dividing line. Dennis Pennington, the representative from this county, voted first with one side and then with the other. The majority clearly demonstrated that it would not accept the leadership of David Robb, one of the Harrison leaders from the Wabash Valley. The legislative council, the upper house of the territorial assembly, rejected the bill "more effectually to prohibit the introduction of slaves, negroes or mulattoes" and the bill to move the capital farther eastward. Control of the legislative council was not in the hands of the eastern members, for only one councilor out of five came from that section, and it is obvious from the journal that he was in the minority.[6]

The territory had increased in population until the lower house included five members from the southeastern part, one from Harrison County, and three from the southwest. In contrast, the legislative council included two members from Knox County and one each from Harrison, Clark, and Dearborn. Only the member from the last was aligned with the majority in the house. But on March 4, 1814, Congress authorized the house of representatives to redistrict the territory for the election of members of the legislative council.[7] The governor called the house in special session on June 1, in which the partisan alignment became very clear. The majority included the members from the southeast and the minority those from the southwest. Pennington of Harrison voted with the minority and Isaac Montgomery from Knox divided his votes about equally between the two groups. David Robb led the southwestern members in asserting that the governor could not assemble the lower house without the council and that the session was illegal and could not act. The majority proceeded to redistrict the territory. No other issues obscured the picture.[8]

The first session of the fifth general assembly, August 15 to September 10, 1814, gave evidence of the continuing political division, but not so clearly. Although the territory had been redistricted for the election of the legislative council, that body again rejected a house bill to prevent the introduction of Negroes into the territory. The legislators seem to have been chiefly concerned with the courts and to have endeavored to control the judiciary as they had previously dominated the administrative department.[9] On several occasions on such issues as the regulation of the courts, the moving of the capital, and the introduction of Negroes, the partisan alignment was evident. In general, the southwestern representatives formed the minority on these issues and the southeastern the majority. During this session a joint resolution was passed for the enumeration of the inhabitants of the territory. Although it was a step in the movement for statehood, a recorded roll call was not demanded.[10]

The memorial to Congress requesting statehood was passed in the second session of the fifth assembly. Although the council rejected house bills on slaves and a new reapportionment of representation, it passed the memorial.[11] In the house of representatives the same sectional and partisan alignment was indicated by the recorded votes. The majority, which came chiefly from the southeast, favored the request for statehood, a bill to prevent the introduction of slaves into the territory, and a bill to reapportion representation in the house. Evidently the southeast had not yet gained control of the council, but the failure of the councilors to defeat the memorial for statehood is significant. Furthermore, neither the newspapers nor the house journal give evidence of strong feeling between the two groups.

Because of this absence of partisan hostility and because of the passage of the census act and the statehood memorial, the conclusion must be accepted that statehood was generally considered as the normal procedure and the capstone of the territorial structure. It would give to the popular party a victorious conclusion to its long struggle. As the people became citizens of the new state, they would choose their highest officials rather than have them appointed by the federal government. They would make their own state laws without the possibility of an absolute veto by a governor they did not choose. In addition to local self-government, they would participate in national affairs; and they were very conscious at this time of the importance of national policies respecting Indians, defense, and the disposal of land by the national government. They were even interested in foreign relations. And, considering the situation realistically, as the politicians did, we can see that more offices would have to be filled and more money spent.

Shortly after the legislature adopted the statehood memorial, "B. Whitson," of Lexington, Indiana, wrote "to the inhabitants of Jefferson County" asserting that statehood was near and that men opposed to slavery should be chosen to form the constitution.[12] A correspondent, who wrote under the name "Farmers & Patriots Rights," contributed five letters attacking Delegate Jonathan Jennings because a proclamation had recently been issued warning "uninformed and evil disposed persons" off the public lands and because Jennings had recently voted to give land to Canadian refugees.[13] "A Settler" stated that the people had been permitted for the last eight years to settle and make improvements on the public lands and that in times of danger they had been called the "bulwark of our frontier," but now they were ordered to cease.[14] In a "Circular Address to the Citizens of Indiana," Moses Wiley wrote vigorously of the impolicy of accepting slavery even partially. Once admitted, he asserted, it would be impossible to stop it.[15] "A Citizen of Gibson" assured the "Citizens of Indiana" that they were not being called upon to settle the existence of slavery but only the question of its admission into Indiana. He thought that it would be humane to admit the slaves.[16] "Another Citizen of Gibson" replied by asserting that slavery would not increase the happiness or wealth of the people, that whites who labored among slaves were held in contempt by those who owned slaves and who lived in idleness, that equality vanished when slavery was admitted, and that vice was common among slaveowners.[17] "A Farmer of Knox County" doubted the desirability of statehood because it would involve an increase in the cost of government. He, too, attacked Jennings in respect to the public land policy.[18] The editor of the *Western Sun* criticized the delegate to Congress for trying to secure an investigation of Harrison's alleged interest in the Indian trade while superintendent of Indian affairs.[19]

News of the passage of the enabling act by Congress arrived in Vincennes at this time. The editor of the *Western Sun* protested that the late arrival of the law left only eleven days to choose delegates to the convention.[20] A week later he dignified the attack on Jennings in regard to the public lands, but the editorial lacked relevancy to the issue of the day.[21] The expressed opposition to statehood was surprisingly small. The opposition revealed its unhappiness about the course of events, but it did little to meet the issue directly. Shortly before the meeting of the convention, "A Republican" advised the postponement of statehood until the citizens were better able to bear the additional costs. He asserted that no advantages would be gained from the change and that the governor was not a tyrannical ruler. He suggested waiting for five years until the lands of the New Purchase should become taxable.[22] One other contemporary comment has been preserved. Timothy Flint, who was passing through Indiana at this time, wrote: "The question in all its magnitude, whether it should be a slaveholding state or not, was just now agitating. I was often compelled to hear the question debated by those in opposite interests, with no small degree of asperity." [23] The petulance of the group that had lost control was clearly indicated by the editor when he announced a little later: "The convention have determined by a majority of 33 to 8, to launch our political vessel of state, and I am afraid without having a sufficient number of skilful navigators on board, at least to manage the vessel in case of a storm." [24]

In the light of this evidence of the resumption of the controversy between members of the old Harrison group and the popular party, it is not possible to agree that the old alignment or the old issues were forgotten. Obviously, too, the controversy was much broader than the slavery issue.[25] The contest was largely political, but it involved the character and quality of the civilization of the new state. To what degree was it to be democratic or aristocratic? What was to be the position of the Negro? Was he to be a slave, a servant, or a freeman, or was he to be shut out of the new state as much as possible? A review of the two groups will serve to bring forth the character of the alignment.

The officeholders and their friends were satisfied with the territorial status. They had generally opposed the changes of the period: the division of the territory, the reapportionment of seats in the legislature, the removal of the capital to a more central location, the repeal of the indenture act, the election of Jennings as delegate to the Congress of the United States, and the democratization of the government. Generally speaking, they were committed to a social order patterned upon the Southern ideal of the country gentleman. They thought of themselves as democrats and Jeffersonians, but they saw no reason to surrender their control of government just because their opponents were in the majority or to hasten into a state government just because it would be done eventually. They were especially numerous in the southwestern part of the territory, and they were defending the established position of their section against a newer and a more rapidly growing southeast.

The attitude of the officeholders, with its strain of aristocratic smug superiority, was well expressed by Governor Thomas Posey in a letter requesting reappointment to the governorship. He thought the people of the territory would not be ready for statehood until he had served another term of three years. He wrote:

Some of our citizens are very restless to go into a State government. I wish the people were well prepared for the measure, but I may say with propriety that at least two-thirds, or three-fourths, are not able to contribute but very little, if anything to the Support of a State; and there is also a very great scarcity of talents, or men of such information as are necessary to fill the respective Stations, & offices of government. No doubt you have seen the memorial of the two Houses of our Legislature to Congress for the purpose of going into a State government. If Congress should be so benevolent as to grant all ask'd for, there would be no difficulty except the want of men of good information.

It is calculated that we shall go into a State government in twelve or eighteen months. I think three years would be short enough to place the Territory in a situation for the change. But so anxious are many, that no doubt they will be ready to accept of any terms. We have numbers sufficient, & that is all we can boast of.[26]

In contrast, the supporters of statehood included individuals who had received few if any appointments to office, who were dissatisfied with the arbitrary features of the territorial government, and who were opposed to the introduction of Negroes either as slaves or servants. They had helped to divide the territory; reapportioned representation in the legislature in order to bring it up to date with the latest migration and to give increased influence to the southeast; and removed the capital from Vincennes, where the Harrisonian group was intrenched. They supported Jennings for Congress, the democratization of the territorial government, and statehood as the culmination of the struggle for self-government. Among them were many Quakers and other former Southern farmers who opposed slavery, but who were not agreed in their attitude toward the Negroes. More numerous in the southeastern part of Indiana, they were probably in a minority only in the Wabash Valley.

The late arrival of information about the passage of the enabling act, only eleven days before the date set for the election of delegates to the convention, left little time to choose candidates or to wage a campaign in which the issues could be discussed pro and con. The result of the election was obviously a victory of the Jennings party, perhaps as decisive as two to one. When the convention assembled, on June 10, 1816, it chose Jennings as its president and authorized him to appoint a number of committees to prepare portions of the new constitution. William Hendricks, who had been one of the owners of the *Western Eagle,* a paper friendly to the Jennings group, and who had served as a clerk of the territorial house of representatives and as a representative, was elected secretary.[27]

The nativity and prior residence of the delegates indicated the source and the character of the people of early Indiana. The largest number of the delegates to have been born in one state or country were the Virginians, probably twelve in number. Seven were natives of Pennsylvania, six of Kentucky, five of Maryland, two of New Jersey, two of Connecticut, one of North Carolina, one of South Carolina, one of Delaware, four of Ireland, one of Switzerland, and one of Germany.[28] Altogether twenty-six of the forty-three were natives of the Southern states. Eleven had been born in Northern states and six in Europe. Only one of the Virginians is known to have been born in the Coastal Plain, while six were born in the Piedmont, one in the Valley, and one near the Ohio above Wheeling. The Marylanders and Carolinians were probably also from the upland district of their states. Many of the delegates seem to have been identified with the Old West.

The migrations of the delegates from their birthplaces to Indiana not only established this point but revealed that they were a part of the expansion of the Old West into the Ohio Valley. Twenty-seven of the forty-three had lived for a time in Kentucky before coming to Indiana, but only six had been born there. The former residents of the Bluegrass State constituted nearly two thirds of the convention. One of the Pennsylvanians had lived in North Carolina before coming to Indiana, and one of the Irishmen had come by way of Pennsylvania, North Carolina, and Tennessee. Two of the Virginians had come directly to Indiana, four of the five Marylanders had lived in Kentucky, and the South Carolinian may have resided in Virginia during his youth.

In contrast to these natives and residents of the South, eight of the forty-three, or approximately one fifth of the delegates, had not lived below the Mason and Dixon Line or the Ohio River. The two New Englanders, the two natives of New Jersey, three of the Pennsylvanians, and the lone German had not lived in the South.

Partisan differences had existed during the period when the territory possessed a legislature, except the two years when the frontier was enmeshed in war.[29] After the constitution was adopted, the offices of the new state were divided according to the wishes of the Jennings group, which had triumphed in the territorial contest.[30] Little reason exists for assuming that politics were forgotten during the convention, and the choice of officers and the contests arising while the constitution was being written indicate that they were not. To divide the delegates according to their partisan loyalties, however, is difficult, because the members were individualists and the party groups were not rigid or organized. They represented allegiance to ideas or to a way of life, not to an organization.

Four of the most prominent early friends of Harrison were members of the convention: Benjamin Parke, John Johnson, David Robb, and James Dill. As leaders of a minority group in the convention, they were opposed by a majority of the delegates. The recorded votes make possible a division of the members into the majority and the minority,[31] but the independent voting of some of the delegates makes the division at some points rather uncertain. The opposition seems to have had less cohesion than the majority, but the latter sometimes separated into two divisions which may be called the regulars and the independents. Fundamentally, the Jennings group agreed upon the main issues and usually differed only upon what may be called minor questions.

Parke and Johnson were elected from Knox County, and with them came William Polke, John Badollet, and John Bennefield. Badollet was the register of the land office at Vincennes and a friend of Albert Gallatin, secretary of the treasury of the United States. He had become active in the movement against slavery and his friendship for Harrison cooled perceptibly. An open break, however, did not occur and in the convention he voted with Harrison's friends.[32] Parke was Harrison's chief defender in the controversy over the passage to the semirepresentative stage of territorial government. A native of New Jersey, he had moved to Kentucky as a young man, studied law, and was married before emigrating to Vincennes, where he became an intimate friend and partisan of Harrison. He was appointed attorney general, was a member of the legislature, was chosen delegate to Congress, and in 1808 was appointed territorial judge.[33] Johnson supported Harrison in the beginning and remained a proslavery leader in the territory and in the convention.[34] William Polke seemingly followed the leadership of Johnson and Parke, but Bennefield adhered to the Jennings group. David Robb was another of Harrison's friends who had frequently been appointed to office and who served in the territorial legislature, where he was one of the Harrison supporters rebuffed by the Jennings group.[35] Other members of the opposition from the southwestern counties were less prominent in the work of the convention but can be identified by their votes.[36]

Dr. David Maxwell, from Jefferson County, and James Dill, from Dearborn County, complete the ranks of the opposition. Like Parke, Johnson, and Scott, they were able men. Maxwell was born in Kentucky in a family that had migrated from Pennsylvania to Virginia and from Virginia to Kentucky. Both he and his wife inherited slaves, but their descendants believed that they moved to Indiana to escape the institution of slavery. His recorded votes were about equally divided between the two groups, but he voted against statehood.[37] Dill was a friend of Governor Arthur St. Clair as well as of Harrison, by whom he was frequently appointed to office. He was born in Ireland and was a former resident of Kentucky and Ohio. In the latter, he had married a daughter of Governor St. Clair.[38] Perhaps his character was accurately reflected by the local county history which states: "He was the last of our gentlemen of the old school. . . . When Gen. Dill appeared in court, it was in the full costume of the gentlemen of the last century—his knee breeches and silver buckles and venerable cue neatly plaited and flowing over his shoulders, seemed a mild protest against the leveling tendencies of the age; but nothing could impair the hold which the gallant soldier and courtly and witty Irishman had on the friendship of the people of this county." [39]

If the above classification is correct, the opposition included all but one of the delegates from the Wabash Valley, that is, four of the five from Knox County, the four members from Gibson County, and the delegate from Posey County. In contrast, not a member from the Whitewater Valley co-operated with the opposition. In the counties of Perry, Harrison, Clark, Jefferson, and Dearborn, which were located in between, the opposition managed to secure some of the delegates. Two of the territorial judges and several individuals, with considerable legislative experience, who were among the most able men in the territory were members of the minority.

The Jennings group did not contain so many prominent leaders. In general, they represented the frontier farmers chosen from the people. Jonathan Jennings and James Noble were the most notable exceptions. Dunn pictured Jennings as "a young Hercules, stripped for the fray, and wielding the mighty bludgeon of 'No Slavery in Indiana,' " but his letters and speeches give the impression that he was a shrewd politician rather than a statesman. His leadership is not evident in the convention.[40] James Noble was the son of Virginia parents who moved to Kentucky. He was followed to Indiana by two brothers, one of whom became governor of Indiana in 1831 and again in 1834. James was chosen one of the first members of the United States Senate from Indiana. He had been a member of the territorial legislature, where he served as speaker during the winter session, 1813–1814.[41]

The Jennings group was strongest in the east and southeast, especially in the Whitewater Valley. The delegation from Wayne

County included three Quakers and a local Methodist preacher. With Noble from Franklin County came a native of each of the four states, Pennsylvania, Maryland, Virginia, and South Carolina, two of whom had lived for a time in Kentucky. The South Carolinian, Robert Hanna, had "an innate prejudice against slavery and slaveholders—peculiar to those who live in the south and are not owners of slaves." [42] Dearborn County sent two delegates, one of whom was a native of Connecticut and the other of Delaware, but neither of them followed the leadership of their colleague, James Dill. The delegate from Switzerland County and two of the three from Jefferson County belonged to the Jennings group, except that Nathaniel Hunt, a New Englander from Jefferson County, voted against statehood. Jennings was elected from Clark County, and the other four members from this county were equally divided between the two groups. Washington, an interior county, sent five delegates who voted with the statehood group and who were typical of the frontier stretching from Pennsylvania to North Carolina and westward to Kentucky. Harrison County elected three adherents of the popular party and two of the opposition. Davis Floyd and Dennis Pennington had formerly co-operated with Harrison's friends but recently had come over to the statehood movement. They were prominent leaders and in the convention proved to be rather independent members of the Jennings forces. Pennington left a tradition of marked hostility to slavery. From the Wabash Valley only one delegate, Bennefield, voted with the popular party. Daniel Grass answered four recorded roll calls before his fatal illness, and on three of these he voted with the statehood group, which record may entitle him to be regarded as a member of the majority.

The popular party included two New Englanders and seven natives of the Middle Atlantic states, a total of nine who were born in the North, or a third of the group. Fifteen and possibly sixteen were natives of Southern states and two of Ireland. The Southerners were from the Upland; they were a part of the migration into the mountain South, and also a part of the frontier expansion into the Ohio Valley. Not more than a third of them had been appointed to office by Governor Harrison. One could not expect them to be representatives of the plantation regime or enthusiastic about the efforts of the territorial official group to imitate that style of living.

The committees appointed by President Jennings to report portions of the proposed constitution were not appointed in a partisan manner, although most of them were in control of the majority. Seven of the twelve important committees had chairmen, and three contained a majority from the opposition. Later a committee of revision was appointed almost entirely from the opposition.[43] Undoubtedly the ability of several of the old leaders whose services and experience began in Harrison's administration was responsible for these assignments and for the prominent part played by these territorial officeholders in the convention. The majority, however, scrutinized the leadership of these men and on occasion defeated their proposals. On the second day, James Dill, a friend and appointee of Harrison, reported rules by which the convention was to be governed. One rule called for two thirds of the members to form a quorum; because this might have enabled the opposition to prevent the convention from proceeding to business, the Jennings group replaced it with a quorum of a simple majority.[44] In the middle of the second week Johnson of Knox, a proslavery, anti-statehood leader, attempted to change the reported article on amendment, apparently to eliminate the authority of the state legislature to call a constitutional convention. Perhaps to conceal his real intention, he moved to substitute a provision that the constitution could not be amended to admit slavery. The antislavery, statehood group, however, rejected his proposal. He then made a straightforward motion to take from a convention the power to amend the constitution. It too was defeated. He then moved to strike out the reference to "involuntary servitude"; this motion led to his third consecutive defeat.[45] Whether he had in mind another method of amendment or whether he sought to make the constitution unacceptable is not clear, but the majority decisively rejected his leadership.

A somewhat similar defeat was administered to David Robb, another Harrisonite, on June 24 and 25. He first moved to give the legislature authority to divide the state for the three circuit courts rather than include the division in the constitution. Failing in this attempt, he moved to give the legislature authority to determine the place of the meeting of the supreme court. This measure also was defeated. On the next day he introduced a motion to empower the legislature to limit the supreme court to one or more judges, and this suggestion, too, was defeated. The majority may have acted upon principle or policy, or it may have been a personal or political rebuff. The constitution gave the legislature considerable authority over the courts, and Robb's amendments would have extended this control only a little; but the convention defeated them decisively.[46] On June 27 Robb endeavored to reduce the maximum salaries to be paid state officials, and Johnson tried to reduce the pay of the legislators; but on three consecutive votes they were again defeated.[47]

There were, however, several important issues before the convention that struck deeper than hostility to the old Harrison leaders. Of the eight members of the convention who voted against statehood, six were in the opposition.[48] The Jennings partisans endeavored to preserve three independent divisions of government, refusing to give the legislature additional control over the courts, to expand the governor's appointive power, and to reduce the salary of legislators. Near the end of the session they increased the representation of the southwestern counties in the house of representatives, thereby assuring control in the state legislature to the section which supported them and favored their ideas.[49]

Undoubtedly the question of the Negro's position was vital, but no evidence has been found that anyone in the convention endeavored to legalize slavery. The effort to insert a statement declaring that the constitution ought not to be amended so as to admit slavery was rejected at first by the Jennings group possibly because Johnson was seeking to accomplish another purpose. Although the journal does not indicate when or in what manner it was inserted, the constitution eventually emerged with a provision that "no alteration of this constitution shall ever take place so as to introduce slavery or involuntary servitude in this State. . . ."[50] A significant compromise was adopted without a recorded roll call or the publication of any details in the journal. The original report of Article XI contained a long section prohibiting slavery and indentured servitude for males above twenty-one and females above eighteen years and declaring illegal the indentures of Negroes and mulattoes whether made within or without the state, except apprenticeships. In the committee of the whole it was reduced to a simple prohibition of slavery and a declaration that any indenture hereafter made and executed out of the state should not be valid within the state. This change saved the indenture contracts already in existence. Article VII excluded "Negroes, Mulattoes and Indians" from serving in the militia. Article VI restricted the franchise to white adult male citizens of the United States. According to Article III representation in the legislature was to be apportioned upon the basis of white adult male inhabitants. Taken all together, the action of the convention indicates not only hostility to slavery but a lack of friendship for the Negro. No welcome greeting was extended to the black, but, on the contrary, a determination was expressed to establish a white man's civilization. This attitude, of course, was an additional link between the yeomen of the Upland South and the pioneers of early Indiana.[51]

If any further evidence were required to indicate the influence of the migration from the Old West to the Ohio Valley, the relationship between the constitution which the convention adopted and the organic laws of Kentucky, Ohio, Tennessee, and Pennsylvania would clinch the point. A large part of Indiana's first constitution was taken from the earlier Ohio Valley constitutions. The portions that were not copied constitute less than ten per cent of the entire document. The process of writing, however, was not the simple method of copying the constitutional law of another state, but was a method of selection. Apparently the members of the convention had before them copies of the constitutions of the nation and the various states. As a general rule, they did not draw entire articles from a single constitution but seem to have searched through these documents to find the sections which embodied the provisions they considered preferable for the government of the new state. Occasionally they wrote a new section when a suitable one was not found in the older documents.[52] This process of selection resulted in a significant constitution.

The preamble, closely patterned after Ohio's preamble, shows the influence of the Northwest Ordinance. It began by asserting the right of admission into the Union on an equal footing with the original states, thus reiterating the right of a territory to escape the subordinate colonial status. Statehood gave to Indiana, as to other states, the right of self-government and the right of participating in the determination of national policies.

The bill of rights, which was the first article and which may have been placed in a primary position as a recognition of its importance, could be read by the citizen of the new state with the conviction that it protected him from tyranny and oppression. Like the preamble, this article resembled the Ohio constitution, especially where it followed rather closely the organic laws of Kentucky, Tennessee, and Pennsylvania. Approximately one third of this article is more like these documents than that of Ohio, and this similarity is strengthened by the omission of some of the more original sections of the Ohio bill of rights.

The government was divided into three separate and independent departments by the second article, which was almost exactly a reproduction of a part of the constitution of Kentucky. The latter was, word for word, a portion of Jefferson's proposed constitution of Virginia. The purpose of the article was to prevent excessive power from falling into the hands of one man or group of men who might thereby be enabled to oppress the people.

The legislature was to be composed of two houses, the members of which were to be apportioned according to the number of adult white males and reapportioned every five years. All of the representatives and one third of the senators were to be elected every year, thus making it possible to change the legislators in a comparatively short time. These provisions resembled the first article of the Ohio constitution, which was largely modeled upon that of Tennessee.

The executive division followed the Kentucky constitution, which was very similar to that of Pennsylvania. Ohio established a very weak executive, perhaps because of the difficulties of the territorial period between the governor and the legislature. Indiana, however, gave its governor powers of appointment, remission of fines and forfeitures, and the veto. The governor and lieutenant governor were popularly elected; and the secretary of state, treasurer, and auditor were chosen by the legislature. The governor could not hold other offices, and his salary could not be changed during his term of three years.

The judiciary article was more original than any of the preceding articles, and the division of government it established was reasonably independent of the legislative and executive branches. The judges were elected or appointed for terms of seven years. The appointment of the supreme court judges by the governor was later the subject of considerable criticism.

The right to vote was given, by the sixth article, to all adult white males who had resided in the state one year immediately preceding the election, except members of the armed forces of the nation. This article resembled the similar portion of Ohio's constitution, but the regulations regarding the suffrage and elections were more liberal in Indiana. Voting was to be by ballot, but the legislature was given the privilege of restoring viva-voce voting.

The provisions for the militia were taken from the constitutions of Ohio and Kentucky. The eighth article, which described the method of amendment, was different from other constitutions, except for the statement that an amendment could not legalize slavery. This was copied from Ohio. The plan for altering the constitution proved to be so cumbersome that it was never used.

An idealistic system of state-supported education was authorized by the ninth article, which was probably original but with a possible debt to the New Hampshire constitution. Not being obligatory, these sections were largely unobserved. They remain, however, as a remarkable statement of the ideal of a democratic people "for a general system of education, ascending in a regular gradation, from township schools to a state university, wherein tuition shall be gratis and equally open to all." Penal reform, poor farms, and county libraries were also to be established.

Banks or banking companies issuing bills of credit were prohibited by the tenth article, unless the legislature established a state bank. This provision, which was not found in earlier constitutions, preceded by more than a decade the Jacksonian opposition to banks.

The prohibition of slavery and of the further introduction of indentured servitude were included in the eleventh and final article. It combined several miscellaneous matters and was copied from various constitutions, especially those in force in Ohio and Kentucky.

The table on page 194 gives a comparison of the Indiana constitution with other constitutions.

The significance of this democratic government may not be recognized by comparing it with the Ohio, Kentucky, or Tennessee constitutions. It did not include Ohio's tax requirement for voting, or Kentucky's denial to the legislature of the power to abolish slavery, or Tennessee's property qualifications for officeholders. Its true significance is seen when compared with the early constitutions of the Southern states, with their property qualifications, unequal apportionment of representation, protection of slavery, and control by an aristocratic group of planters.

The struggle in Indiana also needs to be viewed in broad perspective. It is now possible to note the development, in the early

Article	Subject Matter	No. of Sections	No. of Sections like Ohio	No. of Sections like Ky.	No. of Original Sections	No. of Sections like Other Constitutions	
	Preamble	1	1				
I.	Bill of rights	24	9¾	1¾	1	2½	Pa.
						6	Ky., Pa., Tenn.
						1	Ohio, Tenn.
						1	Tenn.
						1	U.S.
II.	Separation of powers	1		1			
III.	Legislature	26	17	1	1	1	Tenn.
						4	Ohio, Tenn., Pa.
						1	Ky., Pa.
						1	Ohio, Tenn., N. C.
IV.	Executive	26	1½	12	1½	3	Pa.
						1½	La.
						2	Ky., Tenn., Del., Pa., La.
						2½	Ohio, Ky., Tenn., La.
						2	Miscellaneous
V.	Judiciary	12	6½	½	5		
VI.	Elections	5	4		1		
VII.	Militia	10	3	1	2½	2½	Tenn.
						1	Ky., Pa.
VIII.	Amendment	1	⅛		¾	⅛	N.W.O.
IX.	Education	5			4½	½	N. H.
X.	Banks	1			1		
XI.	Miscellaneous	17	7	3	3	2	Ky., La.
						1	U. S.
						1	N. C.
	Total	129	49⅞	20¼	21¼	37⅝	

days of the territory, of a society that was aristocratic in spirit even though crude in form. The French population, the territorial officials who aspired to be Southern gentlemen, and a few men of more than average wealth were largely responsible for this development. They were more or less satisfied with the undemocratic territorial government, the offices of which some of them held. They sought to emulate the organization of Southern society, with its servants at the base and its gentlemen who devoted themselves to politics at the top. The common citizens they sometimes regarded as unworthy of a place in the discussion of public policy and of presuming to criticize the conduct of officials, as too inexperienced to take upon themselves governmental responsibility, and as too uninformed to frame a constitution for their government. Generally these sentiments were not expressed except in unguarded moments, but the occasional utterances and the conduct of the official class give sufficient evidence. To achieve their purpose, it seemed desirable to repeal the prohibition of slavery in the Northwest Ordinance or at least to evade its intended purpose. Hence, a system of indentured servitude was established.

Into the territory in increasing numbers came the poor pioneers from the Upland South and the early settlements of the Ohio Valley, and with them a few from the Middle Atlantic states, New England, and Europe. These were the men of the frontier, individualistic, comparatively unrestrained by the conventionalities of society, and unafraid of gentlemen and officeholders. Many had suffered discriminations, inequalities, and injustices at the hands of the governing classes in the old states. Some of them listened to ministers who declared that slavery and the ways of the rich were doings of the devil. They began to feel that even the poorest had a right to a voice in the determination of the policies which affected his life as well as the career of the richest. Gradually they gained control of the territorial legislature. They refused to be browbeaten by the important men. They secured the repeal of the indenture law, moved the territorial capital, aided in democratizing the territorial government, and carried the statehood movement to success. They were opposed by the aristocratic leaders of superior talents, but they pressed on, and they won. Even in the convention the men who tried to establish a dangerously large quorum, who voted against statehood, and who sometimes seemed to be trying to make the constitution unacceptable were of this territorial aristocracy.

But the convention picked and chose from the older constitutions the more democratic features and, with the aid of the enlightened men of the opposition, added new features of considerable significance. The constitution was not perfect, but the government it established was in the hands of the people.

The constitution contained the ideals of the frontier. It was not intended to solve the economic problems of the poor, for the frontiersmen had confidence that they could do that for themselves, provided they did not have to meet a legally favored and intrenched governing class capable of using its superior talents, wealth, social position, and the powers of government against them. What the frontiersmen asked was not government aid, but freedom to achieve their own destiny, the opportunity to secure land, and the right to live in a free white man's society.

13

A Blazed Trail: Illinois

ILLINOIS Territory was born amidst harsh political differences "raised by the violence and disorder that had for years rent Kaskaskia." [1] The anti-Harrison party gained sufficient strength in the Indiana territorial legislature in 1808 to pass resolutions in favor of dividing the territory and to secure the election of Jesse B. Thomas as delegate to Congress under a pledge to work for division. These developments in turn culminated in the passage of an act providing for the establishment of the Territory of Illinois. [2] The bitterness of partisan strife, added to the hostilities engendered by the land commissioners' investigation of land titles, led to the murder of Rice Jones, the son of John Rice Jones whose abandonment of the Harrison party had contributed to these events. [3]

Contrary to conditions which prevailed at the beginning, the progress of Illinois Territory was to be less filled with strife than was the advancement of the other Ohio Valley territories. Partisan bitterness had discredited itself and in part had been consumed in its own fire. Illinois Territory passed in normal succession through the first to the second stage of government as though following an old and plainly marked path to statehood. Actually, however, its progress was not that simple, for there were differences among the leaders and people as to the character of the civilization they wished to establish for the future state. The contest between forces of an aristocratic bearing and forces of a democratic character came out in the open only at the end of the territorial period. It was the same struggle which developed in the other Ohio Valley states, a continuation of the conflict in the states east of the mountains.

Among the conservative influences were the nonrepresentative features of the territorial government, the inexperience of the French population with American democracy, the presence of slavery and indentured servitude, and the development of an upper class which imitated Southern plantation society.

The act creating Illinois Territory, February 3, 1809, returned the people once more to the type of government in force in the early years of the Northwest Territory, 1788–1798, and of the Indiana Territory, 1800–1805. A governor, a secretary, and three judges appointed by the President governed the people without their participation or their consent to individual measures.[4] Not until 1812 did the territory have a representative assembly.

The grievances of the French inhabitants did not include the undemocratic character of the government, for they were satisfied with its paternalistic features. The unimportance of land in their existence, the uncertainty of their titles, and their ignorance of American ways offered an environment quite conducive to a type of trader and land speculator that was not particularly interested in democracy. Virginia's requirement that the possession and titles of the French be confirmed was interpreted as protecting their property in slaves, thus making the enforcement of the prohibition of slavery difficult.

In addition to the slaves of the French, other slaves and servants were held in the new territory. The census of 1810 gave the number of all Negroes as 629, of which 500 were free blacks, probably servants, and 129 slaves.[5] Ten years later they were counted as 917 slaves and 506 free Negroes.[6] The classification as slave or free may not have been very accurate, but the figures indicated at least a growing servant class. The passage of the indenture act by the legislature of Indiana Territory and its recognition as a law by the territorial government of Illinois were no doubt partly responsible for the larger number of Negroes.

Many of the Negroes were held by the rising upper class, which was made up largely of the territorial officials, traders, speculators, and an occasional Frenchman. Many of them imitated the manners of the Southern planters so far as frontier conditions permitted. Among the holders of slaves or servants were Governor Ninian Edwards, Secretary Nathaniel Pope, Judge Jesse B. Thomas; Councilors Pierre Menard, Thomas Ferguson, and Samuel Judy; Representatives Alexander Wilson and Jacob Short; and Delegates Benjamin Stephenson and Shadrach Bond. Other prominent men who held blacks were John Edgar and William Morrison, leaders of the former anti-Harrison group; members of the Reynolds family, and

H. Ferguson and Willis Hargrave among the more recent arrivals. A considerable number of Negroes were to be found in Gallatin County, where slaves were used in operating the saltworks.[7] One individual held 40, a second 34, a third 33, a fourth 23, and a fifth 19. The French generally held smaller numbers.

Officials and other prominent persons were often natives of Southern states, who brought to the Old Northwest the social ideals and customs of the planter class.[8] Dinners, balls, dances, horse races, and even fox hunts were held. Ladies from Southern plantations and finishing schools were not unknown. A traveler in 1819 wrote: "After dinner I had the honor of being invited to tea at the home of Governor Bond where I, for the first time in the new world, found myself in a company of distinguished ladies." [9] The "society" of the capital city of Springfield, at a latter day, which centered around the Edwards family and the Todd sisters, indicates that considerable success attended the efforts of the official class even though it was accomplished without the help of slaves.[10]

The democratic influences which were present in Illinois Territory included the federal land system, which was much fairer to the smaller purchaser than the system followed in Kentucky and Tennessee; a climate and soil that were unsuitable for large-scale production of Southern staples; the prohibition of slavery by the sixth article of the Ordinance of 1787, which discouraged the immigration of the Southern planter class; the coming of large numbers of the pioneers from the older states of the Ohio Valley and the Atlantic coast; and the appointment of a democratic Jeffersonian as governor of the territory.

The land system of the United States was always far from perfect, and the acts passed in the period of this study represent a compromise between the interests of speculators, government, and settlers. The measures adopted did not meet entirely the wishes of any one interest. But in contrast to the system in Kentucky and Tennessee, the federal laws offered less opportunity for the wealthy to gain special privileges and to engross excessive acreages for private advantage. The definite titles lessened costly court procedure which the poor could not afford and saved thousands from the fate of being dispossessed of land because of technicalities or costs.

Congress had confirmed the land holdings of the French and the early grants to American frontiersmen. In 1813–1816 the government extended to the settlers in Illinois the right of pre-emption

on a quarter section of land if they actually inhabited and cultivated it.[11] Moreover, the credit system of the Harrison Act gave
them five years in which to pay and the Act of 1804 made it possible to buy as little as 160 acres, if they could raise the first payment of eighty dollars. The poor were no doubt at a disadvantage
at the public auctions, but the right of pre-emption and the existence of large quantities of unsold land greatly minimized the significance of this disadvantage. Speculators and large purchasers
were present and active, and the very poor could not take advantage of the pre-emption laws or the minimum purchases under
the credit system after the auction sale, but most of the purchases
were made in the minimum amount and under the credit provision.[12]

Although the prohibition of slavery by the sixth article of the
Ordinance of 1787 was continuously violated, it discouraged the
immigration of the Southern planter class. Not much slave property was imported under the indenture act or the lax enforcement
of the Ordinance. Not a constitutional convention in the Old
Northwest chanced the rejection of its labors by Congress because of
a provision to legalize slavery. Some of the proslavery sentiment in
Indiana and Illinois was caused by the migration of planters
through these territories on their way to Missouri with their slaves
and wealth; such transits in themselves indicate that the sixth article
of the Ordinance was effective.

Probably the strongest influence for democracy was the frontiersmen. No doubt they were handicapped by lack of education and
organization and were generally too busy with their everyday activities to plan any conscious effort to reform society, but they lived
democratically and at times used their political privileges to secure
more democratic government. They came in greater numbers than
the wealthy. Many of them had experienced injustices in the Eastern states at the hands of aristocracies that had often failed to prove
their superior ability to govern.

The appointment of Ninian Edwards to the governorship was
another factor contributing to the advance of democracy in Illinois
Territory. His early career reads like fiction. He was born in a
wealthy planter family in Maryland, Virginians on his father's
side and Marylanders on his mother's. After early training with
tutors, he had studied law and medicine. Moving to Kentucky, he
had wasted two or three years of his young life and much of his

patrimony in riotous living. Before coming of age he had served in the Kentucky legislature, had given up his dissipation, and amassing a large fortune had ascended in ten years to the chief justiceship of the state.[13]

More important than the events of his earlier life was his political philosophy. A follower of Thomas Jefferson, he trusted the people and applied democratic principles to the territorial government. The militia was permitted to choose its own officers for the governor to appoint.[14] He endeavored to follow the popular will in other local appointments and refused to identify himself with either of the existing political factions.[15] After three years of nonrepresentative government, petitions were presented to the executive asking for a territorial legislature. He called an election to determine whether the people wished to advance to the second stage of government.[16] The votes were nearly all favorable, but, because the federal government had not yet put the public domain on the market in Illinois,[17] very few could meet the requirements for voting for the members of the territorial legislature which would come into existence with the change. It was estimated that not more than two per cent of the people could vote. Governor Edwards wrote a statesmanlike letter to Congressman Richard M. Johnson, of Kentucky, requesting him to advocate a change in the law. He explained that a rapid increase in the number of people would make the government even less representative within the five-year term of the members of the upper house. He requested that the franchise be extended to non-landowners and that the delegate to Congress should be popularly elected rather than chosen by the territorial legislature.[18]

The law which Congress passed on May 20, 1812, in response to this appeal authorized the governor to proportion representation according to population, extended the franchise to adult male taxpayers with one year's residence, and made the members of the upper house and the delegate to Congress subject to popular election. This act brought Illinois Territory abreast of the democratic government of Indiana Territory except for the Indiana elections act.[19]

After the War of 1812 a large number of people moved from all parts of the nation into the West, a movement which has been called the "Great Migration." Although it differed in some respects from the preceding movements, it continued to draw heavily on the people of the Upland South and to distribute a large portion of them throughout the Ohio Valley. They were joined by others from Pennsylvania and the older states of the Ohio Valley and by a smaller number from as far north as New York and New England.

From the Carolinas and Georgia they came through Saluda and Swannanoa gaps to the French Broad and the upper Tennessee, where they joined the Quakers of North Carolina and numerous Virginians along the Wilderness Road or the route that followed the New and Kanawha rivers. North of the Potomac were improved roads in the areas that once resounded to the troops of Generals Braddock and Forbes. By 1817 and 1818, stages, freight wagons, and a mass of humanity were following these thoroughfares to the Ohio Valley. Through central and western New York by 1809 or 1810 the movement of people reached the headwaters of the Allegheny River, where northern immigrants entered the Ohio Valley. After the war their number increased, and in the spring of 1818 as many as three thousand were said to be waiting for the ice to break in the river.[20]

The trend of this large migration turned from Kentucky and Tennessee to the lands north of the Ohio. Illinois was only a distant segment of the Ohio Valley frontier, but the restoration of peace and the opening of land sales led to a rush of settlers which has been likened to a flood and the results they produced to a miracle.[21] The changes may have looked big to the people of Illinois, but more settlers were stopping in Ohio, Indiana, Kentucky, and Tennessee than in Illinois. The territorial census of 1818 was thought to indicate a population slightly in excess of 40,000.[22] Although some doubt has been cast upon this territorial count, the federal census two years later reported a population of 55,211.[23] This migration not only justified the second stage of territorial government but also seemed to indicate that statehood could be under taken. It also made necessary a decision about the character of its civilization—between democracy and aristocracy.

The suggestion of statehood for Illinois was not opposed, as in Ohio by the territorial administration,[24] but was advanced by the Edwards group. The idea was sponsored by Daniel Pope Cook, a talented young immigrant from Kentucky, a member of the Edwards party, a nephew of the congressional delegate and of John Pope of Kentucky, both of whom were close friends of Governor Edwards.[25] Writing in the *Western Intelligencer* under the name of

"A Republican," he suggested statehood. He argued that the people were sufficiently numerous, that the cost would not be excessively burdensome, that nine tenths of the people had had experience in government in the different states of the Union, and that the French were firmly attached to the principles of our government. He objected to the territorial status because an executive who was not responsible to the people had the authority to dissolve the legislature or to apply an absolute veto to its acts, and because the division of powers between Congress and the territorial legislature had resulted in enervating the judicial branch of the government for almost three years. He believed that Congress would admit Illinois to the Union because the consequent encouragement of immigration would stimulate the sales of land and increase the federal income.[26]

When the territorial legislature met three days later, Governor Edwards approved the idea and recommended the taking of a census. The assembly, however, moved even more rapidly by drawing up and adopting a memorial to Congress which requested authorization to form a state government.[27] The memorial declared that the territorial government was "a species of despotism in direct hostility with the principles of a republican government," which "ought to exist no longer than absolute necessity may require it," and that there was "an unusual coincidence of sentiment as to the propriety of forming a state government." [28] To keep the record clear the editor of the *Western Intelligencer* declared: "It is true that the government of our territory has been as ably administered as any other in the union, and perhaps with as much satisfaction to the people generally as is possible under existing circumstances. Yet to remain longer in this negative situation than absolute necessity requires, is too humiliating for a people, who possess the talents and means of self-government. That this necessity is at an end we are convinced. . . ." [29] Do these communications not indicate that the people had few grievances against the territorial administration but that they were dissatisfied with the colonial system of the Ordinance of 1787 and that they considered the subordinate status no longer necessary? In order to achieve statehood they exaggerated their discontent.

The effort to secure statehood touched off a discussion of indentured servitude and slavery. Before the council or upper house passed the memorial, the representatives were considering a bill to repeal the act legalizing indentured servitude. In the preamble of the measure was a statement questioning whether the governor and judges in adopting the law had acted constitutionally and whether the act was not contrary to the Ordinance of 1787. The governor would not accept the charge of acting unconstitutionally and therefore vetoed the bill, directing attention to the preamble. Evidently disappointed that the legislature did not repass the meas- use without the preamble, he stated in his message proroguing the legislature that he was opposed not to the bill but only to the preamble.[30]

If this maneuver was intended to check the chances of continuing indentured servitude under the proposed state constitution, other Illinoisians were equally anxious to prohibit slavery in the new state. Daniel P. Cook, who introduced the subject of statehood, also opened the discussion of slavery. In his letter suggesting statehood he wrote that a decision in respect to slavery would relieve persons on both sides of the question and thereby encourage immigration.[31] The following spring when the enabling act was before Congress he expressed his views at some length. He denied that slavery would increase the tide of emigration or convert the forests into the cul- tivated habitations of men. A free people was safer, happier, and stronger than a mixture of slaves and free men, he stated, and a landed aristocracy and a poor tenant class were the likely results of slavery. Because he believed that the Ordinance of 1787 pre- vented the possibility of a slave state, he suggested that the subject be dropped and all energy devoted to obtaining the best possible constitution.[32]

"Caution" expressed the conservative Northern point of view by questioning whether the increasing emigration from the Northern states would not improve the chance of eliminating slavery five years later, whether the men of talents were sufficiently numerous, and whether the territory was able financially to support a state government?[33] "Candor" took issue with Cook about the Ordi- nance, and insisted that it was effective only during the territorial period. He thought that a great majority of the people were op- posed to the toleration of slavery but warned that they might be defeated by the cunning of those having a contrary interest.[34]

The ablest writer of the antislavery movement was "Agis," who was probably Edward Coles. The general drift of his thought was quickly revealed when he wrote, "I trust that I shall not be called upon to prove the injustice of African slavery, either by the professors of that religion which commands us to 'do unto others whatsoever we would that others should do unto us' ; or by those politicians who, with the immortal authors of our declaration of independence, 'hold these truths to be self-evident, that all mankind are created equal; that they are endowed by their creator with certain unalienable rights; that among these are life, LIBERTY, and the pursuit of happiness.' " He denied that slaveowners had an equitable title to the slaves and declared that the territorial indenture act was contrary to the Ordinance of 1787 because the contracts were not made voluntarily by free persons.[35]

In a second article he asserted that slavery placed in the home an inveterate enemy, that it produced the grossest corruption of public morals, and that it placed on labor a badge of servility and disgrace. He warned the people to "beware of those who, while they pretend opposition to slavery, are still desirious to uphold the present method of introducing slaves by indenturing. This half-way is satisfactory neither to the advocates of slavery, nor to the friends of liberty. Let no one enjoy your confidence who will not zealously advocate the entire exclusion of slavery from the state." He called on the people to decide whether they were to live in "simple and happy freedom," or one half in "abject and cruel servitude to support the splendid misery and sickly pomp of the other half," and declared that he would rather see "our rich meadows and fertile woodlands inhabited alone by wild beasts . . . than that they should ever echo the sound of the slave driver's scourge, or resound with the cries of the oppressed African." [36]

Just before the election of delegates to the convention, Cook returned to the attack on slavery, asserting that he opposed the toleration of slavery because it was repugnant to the principles of humanity, to the policy of the general government, and to the best interest of the territory. He pictured vast tracts of uncultivated lands in the hands of slaveowning families and a social order in which labor was associated with servitude and in which the fear of a slave insurrection was constantly felt.[37]

The advocates of unlimited slavery did not resort to the *Intelligencer* to gain support. There is now no way of estimating their number or importance. Persons who appealed to the public through the press were either opposed to any form of slavery or in favor of a modified type of limited slavery. The most able appeal of the

latter group was contributed by "Pacificus," who presented a plan
by which slaves could be held until a stated age, their children freed
at a slightly younger age, and the plan itself not to last beyond
1860. He pleaded that there was "a large and respectable portion
of the inhabitants of this territory who are anxious to be permitted to live as they have hitherto done—to retain in their families those whom they have brought with them into the country,
perhaps raised among their children, or purchased with their money
for the purpose of relieving the toils and burdens of domestic life.
. . . Is not a portion of the community amounting to at least one
third of the actual population of the territory entitled to some
little degree of attention and indulgence?" He thought that his
plan would induce "thousands of the wealthier and more enlightened individuals of the southern states to come and settle among
us." He scarcely understood the frontiersmen when he stated that
"all aristocracies necessarily produce a species of slavery," or when
he pleaded for the thousands of poor and unfortunate beings im-
mersed in deepest ignorance who were treated little, if at all, better
than the horse, the ox, or the mule. He also revealed his real purpose when he objected to the "utter impolicy of so tying up our
hands as to prevent all future legislation upon the subject." [38]

The appeal to aid the slaves by allowing them to be brought to
Illinois was rejected by "Prudence" as the last resort of "an expiring
party, who finding that the naked hook of unconditional slavery,
will not be swallowed by the people, have adroitly enough, gilded
it over with the form of general humanity." He warned them
against "the serious evils arising from admitting among us a host
of free negroes. . . ." [39]

While the convention was at work, "Independence" warned "that
if a constitution should be formed so far 'transcending the authority prescribed,' as to even tolerate slavery, of any kind in the state,
that it would be rejected by Congress upon the same principle, and
for the same reason, that it was prohibited by the Congress in 1787,
in the ordinance for the government of the territory northwest of
the river Ohio." [40]

This line was also taken by a small group which met in St. Clair
County and warned that strong exertions would be made in the
convention to sanction slavery. They urged the friends of freedom
to unite in opposing it by the election of a delegate to Congress
and in preparing remonstrances to Congress against it. [41]

These later appeals which were directed to the convention may have indicated that the extreme antislavery group had been defeated in the elections. They may, however, have indicated only the intensity of the feelings which the contest excited. The elections were held on July 6, 7, and 8, but little is known about the defeated candidates or about the campaign that they may have waged.[42]

The previous records of the delegates elected to the constitutional convention give some idea of the population of Illinois in 1818 and of the men who framed its constitution. Six of the thirty-three delegates seem to have been born north of the Mason and Dixon Line. One of these was a native of Massachusetts, another of New York, three of Pennsylvania, and one was probably from New Jersey. The New Englander had moved to Vermont and then to Kentucky before coming to Illinois.[43] The New Yorker had come by way of Tennessee,[44] while one of the Pennsylvanians had probably lived in Virginia and Kentucky.[45] Two of the men from the Quaker State seem to have come directly to Illinois.[46] Some of the writers during the preconvention campaign indicated that a large migration from the North had begun, but, if true, it came too late to affect the membership of the convention.[47] Northerners were, however, relatively more important in Illinois than in the other states except Ohio.

Natives of Virginia who were members of the convention were as numerous as the delegates who were born in the Middle Atlantic states. One of the five was born in the Piedmont [48] and two in the Valley of Virginia in what is now West Virginia.[49] Two members of the convention were born in the Piedmont of Maryland, in Frederick County. One had moved to the up country of South Carolina before making his way to Illinois; [50] the other had come to Indiana and then Illinois.[51] Only one delegate originated in the Carolinas [52] and possibly one in Georgia. Two natives of Ireland seem to have resided temporarily in the Carolinas, one in Charleston and one in North Carolina and Tennessee.[53] Two men from Tennessee had seats in the convention, but the record is not clear that they were born in that state.[54] Five former Kentuckians were also elected, but only one was known to have been a native of the state.[55] Two of the delegates were born in the Illinois Country of parents from Maryland and Virginia, who seem to have lived in the Appalachian Valley.[56] Finally, eight members of the convention left insufficient records to enable one to determine their place of origin.[57]

The evidence does not indicate clearly that any member of the convention came from a planter family of the Tidewater, although it has been claimed that Jesse B. Thomas was a descendant of Lord Baltimore and that Isham Harrison was related to the Harrisons of Virginia.[58] The planter element in the population was certainly less prominent than in Kentucky and Tennessee and even in Ohio. Perhaps it was unwilling to move so far into a territory where no government land could be purchased before 1814 and where slavery was inadequately protected.

The records that have been preserved as well as the lack of information point to the frontier character of the delegates. Like the people who elected them, they were frontiersmen of the Ohio Valley migration and were a part of the expansion of the Old West. Only four are known to have come directly from the East to Illinois, while twenty of those whose routes of immigration can be traced lived for a while in other parts of the Ohio Valley before settling in Illinois.

The convention, which assembled on August 3, 1818, chose Jesse B. Thomas of the anti-Edwards group to be president. He appointed the lesser committees so as to give the impression that factional politics were not involved, but the three most important committees were safely placed in the hands of the anti-Edwards faction. They were the committees to report on the sufficiency of the census, to prepare a first draft of the constitution, and to make the final revision. Elias K. Kane, a member of the Antis, was chairman of one of these, a member of the other two, chairman of two less important committees, and easily the busiest man in the convention. The secretary of the convention, William C. Greenup, was also not a supporter of Governor Edwards.[59] It thus appears that the partisan alignment of territorial days was carried into the framing of the constitution and that the Edwards group failed to control the movement which it had started.[60]

The partisan alignment is very difficult to reconstruct because of efforts at nonpartisan co-operation, because the slavery issue cut across the alignment, and because of the scarcity of informative records. It is possible, however, to distinguish two groups of almost equal strength, each of whose members voted fairly consistently together. In the smaller of these were several of the leaders of the

Edwards faction, the members of which had received during the territorial period an average of four appointments each from the governor.[61] The persons interested in the salines were prominent among them. In the larger anti-Edwards group the members had each been appointed to office on an average of two and two-thirds times,[62] and among them were anti-Edwards leaders. There was also a third group, the members of which voted too independently to be classified with the above factions.[63]

On the third day of the convention, Kane reported that the population of the territory exceeded the required 40,000 by 258. Prickett, an Edwards supporter, moved that it was expedient to form a state government. Kane failed in an attempt to postpone consideration of the question, and the convention decided to proceed with the constitution.[64]

An important decision concerning the prohibition of slavery was made during the second reading of the constitution. The original draft, which followed the Ohio constitution, stated that "There shall be neither slavery nor involuntary servitude in this state . . . ; nor shall any male person, arrived at the age of 21 years, nor female person arrived at the age of 18 years, be held to serve any person as servant under pretence of indenture or otherwise, unless such person shall enter into such indenture while in a state of perfect freedom . . . ." In this form, the constitution prohibited slavery and indentured servitude.[65] It was changed, however, to read: "Neither slavery nor involuntary servitude shall hereafter be introduced into this state . . . ; nor shall any male person arrived at the age of twenty-one years nor female person arrived at the age of eighteen years, be held to serve any person as a servant under any indenture hereafter made, unless such person shall enter into such indenture while in a state of perfect freedom. . . ." This change protected the owners of slaves and indentured servants already in the territory and made the prohibition apply only in the future. It caused the first recorded vote in the convention. It was supported by nine of the Edwards faction, five of the anti-Edwards group, and three of the independents and was opposed by four, eight, and two of these groups, respectively.[66] The Edwards group of politicians five years later vigorously opposed a convention to legalize slavery, but at this time they occupied a middle position. This attitude of 1818 may have been caused by the manner in which the issue was raised in the territorial assembly and by the influence of

Leonard White, who was United States agent at the salines and a member of the Edwards group. Actually there were more holders of servants or slaves among their rivals than among their own adherents in the convention.

When the constitution was being read the third time, White moved to substitute a new section to protect indenture contracts. It required specific performance of such contracts made without fraud and stipulated that the descendants of such servants should be freed at the age of twenty-five. This issue led to the second recorded vote. All but one of the Edwards men voted favorably and all but three of their rivals voted unfavorably. It was passed by a close vote. The next day a small number of the anti-Edwards men tried to secure a reconsideration of the vote which exempted the saltworks from the prohibition of slavery and servitude, but it was defeated by a large vote in which the Edwards delegates were almost unanimously in the opposition. Since there were no other votes concerning slavery, it should be clear that there was no issue made on the legalization of slavery, other than the protection of existing slavery and indentured servitude.[67]

The constitution which the convention put together was neither an original document nor did it contain unique and unusual provisions. The various articles and even sections were patterned after or copied from the constitutions of the other Ohio Valley states and, like them, may be traced back to the constitutional law of Pennsylvania both in broad outline and in many details. Except for the description of the state boundaries, the preamble was almost identical with the preamble of Ohio's constitution. Jefferson's statement of the doctrine of the separation of powers which he embodied in a proposed constitution for Virginia was copied by Kentucky and the latter was then copied in Article I of the Illinois constitution. The close relationship of the constitutions of the Ohio Valley states becomes quite clear when the origin of the second article is sought. Illinois seems to have followed in general the labors of the Ohio convention, although some sections showed greater resemblance to corresponding sections adopted by Indiana, Kentucky, Tennessee, and Pennsylvania. Since two thirds of the sections copied from the Ohio document had in turn been copied from the Tennessee constitution, the Illinois article which provided for the legislature was more closely modeled on Tennessee than any other constitution except that of Ohio.

The first twelve sections of Article III, which established the executive department, were drawn from the similar article of Ohio's constitution, but more than half of them resembled sections of the constitutional law of Tennessee as much as Ohio. The remaining ten sections were quite similar to Kentucky's constitution of 1799, except that one was copied from New York's and another from Ohio's constitution. Since Indiana had also copied this part of her constitution from Kentucky, at least three of the Illinois sections were almost identical with similar sections of Indiana's constitution. In terms of the structure of government, Illinois borrowed her legislature, governor, and secretary of state from Ohio, her lieutenant-governor and treasurer from Kentucky, and her council of revision from New York.

If any part of the labor of the delegates was original, it was the fourth article, which provided a judiciary for the new state. One of the most persistently unsatisfactory features of territorial government from the beginning of trans-Appalachian expansion had been the courts, and the lawyers and politicians felt more keenly the need of changing the territorial system.

The provisions for the militia (Article V) were patterned after corresponding provisions for the militia of Indiana, three of the sections very closely, two in an abbreviated form, and a sixth showed much resemblance to the constitution of Tennessee.

The original draft, which prohibited slavery and indentured servitude, and the votes on the question in the convention would seem to justify the classification of the anti-Edwards faction as an antislavery group although some of its members were proslavery. This portion of the draft was changed, as has been noticed, so that it applied only as a prohibition of future introduction of slavery and servitude. Written into the article were an exemption of the saltworks to last until 1825 and a provision requiring observance of existing indenture contracts. Unlike Ohio and Indiana, the Illinois convention did not adopt a provision prohibiting the amendment of the constitution to legalize slavery. These provisions in the constitutional law of Ohio and Indiana seemed to be futile and impotent gestures indicating a policy rather than an unalterable law, but the omission of such a provision from the Illinois document may have revealed the intentions of the proslavery group.

The method of amendment seems to have been copied from Ohio, although the procedure which was adopted was common to both Ohio and Tennessee. The bill of rights in the eighth article also illustrates the close relationship of the Ohio Valley states. Ten of the twenty-three sections were almost identical with similar provisions of Pennsylvania's bill of rights, while seven were like Ohio's, six like Kentucky's, a similar number like Indiana's, and eight like Tennessee's. Actually half of the sections were included almost exactly in any one of these constitutions, and few were original either in statement or idea.

The following table gives a comparison of the constitution of Illinois with other constitutions.[68]

Article	Subject Matter	No. of Sections	No. of Sections like				Original	Common to many	No. of Sections like Other Constitutions	
			Ohio	Ind.	Ky.	Tenn.				
	Preamble	1	1							
I.	Separation of powers	2			2					
II.	Legislature	32	16	3	1	1	1	6	2	Ohio, Ind.
									1	Ohio, Del.
									1	Ohio, Pa.
III.	Executive	22	5		6½	2	1½	4	1	Ind., Ky.
									1	N. Y.
									1	Pa.
IV.	Judiciary	8	1				4		2	Pa.
									1	U. S.
V.	Militia	6		3			3			
VI.	Slavery	3	1				2			
VII.	Amendment	1							1	Ohio, Tenn.
VIII.	Bill of rights	23	5			3½	3½	3	3	Pa.
									3	Pa., Ky.
									1	Ohio, Ind.
									1	Vt.
	Total	98	29	6	9½	6½	15	13	19	

The government which this constitution provided was neither perfect nor completely democratic, but it did embody rather well the ideas of the people of the West at the end of the second decade of the nineteenth century. The legislature and the governor, with some lesser officials, were elected by the adult white males. As the more immediate representatives of the people, the members of the general assembly formed the dominant branch of the government. Representation was based upon numbers and was to be revised after a census to be taken every five years. Voting was extended to all adult male whites after six months' residence, whether they were citizens or not.

The controlling element in the convention was evidently unwilling to go as far as Indiana had in creating a strong and efficient executive. The governor was elected for a four-year term, but was denied the power of veto, and the power of appointment was divided unsatisfactorily with the legislature. The veto, probably in imitation of the New York constitution and because of the influence of delegate Kane who came from that state, was given to a council of revision composed of the supreme court justices and the governor. It was to be an unsuccessful experiment. The judiciary was to be composed of a supreme court and such inferior courts as the legislature should establish. The judges were to be chosen by the legislature and to serve during good behavior after 1824. Probably the contest between the territorial assembly and the general court led to this method of election, while the postponement of judicial security to 1824 may have been due to the expected immigration of additional able lawyers. The supreme justices were to serve as circuit judges at least until 1824. Judges were subject to removal for reasonable cause by a two thirds vote of the legislature. When two thirds of the legislators and a majority of the electors of the representatives should agree, a constitutional convention was to be called by the general assembly.

Although the history of Illinois Territory and the formation of its first state constitution was almost completely devoid of the spectacular and the dramatic, there was significance in its quiet development. The men of the Western Waters had been expressing their ideals in petitions and memorials about government and society since before the American Revolution. They had struggled to secure their freedom from the East, to have their own government, to be free from competition with an intrenched favored class, to determine the character of their government, and to be consulted about the laws which ruled them and the taxes they were required to pay. They wanted to obtain land to give them security, respectability, and a livelihood. A large number of them were interested in living in a democratic society that was not dominated by a so-called superior class at the top and unsoundly based upon an enslaved laboring class at the bottom. Little by little they had gained their points. Kentucky and Tennessee were freed from Virginia and North Carolina, state claims to western lands were surrendered to the national government, laws were adopted providing the means by which an increasing number of settlers were able to acquire their own farms, and a scheme of government was evolved which advanced the pioneers to local self-government in states which were admitted into the federal union on a parity with the older states.

Frontiersmen made considerable progress in securing democratic government in Kentucky and Tennessee, but the inequitable land system and the advance of slavery limited their achievements. North of the Ohio, democratic society as well as democratic government was established. In the founding of the state of Ohio, the democratic forces not only defeated the conservative elements but demonstrated the unsuitableness of the Federalist philosophy on the frontier. In the founding of Indiana, the frontiersmen learned how to overcome the arbitrary authority with which the territorial governor was clothed by the Northwest Ordinance. The constitution of Indiana demonstrated the ability of the pioneers to frame a suitable and democratic government. In both states the wisdom of the people in rejecting the institution of slavery has been recognized. It was fairly clear when Illinois became a separate territory that the territorial governor should be careful how he used the almost absolute authority with which he was vested, that the people of the territory could and should be permitted to determine their own affairs when they passed to the semirepresentative stage, that they should be permitted to become a state in the Union with a constitution written by their representatives whenever the population was large enough to support such a government, and that they should be permitted to reject slavery and the influence which it would exert upon the character of the society which they were forming. The violence of the early period disappeared when territorial government was established in 1809 for Illinois, the right to vote without being a landowner was extended to the new territory without a struggle, and statehood came naturally as though the people were following a marked trail. Actually the colonial system of the United States was now embodied in the Northwest Ordinance, in the laws which made it more democratic by providing for the popular election of the legislative councilors and the delegate to Congress and extending the right to vote to taxpayers, and in the precedents growing out of the experiences of St. Clair, Sargent, and Harrison. The trail had been blazed, and Illinois followed it without difficulty as she marched to self-government in the years from 1809 to 1818, a fact which appears very clearly in a comparison of the experience of Illinois with that of Kentucky in the period from 1784 to 1792.

14

The Democracy of the Valley

THE TRAILS by which the people of the Ohio Valley had reached their destination led back to Ireland, Scotland, Wales, and England; to France, the Low Countries, and the Germanies; to New England, the Middle Colonies, the Southern coastal plain, and especially to the Old West south of New York. The heritage of the people was as varied as their origins; they remembered the injustice that was Ireland as well as the stories of want and cruelty in Germany during and after the Thirty Years' War. Their European ancestors had come to America, just as the frontiersmen had crossed the mountains, for a variety of reasons. And both carried visions and ideals of what ought to be. The Old World heritage of the Ohio Valley was vital, but it included both positive and negative influences. In social and religious matters, it was often held fast as something precious. In the monarchical levels of politics and government, it was considered something that ought to be rejected. But the adoption of the English common law, county government, and the form of the English legislative system indicates that only a new spirit of democracy was needed to make many of the institutions acceptable to the Valley.

Many of these people had been born before the American Revolution and had lived through its campaigns and battles. They had listened to the glorious words of the Declaration of Independence about all men being equal and endowed by their Creator with unalienable rights, among which was liberty. Government, it said, received its just powers from the consent of the governed. Its purpose was to protect the rights of the people; and, whenever it destroyed those rights it was supposed to protect, the people were justified in changing or abolishing it and in forming a new government to secure their safety and happiness. And as they sought new homes on the frontier, moving southwest along the back country of the Southern states, they had occasion to remember and to think about these words. The Declaration, like Europe, was a part of the patrimony of the Ohio Valley.

A third heritage of the Valley was the contest between the aristocracy of the seacoast and the yeomanry of the back country and the poor of the towns. When the trans-Allegheny movement began, the frontier stretched along the Appalachian Valley and the Piedmont. The planter class was engaged in its struggle to perpetuate the colonial aristocracy, while the frontiersmen sought a more democratic system which would include white manhood suffrage, the removal of property qualifications for office holding, the apportionment of representation in the state legislatures according to numbers, and the disestablishment of the Anglican church. They sought to remove the discriminations which handicapped their democratic society. They expected to receive more adequate assistance in their warfare with the Indians, a more serviceable judicial system, and equal treatment in such matters as taxes and internal improvements. Some of them hoped for better educational opportunities for their children and some opposed slavery. The pressure for democratic reforms came largely from the counties of the Piedmont and the Valley, where frontier conditions still prevailed.

The planters, however, preferred to pattern their social order after that of the English country gentlemen. They were committed to the plantation system with its large estate, staple crops, and slave labor. They enjoyed the society of gentlemen and ladies and believed that government was the proper function of the well-born. They were so firmly intrenched behind property qualifications, restrictions on the right to vote, and unequal representation that they were able to prevent or delay the democratization of state governments below the Mason and Dixon Line until the Ohio Valley had established the foundations of its civilization. The Tidewater, in which the planters were most numerous, was the older settled area, the region in which European ideas were more strongly held, and the source of aristocratic influence both in politics and culture even though individual planters sometimes held democratic views.

This struggle in the older states formed the background for the later contests in the Ohio Valley. The frontiersmen experienced discriminations at the hands of the planters, learned what aristocracy and slavery meant to the small farmer and the free laborer, and under these influences formed their prejudicies, opinions, and ideals about the political and social order. Thus were the advantages of democracy kept alive in the minds of the people who might have forgotten or become disinterested if the planters had been more attentive to the needs of their poorer brothers. Even as late as the middle of the nineteenth century, in Illinois and Indiana the attitudes developed by the conflict between the frontier way of life and the plantation régime were expressed in the debates of the constitutional conventions when there was little likelihood that slavery could cross the Ohio.

Still another heritage of the trans-Appalachian frontier was the experience of the passage through the mountains. It was a long, hard journey which some families made by installments or in some instances took two or three generations to complete. But it brought the pioneer out of the older settlements into the wilderness where the individual was not only freer to act as he pleased but where his very existence depended upon his own wisdom and skill. The development of individualism was one of the results of this experience. It was also a journey that sifted the people. Persons who were satisfied and whose wealth seemed to give them almost all they could wish were more likely to remain behind. Men who were dissatisfied because of their poverty, whose sense of justice had been deeply injured, those who were driven by religious zeal, and those who were ambitious to take advantage of the many fluid conditions of the frontier were the more likely to make the crossing.

The pioneers were no more than beyond the effective jurisdiction of the Atlantic states than they began to insist that settlers in vacant lands had the right to establish their own government. Contemporaneously with the early efforts of the frontiersmen of the Old West to democratize the governments of the South Atlantic states, other frontiersmen in the upper Tennessee Valley, the Monongahela Valley, the Bluegrass Basin of Kentucky, and the Nashville Basin of Tennessee undertook to set up their own governments. They based their actions upon the sovereignty of the people, insisted upon self-government, and acted only with the consent of the people.

Where governmental services were lacking and organization was needed to settle disputes, establish order, aid defense, and keep records of marriages, inheritance, and property, the task was generally not difficult and the resulting government was simple and democratic. Such instances include Watagua and the Cumberland community.

Where conditions were more complicated and not subject to such an easy solution, various developments resulted. The first problem was to secure freedom from older governments. This was the rock upon which many of the dreams were dashed to pieces. Until the states surrendered their western claims, Congress was not able to assist in this matter. The states were unwilling to see new colonies founded in their western parts. Since the states which claimed most of the Ohio Valley were in the hands of the planter aristocracy which refused to democratize their own governments, the achievement of separation was always a step toward greater democracy.

The earlier efforts to acquire independence and self-determination, as in Franklin, Westsylvania, and Kentucky, were unsuccessful. Their statements of explanation, the petitions and resolutions from these and other areas, give ample evidence of their grievances, of the inadequacy of existing policies and agencies, and of the widespread demand for self-government and a more sympathetic treatment of western problems.

In addition to the heritage of European countries, the American Revolutionary political philosophy, the contest between the planters and the men of the back country, the passage through the mountains, and the earlier unsuccessful efforts to found their own governments, there was the example of the state of Pennsylvania. The frontiersmen of the Quaker colony and the laborers of Philadelphia overthrew the established aristocracy and formed a system of committees and a radical democratic constitution. The committees, which directed their revolutionary activity, as well as the constitution, influenced the men who were expanding the Old West beyond the mountains. The influence was probably greater because so many of the families which moved along the Valley of Virginia or crossed the mountains on their way to the Ohio Valley had lived for a time in Pennsylvania. It was only natural that they should bring with them the ideas about government which they had learned there.

The first successful effort to secure self-government in the Ohio Valley was the statehood movement in Kentucky. The first and most difficult task was that of securing independence from Virginia. The eight years which followed the American Revolution were spent in gaining this point, and if the earliest and premature efforts to organize an independent government are included the period is twice as long. Independence from Virginia was in itself an important achievement, for it meant escape from a subordinate colonial status and freedom from a distant aristocracy, while at the same time it was a defeat for the most conservative group in Kentucky.

An unusual degree of radicalism was revealed in the discussions which accompanied these efforts to secure self-government. The hardships of the war years, the continuation of Indian warfare, the failure of Virginia to adopt equitable land laws and adequate systems of defense and judicature increased their dissatisfaction and determination. A scheme of government was proposed that resembled the committee system and the constitution of Pennsylvania. Some of the radicals favored the gradual abolition of slavery. The organization of the radicals was fairly effective, and its defeat was probably not achieved in the election of delegates to the constitutional convention, but only by the careful co-operation of the conservatives and moderates in the convention. What the outcome might have been without the great ability of George Nicholas is difficult to imagine.

The two most prominent issues between the delegates to the Kentucky constitutional convention concerned the proposals to eliminate slavery and to assign original jurisdiction to the supreme court in cases involving land titles. That these were the chief issues was little less than remarkable, for the preservation of slavery and large estates was essential to the maintenance of the plantation system.

The constitution which the Kentuckians adopted was democratic but moderately so. It resembled very much the new government which Pennsylvania prepared in 1790. The radical features of the first constitution of the Quaker State had been eliminated; and the new scheme, which resembled the new federal constitution, possessed greater efficiency without surrending the democracy of the first. Kentucky, therefore, secured a democratic constitutional law by which the will of the people could be delayed rather than defeated. The conservative features included a thorough system of checks and balances, a provision denying to the legislature the power to emancipate slaves without the consent and remuneration of the owners, and the recently mentioned provision entrusting adjudication of land titles to the supreme court. Politically the frontiersmen gained the chief points that were at issue east of the mountains, and the constitution was more democratic than those of the South Atlantic states.

A political decision of this type was, however, not sufficient to check the growth of the plantation system. Virginia had retained control of Kentucky until slavery was established, until her land laws had created an economic basis for an aristocratic order of society, and until a sufficient number of her planter sons had migrated to protect slavery and to develop the plantation system. Negroes, mostly enslaved, constituted 17 per cent of the population in 1790. By 1830 they had increased to 25 per cent.[1] There is little reason to suppose they were distributed any more equally than was the land. These figures indicate roughly the growing importance of the plantation system in Kentucky.

While planters and Negroes continued to increase, a large number of the poorer early settlers moved across the Ohio to the Northwestern frontier in the area that became Ohio, Indiana, and Illinois, where they hoped to obtain land and to escape competition with slave labor and the plantation system. The frontier period in Kentucky came to an end and planter civilization became dominant. The pioneers had given Kentucky a notable history in the early period, had aided in securing independence from Virginia, and had helped in adopting a democratic government. Although Kentucky followed in the footsteps of the Old Dominion, the frontier influence did not die and Kentucky did not become a new Virginia.

The radical period in Tennessee's progress came in the years when the state of Franklin was in existence and when little had been done to extend political control or military assistance beyond the mountains. After the nation took charge, in 1790, and an effective government was given to the Tennesseans—one that helped to defeat the Indians and that was primarily concerned with the settlers' needs—the people showed relatively little discontent or restlessness. When the opportunity came, they formed a state without much quarreling over its details. As in Kentucky, slavery was continued and protected. In Tennessee property qualifications were retained for office holding, an undemocratic county court system was adopted, and a system of taxation which gave advantage to the wealthy was embedded in the constitution. These revealed the con-

servative spirit of the planter group which looked across the mountains to the Old North State and copied parts of its constitution.
On the other hand, suffrage for free men, representation apportioned according to the number of taxpayers, and popular election
of officials indicated the democratic tendencies of the frontiersmen,
many of whom had moved through the Valley of Virginia and many
of whom looked back to Pennsylvania for liberal provisions for the
new constitution of Tennessee.

As the state developed after 1796, frontier conditions tended to
disappear. The proportion of Negroes, which indicates the expansion of the planter economy, increased from 11 per cent in 1800 to
25 per cent in 1850.[2] Emigration from the state also began, drain-
ing off some of the poorer and more independent frontiersmen.
Tennessee became a part of the Old South, but the assimilation of
the Valley of East Tennessee was not complete in 1860. The state
continues to glory in the history of its pioneer period and its gift
to the nation of three of its sons, Andrew Jackson, Samuel Houston,
and Andrew Johnson, whose careers indicated that frontier ideals
had not been entirely destroyed by the advance of the plantation.

North of the Ohio River the struggle of the frontiersmen for self-
government was continued under different conditions. The imperialistic tendencies of the states were eliminated when the land
claims were surrendered to the national government. Republican
states were to be formed, which were to have equal powers with the
original commonwealths. Land was sold on equal terms to all and
not in great quantities to a few. The Northwest Ordinance established the rules by which the settlers were to be governed and by
which they would pass from a nonrepresentative to a semirepresentative government and finally acquire complete local self-government as a member state in a nation of equal states. While in
a territorial status slavery was prohibited, property of an intestate
was equally distributed, and civil rights were guaranteed. Although
the government under St. Clair and Sargent was often arbitrary,
the progress toward democracy was only delayed. The constitution
of Ohio, which was definitely democratic, prohibited slavery and
indentured servitude.

Before the state of Ohio came into existence, the frontiersmen of
Indiana Territory began the struggle that was to democratize terri-
torial government. Harrison and his friends, who were called the
Virginia Aristocrats, endeavored to preserve their control of gov-

ernment and maintain an even balance between divergent interests. Their opponents, the popular party, opposed their conduct of government, resisted the admission of slavery and indentured servitude, and sought to make the government more democratic. With the aid of Congress, substantial changes were made in the government established by the Northwest Ordinance. The legislative council and the delegate to Congress were made elective and were therefore the agents of the people and not of the governor. The franchise was extended to taxpayers. The territorial assembly proceeded thereafter to pass a democratic election law, to locate the capital near the center of the territory, and to repeal the indenture act by which the official group tried to circumvent the prohibition of slavery. This substantial popular victory came in the territorial period and was the result of the activity of democratic frontiersmen.

The statehood movement in Indiana was the continuation and the culmination of the struggle to make the territorial government subject to popular control. The popular party was not satisfied until it secured complete local self-government and participation in the councils of the nation. The opposition was powerless to prevent statehood, but expressed dissatisfaction and doubt of the ability of the frontier people to form a satisfactory constitution. The convention, however, proceeded quite successfully to frame and adopt a constitution under which the state lived for thirty-five years. It was closely patterned on the older Ohio Valley constitutions, particularly those of Ohio and Kentucky, and embodied the principles for which frontiersmen had been struggling since 1776.

The frontiersmen of Illinois, like the men of the older frontiers, passed through a colonial period and participated in a struggle for democratic government. Their years in a subordinate status were regulated by the Northwest Ordinance as in Indiana and Ohio, but Illinois profited by the democratization of the territorial government of Indiana and after three years quietly gained the more democratic features which the Hoosier pioneers had secured only after years of struggle. Statehood came naturally and peacefully with the blessing of the territorial administration. Although the aristocratic element did not seek to legalize slavery, it was careful not to destroy existing slavery but to keep the door open for a future amendment after statehood was achieved. The democratic forces, however, were strong enough to defeat decisively the effort to amend the constitution in 1823–1824.

This survey of the development of democratic government in the Ohio Valley raises a question about the influence of the frontier and the character of its democracy. Was it the product of European democracy or was it the result of the experience of the American people on the frontier? The question is in reality a part of a larger and more fundamental interrogation about the United States. Is the United States merely a continuation and an expansion of western Europe and is it likely to develop the weaknesses already evident in European nations, or is there a difference about its record that makes its history peculiar to itself and therefore gives hope that the United States may continue to follow a path of its own and escape some of the ills suffered by European peoples?

In the historical sphere the question is in reality one which Frederick Jackson Turner endeavored to answer in his articles and books on the frontier. As a young man he revolted against the attention which historians were then giving to European influences, in this case Germanic origins, and insisted that American environment which produced frontier experiences gave to the United States a unique history. This question of historiography is fundamentally today's question about the United States. Unfortunately, few critics appeared during Turner's life when he could have answered their objections.

The Turner interpretation with its emphasis on American and frontier influences needs to be tested by the history of a definite place and time. For this purpose the story of the Ohio Valley, which has been here narrated, is well suited. It was an early part of our national history when the European heritage was still strong along the Atlantic coast, and the Ohio Valley included two Southern states where the plantation offered a competing way of life. The significance of the frontier is more clearly revealed when contrasted with the European influence in the East and the plantation system of the South.

Turner suggested that American history before 1890 was to a large degree the story of the colonization of the West. American development was explained by the existence of an area of free land, its continuous recession, and the advance of settlement westward. "Our early history is the study of European germs developing in an American environment," and "American social development has

been continually beginning over again on the frontier." The source
of its uniqueness was the fluid condition along the receding frontier where institutions were adapted to new circumstances.[3]

In a few sentences Turner described the process. "The wilderness masters the colonist. It finds him a European in dress, indus-
tries, tools, modes of travel, and thought. . . . It strips off the gar-
ments of civilization and arrays him in the hunting shirt and the
moccasin. It puts him in the log cabin of the Cherokee and the
Iroquois and runs an Indian palisade around him. Before long he
has gone to planting Indian corn and plowing with a sharp stick;
he shouts the war cry and takes the scalp in orthodox Indian
fashion. In short, at the frontier the environment is at first too
strong for the man. He must accept the conditions which it fur-
nishes, or perish, and so he fits himself into the Indian clearings
and follows the Indian trails. Little by little he transforms the
wilderness, but the outcome is not the old Europe, not simply the
development of Germanic germs. . . ."[4]

Four divisions of frontier development have been described in
the present study: first, the struggle of the frontiersmen east of the
mountains to make the early Southern states more democratic;
second, the early expansion of the frontier into and beyond the
Appalachian Valley, and the efforts of the settlers to free themselves from Eastern control; third, the frontier of the southern half
of the Ohio Valley, where two new states were formed after that
area had freed itself from the Atlantic states; and fourth, the North-
western frontier, where national policies rather than state policies
were dominant.

In his article, "The Old West," Turner considered at some
length the first of these frontiers in the years preceding the Revolution. He noted a westward movement of settlers from the Tidewater, the development of large estates, and the extension of the
older aristocratic social order to the Piedmont and the Valley.
From the north poured through the Valley an extensive migration
of Germans, Scotch-Irish, and other non-English settlers, who created a new continuous social and economic order which cut across
artificial colonial boundaries and built a new South in contrast
with the Tidewater. It was democratic, self-sufficient, primitive, and
individualistic. It was characterized by the yeoman farmer, free
labor, non-English settlers, and a multiplicity of Protestant sects.
Recruits from the north strengthened the democratic forces and

delayed the assimilation of the backwoods by the Tidewater so
ciety. Between the frontier and the coast a contest developed over
the control of the state governments and their policies. Involved
were the questions of currency, taxes, internal improvements,
slavery, representation, franchise restrictions, and defense. The new
state governments were more democratic because of this pressure,
and the ideals of the Old West influenced the trans-Allegheny
West.[5]

Writings on the South Atlantic states covering this period are in
substantial agreement with Turner's views. Among the earlier
writers, whose work was available when he published "The Old
West" in 1908, were three of his own students, Charles H. Ambler,
Orin G. Libby, and William A. Schaper.[6] Among more recent historians, the work of Fletcher M. Green, Thomas P. Abernethy, and
Thomas J. Wertenbaker may be noted.

Green's *Constitutional Development in the South Atlantic States*
is in general harmony with the works just mentioned. Thomas P.
Abernethy in his little volume, *Three Virginia Frontiers*, emphasized the expansion of the plantation social order into the Old
West. "The aristocratic institutions which prevailed in tidewater
were transferred to the piedmont virtually without change. . . .
On the other hand, the Valley and the Southwest were dissimilar
both in population and in economic position. The greater democracy of the last-named areas was not due solely to the fact that yeomen farmers predominated, for this element was more numerous
than were large landowners in all sections of Virginia. It was due
partly to the lack of aristocratic tradition, and of the aristocrats. . . .
Law and the necessity for leadership were stronger than democracy
even on the frontier. . . . The piedmont and Valley regions thus
furnish another illustration of the fact that frontier conditions do
not necessarily produce democratic institutions, even when the
lands are easily accessible to independent small farmers."[7]

In contrast to Abernethy's point of view is the treatment of *The
Old South* by Thomas J. Wertenbaker. "In the first stages of settlement the influence of the frontier was profound." Since this statement refers to the region along the Atlantic coast, it may indicate
that Wertenbaker regarded the frontier influence in this region as
even more significant than did Turner, for the latter placed his
chief emphasis on the area west of the Appalachians. "The records
of one frontier county after another tell the same story. . . . So-

ciety is still primitive, still democratic. . . ." His chapter, "Tucka-
hoe and Cohee," which treats the occupation of the Appalachian
Valley, is certainly not in disagreement with Turner's writings.[8]

From these various works one might conclude that if Turner's
treatment of the frontier of the Old West requires serious modification or rejection, the proof is yet to be submitted. Abernethy's
suggestions that the plantation was not modified by the frontier
and that the need for leadership sometimes defeated the democratic
tendencies of the frontier serve to limit and clarify the interpretation rather than refute it.

The second of the frontiers was described by Turner in "Western
State-making in the Revolutionary Era." "Men who had lived under developed institutions were transplanted into the wilderness,
with the opportunity and the necessity of adapting their institutions to their environment, or of creating new ones capable of meeting the changed conditions." The pioneers preferred to establish
government by social compact rather than to live under proprietary
government or the control of large companies like the Vandalia
Company. The presence of free lands broke down social distinctions, created economic equality, and promoted political equality,
democracy, and individualism. There were four areas in the West
where new governments were desired: the upper Tennessee Valley;
the land between the Youghiogheny, Kanawha, and the Ohio; the
combined Bluegrass basins of Kentucky and the Cumberland; and
finally the Old Northwest. He briefly described the Watauga and
Cumberland compacts, the proprietary experiment of Transylvania,
the petitions of the Westsylvania settlers, the state of Franklin, and
the early efforts of the Kentuckians to secure freedom from Virginia. Through these petitions and schemes of government ran
certain ideas, such as "The people in an unoccupied land have
the right to determine their own political institutions." Real grievances stimulated the efforts to secure independence from the East.
Congress was expected, even urged, to assert control over the West
and to permit the people to organize their own states within the
nation.[9]

Turner recognized the activities of speculators who were obtaining vast estates in the wilderness and establishing the foundations
for a later aristocracy. Professor Abernethy has pursued this subject much further than Turner. He has suggested that many of the
separatist movements were the work of the speculators rather than

of the democratic frontiersmen, that the grievances were not very serious, that the frontier offered the speculators so much opportunity that the result was sometimes the encouragement of aristocracy rather than democracy.[10]

Undoubtedly the initiative came from the speculators in a number of instances, but the hope of remedying frontier grievances rather than the initiative of the speculators gave life to the movements. In all probability historians have or will come to believe that the work of Abernethy necessitates a departure from the Turner point of view. Turner paid too little attention to the speculators and to the planter civilization of the South Atlantic states, which was endeavoring to dominate expansion into the lands beyond the Blue Ridge. The power of the older states was too great for the frontier associations and governments and the frontiersmen were defeated. The lack of victory does not disprove the democratic influence of the frontier, but merely makes it evident that it could not win under all circumstances. It must not be forgotten that frontier ideals were enunciated, that they were brought to the attention of Congress, and that they were embodied for a time in temporary governments.

In words that obviously referred to the early occupation of the southern half of the Ohio Valley, Turner wrote: "The 'men of the Western Waters' broke with the old order of things, . . . hotly challenged the right of the East to rule them, demanded their own States, and would not be refused, spoke with contempt of the old social order of ranks and classes in the lands between the Alleghanies and the Atlantic, and proclaimed the ideal of democracy for the vast country which they had entered." [11]

Referring to the Ohio Valley, he declared that it was an extension of the Upland South and that it gave new life to the ideals which were lost in the former region by its assimilation to the Tidewater. As slavery and the plantation system spread, the children of the Old West passed through the mountains. Their society was "characterized by the small farmer, building his log cabin in the wilderness, raising a small crop and a few animals for family use." They founded the Ohio Valley states which entered the Union with manhood suffrage and strengthened the forces of democracy in the nation.[12]

While Turner was producing his articles on various aspects of frontier history, a younger colleague, Ulrich B. Phillips, was be-

ginning a series of publications on the history of the South. An
evaluation offered by him is particularly significant because of his
knowledge of the South, because he knew Turner and his work,
and because he considered the relationship between the frontier
and the plantation system.

> The frontier performed its mission in one area after another, giving place
> in each to a more complex society which grew out of the frontier regime and
> supplanted it. By this process the whole vast region of the United States,
> within the limits where rainfall is sufficient for tillage, has been reduced to
> occupation in a phenomenally rapid process. The extension of settlement
> being now ended, the system has died for want of room.[13]

Phillips recognized three economic types, the frontier, the farm,
and the plantation. "Where two or all three coexisted in a single
area, the systems usually competed for supremacy; and in the outcome the most efficient for the main purpose at hand would con-
quer. The representatives of the other types would mostly have to
move on." [14]

Professor Avery O. Craven reviewed the "Turner Theories" and
their usefulness in studying Southern history. He is one of Turner's
students and the editor of two of Turner's works which were published posthumously. He found the three economic types which
Phillips described and noted that the first two, the frontier and
the farm, were also to be found in the North. The plantation represented the coming of men of capital, a development which corre-
sponded to the rise of urban industrialism in the North, and in
either area marked the end of the frontier period.[15]

Abernethy views the development of Kentucky and Tennessee in
the same light as he describes the earlier separatist movements. The
chief instigators were the land speculators, the radical movement
in Kentucky was totalitarianism, the frontiersmen were defeated in
the formation of both states, and the democratic influence of the
frontier is open to serious question. He discredits the democratic
political aspirations of the frontiersmen and considers the reforms
which were adopted as mere concessions thrown to the masses by
the speculators who were interested chiefly in getting land.[16]

In a comparison of the interpretations of the various writers on
the early expansion of the frontier into the southern half of the
Ohio Valley, a larger place must be accorded to speculation but
not the place which Abernethy has indicated. Virginia had treated

the members of the Kentucky conventions too well for them to have inaugurated a separatist movement in order to get land. The chief speculators in Tennessee had also secured much land from North Carolina. More study of speculation and speculators is needed before the implications of the subject can be accurately stated.

Furthermore, frontier radicalism cannot be democracy in Franklin and totalitarianism in Kentucky. Abernethy also underestimates the reality of frontier grievances and the victory for self-government in the separation of Kentucky and Tennessee from Virginia and North Carolina. Equal representation and white manhood suffrage were not empty concessions. Historians must recognize the valuable contributions to the history of the Old Southwest which Abernethy has made, but will they prefer his interpretation or that outlined by Turner, Phillips, and Craven?

Turner did not treat in any detail the settlement of the Old Northwest or the evolution of government there. He re-explained the frontier and its influence in "The Problem of the West," but treated national rather than local developments. The West, he wrote,

is a form of society, rather than an area . . . , whose social conditions result from the application of older institutions and ideas to the transforming influence of free land. . . . The cake of custom is broken, and new activities, new lines of growth, new institutions and new ideals are brought into existence. The wilderness disappears, the 'West' proper passes on to a new frontier, and in the former area, a new society has emerged from its contact with the backwoods. . . . Decade after decade, West after West, this rebirth of American society has gone on. . . . The history of our political institutions, our democracy, is not a history of imitation, of simple borrowing; it is a history of the evolution and adaptation of organs in response to changed environment, a history of the origin of new political species. . . . This new democracy . . . came, stark and strong and full of life, from the American forest.[17]

As if to meet a critic who might fail to understand that he wrote not of democracy as a philosophy, but of American or frontier democracy, Turner published his "Contributions of the West to American Democracy." "Political thought in the period of the French Revolution tended to treat democracy as an absolute system applicable to all times and all people, a system that was to be created by the act of the people themselves on philosophical principles. Ever since that era there has been an inclination on the part of writers to emphasize the analytical and theoretical treatment to the neglect of the underlying factors of historical development. . . . The careful student of history must, therefore, seek the explanation of the forms and changes of political institutions in the social and economic forces that determine them." He concluded that "American democracy is fundamentally the outcome of the experiences of the American people in dealing with the West." [18]

This résumé of Turner's interpretation of the advance of the frontier into the Ohio Valley and particularly of the relationship of the frontier and democracy may be closed with a quotation from "The West and American Ideals." This was a commencement address delivered in June, 1914, as the world was about to fly to arms. In it he reviewed conditions in the United States in 1914 and its historical developments, particularly the evolution of its ideals. He asserted: "American democracy was born of no theorist's dream; it was not carried in the *Susan Constant* to Virginia, nor in the *Mayflower* to Plymouth. It came out of the American forest, and it gained new strength each time it touched a new frontier. Not the constitution, but free land and an abundance of natural resources open to a fit people, made the democratic type of society in America. . . ." [19]

It is quite interesting that Turner began his career protesting the overemphasis upon European origins and insisting upon the importance of American influences but lived to be criticized for swinging the balance too far to the American side. His major suggestion was that the frontier, the process of beginning over again in that primitive environment, exerted the dominant forces in American history. Professor Benjamin F. Wright, of Harvard, declared that the greatest shortcoming of Turner's interpretation was its tendency to isolate the growth of American democracy from the general course of Western civilization. No frontier was free from the influence of European ideas, Wright asserted, and the colonists altered remarkably little the principles inherited from Europe. Although he was unwilling to recognize the great influence of the frontier, he was inclined to hold its historian in part responsible for the strength of isolationism in the Middle West.

The suggestion that American democracy was essentially a product of the frontier was also rejected by Professor Wright. He insisted that the men of the Middle West were imitative, not creative, that their action seems to have accelerated the rate of growth of the democratic movement but not to have changed its direction, and that "the 'transforming influence' of the frontier, as it appears in Turner's essays, is largely a myth." He summarized his views by saying that "democracy did not come out of the American forest unless it was first carried there. On some frontiers democracy was not strengthened, rather the reverse." [20]

Another Eastern criticism was written by Professor George W. Pierson, of Yale, who suggested that although the frontier influence may have been genuine, it has been exaggerated and magnified into a legend, and that Turner's views are no longer a safe guide to the student, but are sectional, emotional, and illogical. Pierson felt that some physical aspects of the frontier were inadequately considered but that free land was exaggerated and that the term "frontier" was not exactly defined. He questioned the transforming influence of the frontier, its individualism, and its promotion of democracy.[21]

Several prominent scholars have found little to criticize in Turner's work. Frederic L. Paxson, who succeeded him at Wisconsin, wrote in 1932 that his interpretation when "used as its framer framed it, . . . is as useful a guide as it ever was." He added, "We may perhaps account for the weakness of the straggling attacks upon his hypothesis by the inherent weakness of the case against it." [22] Others who wrote about Turner and who found little that was objectionable in his work include Joseph Schafer, John D. Hicks, Merle Curti, and Carl Becker.[23]

The frontier was not a line or a place, but an area or zone where fluid economic and social conditions prevailed. A small density of population merely marked an area that was in its frontier period, when civilization was being reduced to the essentials by the wilderness and where the process of beginning anew was taking place. Turner may have used the term in different senses and even loosely, but this point ought not to be hard to grasp. Without it the Turner interpretation can have little meaning. Another deficiency in understanding the frontier influence is the lack of attention to the end of the pioneer period. Turner recognized the assimilation of the Piedmont by the civilization of the Tidewater by the time the Ohio Valley was able to take its place. The nature of the frontier period will appear more clearly when this is attempted for various sectional frontiers.

Another misconception that is quite pertinent to this discussion concerns the effect of the frontier upon democracy. The statement, "Democracy did not come out of the American forest unless it was first carried there," betrays a failure to read Turner's words with precision. Turner recognized the existence of theoretical democracy, of different types of democracy in other countries, and of the influence of Revolutionary ideas which he did not attribute to the frontier. He even observed that "the peculiar democracy of the frontier has passed away with the conditions that produced it. . . ." Is it not reasonable to point out that the frontier did not originate democracy, but rather those characteristics which made it Western or American? Of course, someone carried democracy to the frontier and to the forest in the beginning, but as it was carried to frontier after frontier, forest after forest, it was less European and more American. Democracy was carried on the *Susan Constant* and the *Mayflower*, but it was not American democracy. It was the European "germ" which Turner maintained was changed by its experience on the frontier until it ceased to be European and became American. Professor Wertenbaker's statement that American democracy was born in Westminster Hall should be taken in the same manner.[24]

Perhaps this will appear a little clearer if the characteristics which distinguished the frontier or Western type from the European are noted. Turner frequently referred to equality, freedom of opportunity, and faith in the common man. These features, however, must be understood in the light of the frontiersmen's struggle against the aristocracy which controlled the colonial and state governments at the beginning of the Revolution. Frontiersmen thought that all would be well if they could destroy that control and establish a democracy of free men. Bonds of social caste, government favoritism, and hopeless inequality had to be destroyed—and the result would be equality. Freedom for the individual to work out his own destiny without artificial limitations or arbitrary obstacles constituted freedom of opportunity. Faith in the common man included the belief that the plain people were worthy of equality, of freedom, and of a share in government, that they possessed an intrinsic value and dependability which would enable them successfully to undertake the responsibilities imposed by these opportunities.

Finally, the occupation and development of government in the Ohio Valley was a story of conflict, of a struggle between aristo-

cratic forces and democratic forces. Aristocracy was largely represented by planters, slaveowners, and large speculators—men who
were or who aspired to become large landholders, masters of slaves,
and founders of established families. Their ideals did not include
democracy or faith in the common people. Along the Eastern coast
they had insisted upon preserving as much as possible of the colonial aristocracy and had sought to retain the western lands under
their control. In the West they endeavored, with the assistance of
Virginia and North Carolina, to found an economic, social, and
political order like that of the plantation South.

But the frontiersmen, who were generally poor, sought on each
of the four frontiers to establish a democratic government which
would be controlled by the common people in whom they had
confidence. They failed in the South Atlantic states and in their
earliest efforts beyond the Blue Ridge Mountains, but they were
partially successful in the founding of Kentucky and Tennessee.
North of the Ohio River, where they were not handicapped by
state governments in the control of planters, they democratized the
colonial system of the nation and founded three democratic states
by 1820. The frontier had finally triumphed over the ideal of the
English country gentleman as held in the South Atlantic states.

The story conforms very closely to the interpretation offered by
Frederick Jackson Turner. Of the democratic influence of the
frontier and its importance there is ample evidence. If the differences between American and European democracies are being
sought, then the frontier influences should be studied, for in this
case they are more significant. The history of democracy in the
Ohio Valley reveals the differences between the civilization of
Europe and that of the United States and gives us an historical
basis for the hope that we as a people may continue to have a history of our own, a history that is unique.

Whether the frontier influences were more important than European will probably remain a matter of opinion and will not be
susceptible of proof. Turner did not claim that democracy originated on the frontier, merely those characteristics which distinguished it from European democracy. The history of the Ohio
Valley supports this point as well as the democratic influence of the
frontier.

Finally, the story of the Ohio Valley where the democratic frontier forces struggled with the aristocratic ideal of the English coun-

try gentlemen is a unique story. The achievement of separation from the South Atlantic states, the democratization of the colonial system of the Northwest Ordinance, the establishment of majority rule in the new states, and the development of individualistic frontier democracy based upon faith in the common man are the notable accomplishments of the pioneers of the Ohio Valley.

Bibliographical Notes

I. SOURCES

UNPUBLISHED MANUSCRIPT SOURCES

THE LYMAN C. Draper Collection at the Wisconsin State Historical Society Library, Madison, Wisconsin, is the largest individual collection of manuscripts relating to western history in this period. It is subdivided into fifty divisions, which vary in size from a single volume in some of the divisions to sixty-four volumes in the George Rogers Clark manuscripts. Draper was interested chiefly in the campaigns of the Revolution and of the Indian wars of the West, but in this large collection are many papers and letters of a wider significance. Reuben G. Thwaites, *Descriptive List of Manuscript Collections of the State Historical Society of Wisconsin* (Madison, Wisconsin, 1906), and the two volumes of the *Publications* of the State Historical Society of Wisconsin, Calendar Series, are very helpful in making use of the collection. Parts of the material have been published in the volumes listed below (Published Documentary and Manuscript Materials) and edited by James A. James, Louise P. Kellogg, and Reuben G. Thwaites. The entire collection is now being made available to other libraries by means of microfilm. Some of the divisions have been acquired by the library of Indiana University.

The Reuben T. Durrett Collection in the University of Chicago Library was also important for this research, particularly because it contains the George Nicholas Papers. For a statement about the Nicholas Papers see *ante,* 92 and note 4, 95–104. These papers have been in the past very slightly used because of their illegibility, but in this instance they have been enlarged and read.

The William H. English Collection in the University of Chicago Library is much less well known. It contains several of the manuscript journals of the assembly of the Territory of Indiana. Recently these journals have been returned to Indiana and the Indiana Historical Bureau has published them. The English Collection also contains much biographical information about territorial and state leaders, letters to early governors of the territory and state, newspaper clippings, and a manuscript of the early history of Indiana to 1800.

The Indiana State Library now has the following manuscript copies of the Journals of the House of Representatives of the Indiana Territory: 1 Assembly, 1 Sess., July 29, 1805; 2 Assembly, 2 Sess., September 26, 1808; October 16, 1809; 3 Assembly, 2 Sess., November 11, 1811; 4 Assembly, 1 Sess., February 1, 1813; 4 Assembly, 2 Sess., December 6, 1813; 5 Assembly, 1 Sess., August 15, 1814; 5 Assembly, 2 Sess., December 4, 1815; and the Journal of the Legislative Council, 4 Assembly, 2 Sess., December 6, 1813. These have been published; see *post,* Publications of state . . . , Indiana.

In addition to these, various less important collections and documents have been consulted. They include the Constitution of the State of Indiana in the Indiana History Division, Indiana State Library, and another manuscript of the same in the William Henry Smith Memorial Library of the Indiana Historical Society; the Minute Book, No. 1, Board of Trustees, Town of Clarksville, Indiana, 1784–1789, and the Albert Gallatin Porter Collection in the Indiana State Library; the Constitution of Tennessee in the State Library, Nashville, Tennessee; the Journals of the various Kentucky conventions from July, 1788, to the Constitutional Convention of 1792 in the Kentucky State Library, Frankfort, Kentucky. The Journals of the Kentucky conventions are as follows:

At a Convention begun and held for the District of Kentucky at the Courthouse in Danville in the County of Mercer on Monday the Twentyeighth day of July in the Year of our Lord one Thousand Seven hundred and eightyeight

At a Convention begun and held for the District of Kentucky at the Courthouse in Danville in the County of Mercer on Monday the third day of November in the Year of Our Lord One Thousand Seven Hundred and Eightycight

At a Convention begun and held for the District of Kentucky at the Courthouse in Danville in the County of Mercer on Monday the Twentieth day of July in the Year of our Lord One Thousand seven Hundred and eighty nine

At a Convention begun and held for the District of Kentucky at the Courthouse in Danville in the County of Mercer on Monday the Twentysixth day of July in the Year of Our Lord One Thousand Seven hundred Ninety

At a Convention begun and held at Danville in the County of Mercer on Monday the second day of April in the year of our Lord One Thousand seven hundred and Ninetytwo

An effort was made to secure photostat copies of early state constitutions, but the secretaries of the states of Ohio and Georgia refused to permit copies to be made.

Photostat copies of the original returns of the Fourth and Fifth Census and microfilm copies of the original returns of the Seventh and Eighth Census for Indiana have been used in the Indiana State Library and the library of Indiana University, the latter in Bloomington, Indiana.

Other collections include the William Blount Papers in the Lawson McGhee Library, Knoxville, Tennessee; the Breckinridge Papers in the Library of Congress, which include those of John Breckinridge, the elder;

the Harry Innes Papers, the Duncan McArthur Papers, which deal largely with land; and the diary and letter books of Thomas Worthington, all in the Library of Congress. The Ohio State Library and the library of the Ohio Archaeological and Historical Society have additional manuscripts of Thomas Worthington. The Paul Fearing MSS and the Griffin Green MSS in the Marietta College Library and the Winthrop Sargent Papers in the Ohio Archaeological and Historical Society Library were also examined.

PUBLISHED DOCUMENTARY AND MANUSCRIPT MATERIALS

A vast amount of manuscript and documentary material relating to the advance of the frontier to the Ohio Valley has been published. A number of prominent historians have devoted their talents to this type of historical work. From their labors have come such significant volumes as the *Cahokia Records, 1778–1790*, the *Kaskaskia Records, 1778–1790* in the Illinois State Historical Library *Collections* (vols. II and V, Springfield, Illinois, 1907, 1909) edited by Clarence W. Alvord; *The Records of the Original Proceedings of the Ohio Company* and *Ohio in the Time of the Confederation* in the Marietta College Historical *Collections* (vols. I, II, and III, Marietta, Ohio, 1917–1918), edited by Archer B. Hulbert; the *George Rogers Clark Papers* in the Illinois State Historical Library *Collections* (vols. VIII and XIX, 1912, 1926), edited by James A. James; *Documentary History of Dunmore's War, 1774* (Madison, Wisconsin, 1905), *The Revolution on the Upper Ohio, 1775–1777* (Madison, Wisconsin, 1908), and *Frontier Defense on the Upper Ohio, 1777–1778* (Madison, Wisconsin, 1912, edited by Reuben G. Thwaites and Louise P. Kellogg; *Frontier Advance on the Upper Ohio, 1778–1779* and *Frontier Retreat on the Upper Ohio, 1779–1781* in Wisconsin State Historical Society *Collections* (vols. XXIII and XXIV, Madison, Wisconsin, 1916 and 1917), edited by Louise P. Kellogg; *Religion on the American Frontier, The Baptists, 1783–1830* and *The Presbyterians, 1783–1840* (New York, 1931 and 1936), edited by William W. Sweet; and *Plantation and Frontier Documents, 1649–1863* (2 vols., Cleveland, Ohio, 1909), edited by Ulrich B. Phillips. Collectively the above ably edited volumes form an exceedingly important body of historical literature on the Middle West.

Other publications of value include the following:

BLOUNT, WILLIAM. Journal and Letters of Governor William Blount in *American Historical Magazine* (Nashville, Tenn., 1896–1904), I–IV. "Documents on the Blount Conspiracy, 1795–1797," ed. by Frederick J. Turner, in *American Historical Review*, X (1904–1905), 574–606.

Bond, Beverley W., Jr. (ed.), *The Correspondence of John Cleves Symmes* (New York, 1926).

Butterfield, Consul W. (ed.), *Washington–Irvine Correspondence* (Madison, Wis., 1882); *Journal of Capt. Jonathan Heart . . . 1785, to which is added the Dickinson–Harmar Correspondence of 1784–85* (Albany, N. Y., 1885).

Dunn, Jacob P., "Slavery Petitions and Papers," Indiana Historical Society *Publications*, II (1895), 443–529.

EDWARDS, NINIAN. *The Edwards Papers*, ed. by E. B. Washburne, in Chicago Historical Society *Collections*, III (1884).

Esarey, Logan (ed.), *Messages and Letters of William Henry Harrison* (2 vols., Indiana Historical *Collections*, VII and IX, 1922); *Messages and Papers of Jonathan Jennings . . .* , Indiana Historical *Collections*, XII (1924).

Hoyt, William H. (ed.), *The Papers of Archibald D. Murphey* (2 vols., Raleigh, N. C., 1914).

"Indiana Historical Society, Minutes of the," in Indiana Historical Society *Publications*, I (1897), 3–76.

Kellogg, Louise P., "A Memorial of Some Trans-Allegheny Inhabitants" in *Mississippi Valley Historical Review*, I, 267–269; "Petition for a Western State, 1780," in *ibid.*, I, 265–267.

Kimball, Gertrude S. (ed.), *Correspondence of William Pitt . . . with the Colonial Governors and Military . . . Commissioners in America* (2 vols., New York, 1906). This work contains letters reporting on Forbes's campaign.

McMinn Correspondence in *American Historical Magazine*, IV (1899), 319–335.

Methodist Episcopal Church, Minutes of the Annual Conference of the, for the Years 1773–1828 (New York, 1840).

"Nourse–Chaplin Letters," in the Kentucky State Historical Society *Register*, XXXI (1933), 152–167.

Old South Leaflets (8 vols., Boston, 1888–1904).

Robertson, James, *Petitions of the Early Inhabitants of Kentucky*, Filson Club *Publications*, XXVII (1914).

ST. CLAIR, ARTHUR. *The St. Clair Papers—The Life and Public Services of Arthur St. Clair*, ed. by William H. Smith (2 vols., Cincinnati, Ohio, 1882).

Sargent, Winthrop, *The History of an Expedition Against Fort Du Quesne, in 1755* (*Memoirs* of the Historical Society of Pennsylvania, V, Philadelphia, 1855); "Winthrop Sargent's Diary while with General Arthur St. Clair's Expedition against the Indians," in *Ohio Archaeological and Historical Quarterly*, XXXIII (1924), 237–273.

Stubbs, William, *Select Charters* (Oxford, 1900).

THOMPSON, CHARLES. "The Papers of Charles Thompson, Secretary of the Continental Congress," *Collections* of the New York Historical Society, XI (1879), 1–286.

WASHINGTON, GEORGE. *Diaries of George Washington,* ed. by John C. Fitzpatrick (4 vols., Boston, 1925).

Whitaker, Arthur P. (ed.), "Letters of James Robertson and Daniel Smith," in *Mississippi Valley Historical Review,* XII (1925–1926), 409–412.

Williams, Samuel C., *Early Travels in the Tennessee Country, 1540–1800* (Johnson City, Tenn., 1928).

JOURNALS, AUTOBIOGRAPHIES, AND MEMOIRS

ASBURY, FRANCIS. *The Journal of the Rev. Francis Asbury, Bishop of the Methodist Episcopal Church, from August 7, 1771, to December 7, 1815* (3 vols., New York, 1821). Asbury traveled along the frontier of the Old West each year and his Journal contains numerous references to the people, the inns, and the roads. He tried all of the main routes of travel.

Baily, Francis, *A Tour of the Unsettled Parts of North America in 1796 & 1797* (London, 1856). The author was an intelligent young Englishman who traveled through the Ohio Valley when the Indian menace had only recently been removed and a large migration was under way.

Birkbeck, Morris, *Notes on a Journal in America* (Philadelphia, 1817). This is a well-known account of a journey from Virginia to Illinois in 1817, by way of the Ohio River.

Blount, William, Journal and Letters, see *ante,* Published Documentary and Manuscript Materials.

BOEHM, HENRY. *Reminiscences, Historical and Biographical, of Sixty-four Years in the Ministry,* ed. by Rev. Joseph B. Wakeley (New York, 1865). The author traveled for a time with Bishop Asbury and his account supplements and confirms Asbury's statements.

Bond, Beverley W., Jr. (ed.), "Memoirs of Benjamin Van Cleve," *Quarterly Publication* of the Historical and Philosophical Society of Ohio, XVII (1922), 1–71; "Dr. Daniel Drake's Memoir of the Miami Country, 1779–1794," in *ibid.,* XVIII (1923), 37–117. Both of these memoirs are important for the early history of the Miami Valley and vicinity.

BROWN, JOSEPH. "Sketch of the Captivity of Colonel Joseph Brown," in *South-Western Monthly,* I (1852), 10–16, 72–78.

Brown, William H., "Memoirs of the Late Hon. Daniel P. Cook," in Ninian W. Edwards, *History of Illinois,* 253–268.

Buell, Rowena (comp.), *The Memoirs of Rufus Putnam* (Boston, 1903).

Burnaby, Rev. Andrew, *Travels through the Middle Settlements in North America* (London, 1775). This contains a description of the Winchester area in 1759–1760.

BUTLER, RICHARD. "Journal of Richard Butler" in *Olden Times,* II, 433–464, 481–525, 529–531.

Butterfield, Consul W. (ed.), *Journal of Capt. Jonathan Heart;* see under

Published Documentary and Manuscript Materials for the works of Butterfield.

Buttrick, Tilly, Jr., *Voyages, Travels and Discoveries* (Boston, 1831), reprinted in Thwaites, *Early Western Travels, 1748–1846*, VIII (1904). This is a brief account of two journeys into the West in 1812 and 1815. The latter included the Allegheny River and the Natchez Trace.

CARR, JOHN. "Narrative of John Carr," in the *South-Western Monthly*, II (1852), 73–80.

CARTWRIGHT, PETER. *Autobiography of Peter Cartwright, the backwoods preacher*, ed. by W. P. Strickland (New York, 1857). This is a frontier classic.

Chastellux, Marquis de, *Travels in North America, in the Years 1780, 1781, and 1782* (2 vols., Dublin, 1787).

CLARK, JOHN. *"Father Clark,"* or the Pioneer Preacher, Sketches and Incidents of Rev. John Clark, by an Old Pioneer, ed. by John M. Peck (New York, 1855).

COFFIN, ELIJAH. "Autobiography" of Elijah Coffin in *The Life of Elijah Coffin with a Reminiscence by his son Charles F. Coffin*, ed. by Mary C. Johnson (n.p., 1863).

COFFIN, LEVI. *Reminiscences of Levi Coffin* (Cincinnati, Ohio, 1876). A vivid picture of the Quaker migration to the West and of opposition to slavery is given by this shrewd Friend.

COOK, DANIEL P., see William H. Brown.

CRESSWELL, NICHOLAS. *The Journal of Nicholas Cresswell, 1774–1777* (New York, 1928). A journey over Braddock's Road and down the Ohio River to Kentucky is recorded by this loyal Englishman as the Revolution began.

Crèvecoeur, Hector St. John de, *Lettres d'un Cultivateur Américain . . .* (3 vols., Paris, 1787), III.

Cuming, Fortesque, *Sketches of a Tour to the Western Country . . .* (Pittsburgh, Pa., 1810). The author pictured Forbes's Road and the Ohio Valley in 1807 and 1808.

Cutler, Julia P., *Life and Times of Ephraim Cutler, prepared from his Journal and Correspondence* (Cincinnati, Ohio, 1890).

Cutler, William P., and Julia P., *Life, Journals and Correspondence of Rev. Manasseh Cutler* (2 vols., Cincinnati, Ohio, 1888).

DENNY, EBENEZER. *Military Journal of Major Ebenezer Denny . . .* (Philadelphia, 1859). The important military activities and travel conditions from 1781 to 1795 are described by the author.

Dewees, Mary C., *Journal of a Trip from Philadelphia to Lexington in Kentucky* (Crawfordsville, Ind., 1936). This is an account of a journey of 1787 into the Ohio Valley.

DRAKE, DANIEL, "Memoir," see Bond, Beverley W., Jr.

Ernst, Ferdinand, "Travels in Illinois in 1819," in Illinois Historical Society *Transactions, 1903* (1904), 150–165.

FINLEY, JAMES B. *Autobiography of Rev. James B. Finley,* ed. by W. P. Strickland (Cincinnati, Ohio, n.d.). The author also wrote *Sketches of Western Methodism* (Cincinnati, Ohio, 1856).

Flint, Timothy, *Recollections of the Last Ten Years* (Boston, 1826). In addition to an excellent general narrative of Western conditions from 1815 to 1825, Flint described Indiana during the transition to statehood.

Gipson, Lawrence H. (ed.), *The Moravian Indian Mission on White River* in Indiana Historical *Collections,* XXIII (1939).

GRELLET, STEPHEN. *Memoirs of the Life and Gospel Labors of Stephen Grellet* (Philadelphia, n.d.).

HOOVER, DAVID. "Memoir of David Hoover," in *Indiana Magazine of History,* II (1906), 17–27.

The three preceding accounts give information on the settlement of the Whitewater Valley in early Indiana.

James, Edwin, *Account of an Expedition from Pittsburgh to the Rocky Mountains, performed in the Years, 1819, 1820 . . . under the command of Maj. S. H. Long . . .* (London, 1823), reprinted in Thwaites, *Early Western Travels, 1748–1846,* XIV and XV (1905).

Johnston, J. Stoddard, *First Explorations of Kentucky; Doctor Thomas Walker's Journal . . . also Colonel Gist's Journal* in Filson Club *Publications,* XIII (1898). These journals describe the route from the Valley of Virginia to Kentucky.

Melish, John, *Information and Advice to Emigrants to the United States: and from the Eastern to the Western States* (Philadelphia, 1819); *A Military and Topographical Atlas of the United States* (Philadelphia, 1815).

MICHAUX, ANDRÉ. "Journal of Travels into Kentucky; July 15, 1793–April 11, 1796," in Thwaites, *Early Western Travels, 1748–1846,* III (1904), 25–104. This is only a portion of the extant journals of André Michaux. "Portions of the Journal of André Michaux, Botanist, written during his Travels in the United States and Canada, 1785 to 1796, with an Introduction and Explanatory Notes," by C. S. Sargent, in *Proceedings* of the American Philosophical Society, XXVI (1889), 1–145. This contains all of the journals of Michaux that are known to be in existence. Travel conditions through the Carolina mountains and into the Ohio Valley are described in these journals.

Michaux, François A., "Travels to the West of the Alleghany Mountains . . . 1802," in Thwaites, *Early Western Travels, 1748–1846,* III, 105–306. A later description of travel conditions is given by the son of André Michaux.

Polke, James, "Some Memoirs of the Polke . . . and Mathes Families," in *Indiana Magazine of History,* X (1914), 83–109.

Pope, John, *A Tour through the Southern and Western Territories of the United States* (Richmond, Va., 1792).

Reed, Isaac, *The Christian Traveller* (New York, 1828). The author traveled through the Kanawha Valley in 1817 and labored in Kentucky and Indiana until 1826.

Schoepf, John D., *Travels in the Confederation* (2 vols., Philadelphia, 1911). Schoepf journeyed over Forbes's Road and into the Valley of Virginia at the close of the Revolution.

Selter, H. Fouré (ed.), *L'Odyssée Américaine d'une Famille Française* (Baltimore, Md., 1936). A brief account of the dangers of travel on the Ohio River in 1788 is included in this little volume.

SLADE, JEREMIAH. "General Slade's Journal of a Trip to Tennessee," in *An Annual Publication of Historical Papers* of the Historical Society of Trinity College, VI (1906), 37–56. This is a narrative of a journey through Flower or Wood's Gap in the Blue Ridge Mountains to Tennessee.

SMITH, DANIEL. "The Journal of General Daniel Smith . . . ," ed. by St. George L. Sioussat, in the *Tennessee Historical Magazine,* I (1915), 40–65.

Thwaites, Reuben G., *Early Western Travels, 1748–1846* . . . (32 vols., Cleveland, Ohio, 1904–1907).

VAN CLEVE, BENJAMIN, "Memoirs," see Bond, Beverley W., Jr.

Woods, John, *Two Years' Residence in the Settlement on the English Prairie in the Illinois Country* (London, 1822).

HISTORIES, BIOGRAPHIES, AND PAMPHLETS

BRADFORD, JOHN. *John Bradford's Historical &c Notes on Kentucky,* compiled by G. W. Stipp in 1827 (San Francisco, Calif., 1932). Bradford came to Kentucky in 1779 and became the founder and editor of the *Kentucky Gazette* in 1787. His account of the contest to free Kentucky from Virginia and found a new state is brief but significant.

Burnet, Jacob, *Notes on the Early Settlement of the North-Western Territory* (New York, 1847). This is a classic account of the Old Northwest by an early lawyer and Federalist of Cincinnati.

Cramer, Zadok, *The Navigator* (Pittsburgh, Pa., 1811).

[Darneille, Isaac], *Letters of Decius* . . . (Louisville, Ky., 1805). This early criticism of Harrison's administration of Indiana Territory has not received the attention it seems to deserve.

Doddridge, Joseph, *Notes on the Settlement and Indian Wars of the Western Parts of Virginia and Pennsylvania from 1763 to 1783,* . . . (Pittsburgh, Pa., 1912). This is a republication of an early and significant work. It compares with Bradford's, and Burnet's *Notes*.

Ferris, Ezra, "The Early Settlement of the Miami Country," in Indiana

Historical Society *Publications,* I, 245–364. This is not so discriminating nor so valuable an account as those of Drake and Van Cleve, but it is useful.

Finley, James B., *Sketches of Western Methodism* (Cincinnati, Ohio, 1856). See also his *Autobiography,* listed under Journals, Autobiographies, and Memoirs. He participated in the early settlement of the Virginia Military District.

Jefferson, Thomas, *Notes on the State of Virginia* (Boston, 1829). This valuable little book on Virginia was written originally in 1781 and has been reprinted many times. It gives a detailed description of Virginia as it emerged from the Revolution.

LITTELL, WILLIAM. *Reprints of Littell's Political Transactions . . . and Letter of George Nicholas,* ed. by Temple Bodley, in Filson Club *Publications,* XXXI (1926). Littell was not an observer of the struggle to make Kentucky a state, but wrote an account which represented the view of Harry Innes and Caleb Wallace and their friends. As reprinted by Bodley, it is supplemented with the contemporary documents. Nicholas participated in the end of the struggle.

McDonald, John, *Biographical Sketches of General Nathaniel Massie* (Cincinnati, Ohio, 1838).

Marshall, Humphrey, *History of Kentucky* (2 vols., Frankfort, Ky., 1812). This is the first formal history of the state of Kentucky but is marred by the bitter prejudices of its author, who was a Federalist to the end.

Massie, David M., *Nathaniel Massie, A Pioneer of Ohio* (Cincinnati, Ohio, 1896). This biography contains many letters of Nathaniel Massie, but the narrative was written by a grandson and is not therefore a source.

Reynolds, John, *The Pioneer History of Illinois . . . to the Year 1818* (Chicago, 1887); *My Own Times* (Chicago, 1879). The author moved to Illinois at an early date and therefore witnessed the events of this period. By the time he began writing his memory was no doubt not an infallible guide.

[Rice, David], "Philanthropos," *Slavery, Inconsistent with Justice and Good Policy* (Lexington, Ky., 1792). This pamphlet was published as the constitutional convention was about to assemble. It represents a point of view of some of the Kentucky radicals.

PUBLICATIONS OF THE FEDERAL GOVERNMENT

The most important federal publication for this study is *The Territorial Papers of the United States* (Washington, 1934–   ), edited by Clarence E. Carter. It has made available a large number of documents from various government departments which could have been found by the individual researcher only after long periods of tedious investigation. The volumes which have been used include II and III, *The Territory Northwest of the River Ohio, 1787–1803;* IV, *The Territory South of the River Ohio, 1790–1796;* VII and VIII, *Indiana Territory,* 1800–*1816;* XVI and XVII, *Illinois Territory, 1809–1818.*

Other publications of importance include the *American State Papers: Documents, Legislative and Executive* (38 vols., Washington, 1832–1861), particularly volumes XXVIII to XXXV which relate to *Public Lands; Annals of the Congress of the United States* (42 vols., Washington, 1834–1856); and *Journals of the Continental Congress, 1774–1789* (34 vols., Washington, 1904–1937). The publication of the decennial census furnish the most reliable information about the advance of settlement. The following were used: *Heads of Families at the First Census of the United States taken in the Year 1790* (12 vols., Washington, 1907–1908); *Return of the Whole Number of Persons within the Several Districts of the United States: according to . . . the second census* (Washington City, 1802); *Aggregate Amount of each description of Persons within the United States of America, and the Territories thereof, agreeably to actual enumeration made according to law, in the year 1810* (Washington, 1811); *Census for 1820* (Washington, 1821); *Ninth Census of the United States, 1870, Statistics of Population,* I (Washington, 1872); and *Twelfth Census of the United States, 1900, Population,* I (Washington, 1901). The returns for 1790 were secured from the last of these volumes. (The original returns of the fourth and fifth, and the seventh and eighth census, population schedules, have been used for Indiana by means of photostat and microfilm copies in the Indiana State Library, Indianapolis, Indiana, and the Indiana University Library, Bloomington, Indiana.)

The Report of the Secretary of War in Relation to the Pension Establishment of the United States (3 vols., in *Senate Documents,* 23 Cong., 1 Sess., XII–XIV), gave some information about members of the conventions who had been Revolutionary soldiers. Indian treaties were found in *Treaties between the United States of America and the Several Indian Tribes from 1778 to 1837* comp. by . . . the Commissioner of Indian Affairs (Washington, 1837), and C. J. Kappler (comp.), *Indian Affairs; Laws and Treaties in Senate Documents,* 57 Cong., 1 Sess., No. 452. Useful maps and digests of Indian treaties are included in the *Eighteenth Annual Report of the Bureau of American Ethnology* (Washington, 1899).

The United States Statutes at Large (Philadelphia and Washington, 1796–   ), were consulted for the laws of the federal government respecting the territories. Francis N. Thorpe (comp.), *The Federal and State Constitutions . . . and other Organic Laws . . .* (7 vols., Washington, 1909), contains satisfactory reprints of the various state constitutions.

They were checked against earlier publications and manuscript copies. A few documents pertaining to this investigation were found in *American Archives . . . A Documentary History of . . . the North American Colonies,* comp. by Peter Force, 4th series, 6 vols., 5th series, 3 vols. (Washington, 1837–1853).

PUBLICATIONS OF STATE, TERRITORIAL, AND LOCAL GOVERNMENTS

It was often necessary to consult various official documents and publications of the states and among these the following were the more useful. Some of them were printed by private organizations, but are included here because of their public character.

FRANKLIN

A Declaration of Rights, also, The Constitution, or Form of Government . . . of the State of Frankland . . . 1785 (Philadelphia, 1786), as reprinted in the *American Historical Magazine,* I, 48–63.

ILLINOIS

The Governors' Letter Books, 1818–1834, ed. by Evarts B. Greene and Clarence W. Alvord, in Illinois State Historical Library *Collections,* IV (1909).

Illinois Census Returns, 1810, 1818, ed. by Margaret C. Norton, in Illinois State Historical Library *Collections,* XXIV (1935).

Illinois Census Returns, 1820, ed. by Margaret C. Norton, in Illinois State Historical Library *Collections,* XXVI (1934).

Illinois Constitutions, ed. by Emil J. Verlie, in Illinois State Historical Library *Collections,* XIII (1919).

"Journal of the Convention," in Illinois State Historical Society *Journal,* VI (1913), 355–424.

Journal of the House of Representatives of the State of Illinois, 3 General Assembly, 1 Sess., 1822 (Vandalia, Ill., 1823).

The Laws of Illinois Territory, 1809–1818, ed. by Francis S. Philbrick, in Illinois State Historical Library *Collections,* XXV (1950).

The Territorial Records of Illinois, ed. by Edmund J. James, in Illinois State Historical Library *Publications,* III (1901). Dr. Clarence E. Carter published a more complete copy of this document in the *Territorial Papers,* XVII, 617–72.

INDIANA

Constitution Making in Indiana, by Charles Kettleborough in Indiana Historical *Collections,* I, II, XVII (1916, 1930). Much documentary material is included in these volumes.

"Executive Journal of Indiana Territory, 1800–1816," ed. by William
   Wesley Woollen, et al., in Indiana Historical Society *Publications*, III
   (1900), 63–252.
Journal of the Convention of the Indiana Territory . . . (Louisville, Ky.,
   1816).
"Journal of the Convention of the Indiana Territory, begun and held at
   the Town of Corydon . . . [June 10, 1816]," reprinted in the *Report* of
   the Sixteenth Annual Meeting of the State Bar Association . . . 1912
   (Indianapolis, Ind., 1912), 137–231.
"Journal of the house of Representatives of the Indiana Territory, convened at the town of Corydon, in the county of Harrison, on Wednes-.
   day the first day of June, in the year of our Lord, 1814," in the Vincennes, Ind., *Western Sun*, July 2, 1814.
Journals of the General Assembly of Indiana Territory, 1805–1815, ed. by
   Gayle Thornbrough and Dorothy Riker, Vol. XXXII of Indiana His-
   torical *Collections* (Indiana Historical Bureau, Indianapolis, Ind., 1950).
The Laws of Indiana Territory, 1801–1809, ed. by Francis S. Philbrick, in
   Illinois State Historical Library *Collections*, XXI (1930). This volume
   contains an excellent historical introduction by the editor.
The Laws of Indiana Territory, 1809–1816, ed. by Louis B. Ewbank and
   Dorothy Riker, in Indiana Historical *Collections*, XX (1934).

KENTUCKY

"Journal of the First Kentucky Convention, Dec. 27, 1784–January 5,
   1785," ed. by Thomas P. Abernethy, in *Journal of Southern History*, I
   (1935), 67–78. For other extant journals of Kentucky conventions,
   1788–1792, see *ante*, Unpublished Manuscript Sources.
Bennett H. Young, *History and Texts of the Three Constitutions of Kentucky* (Louisville, Ky., 1890).

MARYLAND

Laws of Maryland made and passed at a session of Assembly, begun . . .
   the sixth of November [1786] . . . (Printed by Frederick Green, Annapolis, Md., n.d.).
Laws of Maryland, made since M,DCC, LXIII . . . (Printed by Frederick
   Green, Annapolis, Md., 1787).

MISSISSIPPI

The Official Letter Books of W. C. C. Claiborne, ed. by Dunbar Rowland
   (6 vols., Jackson, Miss., 1917).

NORTH CAROLINA

The Colonial Records of North Carolina, ed. by William L. Saunders (10 vols., Raleigh, N. C., 1886–1890).

The State Records of North Carolina, ed. by Walter Clark (16 vols., Winston and Goldsboro, N. C., 1895–1907). The *State Records* are a continuation of the *Colonial Records* and the volumes are numbered consecutively.

OHIO and the NORTHWEST TERRITORY

The Constitutions of Ohio, compiled by Isaac F. Patterson (Cleveland, Ohio, 1912).

"Journal of the Convention," in Ohio Archaeological and Historical *Quarterly,* V (1897), 80–132.

Journal of the House of Representatives of the Territory of the United States Northwest of the River Ohio . . . 1799 (Cincinnati, Ohio, 1800).

Journal of the House of Representatives of the Territory of the United States, North-west of the river Ohio at the Second Session of the First General Assembly, A.D. 1800 (Chillicothe, Ohio, 1800).

Journal of the House of Representatives of the Territory of the United States, North-west of the Ohio, at the First Session of the Second General Assembly, A.D. 1801 (Chillicothe, Ohio, 1801).

Journal of the Legislative Council of the Territory of the United States, North-west of the River Ohio . . . One Thousand, Seven Hundred and Ninety Nine (Cincinnati, Ohio, n.d.).

Laws of the Territory of the United States North-west of the Ohio (Cincinnati, Ohio, printed by W. Maxwell, 1796). This is a copy of the laws known as the Maxwell Code.

Laws of the Northwest Territory, 1788–1800, ed. by Theodore C. Pease, in Illinois State Historical Library *Collections,* XVII (1925).

PENNSYLVANIA

Laws of the Commonwealth of Pennsylvania, compiled by Alexander J. Dallas (4 vols., Philadelphia, 1793–1797).

Pennsylvania Archives (9 series, 119 vols., Philadelphia, 1852–1935).

SOUTH CAROLINA

The Statutes at Large of South Carolina, ed. by Thomas Cooper (5 vols., Columbia, S. C., 1836–1839).

TENNESSEE and the TERRITORY SOUTH OF THE RIVER OHIO

Journal of the Proceedings of a Convention, began and held in Knoxville on the eleventh day of January, 1796, for the purpose of forming a constitution . . . (Knoxville, Tenn., 1796).

Journal of the Proceedings of the House of Representatives of the Territory of the United States of America, South of the River Ohio . . . 1795 (Knoxville, Tenn., 1795, reprinted, Nashville, Tenn., 1852).

VIRGINIA

Calendar of Virginia State Papers (11 vols., Richmond, Va., 1875–1893), ed. by William P. Palmer.

Proceedings and Debates of the Virginia State Convention of 1829–30 (Richmond, Va., 1830).

The Statutes at Large: Being a Collection of all the Laws of Virginia (13 vols., Richmond, Va., 1809–1823), ed. by William W. Hening.

Hugh B. Grigsby, *The History of the Virginia Federal Convention of 1788* (2 vols. in *Collections* of the Virginia Historical Society N.S. IX and X, 1890, 1891).

NEWSPAPERS

One of the most important sources of information about the territorial period in each of the five states of the Ohio Valley was the newspapers or papers published at the time. The history of these territories could not be written without them. The following have been very carefully studied after files have been collected from several libraries in part through the use of microfilm and photostat. The dates indicate the years for which the paper was used.

Baltimore, Md., *Niles' Weekly Register,* 1811–1849.

Chillicothe, Ohio, *Scioto Gazette,* 1800–1802.

Cincinnati, Ohio, *Centinel of the North-Western Territory,* 1793–1796.

Cincinnati, Ohio, *Freeman's Journal,* 1796–1799.

Cincinnati, Ohio, *Liberty Hall,* 1804–1809.

Cincinnati, Ohio, *Western Spy,* 1800–1802.

Edwardsville, Ill., *Spectator,* 1822–1824.

Kaskaskia, Ill., *Illinois Intelligencer,* 1818, 1822–1824.

Kaskaskia, Ill., *Western Intelligencer,* 1816–1818.

Knoxville, Tenn., *Gazette,* 1791–1796.

Lexington, Ind., *Western Eagle,* 1815–1816.

Lexington, Ky., *Kentucky Gazette,* 1787–1792.

Philadelphia, Pa., *Pennsylvania Gazette,* 1777–1780, 1786–1787. Reel No.

18 of the microfilm was used and a few scattered numbers consulted in 1786–1787.

Pittsburgh, Pa., *Gazette*, 1786–1795.

Vincennes, Ind., *Indiana Gazette*, 1804–1806.

Vincennes, Ind., *Western Sun*, 1807–1816, 1822–1823.

One or more numbers of the following were examined:

Indianapolis, Ind., *Indiana Journal* (1858).

Knoxville, Tenn., *Register*.

Princeton, N. J., *Independent Gazetteer*.

ATLASES AND MAPS

Carey, John, *A New Map of part of the United States of North America* (n.p., 1805).

Fite, Emerson D., and Freeman, Archibald, (eds.), *A Book of Old Maps* (Cambridge, Mass., 1926).

Jefferys, Thomas, *The American Atlas: or, A Geographical Description of the Whole Continent of America:* . . . (London, 1776).

Melish, John, *A Military and Topographical Atlas of the United States* (Philadelphia, 1815).

Tanner, Henry S., *The New American Atlas* (3 parts, Philadelphia, 1818, 1819, and 1821).

Tanner, Henry S., *The New American Atlas* (Philadelphia, 1823).

Tanner, Henry S., *A New Universal Atlas* . . . *of the World* (Philadelphia, 1836).

United States Constitution Sesquicentennial Commission, *Maps depicting the 13 original States from New Hampshire to Georgia at the time of the Constitution* (n.p., n.d.). These maps are reprinted from early maps.

II. SECONDARY ACCOUNTS

HISTORIES, BIOGRAPHIES, AND MONOGRAPHS

Abernethy, Thomas P., *From Frontier to Plantation in Tennessee* (Chapel Hill, N. C., 1932); *Western Lands and the American Revolution* (New York, 1937); *Three Virginia Frontiers* (University, La., 1940). The first of these is a substantial piece of historical writing. The second brings out considerable new information and makes an important contribution to our knowledge of speculation, but seems to overemphasize the part of speculators in historical developments. The third is a brief interpretation somewhat marred by overemphasis. These works establish their author as a leading authority on the Southern trans-Appalachian frontier.

Adams, Henry, *The Life of Albert Gallatin* (Philadelphia, 1880).

Allison, John, *Notable Men of Tennessee* (2 vols., Atlanta, Ga., 1905).

Alvord, Clarence W., *The Illinois Country, 1673–1818 (Centennial History of Illinois,* I, Chicago, 1922). The scope and importance of this work is much greater than the title indicates.

Ambler, Charles H., *Sectionalism in Virginia from 1776 to 1861* (Chicago, 1910). This is one of the leading works of the Turner school which treats a South Atlantic state.

Armstrong, Zella, *Taylor of Tennessee* (Chattanooga, Tenn., n.d.).

Bailey, Kenneth P., *The Ohio Company of Virginia and the Westward Movement, 1748–1792* (Glendale, Calif., 1939).

Ballagh, James C., *A History of Slavery in Virginia* in Johns Hopkins University *Studies in Historical and Political Science,* Extra Volume XXIV (Baltimore, Md., 1902).

Barber, John M., *History of Ohio Methodism* (Cincinnati, Ohio, 1898).

Barrett, Jay A., *Evolution of the Ordinance of 1787* (New York, 1891). A study of the legislative history of the Northwest Ordinance. It should be compared with John M. Merriam's article, see below. Both were independent studies made at the same time.

Bassett, John S., *The Life of Andrew Jackson* (2 vols. in one, New York, 1931).

Bateman, Newton, and Selby, Paul, *Biographical and Memorial Edition of the Historical Encyclopedia of Illinois* (2 vols., Chicago, 1905).

Beggs, Rev. Stephen R., *Pages from the Early History of the West and Northwest* (Cincinnati, Ohio, 1868).

Bemis, Samuel F., *Jay's Treaty* (New York, 1924).

Beveridge, Albert J., *Abraham Lincoln, 1809–1858* (4 vols., Boston, 1928).

Biographical Cyclopedia of the Commonwealth of Kentucky (Chicago, 1896).

Biographical Directory of the American Congress, 1774–1927 (Washington, 1928).

Biographical Encyclopedia of Kentucky (Cincinnati, Ohio, 1878).

A Biographical History of Eminent and Self-Made Men of the State of Indiana (2 vols., Cincinnati, Ohio, 1890).

Bodley, Temple, *History of Kentucky, Before the Louisiana Purchase in 1803* (Chicago, 1928). This is volume one of a four-volume history of Kentucky published by J. S. Clarke.

Boggess, Arthur C., *The Settlement of Illinois,* in Chicago Historical Society, *Collections,* V (Chicago, 1908).

Bond, Beverley W., Jr., *The Civilization of the Old Northwest* (New York, 1934); *The Foundations of Ohio (The History of the State of Ohio,* Carl F. Wittke, ed., 6 vols., Columbus, Ohio, 1941–1944, I, 1941). The author reveals an extensive knowledge of the Old Northwest and of the early period of Ohio's history.

Brown, John M., *The Political Beginnings of Kentucky,* in Filson Club *Publications,* VI (1889).

Buck, Solon J., *Illinois in 1818* (Springfield, Ill., 1917). This extra volume to the Illinois Centennial History remains the best detailed picture of a Middle Western state in transition from territorial status to statehood.

Buck, Solon J. and Elizabeth H., *The Planting of Civilization in Western Pennsylvania* (n.p., 1939). Mr. and Mrs. Buck give a valuable picture of the early development of the Ohio-Monongahela frontier.

Butler, Mann, *A History of the Commonwealth of Kentucky* (Cincinnati, Ohio, 1836).

Caldwell, Joshua W., *Sketches of the Bench and Bar of Tennessee* (Knoxville, Tenn., 1898).

Cist, Charles, *Sketches and Statistics of Cincinnati in 1859* (n.p., n.d.).

Clack Genealogy (n.p., n.d.).

Cockrum, William M., *Pioneer History of Indiana* (Oakland City, Ind., 1907).

Collins, Richard H., *History of Kentucky* (2 vols., Louisville, Ky., 1924).

Connelley, William E., and Coulter, E. Merton, *History of Kentucky* (5 vols., Chicago, 1933).

Cotterill, Robert S., *History of Pioneer Kentucky* (Cincinnati, Ohio, 1917).

Craven, Avery O., *The Repressible Conflict, 1830–1861* (University, La., 1939).

Dictionary of American Biography ed. by Allen Johnson and Dumas Malone (20 vols., and index, New York, 1928–1937).

Donaldson, Thomas C., *The Public Domain* (Washington, 1884).

Downes, Randolph C., *Frontier Ohio, 1788–1803,* in Ohio Historical Collections, III (1935); *Council Fires on the Upper Ohio* (Pittsburgh, Pa., 1940). The first of these was a doctoral dissertation at Ohio State University. The second is an excellent treatment of Indian relations from 1783 to 1795.

Draper, Lyman C., *King's Mountain and Its Heroes* (New York, 1929).

Driver, Carl S., *John Sevier, Pioneer of the Old Southwest* (Chapel Hill, N. C., 1932).

Dunlevy, H. H., *History of the Miami Baptist Association* (Cincinnati, Ohio, 1869).

Dunn, Jacob P., *Indiana and Indianians* (5 vols., Chicago, 1919); *Indiana, A Redemption from Slavery* (Boston, 1890). Aside from an overstressing of the slavery controversy, these works establish Dunn as a scholarly historian of Indiana.

Edwards, Everett E. (comp.), *The Early Writings of Frederick Jackson Turner* (Madison, Wis., 1938). This volume contains in addition to the early writings of Turner a bibliography of Turner's writings and a chapter on Turner's formative period by Fulmer Mood.

Edwards, Ninian W., *History of Illinois, from 1778 to 1833; and Life and Times of Ninian Edwards* (Springfield, Ill., 1870).

Emerick, C. F., *The Credit System and the Public Domain* (Nashville, Tenn., 1899).

English, William H., *Conquest of the Country Northwest of the River Ohio, 1778–1783* . . . (2 vols., Indianapolis, Ind., 1896). These volumes remain a very useful account.

Esarey, Logan, *A History of Indiana* (2 vols., Indianapolis, Ind., 1915, 1918). These volumes, the three volumes of *Letters* of Harrison, Jennings, and others listed under Published Documentary and Manuscript Materials, with other works and articles gave Esarey first place among Indiana historians. He probably minimized the slavery struggle in territorial days.

Faust, Albert B., *The German Element in the United States* (2 vols., Boston, 1909).

Ford, Henry J., *Washington and His Colleagues (The Chronicles of America Series,* Allen Johnson, ed., 50 vols., New Haven, Conn., 1918–1921, XIV, 1921).

Ford, Thomas, *A History of Illinois* (Chicago, 1854). The author was too young to know very much of the statehood movement although he later knew many of the early leaders.

Fry, J. Reese, and Conrad, Robert T., *A Life of General Zachary Taylor* (Philadelphia, 1847).

Galbreath, Charles S., *History of Ohio* (5 vols., Chicago, 1925).

Gilmore, William E., *Life of Edward Tiffin, First Governor of Ohio* (Chillicothe, Ohio, 1897).

Goebel, Dorothy B., *William Henry Harrison, A Political Biography,* Indiana Historical *Collections,* XIV (1926).

Gray, Lewis C., *History of Agriculture in the United States to 1860* (2 vols., Washington, 1933).

Green, Fletcher M., *Constitutional Development in the South Atlantic States, 1776–1860* (Chapel Hill, N. C., 1930). This treatment of the South Atlantic states is an excellent piece of work. For a brief criticism of Green's monograph and of his presidential address to the Southern Historical Association see *ante,* 18–19 and note 34.

Hale, William T., and Merritt, Dixon L., *A History of Tennessee and Tennesseans* (8 vols., Chicago, 1913).

Hamer, Philip M., *Tennessee, A History* (4 vols., New York, 1933).

Hanna, Charles A., *The Scotch-Irish: or the Scot in North Britain, North Ireland, and North America* (2 vols., New York, 1902); *Ohio Valley Genealogies* (New York, 1909); *The Wilderness Trail* (2 vols., New York, 1911).

Harris, N. Dwight, *The History of Negro Servitude in Illinois* (Chicago, 1904).

Haywood, John, *The Civil and Political History of the State of Tennessee* (Nashville, Tenn., 1891).

Heineman, John L., *The Indian Trail Down the Whitewater Valley* (n.p., 1912).

Henderson, Archibald, *The Conquest of the Old Southwest; the romantic story of the early pioneers into Virginia, the Carolinas, Tennessee, and Kentucky, 1740–1790* (New York, 1920). This volume and the author's articles make him an authority in the early history of Kentucky and Tennessee. He is the chief exponent of the importance of Judge Richard Henderson.

Hibbard, Benjamin H., *A History of the Public Land Policies* (New York, 1924).

Higgins, Ruth L., *Expansion in New York* (Columbus, Ohio, 1931).

Hildreth, Samuel P., *Pioneer History . . . of the Ohio Valley* (Cincinnati, Ohio, 1848); *Memoirs of the Early Pioneer Settlers of Ohio* (Cincinnati, Ohio, 1854).

Hinsdale, Burk A., *The Old Northwest* (New York, 1888).

Hockett, Homer C., *Western Influences on Political Parties to 1825,* in Ohio State University *Contributions in History and Political Science,* IV (1917). See also his "Federalism and the West," *post,* Secondary Accounts, Articles.

Holcombe, Arthur N., *State Government in the United States* (New York, 1926).

Hooper, Osman C., *History of Ohio Journalism, 1793–1933* (Columbus, Ohio, 1933).

Howe, Henry, *Historical Collections of Ohio* (2 vols., Cincinnati, Ohio, 1908).

Hulbert, Archer B., *Historic Highways of America* (16 vols., Cleveland, Ohio, 1902–1905. Volumes III, VI, and IX, *Washington's Road, Boone's Wilderness Road, and Waterways of Western Expansion,* have been the most useful of the set for this work. *Soil, Its Influence on the History of the United States* (New Haven, Conn., 1930).

James, James A., *Life of George Rogers Clark* (Chicago, 1929). This biography and the two volumes of *Clark Papers,* cited *ante* under Published Documentary and Manuscript Materials, establish the author as the leading authority on George R. Clark.

Jillson, Willard R., *The Kentucky Land Grants,* Filson Club *Publications,* XXXIII (1925). A vast amount of information is presented in this volume.

Lester, William S., *The Transylvania Colony* (Spencer, Ind., 1935).

Lincoln, Charles H., *The Revolutionary Movement in Pennsylvania,* in *Publications* of the University of Pennsylvania *Series in History,* I (Philadelphia, 1901).

Lockwood, George B., *The New Harmony Movement* (New York, 1905).

McBride, James, *Pioneer Biography* (2 vols., Cincinnati, Ohio, 1869).

McCarty, Dwight G., *The Territorial Governors of the Old Northwest* (Iowa City, Iowa, 1910).

M'Ferrin, John B., *History of Methodism in Tennessee* (3 vols., Nashville, Tenn., 1875).

McMaster, John B., *A History of the People of the United States* (8 vols., New York, 1883–1913).

Martin, Asa E., *The Anti-Slavery Movement in Kentucky Prior to 1850,* Filson Club *Publications,* XXIX (1918).

Massie, David M., *Nathaniel Massie, A Pioneer of Ohio . . .* (Cincinnati, Ohio, 1896).

Meyer, Leland W., *Life and Times of Colonel Richard M. Johnson* (New York, 1932).

Moore, John T., *Tennessee, The Volunteer State, 1769–1923* (4 vols., Chicago, 1923).

Moses, John, *Illinois, Historical and Statistical* (2 vols., Chicago, 1889–1892).

National Cyclopedia of American Biography (20 vols., New York, 1898–1906).

Nevins, Allan, *The American States during and after the Revolution, 1775–1789* (New York, 1924).

The Official Roster of the Soldiers of the American Revolution Buried in the State of Ohio (Columbus, Ohio, 1929).

Perrin, William H., Battle, J. H., and Kniffin, G. C., *Kentucky, A History of the State* (Louisville, Ky., 1887).

Pusey, William A., *The Wilderness Road to Kentucky* (New York, c. 1921).

Putnam, A. W., *History of Middle Tennessee . . .* (Nashville, Tenn., 1859).

Ramsey, James G., *The Annals of Tennessee* (Charleston, S. C., 1853).

Randall, Emilius O., and Ryan, Daniel J., *History of Ohio* (5 vols., New York, 1912).

Randall, Henry S., *Life of Thomas Jefferson* (3 vols., New York, 1858).

Roosevelt, Theodore, *The Winning of the West* (4 vols., New York, 1900).

Roseboom, Eugene H., and Weisenburger, Francis P., *A History of Ohio* (New York, 1934).

Sakolski, Aaron M., *The Great American Land Bubble* (New York, 1932).

Savelle, Max, *George Morgan, Colony Builder* (New York, 1932).

Selsam, J. Paul, *The Pennsylvania Constitution of 1776, A Study in Revolutionary Democracy* (Philadelphia, 1936).

Semple, Robert B., *A History of the Rise and Progress of the Baptists in Virginia* (Richmond. Va., 1894).

Smith, Oliver H., *Early Indiana Trials and Sketches* (Cincinnati, Ohio, 1858).

Speed, Thomas, *The Political Club,* in Filson Club *Publications,* IX (1894); *The Wilderness Road,* in Filson Club *Publications,* II (1886). This volume contains two valuable early accounts of the road, the journals of William Brown and William Calk.

Some Tennessee Heroes of the Revolution (Chattanooga, Tenn., n.d.).

Thorpe, Francis N., *A Constitutional History of the American People, 1776–1850* (2 vols., New York, 1898).

Treat, Payson J., *The National Land System, 1785–1820* (New York, 1910).

Turner, Frederick J., *The Frontier in American History* (New York, 1920); *Rise of the New West* (*American Nation Series,* 28 vols., New York, 1904–1925, ed. by Albert B. Hart, XIV, 1906); *The Significance of Sections in American History* (New York, 1932). For an evaluation of Turner's work on the Ohio Valley see *ante,* chapter XIV.

Turner, O., *Pioneer History of the Holland Purchase of Western New York* . . . (Buffalo, N. Y., 1849).

Veech, James, *The Monongahela of Old; or, Historical Sketches of South-Western Pennsylvania to the Year 1800* (Pittsburgh, Pa., 1892, reprinted, 1910); *Centenary Memorial of the Planting and Growth of Presbyterianism in Western Pennsylvania* . . . (Pittsburgh, Pa., 1876).

Washburne, Elihu B., *Sketch of Edward Coles* (Chicago, 1882).

Weeks, Stephan B., *Southern Quakers and Slavery,* Johns Hopkins University *Studies in Historical and Political Science,* Extra Volume XV (1896).

Wertenbaker, Thomas J., *The Founding of American Civilization* (3 vols., New York, 1938, 1942, 1947), II, *The Old South.*

Whitaker, Arthur P., *The Mississippi Question, 1795–1803* (New York, 1934); *The Spanish-American Frontier: 1783–1795* (Boston, 1927). An exhaustive treatment of the relations of the Ohio Valley frontiersmen with foreign governments is given in these volumes.

White, Katherine K., *King's Mountain Men* (Dayton, Va., 1924).

White, Henry A., *Southern Presbyterian Leaders* (New York, 1911).

Whitsitt, William H., *The Life and Times of Judge Caleb Wallace,* in Filson Club *Publications,* IV (1886).

Williams, Samuel C., *History of the Lost State of Franklin* (New York, 1933); *Dawn of Tennessee Valley and Tennessee History* (Johnson City, Tenn., 1937).

Woollen, William Wesley, *Biographical and Historical Sketches of Early Indiana* (Indianapolis, Ind., 1883).

Wright, Marcus J., *The Life and Services of William Blount* (Washington, 1884).

ARTICLES

Abernethy, Thomas P., "Democracy and the Southern Frontier," in *Journal of Southern History,* IV (1938), 3–13. This presidential address to the Southern Historical Association reveals Abernethy's point of view, but should be read in connection with his longer works. See *ante*, 62–63, 88 and note 40, 226–30 and note 10, for a discussion of Abernethy's viewpoint.

Adams, Herbert B., "Maryland's Influence upon Land Cessions to the United States," in Johns Hopkins University *Studies in Historical and Political Science*, III (1885), 7–54.

Allen, J. C., "Palestine, Its Early History," in Illinois State Historical Society *Transactions for the Year 1905* (1906), 122–127.

Alvord, Clarence W., "Virginia and the West: An Interpretation," in *Mississippi Valley Historical Review*, III (1916), 19–38. This brief article is Alvord's recognition of the importance of Virginia's influence upon the West.

Angle, Paul M., "Nathaniel Pope, 1784–1850," in Illinois State Historical Society *Transactions for the Year 1936* (n.d.), 111–181.

Bacot, D. Huger, "The Carolina Up Country at the End of the Eighteenth Century," in *American Historical Review*, XXVIII (1923), 682–698. This is an excellent sketch.

Barnhart, John D., "Sources of Southern Migration into the Old Northwest," in *Mississippi Valley Historical Review*, XXII (1935–1936), 49–62; "The Southern Influence in the Formation of Indiana," in *Indiana Magazine of History*, XXXIII (1937), 261–276; "Sources of Indiana's First Constitution," in *ibid.*, XXXIX (1943), 55–94; "Southern Contributions to the Social Order of the Old Northwest," in *The North Carolina Historical Review*, XVII (1940), 237–248; "Frontiersmen and Planters in the Formation of Kentucky," in *Journal of Southern History*, VII (1941), 19–36; "The Tennessee Constitution of 1796: A Product of the Old West," in *ibid.*, IX (1943), 532–548; "The Southern Influence in the Formation of Ohio," in *ibid.*, III (1937), 28–42; "The Southern Influence in the Formation of Illinois," in *Journal of the Illinois State Historical Society*, XXXII (1939), 358–378. These articles include a few citations or develop a few minor points beyond this present work, but are in the main superseded by it.

Bassett, John S., "The Regulators of North Carolina (1765–1771)," in the American Historical Association *Annual Report for the Year 1894* (1895), 141–212; "Slavery in the State of North Carolina," in Johns Hopkins University *Studies in Historical and Political Science*, XVII (1899), nos. 7–8.

Beard, Charles A., "The Frontier in American History," in the *New Republic*, XXV, 349–350, Feb. 16, 1921; "Books That Changed Our Minds," in *ibid.*, XCVII, 359–362, Feb. 1, 1939; "Culture and Agriculture," in *Saturday Review of Literature*, V (1928–1929), 272–273 (Oct. 20, 1928).

Becker, Carl, "Frederick Jackson Turner," in Howard W. Odum (ed.), *American Masters of Social Science* (New York, c. 1927), 273–318. The author was one of Turner's earlier students. This sketch is an excellent picture of Turner, the teacher.

Belting, Natalia M., "Kaskaskia, 'The Versailles of the West,' " in *Indiana Magazine of History*, XLI (1945), 1–18. Specific details of French life are skillfully woven into this picture of one of the old French villages of the Illinois Country.

Bond, Beverley W., Jr., "Some Political Ideals of the Colonial Period as they were Realized in the Old Northwest," in *Essays in Colonial History Presented to Charles McLean Andrews by his Students* (New Haven, Conn., 1931), 299–325.

Brigham, Albert P., "The Great Roads across the Appalachians," in American Geographical Society of New York *Bulletin*, XXXVII, 321–339.

Brooks, Robert P., "The Agrarian Revolution in Georgia, 1865–1912," in University of Wisconsin *Bulletin*, History Series, III (1912–1914), 461–506.

Brown, William H., "Early History of Illinois," in *Fergus Historical Series*, XIV (1880), 81–102.

Burtner, W. H., "Charles Willing Byrd," in *Ohio Archaeological and Historical Quarterly*, XLI (1932), 237–240.

Butler, Amos W., "Notes Concerning Brookville, Ind., A Century Ago," in *Indiana Magazine of History*, XIII (1917), 146–150.

Carmony, Donald F., "Fiscal Objection to Statehood in Indiana," in *Indiana Magazine of History*, XLII (1946), 311–321.

Chaddock, Robert E., "Ohio before 1850. A Study of the Early Influence of Pennsylvania and Southern Populations in Ohio," in Columbia University *Studies in History, Economics and Public Law*, XXX (1908), No. 2, pp. 1–155. The importante of the Southern element in Ohio and its close relations with the Middle States element is clearly set forth in this dissertation.

Chamberlain, Henry B., "Elias Kent Kane," in Illinois State Historical Society *Transactions for the Year 1908* (1909), 162–170.

"William Cocke . . . ," in *The American Historical Magazine*, I (1896), 224–229.

Coulter, E. Merton, "Early Frontier Democracy in the First Kentucky Constitution," in *Political Science Quarterly*, XXXIX (1924), 665–677.

Cox, Isaac J., "The Burr Conspiracy in Indiana," in *Indiana Magazine of History*, XXV (1929), 257–280.

Craven, Avery O., "The 'Turner Theories' and the South," in *Journal of Southern History*, V (1939), 291–314. The author applies and defines Turner's point of view to the South. He differs considerably from Abernethy.

Curti, Merle E., "The Section and the Frontier in American History:

The Methodological Concepts of Frederick Jackson Turner," in Stuart A. Rice (ed.), *Methods in Social Science* (Chicago, c. 1931), 353–367.

Dodd, William E., "The Emergence of the First Social Order in the United States," in *American Historical Review*, XL (1934–1935), 217–231.

Downes, Randolph C., "Ohio's Squatter Governor: William Hogland of Hoglandstown," *Ohio Archaeological and Historical Quarterly*, XLIII (1934), 273–282; "The Statehood Contest in Ohio," in *Mississippi Valley Historical Review*, XVIII (1931–1932), 155–171.

Esarey, Logan, "Indian Captives in Early Indiana," in *Indiana Magazine of History*, IX (1913), 95–112.

Fisk, Moses, "A Summary Notice of the First Settlements made by White People within the Limits which Bound the State of Tennessee," in Massachusetts Historical Society *Collections*, 2nd Series, VII (1818), 58–65. The author was in Tennessee early enough to talk with some of the first settlers, but did not witness the events which he narrated. For a later reprint see Albert V. Goodpasture, "Moses Fisk's Historical Sketch of Tennessee," cited below.

Garber, Blanche G., "Colonel John Paul, Hoosier Pioneer; First Proprietor and Founder of Xenia, Ohio, and Madison, Indiana," in *Indiana Magazine of History*, XIII (1917), 129–145.

Goodpasture, Albert V., "Beginnings of Montgomery County [Tennessee]," in *American Historical Magazine*, VIII (1903), 193–215; "Moses Fisk's Historical Sketch of Tennessee," in *ibid.*, II (1897), 17–26; "Dr. James White, Pioneer, Politician, Lawyer," in *Tennessee Historical Magazine*, I (1915), 282–291.

Green, Fletcher M., "Democracy in the Old South," in *Journal of Southern History*, XII (1946), 3–23. See *ante*, chapter I, 18–19 and note 34, for a comment on this article.

Hacker, Louis M., "Sections or Classes," in *Nation*, CXXXVII, July 26, 1933, pp. 108–110.

Hall, James, "Memoir of Thomas Posey," in Jared Sparks (ed.), *The Library of American Biography*, 2nd Series (15 vols., Boston, 1852–1855), IX (1852), 359–403.

Hamer, Marguerite B., "John Rhea of Tennessee," in East Tennessee Historical Society *Publications*, IV (1932), 35–44.

Harry, James W., "The Maryland Constitution of 1851," in Johns Hopkins University *Studies in Historical and Political Science*, XX (1902), 379–464.

Hayes, C. Willard, "The Southern Appalachians," in J. W. Powell, *et al.*, *The Physiography of the United States* (New York, c. 1896), 305–336.

Hayter, Earl W., "Sources of Early Illinois Culture," in Illinois State Historical Society *Transactions for the Year 1936* (n.d.), 81–96.

Henderson, Archibald, "Richard Henderson: The Authorship of the Cumberland Compact and the Founding of Nashville," in *Tennessee His-*

torical Magazine, II (1916), 155–172; "The Creative Forces in Westward Expansion: Henderson and Boone," in *American Historical Review,* XX (1914–1915), 86–107; "Richard Henderson and the Occupation of Kentucky, 1775," in *Mississippi Valley Historical Review,* I (1914), 341–363; "A Pre-Revolutionary Revolt in the Old Southwest," in *ibid.,* XVII (1930–1931), 191–212. Note the comment on these articles under Henderson's *Conquest of the Old Southwest.*

Henley, Mrs. Charles F., "The Hon. Joseph Anderson . . . ," in *American Historical Magazine,* III (1898), 240–259.

Hicks, John D., "The Development of Civilization in the Middle West, 1860–1900," in Dixon R. Fox (ed.), *Sources of Culture in the Middle West,* 73–101.

Hockett, Homer C., "Federalism and the West," in *Essays in American History Dedicated to Frederick Jackson Turner* (New York, 1910), 113–136.

James, Alfred P., "The First English-Speaking Trans-Appalachian Frontier," in *Mississippi Valley Historical Review,* XVII (1930–1931), 55–71.

James, Herman G., "The Origin and Development of the Bill of Rights in the Constitution of Illinois," in Illinois State Historical Society *Transactions for the Year 1910* (1912), 81–104.

Knollenberg, Bernhard, "Pioneer Sketches of the Upper Whitewater Valley, Quaker Stronghold of the West," in Indiana Historical Society *Publications,* XV (1945), 1–171.

Libby, Orin G., "Geographical Distributions of the Vote of the Thirteen States on the Federal Constitution, 1787–8," in *Bulletin* of the University of Wisconsin, Economic, Political Science, and History Series, I, 1894, pp. 1–116.

Lingley, Charles R., "The Transition from Colony to Commonwealth," in Columbia University *Studies in History, Economics and Public Law,* XXXVI (1910), 325–535.

M'Elwee, W. E., " 'The Old Road,' from Washington and Hamilton Districts to the Cumberland Settlement," in *American Historical Magazine,* VIII (1898), 347–354.

McMillan, Fay E., "A Biographical Sketch of Joseph Anderson," in East Tennessee Historical Society *Publications,* II (1930), 81–93.

Maxwell, Louise, "Sketch of Dr. David H. Maxwell," in *Indiana Magazine of History,* VIII (1912), 101–108.

Martin, Asa E., "The Anti-Slavery Societies of Tennessee," in *Tennessee Historical Magazine,* I (1915), 261–281.

Merriam, John M., "The Legislative History of the Ordinance of 1787," in American Antiquarian Society *Proceedings,* N.S., V (1888), 303–342. See the comment under Jay A. Barrett, *The Evolution of the Ordinance of 1787.*

Mitchell, Waldo F., "Indiana's Growth, 1812–1820," in *Indiana Magazine of History*, X (1914), 369–395.

Nelson, Selden, "The Tipton Family in Tennessee," East Tennessee Historical Society *Publications*, I (1929), 67–76.

Newell, Mason H., "The Attorneys-General of Illinois," in Illinois State Historical Society *Transactions for the Year 1903* (1904), 211–220.

Parkinson, Daniel M., "Pioneer Life in Wisconsin," in Wisconsin State Historical Society *Second Annual Report and Collections* (1856), 226–364.

Paxson, Frederic L., "A Generation of the Frontier Hypothesis, 1893–1932," in *Pacific Historical Review*, II (1933), 34–51; "The Gateways of the Old Northwest," in Michigan Pioneer and Historical Society *Collections*, XXXVIII (1912), 139–148.

Pershing, B. H., "Winthrop Sargent," in *Ohio Archaeological and Historical Quarterly*, XXXV (1926), 583–601.

Phillips, Ulrich B., "The Origin and Growth of the Southern Black Belts," in *American Historical Review*, XI (1905–1906), 798–816.

Pierson, George W., "The Frontier and Frontiersmen of Turner's Essays," in *Pennsylvania Magazine of History and Biography*, LXIV (1940), 449–478. See *ante*, chapter XIV, 232–35, for an evaluation of this article.

Reid, Nina K., "Sketches of Early Indiana Senators—Waller Taylor, 1816–1825," in *Indiana Magazine of History*, IX (1913), 92–95.

Relf, Frances H., "The Two Michael Joneses," in Illinois State Historical Society *Journal*, IX (1916–1917), 146–151.

Riker, Dorothy, "Jonathan Jennings," in *Indiana Magazine of History*, XXVIII (1932), 223–239.

Roberts, Lucien E., "Sectional Factors in the Movements for Legislative Reapportionment and Reduction in Georgia, 1777–1860," in *Studies in Georgia History and Government*, ed. by James C. Bonner and Lucien E. Roberts (Athens, Ga., 1940), 94–122.

Royce, Charles C., "The Cherokee Nation of Indians," in *Fifth Annual Report of the Bureau of Ethnology* (Washington, 1887), 129–378.

Sanford, Edward T., "The Constitutional Convention of Tennessee of 1796," in the *Proceedings* of the Bar Association of Tennessee for 1896 (Nashville, Tenn., 1896), 92–155.

Schafer, Joseph, "Turner's Frontier Philosophy," in *Wisconsin Magazine of History*, XVI (1933), 451–469; "Turner's America," in *ibid.*, XVII (1934), 447–465.

Schaper, William A., "Sectionalism and Representation in South Carolina," in American Historical Association *Annual Report for the Year 1900*, I (1901), 237–463. This work was one of the early productions of the Turner school.

Shepard, Claude L., "The Connecticut Land Company: A Study in the

Beginnings of Colonization of the Western Reserve," in Western Reserve Historical Society, *Tract No. 96* (1916), 59–221.

Skinner, Hubert M., "Brookville's Rounded Century, June, 1908," in *Indiana Magazine of History,* VI (1910), 81–86.

Snyder, John F., "Forgotten Statesmen of Illinois: Hon. Conrad Will," in Illinois State Historical Society *Transactions for the Year 1905* (1906), 349–377; "Forgotten Statesmen of Illinois: Hon. Jesse Burgess Thomas," in Illinois State Historical Society *Transactions for the Year 1904* (1904), 514–523.

Steiner, Bernard C., "Western Maryland in the Revolution," in Johns Hopkins University *Studies in Historical and Political Science,* XX (1902), 5–57.

Turner, Frederick J., "Western State-Making in the Revolutionary Era," in *American Historical Review,* I (1895), 70–87, 251–269; "The Old West," in Frederick J. Turner, *The Frontier in American History* (New York, 1920), 67–125; "Problems in American History," in *The Early Writings of Frederick Jackson Turner* (Madison, Wis., 1938), 71–83; "The Colonization of the West (1820–1830)," in *American Historical Review,* XI (1905–1906), 303–327. See *ante,* chapter XIV, for a discussion of Turner's work.

Wagstaff, Henry M., "State Rights and Political Parties in North Carolina, 1776–1861," in Johns Hopkins University *Studies in Historical and Political Science,* XXIV (1906), 445–599.

Webster, Homer G., "William Henry Harrison's Administration of Indiana Territory," in Indiana Historical Society *Publications,* IV (1907), 173–297.

Whitaker, Arthur P., "Spanish Intrigue in the Old Southwest: An Episode, 1788–1789," in *Mississippi Valley Historical Review,* XII (1925–1926), 155–176.

White, Kate, "John Adair, The Entry-Taker," in *Tennessee Historical Magazine,* VIII (1924), 112–118.

Williams, Samuel C., "Tennessee's First Military Expedition," in *Tennessee Historical Magazine,* VIII (1924), 171–190; "The Admission of Tennessee into the Union," *Tennessee Historical Quarterly,* IV (1945), 291–319.

Wilson, George R., "Early Indiana Trails and Surveys," in Indiana Historical Society *Publications,* VI (1919), 347–457.

Willis, Bailey, "The Northern Appalachians," in Powell, *et al., Physiography of the United States,* 169–202.

Wright, Benjamin F., "American Democracy and the Frontier," in the *Yale Review,* N.S., XX (1930), 349–365; "Political Institutions and the Frontier," in *Sources of Culture in the Middle West,* ed. by Dixon R. Fox, 15–38; and book review of Turner's *Significance of the Sections in American History* in the *New England Quarterly,* VI (1933), 630–

634. See *ante,* 231–33, and note 20. Wright is one of the leading critics of the Turner interpretation of American history.

Wright, Frank J., "The Blue Ridge of Southern Virginia and Western North Carolina," in *Journal of the Scientific Laboratories of Denison University* (Granville, Ohio, 1885–   ), XXII (1927), 116–132.

PERIODICALS AND OCCASIONAL PUBLICATIONS

American Antiquarian Society, *Proceedings,* N.S. (Worcester, Mass., 1880–   ).

American Geographical Society of New York, *Bulletin* (47 vols., New York, 1859–1915).

American Historical Magazine (9 vols., Nashville, Tenn., 1896–1904).

American Historical Association, *American Historical Review* (New York, 1895–   ); *Annual Reports* (New York, Washington, 1884–   ).

American Philosophical Society, *Proceedings* (Philadelphia, 1838–   ).

Chicago Historical Society, *Collections* (12 vols., Chicago, 1882–1928).

Columbia University, *Studies in History, Economics and Public Law* (New York, 1891–   ).

Denison University, *Journal of the Scientific Laboratories* (Granville, Ohio, 1885–   ).

East Tennessee Historical Society, *Publications* (Knoxville, Tenn., 1929–   ).

Fergus Historical Series (35 vols., Chicago, 1876–1914).

Filson Club, *History Quarterly* (Louisville, Ky., 1926–   ); *Publications* (Louisville, Ky., 1884–   ).

Historical and Philosophical Society of Ohio, *Quarterly Publications* (18 vols., Cincinnati, Ohio, 1906–1923); *Publications* (Cincinnati, Ohio, 1924–   ).

Illinois State Historical Library, *Collections* (Springfield, Ill., 1903–   ). This is an unusually significant series of publications, some of which were edited by Clarence W. Alvord, Solon J. Buck, James A. James, Francis S. Philbrick, and Theodore C. Pease.

Illinois State Historical Society, *Journal* (Springfield, Ill., 1908–   ); *Transactions* (Springfield, Ill., 1900–1936; and *Papers in Illinois History* (Springfield, Ill., 1937–   ).

Indiana Historical Bureau, Indiana Historical *Collections* (Indianapolis, Ind., 1916–   ). This agency was known as the Indiana Historical Commission, but became the Bureau in 1925. It is supported by the state. It has published a number of very useful volumes.

Indiana Historical Society, *Publications* (Indianapolis, Ind., 1895–   ).

Indiana Magazine of History (Bloomington, Ind., 1905–   ).

Johns Hopkins University, *Studies in Historical and Political Science* (Baltimore, Md., 1883–   ).

Kentucky State Historical Society, *Register* (Frankfort, Ky., 1903–   ).

Marietta College, *Historical Collections* (3 vols., Marietta, Ohio, 1917–1918). These volumes were edited by Archer B. Hulbert and are listed under Published Documentary and Manuscript Materials in this bibliography. They are important to a study of early Ohio.

Massachusetts Historical Society, *Collections* (Boston, Mass., 1792–   ).

Michigan Pioneer and Historical Society, *Collections* (Lansing, Mich., 1877–   ).

Mississippi Valley Historical Association, *Mississippi Valley Historical Review* (Cedar Rapids, Iowa, 1914–   ). Under the able editorship of such men as Clarence W. Alvord, Lester B. Shippee, Milo Quaife, Arthur C. Cole, and Louis Pelzer, this review became the most important organ of Western historians and now of historians of the United States.

Nation (New York, 1865–   ).

New Republic (New York, 1914–   ).

New York Historical Society, *Collections* (5 vols., New York, 1809–1830; 2nd Series, 4 vols., 1841–1859; present series, 1868–   ).

North Carolina Historical Commission, *North Carolina Historical Review* (Raleigh, N. C., 1924–   ).

The Olden Time (2 vols., Pittsburgh, Pa., 1846–1848). A number of early documents of the history of the Ohio Valley were printed in this early magazine, which was reprinted in Cincinnati, Ohio, in 1876.

Ohio State Archaeological and Historical Society, *Quarterly* (Columbus, Ohio, 1887–   ). The bound volumes of the *Quarterly* are published as *Publications; Historical Collections* (Columbus, Ohio, 1931–   ).

Ohio State University, *Contributions in History and Political Science* (Columbus, Ohio, 1913–   ).

Pacific Coast branch, American Historical Association, *Pacific Historical Review* (Glendale, Calif., 1932–   ).

Pennsylvania Historical Society, *Pennsylvania Magazine of History and Biography* (Philadelphia, 1877–   ).

Political Science Quarterly (New York, 1886–   ).

Southern Historical Association, *Journal of Southern History* (Baton Rouge, La., 1935–   ).

South-Western Monthly (2 vols., Nashville, Tenn., 1852).

Tennessee Historical Society, *Tennessee Historical Magazine* (13 vols., Nashville, Tenn., 1915–1937); Tennessee Historical Commission and Tennessee Historical Society, *Tennessee Historical Quarterly* (Nashville, Tenn., 1942–   ).

Trinity College Historical Society, *Historical Papers* (Durham, N. C., 1897–   ).

Virginia Historical Society, *Collections* (Richmond, Va., 1 vol., 1833, N.S., 11 vols., 1882–1892).

Western Reserve Historical Society, *Publications* (110 vols., Cleveland,

Ohio, 1870–1929). Nos. 1–12 were published as Historical and Archaeological Tracts; Nos. 3–97 Tracts.

Wisconsin State Historical Society, *Wisconsin Magazine of History* (Madison, Wis., 1917–   ); *Collections* (Madison, Wis., 1854–   ); *Publications* (Madison, Wis., 1915–   ). The Calendar Series of the *Publications* have been referred to in connection with the Draper Collection of Manuscripts. The important volumes edited by Thwaites and Kellogg containing material from the Draper Collection are mentioned under Published Documentary and Manuscript Materials. The Wisconsin State Historical Society is one of the oldest and most active of western societies. Its publications are very important for a study of the Middle West.

University of Wisconsin, *Bulletin*, Economics, Political Science, and History Series (2 vols., Madison, Wis., 1894–1899).

Yale Review (19 vols., New Haven, Conn., 1892–1911, N.S., 1911–   ).

COUNTY HISTORIES AND ATLASES, AND LOCAL BIOGRAPHICAL WORKS

In searching for the nativities and early careers of the members of the various constitutional conventions, a considerable number of county histories, atlases, and biographical volumes were consulted. The list is too long to include here. This type of work is uncritical and often unreliable. The biographical sketches of local leaders seldom contain anything uncomplimentary to the individuals. Often, however, they preserve details which cannot be found elsewhere. Quite frequently, the biographical sketch was furnished by the descendant of the person described and, therefore, should be reasonably accurate for the type of information sought. Poor as they are, the lack of such studies in certain states leaves the historical investigator with an even greater problem than that occasioned by their deficiencies. Where possible, biographies of the more important leaders written by competent scholars and the sketches in the *Dictionary of American Biography* and other better biographical cyclopedias have been used. Many of the county histories have been cited in the footnotes and additional citations may be found in the author's articles listed under Secondary Accounts, Articles, but they will not be repeated here.

UNPUBLISHED MANUSCRIPTS

Caldemeyer, Richard H., The Career of George Nichols (a Ph.D. dissertation, Indiana University, 1950). This is an excellent study.

Hutchinson, William T., The Bounty Lands of the American Revolution in Ohio (unpublished Ph.D. Thesis, University of Chicago, Department of History, 1927).

Sears, Alfred B., The Public Career of Thomas Worthington (unpublished Ph.D. Thesis, Ohio State University, Columbus, Ohio, 1932).

Smith, Dwight L., Indian Land Cessions in the Old Northwest, 1795–1809 (a Ph.D. dissertation, Indiana University, 1949).

Utter, William T., Ohio Politics and Politicians, 1802–1815 (unpublished Ph.D. Thesis, University of Chicago, 1929).

Uzée, Philip D., The First Louisiana State Constitution: A Study of its Origins (M.A. Thesis, Louisiana State University, Baton Rouge, La., 1938).

MODERN ATLASES AND MAPS

Adams, James T., and Coleman, R. V. (eds.), *Atlas of American History* (New York, 1943).

Paullin, Charles O., and Wright, John K., *Atlas of the Historical Geography of the United States* (Washington and New York, 1932).

United States Geological Survey Topographical Maps.

BIBLIOGRAPHICAL AIDS

The various aids which the bibliographers have created were used in making this study. Among the more helpful were bibliographies of newspapers and serials, lists of manuscript collections, printed catalogues of published books and pamphlets, card catalogues of national, regional, state, and local libraries, and the lists of the publications of historical and other learned societies. The more useful guides to newspaper and serial collections include Clarence S. Brigham, *History and Bibliography of American Newspapers, 1690–1820*, 2 vols. (Worcester, Massachusetts, 1947); Winifred Gregory, *American Newspapers, 1821–1936* (New York, 1937), and *Union List of Serials* (New York, 1943); Franklin W. Scott, *Newspapers and Periodicals of Illinois, 1814–1879 (Collections* of the Illinois State Historical Library, VI, Springfield, Illinois, 1910); Arthur D. Mink, *Union List of Ohio Newspapers Available in Ohio* (Columbus, Ohio, 1946); Charles B. Galbreath, *Newspapers and Periodicals in Ohio State Library, Other Libraries of the State and List of Ohio Newspapers in the Library of Congress and the Historical Society of Wisconsin* (Columbus, Ohio, 1902).

The lists of manuscript collections include *Handbook of Manuscripts in the Library of Congress* (Washington, 1902); "List of Manuscript Collections in the Library of Congress to July 1, 1931," compiled by Curtis W. Garrison, in American Historical Association, *Annual Report for 1930*, I (Washington, 1931), 123–233; The National Archives, *Annual Report of the Archivist of the United States* (Washington, 1936–   ); Library of Congress, *Report of the Librarian of Congress, 1932–   * (Washington, 1932–   );

Reuben G. Thwaites (ed.), *Descriptive List of Manuscript Collections of the State Historical Society of Wisconsin* (Madison, Wisconsin, 1906); Alice E. Smith, *Guide to the Manuscripts of the Wisconsin Historical Society* (Madison, Wisconsin, 1944); *The Preston and Virginia Papers of the Draper Collection of Manuscripts,* in the State Historical Society of Wisconsin, *Publications,* Calendar Series, I (Madison, Wisconsin, 1915); *The Kentucky Papers of the Draper Collection of Manuscripts,* in *ibid.,* II (1925). *Calendar of Virginia State Papers* (11 vols., Richmond, Virginia, 1875–1893), edited by William P. Palmer. Thwaites' *List* gives much detail about the Draper Collection while Miss Smith's later guide treats principally the other collections of the Wisconsin Historical Society. The *Calendar of Virginia State Papers* often quotes portions of the documents.

Among the more useful bibliographies of published works were the following: Charles Evans, *American Bibliography, 1639 to 1820* (12 vols., Chicago, 1902–1934); Joseph Sabin, *et al., A Dictionary of Books relating to America* (29 vols., New York, 1868–1936); *American Catalogue of Books, 1876–1910* (New York, 1881–1911); *Annual American Catalogue, 1886–1910* (New York, 1887–1911); *Cumulative Book Index,* 1898– (New York, 1898–); *United States Catalogue,* 1900– (New York, 1900–); *A Catalogue of Books Represented by Library of Congress Printed Cards* (167 vols., Ann Arbor, Michigan, 1942–1946); *Writings on American History,* 1902, 1903, 1906– (New York and other cities, 1904–); Edward Chaning, Albert B. Hart, and Frederick J. Turner, *Guide to the Study of American History* (Boston, 1912); Peter G. Thompson, *Bibliography of the State of Ohio . . .* (Cincinnati, Ohio, 1880); and Solon J. Buck, *Travel and Description, 1765–1865, together with a list of county histories, atlases, and biographical collections and a list of territorial and state laws* (*Collections* of the Illinois State Historical Library, IX, Springfield, Illinois, 1914).

More useful in this instance were the card catalogues of various libraries visited. In the various localities the leading library usually specialized in the history of the particular state or section of the state. When brought together for a region like the Ohio Valley and added to the accumulations of such leading libraries as the Library of Congress and the University of Chicago Library, the coverage is actually greater than that found in the more usual aids. The following libraries were among those visited: Carnegie Library of Pittsburgh, Pennsylvania; Chillicothe, Ohio, Public Library; Cincinnati, Ohio, Public Library; Illinois State Historical Library, Springfield, Illinois; Indiana State Library, Indianapolis, Indiana; Indiana University Library, Bloomington, Indiana; Knoxville, Tennessee, Public Library; Lawson McGhee Library, Knoxville, Tennessee; Lexington Kentucky, Public Library; Library of Congress, Washington; Louisiana State University Library, Baton Rouge; Memphis, Tennessee, Public Library; Mercantile Library, St. Louis, Missouri; Ohio Archaeological and

Historical Society Library, Columbus, Ohio; Ohio State University Library, Columbus, Ohio; University of Chicago Library; University of Illinois Library, Urbana, Illinois; University of Kentucky Library, Lexington, Kentucky; University of North Carolina Library, Chapel Hill, North Carolina; University of Tennessee Library, Knoxville, Tennessee; University of West Virginia Library, Morgantown, West Virginia; Western Pennsylvania Historical Society Library, Pittsburgh, Pennsylvania; Western Reserve Historical Society Library, Cleveland, Ohio; William and Mary College Library, Williamsburg, Virginia; William Henry Smith Memorial Library, Indianapolis, Indiana; Wisconsin State Historical Society Library, Madison, Wisconsin.

The publications of the Learned Societies and State and Local Historical Societies have been examined and the following bibliographies consulted: Leslie W. Dunlap, *American Historical Societies, 1790–1860* (Madison, Wisconsin, 1944); and Christopher Crittenden and Doris Godard (comps.), *Historical Societies in the United States and Canada, A Handbook* (Washington, 1944).

NOTES

INTRODUCTION AND ACKNOWLEDGMENTS

1. Edwards, Everett E. (comp.), *The Early Writings of Frederick Jackson Turner* (Madison, Wis., 1938), 37 and 72.

2. Frederick J. Turner, "The Significance of the Frontier in American History," in American Historical Association, *Annual Report, 1893* (Washington, 1894), 199–227. This article has been reprinted many times as in Frederick J. Turner, *The Frontier in American History (New York,* 1920), 1–38.

3. John Finley, *Les Français au coeur de L'Amérique* (Paris, 1916), 361; and Meredith Nicholson, *The Valley of Democracy* (New York, 1918).

CHAPTER 1. PLANTERS VERSUS YEOMEN

1. William E. Dodd, "The Emergence of the First Social Order in the United States," in the *American Historical Review* (New York, 1895–), XL (1934–1935), 217–231, gives an interesting description of the rise of the planter civilization. Avery O. Craven in *The Repressible Conflict, 1830–1861* (University, La., 1939), 20–23, recognized this ideal as an important feature of the South.

2. Thomas P. Abernethy, *Three Virginia Frontiers* (University, La., 1940), 1–62. The author presents a view which varies considerably from that of Frederick J. Turner. The undemocratic features of the frontier are emphasized.

3. The well-known article by Frederick J. Turner entitled "The Old West," in *The Frontier in American History* (New York, 1920), 67–125, will always remain a classic description of the frontier in the Upland South. See 83 ff.

4. Charles A. Hanna, *The Scotch-Irish: or the Scot in North Britain, North Ireland, and North America* (2 vols., New York, 1902), and Albert

B. Faust, *The German Element in the United States* (2 vols., Boston, 1909).

5. Thomas J. Wertenbaker, *The Founding of American Civilization* (3 vols., New York, 1938–1947), II, *The Old South* (1942), gives a significant picture of the different social orders of the South. For the civilizations of the Tidewater and Upland, see 1–18, 118–219, and 305–347.

6. J. Paul Selsam, *The Pennsylvania Constitution of 1776, A Study in Revolutionary Democracy* (Philadelphia, 1936), 25–43.

7. *Ibid.*, 4–25; Allan Nevins, *The American States during and after the Revolution, 1775–1789* (New York, 1924), 98–108; and Charles H. Lincoln, *The Revolutionary Movement in Pennsylvania*, in *Publications* of the University of Pennsylvania, *Series in History*, No. 1 (Philadelphia, 1901), 189–287.

8. Selsam, *The Pennsylvania Constitution of 1776*, pp. 49–168; and Lincoln, *Revolutionary Movement in Pennsylvania*, 189–265.

9. The constitution is printed in Francis N. Thorpe (comp.), *Federal and State Constitutions . . . and Other Organic Laws* (7 vols., Washington, 1909), V, 3081–3092. See Selsam, *Pennsylvania Constitution of 1776*, pp. 169–204; and Lincoln, *Revolutionary Movement in Pennsylvania*, 226–287.

10. D. Huger Bacot, "The South Carolina Up Country at the End of the Eighteenth Century," in the *American Historical Review*, XXVIII (1922–1923), 682–698; see 684.

11. William A. Schaper, "Sectionalism and Representation in South Carolina," in the American Historical Association *Annual Report for the Year 1900* (2 vols., Washington, 1901), I, 378.

12. Thomas Cooper (ed.), *The Statutes at Large of South Carolina* (5 vols., Columbia, S. C., 1836–1839), IV (1838), 885.

13. Charles R. Lingley, "The Transition from Colony to Commonwealth," in Columbia University *Studies in History, Economics and Public Law* (New York, 1891–   ), XXXVI (1910), 502–535; Charles H. Ambler, *Sectionalism in Virginia from 1776 to 1861* (Chicago, 1910), 1–60; Fletcher M. Green, *Constitutional Development in the South Atlantic States, 1776–1860* (Chapel Hill, N. C., 1930), 62–65. The constitutions referred to have been reprinted in Thorpe, *Federal and State Constitutions*. The constitutions are arranged by states and under each state chronologically. Each point in the following discussion has been carefully checked, but footnote citations will not be given. The secondary accounts are largely those of Southern writers and do not, therefore, represent a hostile interpretation.

14. Bernard C. Steiner, "Western Maryland in the Revolution," in Johns Hopkins University *Studies in Historical and Political Science* (Baltimore, Md., 1883–   ), XX (1902), 5–57; Green, *Constitutional De-*

velopment in the South Atlantic States, 71–72; Faust, *The German Element in the United States,* I, 161–176.

15. Henry M. Wagstaff, "State Rights and Political Parties in North Carolina: 1776–1861," in Johns Hopkins University *Studies in Historical and Political Science,* XXIV (1906), 457.

16. John S. Bassett, "The Regulators of North Carolina (1765–1771)," in the American Historical Association *Annual Report for the Year 1894* (Washington, 1895), 141–212.

17. Green, *Constitutional Development in the South Atlantic States,* 66–71.

18. Lucien E. Roberts, "Sectional Factors in the Movements for Legislative Reapportionment and Reduction in Georgia, 1777–1860," in James C. Bonner and Lucien E. Roberts (eds.), *Studies in Georgia History and Government* (Athens, Ga., 1940), 94–122.

19. *Laws of Maryland, made since M,DCC,LXIII . . .* (printed by Frederick Green, Annapolis, 1787), see chapter 23, session of 1782–1783; *Laws of Maryland made and passed at a session of Assembly, begun . . . in 1786* (Printed by Frederick Green, Annapolis, n.d.), chapter 45; Nevins, *The American States during and after the Revolution,* 204, 443.

20. Lingley, "Transition from Colony to Commonwealth," in Columbia University *Studies in History, Economics and Public Law,* XXXVI, 502–535; Ambler, *Sectionalism in Virginia,* 1–60.

21. Green, *Constitutional Development in the South Atlantic States,* 115; and Schaper, "Sectionalism and Representation in South Carolina," in the American Historical Association *Annual Report for the Year 1900,* I, 367–369.

22. Green, *Constitutional Development in the South Atlantic States,* 124–137; and Robert P. Brooks, "The Agrarian Revolution in Georgia, 1865–1912," in the *Bulletin* of the University of Wisconsin, *History Series* (Madison, Wis., 1902–1918), III (1912–1914), 461–506.

23. Ambler, *Sectionalism in Virginia,* 93–99; Green, *Constitutional Development in the South Atlantic States,* 203–204.

24. William H. Hoyt (ed.), *The Papers of Archibald D. Murphey* (2 vols., Raleigh, N. C., 1914), II, 58–59; Green, *Constitutional Development in the South Atlantic States,* 204–205.

25. James W. Harry, "The Maryland Constitution of 1851," in the Johns Hopkins University *Studies in Historical and Political Science,* XX, 379–464, see 391; Green, *Constitutional Development in the South Atlantic States,* 201.

26. Schaper, "Sectionalism and Representation in South Carolina," in the American Historical Association *Annual Report for the Year 1900,* I, 433–434.

27. Green, *Constitutional Development in the South Atlantic States,* 202, 207–210.

28. *Proceedings and Debates of the Virginia State Convention of 1829–30* (Richmond, Va., 1830), 25–31, 79–90. These pages give a "Memorial of the Non-Freeholders of the City of Richmond," and the very able speech of Philip Doddridge of Brooke County which is almost a history of representation in Virginia. See also Ambler, *Sectionalism in Virginia,* 137–174; Green, *Constitutional Development in the South Atlantic States,* 210–224.

29. Green, *Constitutional Development in the South Atlantic States,* 233–240; Roberts, "Sectional Factors in the Movements for Legislative Reapportionment," in Bonner and Roberts, *Studies in Georgia History,* 103–120.

30. Green, *Constitutional Development in the South Atlantic States,* 223–233.

31. *Niles' Weekly Register* (Baltimore, Md., 1811–1849), LII (1837), 73–74; Harry, "The Maryland Constitution of 1851," in the Johns Hopkins University *Studies in Historical and Political Science,* XX, 390–396; Green, *Constitutional Development in the South Atlantic States,* 240–248.

32. Green, *Constitutional Development in the South Atlantic States,* 254–296; Ambler, *Sectionalism in Virginia,* 251–299; Harry, "The Maryland Constitution of 1851," in the Johns Hopkins University *Studies in Historical and Political Science,* XX, 387–464.

33. A reference to Bacon's Rebellion in 1676 indicates that this issue was a century-old grievance.

34. Professor Fletcher Green's presidential address to the Southern Historical Association for 1945, "Democracy in the Old South," lays considerable emphasis upon the growing democracy of the South. It is found in the *Journal of Southern History* (Baton Rouge, La., 1935–   ), XII (1946), 3–23. There seems to be no conflict between this chapter and Green's address so far as the reform efforts are concerned. There is a difference in point of view between his book, *Constitutional Development in the South Atlantic States,* and his presidential address; this chapter follows more closely the former. This view is supported by original materials and by the works of several Southern scholars, including Green's excellent volume. If one pays strict attention to the very important exceptions mentioned in the presidential address, the difference becomes largely a matter of emphasis. Both in the book and in the address, however, Green denies the influence of the frontier. "The demands for reform grew out of local conditions and would have arisen had there been no 'New West' beyond the Appalachians." See p. 15 of the address and p. 300 in the longer study. How can anyone know this? As a matter of fact, the frontier existed in each of the Southern states and was one of the "local conditions." The frontier on both sides of the mountains created fluid social and economic conditions which set the stage for reform.

CHAPTER 2. THE HIGHWAYS OF FRONTIER EXPANSION

1. A Map of the most Inhabited part of Virginia, containing the whole Province of Maryland with Part of Pennsylvania, New Jersey and North Carolina, Drawn by Joshua Fry & Peter Jefferson in 1751, in Emerson D. Fite and Archibald Freeman (eds.), *A Book of Old Maps* (Cambridge, Mass., 1926), 242–245; Thomas Jefferys, *The American Atlas: or, A Geographical Description of the Whole Continent of America: . . .* (London, 1776), 20–21. It is difficult to understand why Archer B. Hulbert did not devote a volume in his *Historic Highways of America* to this historic highway. He published fifteen volumes and an index (Cleveland, O., 1902–1905).

2. William L. Saunders (ed.), *The Colonial Records of North Carolina* (10 vols., Raleigh, N. C., 1886–1890), VII (1890), 248.

3. J. Stoddard Johnston, *First Explorations of Kentucky; Doctor Thomas Walker's Journal . . . also Colonel Christopher Gist's Journal* in Filson Club *Publications* (Louisville, Ky., 1884–   ), XIII (1898), 36–44.

4. Samuel C. Williams, *Dawn of Tennessee Valley and Tennessee History* (Johnson City, Tenn., 1937), 265.

5. John Haywood, *The Civil and Political History of the State of Tennessee* (Nashville, Tenn., 1891), 49–50.

6. Johnston, *First Explorations of Kentucky*, 36–37.

7. Walter Clark (ed.), *The State Records of North Carolina* (16 vols., Winston and Goldsboro, N. C., 1895–1907), XXII (1907), 706. The *State Records* are a continuation of the *Colonial Records*, and the volumes are numbered consecutively.

8. Johnston, *First Explorations of Kentucky*, 160–162.

9. *The Journal of the Rev. Francis Asbury, Bishop of the Methodist Episcopal Church . . .* (3 vols., New York, 1821), II, 125; "General Slade's Journal of a Trip to Tennessee," in the Historical Society of Trinity College, *An Annual Publication of Historical Papers* (Durham, N. C., 1897–   ), VI (1906), 37–56; see 43–44.

10. Williams, *Dawn of Tennessee History*, 10, 54. This route which Boone used from the Yadkin Valley over the Appalachian Mountains should not be confused with his later Wilderness Road from the Watauga Valley to the Kentucky Bluegrass.

11. Lyman C. Draper, *King's Mountain and Its Heroes* (New York, 1929), 176–183.

12. "The Journal of André Michaux, 1793–1796," in Reuben G. Thwaites (ed.), *Early Western Travels, 1748–1846* (32 vols., Cleveland, O., 1904–1907), III (1904), 55–62. The above was first published in "Portions of the Journal of André Michaux, Botantist, written during his Travels in the United States and Canada, 1785 to 1796, with an Introduction and Explanatory Notes, by C. S. Sargent," in *Proceedings* of the American Philosophical Society (Philadelphia, 1838–   ), XXVI (1889), 1–145.

13. *Journal of the Rev. Francis Asbury*, II, 69, 248–249, and 284–287.

14. François A. Michaux, "Travels to the West of the Alleghany Mountains, . . . 1802," in Thwaites (ed.), *Early Western Travels*, III, 283–286.

15. *Journal of the Rev. Francis Asbury*, II, 31–32, 69–70, 160–161, and 221–222.

16. These quotations come from the *Journal of the Rev. Francis Asbury*, II, 400, III, 1–2, 83–84, 206, 278, 300–301. See also Henry Boehm, *Reminiscences, Historical and Biographical of Sixty-four Years in the Ministry*, ed. by Rev. Joseph B. Wakeley (New York, 1865), 209–212, 263–266.

17. Thomas P. Abernethy, *From Frontier to Plantation in Tennessee* (Chapel Hill, N. C., 1932), 154–155.

18. *Ibid.*, 7; Williams, *Dawn of Tennessee History*, 437.

19. Williams, *Dawn of Tennessee History*, 361–362.

20. Archer B. Hulbert, *Washington's Road, Historic Highways of America*, III (1903), 91–96; Kenneth P. Bailey, *The Ohio Company of Virginia and the Westward Movement, 1748–1792* (Glendale, Calif., 1939), 153–154.

21. Winthrop Sargent, *The History of an Expedition Against Fort Du Quesne, in 1755 (Memoirs of the Historical Society of Pennsylvania*, V, Philadelphia, 1855), 201. This volume contains two journals kept on the expedition. The entire army was even longer in reaching Little Crossing.

22. See letters of General John Forbes and Governor Horatio Sharpe to William Pitt in Gertrude S. Kimball (ed.), *Correspondence of William Pitt . . . with the Colonial Governors and Military . . . Commissioners in America* (2 vols., New York, 1906), I, 235–238, 245–248, 278–281, 294–297, 327–332, 338–343, 370–375, 410–411, 427.

23. John C. Fitzpatrick (ed.), *Diaries of George Washington* (4 vols., Boston, 1925), I, 441; and Alfred P. James, "The First English-Speaking Trans-Appalachian Frontier," in the *Mississippi Valley Historical Review* (Cedar Rapids, Iowa, 1914–   ), XVII (1930–1931), 55–71.

24. James A. James, *Life of George Rogers Clark* (Chicago, 1929), 10.

25. Thomas Speed, *The Wilderness Road* in Filson Club *Publications*, II (1886). See the Journal of William Brown on pp. 18–20, and the Journal of William Calk on pp. 34–38. Calk went to Kentucky in 1775 and

Brown in 1782. A recent study of the road is *The Wilderness Road* (Indianapolis, c. 1947), by Robert L. Kincaid.

26. Samuel C. Williams, *Early Travels in the Tennessee Country, 1540–1800* (Johnson City, Tenn., 1928), 278.

27. Speed, *The Wilderness Road*, 19; William A. Pusey, *The Wilderness Road to Kentucky* (New York, c. 1921), 102–112. Note the various pictures and the detailed maps on pp. 71–81.

28. Williams, *Early Travels in the Tennessee Country*, 274.

29. Speed, *The Wilderness Road*, 19.

30. W. P. Strickland (ed.), *Autobiography of Peter Cartwright, The Backwoods Preacher* (New York, 1857), 17–18.

31. Robert S. Cotterill, *History of Pioneer Kentucky* (Cincinnati, 1917), 162.

32. James Veech in the *Centenary Memorial of the Planting and Growth of Presbyterianism in Western Pennsylvania . . .* (Pittsburgh, 1876), 340.

33. Archer B. Hulbert, *Boone's Wilderness Road, Historic Highways of America*, VI (1903), 178–181.

34. Archer B. Hulbert, *Waterways of Westward Expansion, Historic Highways of America*, IX (1903), 89–90; Zadok Cramer, *The Navigator* (Pittsburgh, 1811), 35–36.

35. Note the experiences of Francis Baily as recorded in *A Tour of the Unsettled Parts of North America in 1796 & 1797* (London, 1856), 147–195.

36. Mary C. Dewees, *Journal of a Trip from Philadelphia to Lexington in Kentucky* (Crawfordsville, Ind., 1936), 9–11. Mrs. Dewees waited from October 26 to November 18, 1787, for a rise in the river.

37. Pittsburgh, Pa., *Gazette*, Oct. 7, 1786, Feb. 9, 1788, March 29, 1788, June 14, 1788, July 7, 1789, *et passim;* Cramer, *The Navigator*, 34–35.

38. H. Fouré Selter (ed.), *L'Odyssée Américaine d'une Famille Française* (Baltimore, 1936), 49; and Lexington, Ky., *Gazette*, March 29, 1790, April 5, 1790, May 17, 1790, Jan. 15, 1791, March 26, 1791, May 7, 1791, May 14, 1791, July 2, 1791, and July 9, 1791.

CHAPTER 3. O'ER THE MOUNTAINS

1. Hamlin Garland, *A Son of the Middle Border* (New York, 1941), 45–46.

2. William W. Hening (ed.), *The Statutes at Large, Virginia* (13 vols.,

Richmond, Va., 1809–1823), X (1822), 143; Cotterill, *Pioneer History of Kentucky*, 125, 147, 158.

3. Floyd to Preston, May 5, 1780, Draper MSS., 17CC124; Thomas P. Abernethy, *Western Lands and the American Revolution* (New York, 1937), 249; *John Bradford's Historical &c Notes on Kentucky . . .* compiled by G. W. Stipp in 1827 (San Francisco, 1932), 71–72, 92; Hening, *The Statutes at Large, Virginia,* X, 50; Humphrey Marshall, *The History of Kentucky* (2 vols., Frankfort, Ky., 1812), I, 89–90.

4. John Rogers to George Rogers Clark, October 17, 1779, in James A. James (ed.), *George Rogers Clark Papers, 1771–1781,* in Illinois State Historical Library *Collections* (Springfield, Ill., 1903–   ), VIII (1912), 373.

5. General Lachlan McIntosh to General George Washington, Fort Pitt, March 12, 1779, in Louise P. Kellogg (ed.), *Frontier Advance on the Upper Ohio, 1778–1779,* Wisconsin State Historical Society *Collections* (Madison, Wis., 1855–   ), XXIII (1916), 240.

6. Hening, *The Statutes at Large, Virginia,* X, 315–317.

7. George Rogers Clark to Governor Thomas Jefferson, Louisville, Aug. 22, 1780, in James, *George Rogers Clark Papers, 1771–1781,* p. 451; and Joseph Bowman to Isaac Hite, June 14, 1779, in *ibid.,* 333.

8. McAffee MSS, Durrett collection, in Temple Bodley, *History of Kentucky, Before the Louisiana Purchase in 1803* (Chicago, 1928), 213. This is volume one of a four-volume history of Kentucky published by J. S. Clarke.

9. James, "The First English-Speaking Trans-Appalachian Frontier," in the *Mississippi Valley Historical Review,* XVII, 55–71; Solon J. and Elizabeth H. Buck, *The Planting of Civilization in Western Pennsylvania* (n.p., 1939), 135–155.

10. *Pennsylvania Archives* (9 series, 119 vols., Philadelphia, 1852–1935), 1st Series, VIII (1853), 352–354, see 353.

11. See the letters of Colonel Daniel Brodhead in Neville B. Craig (ed.), *The Olden Time* (2 vols., Pittsburgh, 1846–1848, reprinted, Cincinnati, Ohio, 1876), II, 374, 378, 384, 387–388, and 392.

12. "To *his Excellency* John *Earl* of Dunmore, . . . *Governor General . . . of* Virginia . . . *and . . .* the Council *and* House of Burgesses: *The Petition of the Inhabitants settled on the Waters of the* Ohio . . . " in Peter Force, *American Archives,* 4th Series (6 vols., Washington, 1837–1846), I (1837), 275.

13. Veech in the *Centenary Memorial,* 356.

14. Alexander McClean to President Moore, June 27, 1782, in the *Pennsylvania Archives,* 1st Series, IX (1854), 564–566.

15. James Finley to John Dickinson, April 28, 1783, in *ibid.,* 1st Series, X (1854), 41.

16. Thomas Scott to President Reed, Westmoreland, Jan. 24, 1781, in *ibid.,* 1st Series, VIII, 713–714.

17. Alexander J. Dallas, *Laws of the Commonwealth of Pennsylvania* (4 vols., Philadelphia, 1793–1797), II (1793), 82–84, see 83.

18. Veech in the *Centenary Memorial,* 340.

19. Consul W. Butterfield (ed.), *Washington-Irvine Correspondence* (Madison, Wis., 1882), 109, see also 231–233, 244, and 267. A similar letter of Irvine's is found in Craig, *The Olden Time,* II, 479.

20. *John Bradford's . . . Notes on Kentucky,* 101–105; Cotterill, *History of Pioneer Kentucky,* 177; Abernethy, *Western Lands and the American Revolution,* 258–267.

21. William P. Palmer (ed.), *Calendar of Virginia State Papers* (11 vols., Richmond, Va., 1875–1893), III (1883), 301–302. See also Andrew Steele to Governor of Virginia, Lexington, Ky., Sept. 12, 1782, in *ibid.,* 303–304.

22. Williams, *Early Travels in the Tennessee Country,* 274.

23. Pittsburgh *Gazette,* March 29, 1786.

24. Princeton, N. J., *Independent Gazetteer,* July 10, 1787; and Lieutenant Colonel Josiah Harmar to General Henry Knox, Fort Harmar, May 14, 1787, in the *Military Journal of Major Ebenezer Denny* (Philadelphia, 1859), 217–218.

25. Pittsburgh *Gazette,* June 20, 1787; "Nourse-Chapline Letters," in the Kentucky State Historical Society *Register* (Frankfort, Kentucky, 1903–   ), XXXI (1933), 155.

26. "Nourse-Chapline Letters," in the Kentucky State Historical Society *Register,* XXXI, 154–155.

27. Lieutenant Colonel Josiah Harmar to General Henry Knox, Fort Harmar, Dec. 9, 1787, in the *Military Journal of Major Ebenezer Denny,* 221; and in William H. Smith (ed.), *The St. Clair Papers* (2 vols., Cincinnati, 1882), II, 38.

28. Pittsburgh *Gazette,* March 22, 1788.

29. Selter, *L'Odyssée Américaine d'une Famille Française,* 48–49, 64, *et passim.*

30. Pittsburgh *Gazette,* Jan. 24, 1789.

31. *Ibid.,* Nov. 1, 1788.

32. Clarence E. Carter (comp. and ed.), *The Territorial Papers of the United States* (Washington, 1934–   ), II (1934), *The Territory Northwest of the River Ohio, 1787–1803,* pp. 196, 221 note 64, and 224. The last line in the table is from a letter of Winthrop Sargent, the rest from a report by General Knox.

33. Selter, *L'Odyssée Américaine d'une Famille Française,* 49; and Lexington, Ky., *Gazette,* March 29, 1790, April 5, 1790, May 17, 1790, Jan. 15, 1791, March 26, 1791, May 7, 1791, May 14, 1791, July 2, 1791, and July 9, 1791.

34. Payson J. Treat, *The National Land System, 1785–1820* (New York, 1910), 42.

35. Consul W. Butterfield, *Journal of Capt. Jonathan Heart . . . 1785, to which is added the Dickinson-Harmar Correspondence of 1784–85* (Albany, N. Y., 1885), 61–66; Smith, *The St. Clair Papers*, II, 1; and Hulbert, *Waterways of Westward Expansion, Historic Highways of America*, IX, 55. The number and activities of the squatters are described more fully *post*, chapters IV, 58–59, V, and IX, 128–31.

36. William H. Smith (ed.), *The Life and Public Services of Arthur St. Clair* (2 vols., Cincinnati, Ohio, 1882), II, 7, note 1. Hereafter referred to as *St. Clair Papers*.

37. *Journals of the Continental Congress, 1774–1789* (34 vols., Washington, 1904–1937), XXXIII (1936), 602.

38. John M. Brown, *The Political Beginnings of Kentucky*, in Filson Club *Publications*, VI (1889), 254–256.

39. James G. Ramsey, *The Annals of Tennessee* (Charleston, S. C., 1853), 195; "Narrative of John Carr," in *The South-Western Monthly* (2 vols., Nashville, Tenn., 1852–1853), II, 74–75; and "Sketch of the Captivity of Colonel Joseph Brown," in *ibid.*, I, 74, 75, 77.

40. "Journal of a Voyage," in A. W. Putnam, *History of Middle Tennessee* (Nashville, Tenn., 1859), 69–75; and "Sketch of the Captivity of Colonel Joseph Brown," in *The South-Western Monthly*, I, 11–12.

41. Ramsey, *Annals of Tennessee*, 185–186.

42. W. E. M'Elwee, " 'The Old Road,' from Washington and Hamilton districts to the Cumberland Settlement," in the *American Historical Magazine* (9 vols., Nashville, Tenn., 1896–1904), VIII (1898), 347–348. The Crab Orchard of Avery's Trace is not to be confused with the one on Boone's Wilderness Trail.

43. The population figures for 1790 were taken from the *Twelfth Census of the United States, 1900, Population*, I, Table 4, pp. 9–47.

CHAPTER 4. AN EPIDEMIC OF STATE MAKING

1. Abernethy, *Western Lands and the American Revolution*, 228, 261. The act was printed in the *State Records of North Carolina*, XXIV (1905), 478–482.

2. Abernethy, *From Frontier to Plantation in Tennessee*, 54.

3. Ramsey, *The Annals of Tennessee*, 134–138, gives their petition for annexation to North Carolina which contains the only contemporary account of the history of Watauga. It is particularly important because the agreement or constitution has not survived. For the quotation see page

136. Moses Fisk wrote an early account, but he was not an eyewitness of the events described. See "A Summary Notice of the First Settlements Made by White People within the Limits which Bound the State of Tennessee," in the Massachusetts Historical Society, *Collections* (Boston, 1792–   ), 2nd Series, VII (1818), 58–65. See also Albert V. Goodpasture (ed.), "Moses Fisk's Historical Sketch of Tennessee," in the *American Historical Magazine*, II (1897), 17–26. John Haywood wrote another early account, *The Civil and Political History of the State of Tennessee*, 50–61. Judge Haywood was a young man who was living in North Carolina when these events occurred. He could hardly have known of them from his own experiences.

4. Ramsey, *Annals of Tennessee*, 135–136.

5. *Colonial Records of North Carolina*, X (1890), 925–926, 951, 974; Abernethy, *From Frontier to Plantation in Tennessee*, 9–18; Ramsey, *Annals of Tennessee*, 139.

6. "Memorial for the Erection of a New State," in Boyd Crumrine (ed.), *History of Washington County, Pennsylvania (Philadelphia, 1882)*, 187–188.

7. Buck and Buck, *The Planting of Civilization in Western Pennsylvania*, 158–159, 162–169; Joseph Doddridge, *Notes on the Settlement and Indian Wars of the Western Parts of Virginia and Pennsylvania from 1763 to 1783* (Pittsburgh, 1912), 80–86.

8. Buck and Buck, *The Planting of Civilization in Western Pennsylvania*, 179–182.

9. *Ibid.*, 169, 182; Crumrine, *History of Washington County, Pennsylvania*, 225.

10. Abernethy, *Western Lands and the American Revolution*, 175–179.

11. Robert Lettis Hooper, Jr., to William Franklin, Fort Pitt, Sept. 15, 1772, in Crumrine, *History of Washington County, Pennsylvania*, 168.

12. "Memorial for the Erection of a New State," in Crumrine, *History of Washington County, Pennsylvania*, 187–188.

13. *Journals of the Continental Congress, 1774–1789*, XVIII (1910), 915–916. It is to be noted that they were not incorporated in the resolutions of September 6; see *ibid.*, XVII (1910), 808.

14. *Ibid.*, XXVI (1928), 113–116, see 114; and Thorpe, *Federal and State Constitutions*, II, 955–956.

15. *Journals of the Continental Congress, 1774–1789*, XXVI, 274–279.

16. *Ibid.*, XXXII (1936), 334–343, see 342; and Thorpe, *Federal and State Constitutions*, II, 957–962 (Section V).

17. Richard H. Collins, *History of Kentucky* (2 vols., Louisville, Ky., 1924), II, 498–514, contains Henderson's diary, the "Journal of the Proceedings . . . of the Colony of Transylvania," and other documents. See also William S. Lester, *The Transylvania Colony* (Spencer, Ind., 1935); Archibald Henderson, "The Creative Forces in Westward Expansion:

Henderson and Boone," in the *American Historical Review,* XX (1915), 86–107; *idem,* "A Pre-Revolutionary Revolt in the Old Southwest," in the *Mississippi Valley Historical Review,* XVIII (1931–1932), 191–212; *idem,* "Richard Henderson and the Occupation of Kentucky, 1775," in *ibid.,* I, 341–363; Cotterill, *History of Pioneer Kentucky,* 71–107; and Abernethy, *Western Lands and the American Revolution,* 123–135.

18. *Colonial Records of North Carolina,* IX, 1267–1279, see 1272; *American Archives,* 4th Series, IV (1843), 546–553. These volumes give the proceedings of the convention, which is also in Collins.

19. *Colonial Records of North Carolina,* IX, 1277; *American Archives,* 4th Series, IV, 552.

20. James, *George Rogers Clark Papers, 1771–1781,* pp. 11–13.

21. *Ibid.,* 209.

22. Hening, *The Statutes at Large,* IX, (1821), 257–261.

23. James, *George Rogers Clark Papers, 1771–1781,* p. 13.

24. "The Articles of Agreement, or Compact of Government entered into by settlers on the Cumberland river, 1st May, 1780," is printed in Putnam, *History of Middle Tennessee,* 94–102. Archibald Henderson, "Richard Henderson: The Authorship of the Cumberland Compact and the Founding of Nashville," in the *Tennessee Historical Magazine* (13 vols., Nashville, Tenn., 1915–1937), 1st Series, II (1916), 155–172; and Abernethy, *From Frontier to Plantation in Tennessee,* 19–32.

25. James R. Robertson, *Petitions of the Early Inhabitants of Kentucky,* in Filson Club *Publications,* XXVII (1914), 45–47.

26. This is quoted by George Morgan in a letter of September 12, 1780, to Major William Trent, Draper MSS 46J59. The Land Act of 1779 granted to the few persons who were present in Kentucky before January 1, 1778, four hundred acres of land and to those who came after this date and who had improved the land on which they had settled, preemption rights on four hundred acres. Persons of both classes could also have the right of pre-emption on one thousand additional acres. See Hening, *The Statutes at Large, Virginia,* X, 35–50.

27. Letter of John Floyd of May 31, 1780, Draper MSS 17CC128; and Bodley, *History of Kentucky,* 282.

28. The petition is printed in Theodore Roosevelt, *The Winning of the West* (4 vols., New York, 1900), II, 398–399.

29. George Rogers Clark to John Clark, Aug. 23, 1780, in James, *George Rogers Clark Papers, 1771–1781,* p. 453.

30. Abernethy, *Western Lands and the American Revolution,* 249–252, and 262–264.

31. Hening, *The Statutes at Large,* X, 564–567; Abernethy, *Western Lands and the American Revolution,* 244–246; Bodley, *History of Kentucky,* 291–292.

32. John Donelson to Arthur Campbell, Draper MSS 9DD34; Allin to

L. Todd, *ibid.*, 16CC40; Abernethy, *Western Lands and the American Revolution,* 264; Bodley, *History of Kentucky,* 299.

33. "The Papers of Charles Thomson, Secretary of the Continental Congress," New York Historical Society *Collections, 1878* (New York, 1879), 145–150.

34. Robertson, *Petitions of the Early Inhabitants of Kentucky,* 62–66. See also Hening, *The Statutes at Large, Virginia,* X, 431–32. The relief act allowed poor residents 2½ years in which to pay for land.

35. George Rogers Clark to the Governor of Virginia, Fort Nelson, May 2, 1782, *Calendar of Virginia State Papers,* III, 150.

36. Clark to Governor Harrison, Lincoln, Ky., Nov. 30, 1782, *ibid.*, 384.

37. Robertson, *Petitions of the Early Inhabitants of Kentucky,* 78–79. The petition is undated. Bodley, *History of Kentucky,* 304–305.

38. Walker Daniel to Governor Harrison, Lincoln, Ky., Jan. 19, 1784, and *idem* to *idem,* Lincoln, Ky., May 21, 1784, in *Calendar of Virginia State Papers,* III, 555–556, and 584–588.

39. Colonel Daniel Brodhead, commander at Fort Pitt, to General Washington, Fort Pitt, Oct. 17, 1780, in Craig, *The Olden Time,* II, 374; *idem* to Hon. Richard Peters, Fort Pitt, Dec. 7, 1780, *ibid.*, 378; Colonel Daniel Brodhead to General Washington, Fort Pitt, Feb. 18, 1781, *ibid.*, 384; Colonel Daniel Brodhead to Samuel Irwin, Fort Pitt, Feb. 2, 1781, *ibid.*, 387–388; General Wm. Irvine, Brodhead's successor, to [Washington], Fort Pitt, March 30, 1782, in *ibid.*, 479; Butterfield, *Washington-Irvine Correspondence,* 109, 229–232, 241–245, and 266–267; Veech, *Centenary Memorial,* 340; Thomas Scott to Pres. Reed, Westmoreland, Jan. 24, 1781, in *Pennsylvania Archives,* 1st Series, VIII, 713–715. Scott was a member of the Pennsylvania Supreme Executive Council. James Finley to John Dickinson, Cecil County, Md., April 28, 1783, in *ibid.*, X, 40–41; Instructions from John Dickinson to Rev. James Finley, Feb. 6, 1783, *ibid.*, 163–165. Reverend Finley was sent to calm the fears of the people. B. Johnston to Colonel David Shepperd, Yohogania, Oct. 1, 1780, and Nov. 30, 1780, Draper MSS 1SS231, and in Louise P. Kellogg, "Petition for a Western State, 1780," *Mississippi Valley Historical Review,* I, 265–267; B. Johnston to Governor Harrison, June 29, 1784, in *Calendar of Virginia State Papers,* III, 594–595. Johnston was one of the Virginia partisans.

40. Draper MSS 1SS229–230; published by Louise P. Kellogg, "A Memorial of Some Transallegheny Inhabitants," in *Mississippi Valley Historical Review,* I, 267–269.

41. William Irvine to William Moore, Fort Pitt, Dec. 3, 1781, in Butterfield, *Washington-Irvine Correspondence,* 231.

42. See *ante,* 37, and Crumrine, *History of Washington County, Pennsylvania,* 234.

43. *Journals of the Continental Congress, 1774–1789*, XXV (1922), 602; Butterfield, *Journal of Capt. Jonathan Heart*, 62–64.

44. *Maryland Journal*, Dec. 9 and 19, 1783, as quoted in Draper MSS 3JJ114–121.

45. Walker Daniel to the Commissioners for Adjustment of Western Accounts, New Holland, Feb. 3, 1783, in *Calendar of Virginia State Papers*, II, 430–432.

46. The petitions to Virginia and to Congress are printed in Clarence W. Alvord (ed.), *Kaskaskia Records, 1778–1790*, in Illinois State Historical Library *Collections*, V (1909), 329–344, 360–369.

47. Samuel C. Williams, *History of the Lost State of Franklin* (New York, 1933), 6.

48. Frederick J. Turner, *The Significance of Sections in American History* (New York, 1932), 125; Frederick J. Turner, "Western State-Making in the Revolutionary Era," *American Historical Review*, I, 260; *Calendar of Virginia State Papers*, IV (1884), 4–5. Obviously this frontier radical was not socialistic.

49. Williams, *History of the Lost State of Franklin*, 157.

50. Williams, *History of the Lost State of Franklin*, gives the best account of the efforts of the Franklinites to form a state. It also contains a number of the important documents. Abernethy, *From Frontier to Plantation in Tennessee*, 64–90, is more concise but is marked by interpretation that differs from older accounts. See *State Records of North Carolina*, XXII, 637–640, for a letter of March 22, 1785, written by a group of Franklin leaders to Governor Alexander Martin of North Carolina, explaining their procedure. It confirms the immediate causes in particular.

51. *A Declaration of Rights, also, The Constitution, or Form of Government . . . of the State of Frankland . . . 1785* (Philadelphia, 1786), 5, as reprinted in the *American Historical Magazine*, I, 48–63.

52. *Ibid.*

53. Abernethy, *From Frontier to Plantation in Tennessee*, 78–79.

54. *State Records of North Carolina*, XXII, 705–714; Williams, *History of the Lost State of Franklin*, 347 355.

CHAPTER 5. INDEPENDENCE FROM THE TIDEWATER: KENTUCKY

1. Robert Johnson to Governor Henry, Big Crossing, Fayette County, Ky., Dec. 5, 1786, in *Calendar of Virginia State Papers*, IV, 191.

2. See *ante*, chapter IV.

3. Hening, *The Statutes at Large,* XII (1823), 9–24.

4. "Order from Gov. Beverley Randolph, June 1, 1789," in the Lexington, Ky., *Gazette,* Aug. 1, 1789.

5. Colonel John Todd to the Governor of Virginia, Lexington, Ky., Oct. 21, 1781, in the *Calendar of Virginia State Papers,* II (1881), 562–564; Colonel John Floyd to Governor Nelson, Jefferson, Ky., Oct. 6, 1781, *ibid.,* II, 529–531; Samuel McDowell to Governor Henry, Lincoln County, April 18, 1786, in *ibid.,* IV, 118; Benjamin Logan to Governor Henry, Lincoln Courthouse, April 19, 1786, in *ibid.,* IV, 120; Colonel Levi Todd to Governor Henry, Fayette County, June 22, 1786, in *ibid.,* IV, 151; Colonel Levi Todd to Governor Edward Randolph, Fayette County, Ky., Feb. 14, 1787, in *ibid.,* IV, 237–238; Colonel Levi Todd to Governor Edward Randolph, Fayette County, April 30, 1787, in *ibid.,* IV, 277; Alexander S. Bullitt to the Governor of Virginia, Jefferson County, Ky., May 16, 1787, in *ibid.,* IV, 284–285; Harry Innes to Edmund Randolph, Kentucky, July 21, 1787, in *ibid.,* IV, 321–322; statement of Commanding officers, Danville, July 19, 1787, in *ibid.,* IV, 344; John Logan, *et al.* to Governor Randolph, Richmond, June 16, 1788, in *ibid.,* IV, 456; statement of Daniel Boone, *et al.,* Richmond, Jan. 5, 1788, in *ibid.,* IV, 391; and Christopher Greenup to Governor Beverley Randolph, Danville, Ky., June 8, 1789, in *ibid.,* IV, 641.

6. Willard R. Jillson (comp.), *The Kentucky Land Grants* in Filson Club *Publications,* XXXIII (1925). This is a list of grantees and the amounts of land granted them in Kentucky. It is arranged in sections according to the grantor or the time or place of the grants. The first section gives the grants made by Virginia prior to statehood.

7. The grievances of the people of Kentucky were expressed in resolutions, petitions, and letters. In addition to the citations on the following pages, see Robertson, *Petitions of the Early Inhabitants of Kentucky,* petitions numbered 4, 15, 17, 24, 25, and 50.

8. "A Farmer" in Lexington, Ky., *Gazette,* Oct. 18, 1788. "A Farmer" seems to have been well-informed about the conventions. See also Temple Bodley (ed.), *Reprints of Littell's Political Transactions . . . and Letter of George Nicholas* in Filson Club *Publications,* XXX (1926), 6–12.

9. Lexington, Ky., *Gazette,* April 25, 1789; Abernethy, *Western Lands and the American Revolution,* 303.

10. Hening, *The Statutes at Large,* XI (1823), 445.

11. Abernethy, *Western Lands and the American Revolution,* 303–305.

12. Hening, *The Statutes at Large,* XII, 115.

13. Bodley, *Littell's Political Transactions,* 12–13; "A Farmer" in Lexington, Ky., *Gazette,* Oct. 18, 1788; *John Bradford's . . . Notes on Kentucky,* 149.

14. Thomas P. Abernethy (ed.), "Journal of the First Kentucky Convention, Dec. 27, 1784–January 5, 1785," in the *Journal of Southern*

History, I, 67–78. These resolutions, pp. 72–73, include criticisms of the militia law, courts, surveyors, registers, the lack of provisions for the care of orphans and the poor, and the laws respecting horses. They also called attention to the need of a newspaper and requested that the district judges explain their inactivity.

15. *Ibid.,* 75–76. They include protests against taxes which were not impartial, against the five shillings tax on each hundred acres of land held in Kentucky in excess of 1,400 acres, against taxes imposed at Pittsburgh upon goods en route to Kentucky, against the method of paying judges which was thought to be unfair to Kentuckians, against nonresident officials, and against large land grants.

16. *Ibid.,* 77–78. The grievances which it was said Virginia could not remedy included the location of the Court of Appeals at Richmond, the lack of executive and legislative branches of government in Kentucky, the absence of a pardoning power, the inability of the people to know what laws were enacted by the legislature, and finally the drainage of money to the East.

17. Other resolutions provided for the apportionment, election, and meeting of the delegates of the proposed convention. A copy of the minutes of the convention just about to close was to be sent to the commanding officer of each county. Since the existing journal of the convention is incomplete and since Hector St. John de Crèvecoeur published in the Paris edition (1787) of the *Letters of an American Farmer* a somewhat different set of resolutions, it is not clear what may have occurred at the end of the convention. The Crèvecoeur resolutions do not stop with the word *separation* as does the journal, but refers to the erection of a "New State which shall be a member of the Confederation." Hector St. John de Crèvecoeur, *Lettres d'un Cultivateur Américain* (3 vols., Paris, 1787), III, 438–440. "A Farmer" in the Lexington, Ky., *Gazette,* Oct. 18, 1788, stated, "Poplicola [one of the correspondents] is mistaken in supposing this Convention determined on the expedience of a Separate State; a motion was made to that purpose, but it was not seconded."

18. Bodley, *Littell's Political Transactions,* 62–66.

19. Lexington, Ky., *Gazette,* Oct. 18, 1788.

20. Bodley, *Littell's Political Transactions,* 66–70.

21. *Ibid.,* 72–76; Hening, *The Statutes at Large,* XII, 37–40.

22. Bodley, *Littell's Political Transactions,* 16.

23. *Ibid.,* 14–19, 76; Hening, *The Statutes at Large,* XII, 240–243. See also "A Farmer" in Lexington, Ky., *Gazette,* Oct. 18, 1788, and "A Real Friend to the People," in *ibid.,* April 25, 1789.

24. Lexington, Ky., *Gazette,* Aug. 18, 1787.

25. *Ibid.,* Aug. 25, Sept. 1, and Sept. 15, 1787.

26. *Ibid.,* Sept. 8, 1787.

27. *Ibid.,* Sept. 15, 1787.

28. *Ibid.*, Sept. 22, 1787.

29. Bodley, *Littell's Political Transactions,* 24.

30. *Ibid.*, 24–25, 84–88; Hening, *The Statutes at Large,* XII, 240–243.

31. Lexington, Ky., *Gazette,* Feb. 16 and March 1, 1788.

32. *Ibid.*, Feb. 23, 1788.

33. *Ibid.*, May 10, 1788.

34. *Ibid.*, June 14, 1788.

35. *Journals of the Continental Congress,* XXXIV (1937), 72–73, 77, 194, 198, 287–294; Bodley, *Littell's Political Transactions,* 88–93.

36. At a Convention begun and held for the District of Kentucky at the Courthouse in Danville in the County of Mercer on Monday the Twentyeighth day of July in the Year of our Lord one Thousand Seven hundred and eightyeight; Bodley, *Littell's Political Transactions,* 94–95; and Lexington, Ky., *Gazette,* Sept. 6, 1788.

37. Lexington, Ky., *Gazette,* Sept. 13, 1788.

38. *Ibid.*, Oct. 25, 1788.

39. *Ibid.*, Sept. 27, 1788.

40. *Ibid.*, Nov. 8, 1788.

41. *Ibid.*, Oct. 11, 1788.

42. *Ibid.*, Oct. 18, 1788.

43. *Ibid.*, Oct. 18, 1788.

44. *Ibid.*, Oct. 18, 1788.

45. *Ibid.*, Nov. 8, 1788.

46. *Ibid.*, Nov. 15, 1788.

47. Bodley, *Littell's Political Transactions,* 29–30.

48. At a Convention begun and held for the District of Kentucky at the Courthouse in Danville in the County of Mercer on Monday the third day of November in the Year of Our Lord One Thousand Seven hundred and Eightyeight; Bodley, *Littell's Political Transactions,* 99–108; Lexington, Ky., *Gazette,* Jan. 30 and Feb. 5, 1789.

49. Hening, *The Statutes at Large,* XII, 788–791

50. Lexington, Ky., *Gazette,* April 25, 1789.

51. *Ibid.*, May 2, 1789.

52. At a Convention begun and held for the District of Kentucky at the Courthouse in Danville in the County of Mercer on Monday the Twentieth day of July in the Year of our Lord One Thousand seven Hundred and eighty nine; Lexington, Ky., *Gazette,* Aug. 29 and Sept. 5, 1789; and Bodley, *Littell's Political Transactions,* 109–110.

53. Hening, *The Statutes at Large,* XIII (1823), 17–21.

54. Lexington, Ky., *Gazette,* Aug. 15, 1789.

55. At a Convention begun and held for the District of Kentucky at the Courthouse in Danville in the County of Mercer on Monday the Twentysixth day of July in the Year of Our Lord One Thousand Seven

hundred Ninety; Lexington, Ky., *Gazette,* Feb. 12 and 19, 1791; and Bodley, *Littell's Political Transactions,* 111–114.

CHAPTER 6. RADICALISM IN PIONEER KENTUCKY

1. See *ante,* 54.

2. Abernethy, "Journal of the First Kentucky Convention," in the *Journal of Southern History,* I, 73, 75–76.

3. Bodley, *Littell's Political Transactions,* 67.

4. Lexington, Ky., *Gazette,* Oct. 18, 1788.

5. See *ante,* 76, 77.

6. Lexington, Ky., *Gazette,* Oct. 25, 1788, Oct. 15, 1791, Dec. 3, and Dec. 24, 1791, and Jan. 7, 1792. See the letters of conservative writers referred to *post,* p. 86, and the portions of a suggested constitution printed in the *Gazette,* Sept. 17, 24, Oct. 1, 8, and 15, 1791.

7. Note "A Real Friend to the People" in Lexington, Ky., *Gazette,* Aug. 15, 1789; and also "Torismond" in *ibid.,* Jan. 28, 1792.

8. See *ante,* chapter V, 73.

9. Lexington, Ky., *Gazette,* Aug. 23 and Sept. 6, 1788.

10. *Ibid.,* Oct. 4, 1788.

11. *Ibid.,* Oct. 25, 1788.

12. *Ibid.,* Dec. 11, 1790, March 5 and 12, 1791, July 2, 1791, Oct. 22 and 29, 1791, Dec. 31, 1791, and Feb. 11 and 25, 1792.

13. *Ibid.,* Sept. 24, 1791, Oct. 1 and 8, 1791, Dec. 3 and 10, 1791, and Feb. 4, 1792.

14. *Ibid.,* Oct. 15 and 22, 1791.

15. *Ibid.,* Oct. 8, 1791.

16. *Ibid.,* Oct. 1, 1791.

17. *Ibid.,* Oct. 15, 1791.

18. *Ibid.,* Nov. 12, 1791.

19. *Ibid.,* Nov. 19, 1791.

20. *Ibid.,* Nov. 26, 1791.

21. *Ibid.,* Dec. 3, 1791.

22. He devoted his article in *ibid.,* Dec. 24, 1791, largely to this point.

23. *Ibid.,* Nov. 19 and Dec. 24, 1791.

24. *Ibid.,* Nov. 26, 1791, and Feb. 25, 1792.

25. *Ibid.,* Jan. 7, 1792.

26. *Ibid.,* Dec. 17, 1791.

27. *Ibid.,* Dec. 17, 1791.

28. *Ibid.*, Jan. 14, 1792.

29. *Ibid.*, Feb. 18, 1792.

30. *Ibid.*, Dec. 24, 1791.

31. *Ibid.*, Dec. 17 and 24, 1791.

32. *Ibid.*, Nov. 19, 1791.

33. *Ibid.*, Jan. 28, 1792.

34. *Ibid.*, March 10, 1792.

35. *Ibid.*, Feb. 11, 1792.

36. "Philanthropos" [David Rice], *Slavery, Inconsistent with Justice and Good Policy* (Lexington, Ky., 1792).

37. Lexington, Ky., *Gazette*, Jan. 14, 1792.

38. "Philanthropos" [Rice], *Slavery, Inconsistent with Justice*, 21–22, 30.

39. See particularly "H.S.B.M." in Lexington, Ky., *Gazette*, Dec. 24, 1791. See also Selsam, *Pennsylvania Constitution of 1776*, pp. 66–93, *et passim*.

40. See *ante*, chapter IV, 62–63. It is interesting to note that Abernethy in *From Frontier to Plantation in Tennessee*, 79, describes the rejection of the Houston constitution as a defeat of democracy in the wilderness, but the defeat of the Kentucky radicals is described in his *Three Virginia Frontiers*, 95–96, as evidence of the superior wisdom of conservative leaders, and the action of the radicals as totalitarianism. Either it was not democracy in Franklin, or it was not totalitarianism in Kentucky.

41. See *ante*, 86, 87.

42. This is the conclusion of E. Merton Coulter, "Early Frontier Democracy in the First Kentucky Constitution," in *Political Science Quarterly* (Boston and New York, 1886–   ), XXXIX (1924), 675–676.

43. The lists of members are found in Abernethy, "Journal of the First Kentucky Convention," *Journal of Southern History*, I, 67–78; Collins, *History of Kentucky*, I, 354; Bodley, *Littell's Political Transactions*, 68; and the journals of the seventh, eighth, and tenth conventions. Three of the five delegates elected to the constitutional convention from Fayette County were men who received very little land from Virginia and who voted against the provision in the constitution denying to the legislature the authority to emancipate slaves without the consent of their owners and without remuneration. Three of the delegates from Bourbon County also voted against the slavery provision, but three were recipients of large land grants from Virginia, and two had served in seven of the eight conventions of which lists of members have been found. The Fayette election may have been a three to two victory for the radicals, while in Bourbon moderates may have won, but if so three of them had radical leanings. Lincoln County may have returned three moderates and two preachers. The latter opposed the slavery provision and may therefore have been radicals. Among the delegates from Madison County, only one was a preacher, and he alone voted against fastening slavery

on the new state, but none of the five were among those who received
large land grants from the mother state. William Irvine, who had been
a member from this county of the fifth, sixth, seventh, eighth, and probably the ninth, was not in the tenth or constitutional convention. It
would require more evidence than now seems available to justify calling
the election in this county a conservative victory. Mason County was a
new county from which came men only one of whom is known to have
attended a previous convention. Two had not received land from Virginia and two others had only small grants. Three of the five, including
one large recipient of Virginia land grants, voted against the slavery
provision. The safest estimate would be that the results of the election
in this county were gratifying to the radicals. Mercer County was the
home of Samuel McDowell, who had served as president of most of the
conventions, and who was no doubt a moderate. George Nicholas, who
had recently moved to Kentucky and had not served in any of the earlier
conventions, is generally regarded as a conservative, but as will be indicated in the next chapter, he was in reality a Jeffersonian who should
be classed as a moderate. The other three delegates were antislavery men.
This county must be ascribed to the moderates or the radicals, and it
looks like three to two in favor of the radicals.

Two delegates of considerable previous experience in Kentucky conventions, who had received land from Virginia, were elected from Nelson
County. One of them, however, voted against slavery in the convention.
Probably three of the remaining were without convention experience and
two were without Virginia land grants. The delegation does not seem
to have been antislavery, but it did not seem to belong to the conservative group. Woodford County, like Mason County, was new, but unlike
Mason, it showed few effects of the radical campaign. Two of its delegates were large recipients of Virginia land grants, the others were moderate recipients, and all were proslavery. The largest landholder of them
all was declared to be an exponent of the free spirit of democracy and
the principles of liberty. Probably the delegation was composed of moderates and conservatives. Jefferson County's representatives seem not to
have been radicals. For some reason three of the five did not vote on
the slavery provision. All had been granted land by Virginia, and their
tendencies seem to have been towards the conservatives rather than the
radicals.

CHAPTER 7. THE CONTEST IN THE CONVENTION

1. Obituary of Cave Johnson in the Durrett Collection, University of Chicago Library; Leland W. Meyer, *Life and Times of Colonel Richard M. Johnson* (New York, 1932), 13–48; Robert S. Cotterill, "Alexander Scott Bullitt," in *Dictionary of American Biography* (20 vols., and index, New York, 1928–1937), III (1929), 255–256; E. Merton Coulter, "John Edwards," in *ibid.*, VI (1931), 29–30; Wendell H. Stephenson, "Zachary Taylor," in *ibid.*, XVIII (1936), 349–354; J. Reese Fry and Robert T. Conrad, *A Life of General Zachary Taylor* (Philadelphia, 1847), 13–17; *Biographical Directory of the American Congress, 1774–1927* (Washington, 1928), 1664; Thomas Speed, *The Political Club* in Filson Club *Publications*, IX (1894), 75–76; and Holman Hamilton, *Zachary Taylor, Soldier of the Republic* (Indianapolis, 1941), 21–37.

2. Jillson, *The Kentucky Land Grants*. Cf. chapter V, note 6.

3. Abernethy, *Western Lands and the American Revolution*, 303–304; Abernethy, *Three Virginia Frontiers*, 63–70.

4. The Papers, Letters, Speeches, Etc., of George Nicholas, in the Durrett Collection in the University of Chicago Library, manuscript division. In these papers is a Preliminary Biographical Sketch which does not possess great merit. See also Hugh B. Grigsby, *The History of the Virginia Federal Convention of 1788*, in Virginia Historical Society *Collections* (N.S., 11 vols., Richmond, Va., 1882–1892), X (1891), 281–298; Thomas P. Abernethy, "George Nicholas," in *Dictionary of American Biography*, XIII (1934), 482–483; Isaac J. Cox, "Benjamin Sebastian," in *ibid.*, XVI (1935), 543–544; Edward Wiest, "Harry Innes," in *ibid.*, IX (1932), 485–486; Speed, *The Political Club*, 42–45; and Brown, *Political Beginnings of Kentucky*, 109–110. Since this chapter was finished, Richard H. Caldemeyer has written "The Career of George Nicholas" (a Ph.D. dissertation, Indiana University, 1951), which throws much additional light on other phases of Nicholas' life.

5. These and other communications which were printed in the Lexington, Ky., *Gazette* were reviewed in the previous chapter. See also 83–85, 87–88, and note 43 of chapter VI for an analysis of the election.

6. For Benjamin Sebastian, see *ante,* 92, note 4, and for Caleb Wallace, see William H. Whitsitt, *The Life and Times of Judge Caleb Wallace*, in Filson Club *Publications*, IV (1888), and Henry A. White, *Southern Presbyterian Leaders* (New York, 1911), 110, 165–166, *et passim.*

7. "Philanthropos" [Rice], *Slavery, Inconsistent with Justice and Good Policy;* Walter L. Lingle, "David Rice," in *Dictionary of American Biography,* XV (1935), 537–538; Asa E. Martin, *The Anti-Slavery Movement in Kentucky Prior to 1850,* in Filson Club *Publications,* XXIX (1918), 12–13; and White, *Southern Presbyterian Leaders,* 58–59, 110, 206–209. See also *ante,* chapter VI, 87–88.

8. James Garrard, George S. Smith, and John Bailey. The last was one of George Rogers Clark's soldiers before becoming a preacher. Little is known about Smith except that he had an older brother who was a radical opponent of slavery. Garrard came from a Virginia family of importance in Stafford County. He was engaged in the struggle for freedom of religion. Robert S. Cotterill, "James Garrard," in *Dictionary of American Biography,* VII (1931), 159–160; Robert B. Semple, *A History of the Rise and Progress of the Baptists in Virginia* (Richmond, Va., 1894), 407, 474; Reuben G. Thwaites and Louise P. Kellogg, *Frontier Defense on the Upper Ohio, 1777–1778* (Madison, Wis., 1912), 194, note 64.

9. For Benedict Swope see William E. Connelley and E. Merton Coulter, *History of Kentucky* (5 vols., Chicago, 1922), III, 358–359.

10. For Charles Kavanaugh see "Autobiography of Rev. William Burke," in James B. Finley, *Sketches of Western Methodism* (Cincinnati, 1856), 64.

11. William W. Sweet (ed.), *Religion on the American Frontier, The Baptists, 1783–1830* (New York, 1931), 444, 447.

12. At a Convention begun and held at Danville . . . the second day of April in the Year of our Lord One Thousand seven hundred and Ninetytwo, 22, in the state library, Frankfort, Ky.

13. For Miles W. Conway see Connelley and Coulter, *History of Kentucky,* V, 612.

14. For Andrew Hynes see *Biographical Cyclopedia of the Commonwealth of Kentucky* (Chicago, 1896), 32–33.

15. Jacob Froman and Robert Fryer, Connelley and Coulter, *History of Kentucky,* IV, 204. No information has been found about Fryer.

16. John McKinney and John Wilson. Kentucky MSS, XIII, 137, in Draper Collection; Reuben G. Thwaites and Louise P. Kellogg, *Dunmore's War, 1774* (Madison, Wis., 1905), 272, note 87.

17. Samuel M. Wilson, "James Smith," in *Dictionary of American Biography,* XVII (1935), 284–285; Collins, *History of Kentucky,* II, 77.

18. William H. Perrin, J. H. Battle, and G. C. Kniffin, *Kentucky, A History of the State* (Louisville, Ky., 1887), 1014. The individual was Samuel Taylor.

19. Thomas Kennedy and Higgason Grubbs. *Biographical Encyclopedia of Kentucky* (Cincinnati, Ohio, 1878), 359; Connelley and Coulter, *History of Kentucky,* IV, 50; Collins, *History of Kentucky,* II, 61, 71, 510–511, 514.

20. Joseph Kennedy. William H. Perrin, *History of Bourbon, Scott, Harrison, and Nicholas Counties* (Chicago, 1882), 477.

21. Thomas Kennedy. See *ante*, note 19 of this chapter.

22. William Steele. Collins, *History of Kentucky*, II, 326. The other members of this group were Joseph Hobbs, William King, Robert Rankin, Thomas Waring, and John Watkins.

23. Autobiography of Isaac Shelby in the Durrett Collection; Samuel M. Wilson, "Isaac Shelby," in *Dictionary of American Biography*, XVII, 60–62.

24. Statement of Harvey M. McDowell in the Durrett Collection; Speed, *The Political Club*, 56–61; *Biographical Encyclopedia of Kentucky*, 36, 38; Joseph S. Waddell, *Annals of Augusta County, Virginia* (Richmond, Va., 1886), 140–142; Collins, *History of Kentucky*, II, 98; Robert S. Cotterill, "Benjamin Logan," in *Dictionary of American Biography*, XI (1933), 356–357; and *idem, Pioneer Kentucky*, 217–218.

25. See *ante*, 93 and note 6.

26. Speed, *The Political Club*, 38, 111–112, 114, 118, 125, 129, 139, and 151.

27. Journal of the Constitutional Convention. The manuscript copy of the Journal is in the Kentucky State Library, Frankfort. A printed copy without title page is in the Library of Congress.

28. See *ante*, 92, note 4.

29. Marshall, *History of Kentucky*, I, 395–396.

30. In the Nicholas Papers are two sets of notes which are entitled "In 1 Day," which probably means "In the first day." One set, three pages long, is in the handwriting of Nicholas, and, therefore, practically unreadable. The second set is four pages long and in a small, round, straight, and very neat hand. It was corrected by Nicholas in his own hand. Perhaps the second was copied for him from the first, corrected by him, and then used in speaking before the convention. There is also a "Speech in the Kentucky convention," which appears to be an attempt to clothe the above notes in the form of an address as it was imagined that Nicholas delivered it. It was written by a third person, followed a different order, and is not identical in thought. There is no other evidence that Nicholas spoke at all, but his lengthy notes are unexplainable on any other basis.

31. There are six pages of notes entitled "Checks and Division of power." The ideas are fundamental to his theory of government.

32. There are two sets of notes entitled "Senate." One is in Nicholas' writing and the other in that of his secretary or helper, with a few corrections added by Nicholas. There is a third form, in which a third person has given the notes the character of a finished speech. In this instance he has followed very closely the above notes. There are three pages of notes on the House of Representatives and seven pages on the

Powers of the House of Representatives. There is only one copy of each.

33. This is probably one of the more important speeches of Nicholas in this convention. Upon it depended the reaction of the more moderate radicals. It exists only in one form in his own hand and seems not to have received the attention of those who rewrote some of his notes and speeches.

34. There are two sets of notes giving the ideas of Nicholas in regard to the governor. One is in his own hand, and the other in that of his helper. The latter has markings and a few corrections in Nicholas' hand. On the lower half of the last page, which served as an outside cover, was written by Nicholas the title "Governor."

35. "H.S.B.M.," in Lexington, Ky., *Gazette*, Jan. 7, 1792; and "Address to the freemen of the district of Kentucky," in *ibid.*, Oct. 15, 1791.

36. The italics are in the original, but the statements are paraphrases rather than quotations.

37. There are the usual two sets of notes on the subject of "Courts," one in Nicholas' hand and a second in the hand of his helper.

38. The notes on this subject seem to be incomplete. There are two pages and two fractional pages in Nicholas' hand.

39. His notes on "Slaves" exist in the usual two handwritings.

40. The notes in his own hand are entitled "Government for a limited time," and, in the hand of his assistant, "Limitations of Government."

41. Journal of the Convention, 10–20. A copy of these resolutions in Nicholas' hand and with many minor variations in the text is in the Nicholas Papers.

42. *Ibid.*, 21–22.

43. *Ibid.*, 23–47.

44. Francis N. Thorpe, *A Constitutional History of the American People, 1776–1850* (2 vols., New York, 1898), I, 133–134, stated that it closely resembled the constitution of Virginia. The following assert its likeness to the Constitution of the United States: Marshall, *History of Kentucky*, I, 414; Coulter, "Early Frontier Democracy," in *Political Science Quarterly*, XXXIX, 676; and Bennett H. Young, *History and Texts of the Three Constitutions of Kentucky* (Louisville, Ky., 1890), q. It is not unlike the Constitution of the United States, but the Pennsylvania constitution was the one modeled upon the national document, and Kentucky followed Pennsylvania rather than the national constitution.

45. This is stated by Marshall, *History of Kentucky*, I, 414; Mann Butler, *A History of the Commonwealth of Kentucky* (Cincinnati, 1834), 207–211; Brown, *Political Beginnings of Kentucky*, 227–228; and Thorpe, *Constitutional History of the American People*, I, 133–134.

46. The Kentucky constitution of 1792 is included in the Journal of the Convention. It may also be found in Thorpe, *Federal and State Constitutions*, III, 1264–1277. The latter is a substantially correct copy but

is not free from error when compared with the manuscript copy. The Pennsylvania constitution of 1790 is also in *ibid.*, V, 3092–3103.

47. See *ante*, 94, note 17.

48. Selsam, *The Pennsylvania Constitution of 1776*, p. 259.

49. In addition to the following chapters of this study, see Philip D. Uzée, The First Louisiana State Constitution: A Study of its Origins (M.A. Thesis, Louisiana State University, Baton Rouge, La., 1938).

CHAPTER 8. THE FRONTIER IN THE FORMATION OF TENNESSEE

1. Carter (ed.), *The Territorial Papers of the United States*, IV, *The Territory South of the River Ohio, 1790–1796* (1936), 429–442.

2. *Ibid.*, 18–19.

3. *Ibid.*, 368.

4. "Governor Blount to the Secretary of War, Knoxville, January 14, 1793," in *ibid.*, IV, 231.

5. "Andrew Pickens to the Governor of South Carolina, Hopewell, 13th September 1792," in *ibid.*, 169. See also Arthur P. Whitaker, "Spanish Intrigue in the Old Southwest: An Episode, 1788–89," in *Mississippi Valley Historical Review*, XII (1925–1926), 163.

6. The figures for 1795 are taken from the Territorial Census. They may be found in Carter (ed.), *The Territorial Papers of the United States*, IV, 404–405.

7. "The Secretary of War to Governor Blount, 31st *January* 1792," in *ibid.*, 115; "The Secretary of War to Governor Blount, War Department *November* 26. 1792," in *ibid.*, 222; "The Secretary of War to Governor Blount, Department of War *March* 23rd, 1795," in *ibid.*, 389. See also *ibid.*, 299. "The Secretary of War to B. Dandridge [June 27, 1795]," in *ibid.*, 395.

8. *Ibid.*, 245; Abernethy, *From Frontier to Plantation in Tennessee*, 130.

9. Carter, *The Territorial Papers of the United States*, IV, 271, 275, 282; *Calendar of Virginia State Papers*, VI (1886), 409–410.

10. Carter, *The Territorial Papers of the United States*, IV, 281.

11. Ramsey, *Annals of Tennessee*, 578–579.

12. Carter, *The Territorial Papers of the United States*, IV, 307–308.

13. "Governor Blount's Journal," in *American Historical Magazine*, II, 257–259; Abernethy, *From Frontier to Plantation in Tennessee*, 133.

14. Knoxville, Tenn., *Gazette*, March 23, Oct. 17 and Nov. 23, 1793, Jan. 2, Feb. 27, March 13 and 27, 1794; Carter, *The Territorial Papers of the*

United States, IV, 309–319, and 328; Ramsey, *Annals of Tennessee,* 622; and Haywood, *Civil and Political History of Tennessee,* 314. The term Tennessee is used in the name of the *Gazette* before statehood to avoid the longer territorial name.

15. Ramsey, *Annals of Tennessee,* 623–636, quotes several passages from the legislative journal. See 633.

16. *Ibid.,* 633–634; see also William Blount to General James Robertson, Knoxville, Oct. 1, 1794, in *American Historical Magazine,* III (1898), 359.

17. *Journal of the Proceedings of the House of Representatives of the Territory of the United States of America, South of the River Ohio . . . 1795* (Knoxville, 1795, reprinted, Nashville, 1852), 4, 11.

18. Carter, *The Territorial Papers of the United States,* IV, 404.

19. See *post,* chapter X.

20. Carter, *The Territorial Papers of the United States,* IV, 423.

21. When the vote was taken on the question of statehood in the territorial legislature, there was one vote against the change. Thomas Hardiman, a representative from Davidson County, Miro District, explained his opposition by stating that the change would "burden the people with additional taxes, without a certainty of deriving any advantages from it. . . ." He said that the people had not requested it and that the sources of revenue were inadequate. Knoxville, Tenn., *Gazette,* Oct. 23, 1795. Although Sumner County did not express itself on this question, the two other counties of Miro District were opposed in the ratio of five to one. Carter, *The Territorial Papers of the United States,* IV, 404.

22. They were Joseph Anderson, John Galbraith, Thomas Johnson, Charles McClung, Joseph McMinn, William Rankin, Archibald Roane, and James Roddye. For sources of information about these men and the other members of the convention see *post,* notes 23–60.

23. David and John Shelby came from the Valley and John Tipton from the Piedmont.

24. From the Valley were James Berry, Joseph Black, John Crawford, George Doherty, James Houston, and Samuel Wear; from the Piedmont were John and Spencer Clack, William Cocke, William and Edward Douglas, Joel Lewis, James Robertson, Leroy Taylor, and probably Thomas Hardiman; and from the Tidewater were Daniel Smith and W. C. C. Claiborne.

25. John Rhea, George Rutledge, and John Adair were from Ireland, and Richard Gammon probably was born in England.

26. James White, Samuel Frazier, and Samuel Handley.

27. John McNairy.

28. William Blount, Stephen Brooks, and Alexander Outlaw.

29. James Ford, Robert and William Prince, and Andrew Jackson.

30. Information concerning these delegates could change the above

conclusions about the origins of the delegates in the various states. It is the poor, however, who fail to leave records, and the poor were often the ones who were driven along at the edge of the frontier. The delegates in this group were Elisha Baker, Peter Bryan or Bryant, Thomas Buckingham, David Craig, William Fort, Samuel Glass, James Greenaway, Thomas Henderson, Richard Mitchell, James Stuart and Isaac Walton.

31. Ramsey, *Annals of Tennessee,* 650, 652.

32. On the partisan alignment, in addition to references below, see William Blount to General Robertson, Knoxville, Oct. 25, 1795, in *American Historical Magazine, IV* (1899), 77–78, and a letter of Governor Blount probably to Robertson, Knoxville, Oct. 3, 1795, in *ibid., IV,* 74–75; and Abernethy, *From Frontier to Plantation in Tennessee,* 164–165.

33. Philip M. Hamer, "William Blount," in *Dictionary of American Biography,* II (1929), 390–391; Marcus J. Wright, *The Life and Services of William Blount* (Washington, 1884), 7–13.

34. Draper MSS 6XX49, 6XX50; Arthur P. Whitaker (ed.), "Letters of James Robertson and Daniel Smith," *Mississippi Valley Historical Review,* XII, 411–412; St. George L. Sioussat, "The Journal of General Daniel Smith . . ." in *Tennessee Historical Magazine* (10 vols., Nashville, Tenn., 1915–1926), I, 40–65; Carl S. Driver, "Daniel Smith," in *Dictionary of American Biography,* XVII, 254–255; Abernethy, *From Frontier to Plantation in Tennessee,* 164–165.

35. Draper MSS 6XX49, 6XX50; Whitaker, "Letters of James Robertson and Daniel Smith," *Mississippi Valley Historical Review,* XII, 409–410; "The Correspondence of Gen. James Robertson," in *American Historical Magazine,* I, 71–91, 189–194, 280–291, 390–396; II, 59–86, 172–177, 355–375; III, 74–83, 267–298, 348–394; IV, 66–96, 163–192, 247–286, 336–381; Carl S. Driver, "James Robertson," in *Dictionary of American Biography,* XVI, 24–25; Abernethy, *From Frontier to Plantation in Tennessee,* 53, 95–97, 129–130.

36. Abernethy, *From Frontier to Plantation in Tennessee,* 123–124; John S. Bassett, *The Life of Andrew Jackson* (2 vols. in 1, New York, 1931), 11–14.

37. John T. Moore, *Tennessee, The Volunteer State,* 1769–1923 (4 vols., Chicago, 1923), II, 181; Abernethy, *From Frontier to Plantation in Tennessee,* 122, 124–128, 172; Ramsey, *Annals of Tennessee,* 506, 650–653.

38. Thomas P. Abernethy, "Archibald Roane," in *Dictionary of American Biography,* XV, 640–641; and Joshua W. Caldwell, *Sketches of the Bench and Bar of Tennessee* (Knoxville, Tenn., 1898), 19–21.

39. Moore, *Tennessee, The Volunteer State,* IV, 905; Carter, *The Territorial Papers of the United States,* IV, 326, and note 19; Ramsey, *Annals of Tennessee,* 568, 651–655. McClung was a Pennsylvanian who came to the Holston area in 1788 and married a daughter of General James White.

40. Carl S. Driver, "James White," in *Dictionary of American Biography,* XX (1936), 108; Abernethy, *From Frontier to Plantation in Tennessee,* 53, 118–121, 165, 168. White, the founder of Knoxville and an associate of Blount, was a native of the North Carolina Piedmont, a son of Irish parents, and a recipient of local offices by gubernatorial appointment. His son, Hugh Lawson White, was a private secretary of the governor.

41. Charles P. Paullin, "Landon Carter," in *Dictionary of American Biography,* III, 541; and Abernethy, *From Frontier to Plantation in Tennessee,* 3, 174–176. Carter was one of the larger landowners in the territory and had been appointed lieutenant colonel and treasurer of Washington District.

42. Dunbar Rowland (ed.), *The Official Letter Books of W. C. C. Claiborne* (6 vols., Jackson, Miss., 1917), I, 1–5, note 1, contains a brief biographical sketch. Isaac J. Cox, "William Charles Coles Claiborne," in *Dictionary of American Biography,* IV (1930), 115–116. A native of southeastern Virginia, Claiborne studied for a short time at William and Mary before moving to the Nashville region.

43. Marguerite B. Hamer, "John Rhea of Tennessee," in East Tennessee Historical Society *Publications* (Knoxville, Tenn., 1929–   ), IV (1932), 35–44. Rhea was a member of a Scotch-Irish family from the north of Ireland, that moved to Pennsylvania and Maryland. In the convention he favored a unicameral legislature and in later life held mild antislavery and agrarian views. If he is classified in the Blount group, he was one of the least aristocratic members.

44. The following may be listed as probable followers of Blount: Stephen Brooks, Peter Bryan, Edward and William Douglas, James Ford, William Fort, Thomas Henderson, Thomas Johnson, Joel Lewis, Richard Mitchell, Robert and William Prince, James Roddye, David and John Shelby, James Stuart, and Isaac Walton. The nativity of six of these was not found: Bryan, Fort, Henderson, Mitchell, Stuart, and Walton (or Walker). Brooks was a Methodist minister from the coast of North Carolina; see John B. M'Ferrin, *History of Methodism in Tennessee* (3 vols., Nashville, Tenn., 1875), I, 119–120.

45. "William Blount to James Robertson, Mr. Cobb's September 3d 1791," in Carter, *The Territorial Papers of the United States,* IV, 79; and "Governor Blount to James Robertson, April 29, 1792," in *American Historical Magazine,* I, 393; Addison A. Anderson to L. C. Draper, July 7, 1839, in Draper MSS 14DD110; and Frank L. Owsley, "Joseph Anderson," in *Dictionary of American Biography,* I (1928), 267–268.

46. Williams, *History of the Lost State of Franklin,* 324–325; and Caldwell, *Sketches of the Bench and Bar of Tennessee,* 64–66.

47. Marguerite B. Hamer, "Joseph McMinn," in *Dictionary of American Biography,* XII (1933), 145–146; Abernethy, *From Frontier to Plantation*

in Tennessee, 138, 223; McMinn Correspondence in the *American Historical Magazine,* IV, 319–335.

48. These were Joseph McMinn, just referred to, George Doherty, Samuel Wear, Leroy Taylor, George Rutledge and William Cocke. Doherty was an early resident of the Tennessee frontier, who had followed Sevier at King's Mountain and on later campaigns against the Indians, and a leader of one of the expeditions which violated the governor's peace policy. Williams, *History of the Lost State of Franklin,* 317–319; and Landon C. White to Lyman Draper, a memorandum, Draper MSS 14DD14. Wear, who also led an unauthorized attack on the Indians, was a native of the Valley of Virginia and an early settler on the French Broad. He co-operated with Sevier at King's Mountain and throughout the Franklin movement. Williams, *History of the Lost State of Franklin,* 328–329. Probably he and Doherty represented the attitude which Sevier could hardly have taken publicly because of the responsibility of the brigadier generalship. Rutledge was said to have been a native of Ireland who came by way of South Carolina. Katherine K. White, *The King's Mountain Men* (Dayton, Va., 1924), 222; and Oliver Taylor, *Historic Sullivan* (Bristol, Tenn., 1909), 162, note 1. Taylor was a native of the Virginia Piedmont and a resident for a time of western North Carolina. Zella Armstrong, *Taylor of Tennessee* (Chattanooga, Tenn., n.d.), 20–23. Cocke was so much the individualist that it is difficult to asociate him with any group, but he was probably less identified with the governor's friends than any other faction. He opposed the policy of peace with the Indians and the election of White as territorial delegate to Congress. His election to the United States Senate in 1796 was not in accord with the wishes of Blount. William Blount to J. G. Blount, Nov. 7, 1797 (copy in Lawson McGhee Library, Knoxville, Tenn.); William Goodrich, "William Cocke . . . ," in the *American Historical Magazine,* I, 224–229; and Abernethy, *From Frontier to Plantation in Tennessee,* 72, 78–79, 130, 138, 141, and 165.

49. Among these were Samuel Handley, a native of Pennsylvania who lived for a time in the Valley of Virginia; William Rankin, who was born near Carlisle, Pennsylvania; John Galbraith, a native of southwestern Pennsylvania; Richard Gammon, who was of English descent if not nativity and who came by way of Pennsylvania and Virginia; Samuel Frazier, who was said by one writer to have been born in Scotland and by another in North Carolina; and Elisha Baker, whose origin seems not to be known. Williams, *History of the Lost State of Franklin,* 39, 41, 319–320; Draper MSS 6ZZ37; Charles A. Hanna, *The Wilderness Trail* (2 vols., New York, 1911), I, 175, II, 332; *History of Tennessee* [Goodspeed Pub. Co., title page missing], 1245; letter of W. G. Gammon, Nov. 14, 1939; Moore, *Tennessee, The Volunteer State,* II, 210; and John Allison, *Notable Men of Tennessee* (2 vols., Atlanta, Ga., 1905), I, 35.

50. Among them were John Adair, David Craig, Spencer and John Clack,

John Crawford, and James Houston. Adair, the entry taker, was probably a native of Ireland, an early settler, and an associate of Blount's. Knoxville, Tenn., *Gazette,* supplement, July 14, 1792; Kate White, "John Adair, the Entry-Taker," in the *Tennessee Historical Magazine,* VIII (1924), 112–118; and Taylor, *Historic Sullivan,* 98–99. Craig was described by the governor as a frontier man who was "generally viewed by the whites as too great a friend to indians." Carter, *The Territorial Papers of the United States,* IV, 129; Williams, *History of the Lost State of Franklin,* 231; White, *The King's Mountain Men,* 163; Ramsey, *Annals of Tennessee,* 323, 370, 568, 643–644, 650–652. The Clacks were natives of Virginia and, after statehood, local leaders. Knoxville, Tenn., *Register,* July 18, 1832; *Clack Genealogy* (n.p., n.d.); and Ramsey, *Annals of Tennessee,* 340, 651, 652, 658, 669, and 688. Crawford, a native of the Staunton, Virginia, neighborhood, moved east of the Blue Ridge in North Carolina before crossing back to the west of the mountains. *Some Tennessee Heroes of the Revolution* (Chattanooga, Tenn., n.d.), 11; and Ramsey, *Annals of Tennessee,* 564, 589, 651, 658, 663, and 704. Houston, a native of the Valley of Virginia, was a member of the group that produced the Houston constitution for Franklin, and later, an uncle of Sam Houston. Williams, *History of the Lost State of Franklin,* 320–322; and *Tennessee Historical Magazine,* I, 281. Five others, James Berry, Joseph Black, Thomas Buckingham, Samuel Glass, and James Greenaway, left very little record of their lives except the few local offices which they filled from time to time.

51. John Tipton to Lyman C. Draper, Washington, Jan. 2, 1839, Draper MSS 14DD112; Selden Nelson, "The Tipton Family of Tennessee," in the East Tennessee Historical Society *Publications,* I, 67–76; and Williams, *History of the Lost State of Franklin,* 334–335.

52. *Journal of the Proceedings of a Convention, began and held in Knoxville on the eleventh day of January, 1796, for the purpose of forming a constitution, or form of government, for the government of the people ...* (Knoxville, Tenn., 1796), January 18. A copy of the Journal is in the Library of Congress, and a copy of an 1852 edition is in the Library of the University of Tennessee at Knoxville.

53. *Ibid.,* Feb. 3.

54. *Ibid.,* Jan. 30 (see Article I, section 1); Feb. 3 and 4.

55. *Ibid.,* Jan. 12, 18, 19, 20, and Feb. 3.

56. *Ibid.,* Feb. 1 and 4.

57. *Ibid.,* Feb. 1.

58. *Ibid.,* Feb. 1 and 4.

59. *Ibid.,* Feb. 1.

60. *Ibid.,* Jan. 30, Article II, section 22; and Feb. 4; and *North Carolina State Records,* XXIV (1905), 543–544, 807–808, and 952. The latter reference is to the law of 1788, which did not provide equality.

61. *Journal of the Convention held in Knoxville, 1796,* Feb. 2.

62. *Ibid.,* Feb. 2 and 4; see also Article IX, section 4 of the constitution.

63. The constitutions of the various states may be found in Thorpe, *Federal and State Constitutions.* Original MSS have been photostated for the Kentucky and Tennessee constitutions.

64. Articles III, V, VI, IX, and X were different and in places original. Except for the judiciary (Article V), these articles were generally short and less important. The exclusion of ministers as reported to the convention was copied from the New York constitution, but an amendment, taken from the constitution of South Carolina, was substituted for a part of it. The religious test bore some similarity to North Carolina's test.

CHAPTER 9. A NATIONAL FRONTIER: THE OLD NORTHWEST

1. The Territory of the United States south of the river Ohio which developed into the state of Tennessee was subject to national control during the six years of its territorial period, but little of the land was distributed by the federal government, and the mother state exacted the pledge that "no regulations made or to be made by Congress shall tend to emancipate Slaves." It was, therefore, something less than a national frontier, and frontier forces were not free to exert their maximum influence. See *ante,* chapter VIII.

In the eastern portion of the Northwest Territory the amount of land distributed other than under the general acts of 1785 and 1796 forms an important exception before 1800. But Virginia's influence in the Virginia Military District was somewhat counteracted by New England's influence in the Connecticut Reserve and the Ohio Company's purchase, and all were somewhat neutralized or lessened by the areas which were distributed by the national government and the Symmes Purchase. Farther west in Indiana and Illinois the influence of the national land policy was more significant.

2. Beverley W. Bond, Jr., *The Foundations of Ohio* (Vol. I of the *History of the State of Ohio,* Columbus, Ohio, 1941), 356, 370–371; and Randolph C. Downes, *Frontier Ohio, 1788–1803,* Ohio Historical *Collections* (Columbus, 1930–   ), III (1935), 69.

3. Herbert B. Adams, "Maryland's Influence upon Land Cessions to the United States," in Johns Hopkins University *Studies in Historical and Political Science,* III (1885), 7–54; Treat, *The National Land System, 1785–1820,* pp. 1–14; and Benjamin H. Hibbard, *A History of the Public Land Policies* (New York, 1924), 7–14.

4. Carter, *Territorial Papers of the United States,* II, *The Territory*

Northwest of the River Ohio, 1787–1803 (1934), 22–24; Thomas C. Donaldson, *The Public Domain* (Washington, 1884), 72–73; and Treat, *National Land System,* 10–11, 319–325.

5. Hening, *Statutes at Large,* XI, 326–328, or Donaldson, *Public Domain,* 68–69.

6. *Journals of the Continental Congress,* XVIII, 915–916.

7. *Ibid.,* XXVI, 113–116. See p. 114.

8. *Ibid.,* XXVI, 275–279; and Jay A. Barrett, *Evolution of the Ordinance of 1787* (New York, 1891), 17–27.

9. *Journals of the Continental Congress,* XXXII, 342.

10. *Ibid.,* XXV, 684–693, especially 686; Randolph C. Downes, *Council Fires on the Upper Ohio* (Pittsburgh, 1940), 277–289; and Dwight L. Smith, Indian Land Cessions in the Old Northwest, 1795–1809 (a Ph.D. dissertation, Indiana University, 1949).

11. Charles J. Kappler (ed.), *Indian Affairs: Laws and Treaties* (2 vols., Washington, 1903), II, 3–4, 4–5, 12–13; *Military Journal of Ebenezer Denny,* 59–76; and Downes, *Council Fires on the Upper Ohio,* 289–298.

12. *Military Journal of Ebenezer Denny,* 137–138; Selter, *L'Odyssée Américaine,* 49; and the Lexington, Ky., *Gazette,* March 29, April 5, May 17, 1790, Jan. 15, March 26, May 7, May 14, July 2, and July 9, 1791.

13. Carter, *Territorial Papers of the United States,* II, 174–186; Kappler, *Indian Affairs: Laws and Treaties,* II, 13–18, 18–19; *Military Journal of Ebenezer Denny,* 334; Downes, *Council Fires on the Upper Ohio,* 299–309; and Bond, *Foundations of Ohio,* 312–317.

14. *Military Journal of Ebenezer Denny,* 139–149; and Smith, *St. Clair Papers,* II, 188–189.

15. "Winthrop Sargent's Diary while with General Arthur St. Clair's Expedition against the Indians," in *Ohio Archaeological and Historical Quarterly* (Columbus, 1887–   ), XXXIII (1924), 237–273. The bound volumes of the *Quarterly* are published as *Publications.* See also *Military Journal of Ebenezer Denny,* 164–171; Smith, *St. Clair Papers,* II, 262–267; Bond, *Foundations of Ohio,* 322–328; and Downes, *Council Fires on the Upper Ohio,* 310–320.

16. Roosevelt, *The Winning of the West,* IV, 49–52; and Henry J. Ford, *Washington and His Colleagues* (*The Chronicles of America Series,* Allen Johnson, ed., 50 vols., New Haven, Conn., 1918–1921), XIV (1921), 97–103.

17. Samuel F. Bemis, *Jay's Treaty* (New York, 1924), 263; Kappler, *Indian Affairs: Laws and Treaties,* II, 30–34; and Downes, *Council Fires on the Upper Ohio,* 320–338.

18. *Journals of the Continental Congress,* XXVIII, 375–381; Treat, *National Land System,* 15–40. The act of 1785 is also reprinted in the latter, 395–400.

19. Aaron M. Sakolski, *The Great American Land Bubble* (New York, 1932), 29–53.

20. *Journals of the Continental Congress*, XXVIII, 375–381, see 378.

21. *American State Papers: Documents, Legislative and Executive* (38 vols., Washington, 1832–1861), *Public Lands* (1832–1861), II (1834), 442; and Treat, *National Land System*, 15–40, 370–376. Note the emphasis on good titles in "Miami Lands for Sale," in Beverley W. Bond, Jr. (ed.), *Correspondence of John Cleves Symmes* (New York, 1926), 282.

22. "Petition of Inhabitants West of the Ohio River (1785)," in *Ohio in the Time of the Confederation,* edited by Archer B. Hulbert as Vol. III (1918) of the Marietta College *Historical Collections* (3 vols., Marietta, Ohio, 1917–1918), 103–106. See 104–105. See also "John Cleves Symmes to the People of Kentucky," in Bond, *Correspondence of John Cleves Symmes,* 278–281.

23. "Journal of General Butler," in Craig, *The Olden Time,* II, 507.

24. "Governor St. Clair to the Secretary for Foreign Affairs, Fort Harmer Decr 13th 1788," in Carter, *The Territorial Papers of the United States,* II, 169.

25. "Memorial for the Erection of a New State," in Crumrine, *History of Washington County, Pennsylvania,* 187–188. See *ante,* chapter IV, 50-51.

26. *Pennsylvania Archives,* 1st Series, XII (1856), 176–177.

27. William Irvine to William Moore, Fort Pitt, December 3, 1781, "in Butterfield, *Washington-Irvine Correspondence,* 231.

28. *Ibid.,* 109, 244, and 267. See also "General Wm. Irvine to [Washington], Fort Pitt, March 30, 1782," in Craig, *The Olden Time,* II, 479.

29. Butterfield, *Washington-Irvine Correspondence,* 339.

30. *Journals of the Continental Congress,* XXV, 602.

31. Butterfield, *Washington-Irvine Corerspondence,* 196, note 2.

32. The advertisement is reprinted in Hulbert, *Ohio in the Time of the Confederation,* 98–99; and Smith, *St. Clair Papers,* II, 5.

33. "Petition of Inhabitants West of the Ohio River (1785)," in Hulbert, *Ohio in the Time of the Confederation,* 103–105; and "Ensign Armstrong's Report to Colonel Harmar, Fort McIntosh, 12th April, 1785," in *ibid.,* 106–109.

34. Smith, *St. Clair Papers,* II, 3–4; Randolph C. Downes, "Ohio's Squatter Governor: William Hogland of Hoglandstown," in *Ohio Archaeological and Historical Quarterly,* XLIII (1934), 279–280; John B. McMaster, *A History of the People of the United States* (8 vols., New York, 1883–1913), III (1892), 107–108.

35. Pittsburgh *Gazette,* Sept. 29, 1787, as quoted in Downes, "Ohio's Squatter Governor," *Ohio Archaeological and Historical Quarterly,* XLIII, 273.

36. Carter, *Territorial Papers of the United States,* II, 51.

37. Downes, "Ohio's Squatter Governor," *Ohio Archaeological and Historical Quarterly,* XLIII, 281–282; *Military Journal of Major Ebenezer*

Denny, 56–59; "Journal of General Butler," in Craig, *The Olden Time,* II, 433–464, 481–525, 529–531.

38. "Judge Putnam to the President, Marietta *February* 28th 1791," in Carter, *The Territorial Papers of the United States,* II, 338–339.

39. "Governor St. Clair to the Secretary at War, Pittsburgh, *July* 5th 1788," in *ibid.,* II, 119; "Governor St. Clair to the Secretary for Foreign Affairs, Fort Harmar, *Decr* 13th 1788," in *ibid.,* II, 168–169; and "Governor St. Clair to the President [*August,* 1789]," in *ibid.,* II, 208–210.

40. Bond, *The Correspondence of John Cleves Symmes,* 64–65; Archer B. Hulbert (ed.), *The Records of the Original Proceedings of the Ohio Company,* Volumes I and II of the Marietta College *Historical Collections* (1917), I, 70–72; Beverley W. Bond, Jr. (ed.), "Dr. Daniel Drake's Memoir of the Miami Country, 1779–1794," in the *Quarterly Publication* of the Historical and Philosophical Society of Ohio (Cincinnati, 1906–   ), XVIII (1923), 55, 97, and 103; Downes, *Frontier Ohio,* 59–69; and Baily, *A Tour of the Unsettled Parts of North America,* 195–196.

41. *Annals of Congress,* 1 Cong., 1 Sess., 624–625.

42. *Journals of the Continental Congress,* XXXIII, 427–429; Hulbert, *Records of the . . . Ohio Company,* I, 13–15, 29–37; William P. and Julia P. Cutler, *Life, Journals and Correspondence of Rev. Manasseh Cutler* (2 vols., Cincinnati, 1888), I, 326; Treat, *National Land System,* 47–52; and Bond, *Foundations of Ohio,* 275–290. The agreement was made July 27, but the final contract was signed on October 27.

43. Bond, *Correspondence of John Cleves Symmes,* 6–9; Treat, *National Land System,* 52–54.

44. *Journals of the Continental Congress,* XXXII, 334–343; Barrett, *Evolution of the Ordinance of 1787,* pp. 49–80. The Ordinance is also printed in *Old South Leaflets* (8 vols., Boston, 1888–1904), I, No. 13.

45. *Ante,* 123; Jefferson's Report is printed in Henry S. Randall, *Life of Thomas Jefferson* (3 vols., New York, 1858), I, 397–399. It is also printed with several pertinent documents and comments in *Old South Leaflets,* VI, No. 127.

46. This document is printed in John M. Merriam, "The Legislative History of the Ordinance of 1787," in American Antiquarian Society *Proceedings,* N.S. (Worcester, Mass., 1880–   ), V (1888), 303–342, see 321–323. See also *Journals of the Continental Congress,* XXXII, 274–275, 314–320.

47. Barrett, *Evolution of the Ordinance of 1787,* p. 33.

48. Merriam, "Legislative History of the Ordinance of 1787," in American Antiquarian Society *Proceedings,* N.S., V, 336–342.

49. Thorpe, *Federal and State Constitutions,* VII, 3783–3789, see 3788.

50. William Stubbs, *Select Charters* (Oxford, 1900), 523–528.

51. Thorpe, *Federal and State Constitutions,* VII, 3812–3814.

52. See *post,* chapters X, XI, and XIII.

53. See *post*, chapters X, XI, and XII.

54. Smith, *St. Clair Papers*, I, 205–206; "Governor St. Clair to the President, Cahokia *May* 1st 1790," in Carter, *Territorial Papers of the United States*, II, 244–248, see 248, and "By the Governor to Luke Decker, Esquire, *Cincinnati October the* 11th 1793," in *ibid.*, III, 415–416. Dorothy B. Goebel, *William Henry Harrison, A Political Biography*, in Indiana Historical *Collections* (Indianapolis, 1916–   ), XIV (1926), 74–76.

55. See *post*, 204.

56. Since this chapter was written Francis S. Philbrick has published *The Laws of Illinois Territory, 1809–1818* (Illinois State Historical Library *Collections*, XXV, Springfield, Ill., 1950), in which he discusses the Ordinance of 1787, clxxix–ccxlix. He criticizes the Ordinance more vigorously than other writers.

CHAPTER 10. A STATE OF THE NATIONAL FRONTIER: OHIO

1. Rowena Buell (comp.), *The Memoirs of Rufus Putnam* (Boston, 1903), 103–107; Samuel P. Hildreth, *Memoirs of the Early Pioneer Settlers of Ohio* (Cincinnati, 1854), 101–105; *Military Journal of Major Ebenezer Denny*, 119–122; and Bond, *Foundations of Ohio*, 275–290.

2. "Estimate by Mr. Heckenwelder of the Settlers North of the Ohio [1793]," in Carter, *Territorial Papers of the United States*, II, 470.

3. "John Cleves Symmes to Jonathan Dayton, Northbend, May the 18th 19th & 20th 1789" in Bond, *The Correspondence of John Cleves Symmes*, 53–97.

4. Bond, "Dr. Daniel Drake's Memoir," in the *Quarterly Publication* of the Historical and Philosophical Society of Ohio, XVIII, 79, 87, 89–91.

5. "Estimate by Mr. Heckenwelder of the Settlers North of the Ohio [1793]," in Carter, *Territorial Papers of the United States*, II, 470.

6. "Return of Inhabitants of Hamilton County [*July* 12, 1798]," in *ibid.*, II, 648–649.

7. Downes, *Frontier Ohio*, 59–60, 62, and 69; and Bond, *Foundations of Ohio*, 290–301.

8. Bond, *Foundations of Ohio*, 308, 349; Downes, *Frontier Ohio*, 69–72.

9. W. P. Strickland (ed.), *Autobiography of Rev. James B. Finley* (Cincinnati, n.d.), 99–113; John McDonald, *Biographical Sketches of General Nathaniel Massie* ...(Cincinnati, 1838), 7–70; David M. Massie, *Nathaniel Massie, A Pioneer of Ohio* (Cincinnati, 1896), 23–64; and Bond, *Foundations of Ohio*, 349–353.

10. The Duncan McArthur Papers and a collection of Thomas Worthington Papers are in the Library of Congress, Division of Manuscripts. Other papers of Thomas Worthington are in the library of the Ohio Archaeological and Historical Society and the Ohio State Library at Columbus, Ohio. There are biographies of these men in Massie, *Nathaniel Massie*, see 65–92; William E. Gilmore, *Life of Edward Tiffin, First Governor of Ohio* (Chillicothe, Ohio, 1897), see 17–87; and Alfred B. Sears, The Public Career of Thomas Worthington (unpublished Ph.D. thesis, Ohio State University, Columbus, 1932), see 38–70. At this writing, Professor Sears is revising the study for publication. See also Downes, *Frontier Ohio*, 77–82, and William T. Hutchinson, The Bounty Lands of the American Revolution in Ohio (unpublished Ph.D. thesis, Department of History, University of Chicago, 1927), 35–56, 181–196, 247–248.

11. Claude L. Shepard, "The Connecticut Land Company: A Study in the Beginnings of Colonization of the Western Reserve," in Western Reserve Historical Society, *Tract No. 96* (Cleveland, 1916), 59–221, see 74–84 particularly; Bond, *Foundations of Ohio*, 358–372; and Treat, *National Land System*, 319–325.

12. *American State Papers: Public Lands*, II, 442; Treat, *National Land System*, 41–45, 92; Bond, *Foundations of Ohio*, 308–309; Downes, *Frontier Ohio*, 82–83.

13. Treat, *National Land System*, 238–241; and Bond, *Foundations of Ohio*, 376–377.

14. *United States Statutes at Large*, I, 464; Treat, *National Land System*, 91–94.

15. *United States Statutes at Large*, II, 73–78.

16. *American State Papers: Public Lands*, II, 444.

17. Smith, *St. Clair Papers*, I, 1–136, describes his life before his governorship. His early activities as governor are narrated in 137–166.

18. B. H. Pershing, "Winthrop Sargent," in *Ohio Archaeological and Historical Quarterly*, XXXV (1926), 583–601. The Ohio Archaeological and Historical Society has a Winthrop Sargent Collection which includes letters to Sargent, copies of some of his letters to other people, and other documents.

19. "Samuel Holden Parsons," in *Dictionary of American Biography*, XIV, 270–271; and "James Mitchell Varnum," in *ibid.*, XIX (1936), 227–228.

20. Bond, *Correspondence of John Cleves Symmes*. A biographical introduction is given on pp. 1–24. See also Beverley W. Bond, Jr., "John Cleves Symmes," in *Dictionary of American Biography*, XVIII, 258–259.

21. *Journal of the House of Representatives of the Territory of the United States, North-west of the River Ohio ... 1799* (Cincinnati, 1800); Smith, *St. Clair Papers*, I, 137–192.

22. Lexington, Ky., *Gazette*, March 29, April 5, May 17, 1790, Jan. 15,

March 26, May 7, May 14, July 2, and July 9, 1791; Selter, *L'Odyssée Américaine*, 49; Downes, *Council Fires on the Upper Ohio*, 301–320; *Military Journal of Ebenezer Denny*, 123–178.

23. "Report of Governor St. Clair to the Secretary of State [*February* 10, 1791]," in Carter, *Territorial Papers of the United States*, II, 323; "Journal of the Executive Proceedings in the Territory Northwest of the River Ohio," in *ibid.*, III, 278–279, 294–295, 301–303, 311, and 313; Dwight G. McCarty, *The Territorial Governors of the Old Northwest* (Iowa City, Iowa, 1910), 44–74. *Laws of the Territory of the United States North-west of the Ohio* [*Maxwell's Code*] (Cincinnati, Printed by W. Maxwell, 1796). Copies of the latter are in the Library of the Historical and Philosophical Society of Ohio, Cincinnati, and the Indiana University Library, Bloomington. Theodore C. Pease (ed.), *Laws of the Northwest Territory, 1788–1800*, in Illinois State Historical Library *Collections* (Springfield, Ill., 1903–   ), XVII (1925), contains all the laws of the Northwest Territory. Very satisfactory accounts of the territorial period are found in Downes, *Frontier Ohio;* Bond, *Foundations of Ohio*, 437–476; and Beverley W. Bond, Jr., *The Civilization of the Old Northwest* (New York, 1934), 55–119.

24. Cincinnati, Ohio, *Centinel of the North-Western Territory*, Nov. 9, 1793.

25. *Ibid.*, Nov. 23, 1793.

26. *Ibid.*, Nov. 30, 1793.

27. *Ibid.*, July 12, 1794

28. *Ibid.*, Sept. 20, 1794

29. *Ibid.*, Sept. 27, 1794.

30. *Ibid.*, Oct. 4 and 11, 1794.

31. *Ibid.*, Oct. 18, 1794.

32. *Ibid.*, Nov. 1, 1794.

33. *Ibid.*, Jan. 31, 1795. See also the issues of Feb. 7 and 14, 1795.

34. *Ibid.*, July 18, 1795

35. "Hoffel Paugh," in *ibid.*, June 13, 1795, and "Hospes," in *ibid.*, July 4, 1795.

36. *Ibid.*, April 2, 1796. This appears under the title "Christian Sugar-Making."

37. "Dorastius," in *ibid.*, Jan. 31, 1795; Downes, *Frontier Ohio*, 155–163.

38. Note the letters of Sargent in Carter, *Territorial Papers of the United States*, II, 429, 432–434, 622–624, and III, 399–404. See also Downes, *Frontier Ohio*, 127–146.

39. Cincinnati, *Centinel of the North-Western Territory*, Feb. 20, 1796; Carter, *Territorial Papers of the United States*, III, 514–515; Downes, *Frontier Ohio*, 179–186; and Bond, *Foundations of Ohio*, 432–436.

40. *Journal of the House of Representatives of the Territory of the United States, North-west of the River Ohio . . . 1799*, pp. 1, 12, 32, 207–211; *Journal of the Legislative Council of the Territory of the United*

States, North-west of the River Ohio . . . One Thousand, Seven Hundred and Ninety Nine (Cincinnati, n.d.), 3, 19, 98–103; Cincinnati *Western Spy,* June 11, Aug. 27, Sept. 10 and 17, 1800; Cincinnati *Freeman's Journal,* Sept. 26, Oct. 8, 1800; Jacob Burnet, *Notes on the Early Settlement of the North-Western Territory* (New York, 1847), 301–302; Logan Esarey, *Messages and Letters of William Henry Harrison* (2 vols., Indiana Historical *Collections,* VII and IX, 1922), I, 12–18.

41. "Petition to Congress by Inhabitants of the Illinois Country [*February* 7, 1800], in Carter, *Territorial Papers of the United States,* III, 76–78; and the act dividing the territory in *ibid.,* 86–88. There was some opposition to the increased cost in the Cincinnati area. See "A Farmer," in Cincinnati *Western Spy,* Aug. 27, 1800, "The Farmer's Friend," in *ibid.,* Oct. 1, 1800, and "No Lawyer," in *ibid.,* Sept. 3, 1800.

42. *Journal of the House of Representatives of the Territory of the United States, North-west of the river Ohio at the Second Session of the First General Assembly, A.D. 1800* (Chillicothe, Ohio, 1800), 22–23, 56–57, 90, 124–125, *et passim.* See also Burnet, *Notes on the . . . North-Western Territory,* 325–327.

43. *Annals of Congress,* 7 Cong., 1 Sess., 1350–1351.

44. *Journal of the House of Representatives of the Territory of the United States, North-west of the Ohio, at the First Session of the Second General Assembly, A.D. 1801* (Chillicothe, Ohio, 1801), 81–84. The date of publication of the above *Journal* is erroneous as the session lasted from November 23, 1801, to January 23, 1802.

45. See *ante,* chapters IV, VI, VII, and VIII.

46. Cincinnati *Western Spy,* Aug. 21, Sept. 18, and Oct. 9 and 20, 1802. See also Chillicothe, Ohio, *Scioto Gazette,* Sept. 25, 1802; and Downes, *Frontier Ohio,* 241–242, 245–246.

47. Chillicothe, Ohio, *Scioto Gazette,* Aug. 28, Sept. 4, 11, 18, 25, and Oct. 2, and 16, 1802.

48. *Ibid.,* Aug. 7, Sept. 11, and Oct. 9, 1802.

49. *Ibid.,* Sept. 4, 1802; and Julia P. Cutler, *Life and Times of Ephraim Cutler, prepared from his Journal and Correspondence* (Cincinnati, 1890), 66–67.

50. Beverley W. Bond, Jr. (ed.), "Memoirs of Benjamin Van Cleve," in *Quarterly Publication* of the Historical and Philosophical Society of Ohio, XVII (1922), 67–71; and Burnet, *Notes on the . . . North-Western Territory,* 335–349, 496–501. See also Downes, *Frontier Ohio,* 226–233.

51. The letters published in the *Scioto Gazette* might not be accepted at face value if they were not supported by the action of these men in the territorial legislature and in the convention. I believe they were honest statements. See *ante,* note 47.

52. "Thomas Worthington to the President, Chilicothe *Novr* 8th 1802," in Carter, *The Territorial Papers of the United States,* III, 254, estimated

the alignment as twenty-six decided Republicans, seven Federalists, and two doubtful. See also the letters of John Smith, Joseph Darlinton, and Worthington in *ibid.*, III, 254–258. On the basis of the votes in the convention, the delegates might be classified as twenty regular Republicans, eight independent Republicans, and seven Federalists. Two of the latter were also somewhat independent.

53. John Smith was a Virginian, a Baptist preacher, an agent for Symmes, and a politician, who lived for a time in southwestern Pennsylvania. See H. H. Dunlevy, *History of the Miami Baptist Association* (Cincinnati, 1869), 96; and Downes, *Frontier Ohio*, 95, *et passim*.

54. W. H. Burtner, Jr., "Charles Willing Byrd," in *Ohio Archaeological and Historical Quarterly*, XLI (1932), 237–240.

55. Reily was the lone Federalist. See Burnet, *Notes on the ... North-Western Territory*, 469–478; and James McBride, *Pioneer Biography* (2 vols., Cincinnati, 1869), I, 1–105.

56. Blanche G. Garber, "Colonel John Paul, Hoosier Pioneer; First Proprietor and Founder of Xenia, Ohio, and Madison, Indiana," in *Indiana Magazine of History* (Bloomington, Ind., 1905–   ), XIII (1917), 129–145; William H. English, *Conquest of the Country Northwest of the River Ohio* (2 vols., Indianapolis, 1896), II, 941–944; George F. Robinson, *History of Greene County, Ohio* (Chicago, 1902), 36–40.

57. Philip Gatch, one of the delegates, was a Methodist preacher and a friend of Bishop Asbury. He was born near Baltimore in a Quaker family. He became a slaveowner in Virginia but freed his slaves before moving to the West. John M. Barber, *History of Ohio Methodism* (Cincinnati, 1898), 148–150; Henry A. Ford and Kate B. Ford (comps.), *History of Hamilton County, Ohio* (Cleveland, 1881), 251. James Sargent, the other delegate, also freed slaves before migrating to Kentucky. *A History of Clermont County, Ohio* (Cleveland, 1880), 336, and Henry Howe, *Historical Collections of Ohio* (2 vols., Cincinnati, 1908), I, 409.

58. The Virginian was Joseph Darlinton who had lived in southwestern Pennsylvania and had owned slaves. See Nelson W. Evans and Emons B. Stivers, *A History of Adams County, Ohio* (West Union, Ohio, 1900), 251–256, and Charles S. Galbreath, *History of Ohio* (5 vols., Chicago, 1925), II, 20. Israel Donalson, the native of New Jersey, moved to northwestern Virginia and Kentucky, before coming to Adams County. He had been an Indian scout, a soldier with Wayne, and schoolteacher. See Cutler, *Life and Times of Ephraim Cutler*, 260; and Evans and Stivers, *History of Adams County, Ohio*, 66–73, 549–550.

59. For Thomas Kirker see Evans and Stivers, *History of Adams County, Ohio*, 82–83, 256–257; and Galbreath, *History of Ohio*, II, 21–22.

60. For Michael Baldwin see Emilius O. Randall and Daniel J. Ryan, *History of Ohio* (5 vols., New York, 1912), III, 91; and Howe, *Historical Collections of Ohio*, II, 517–518.

61. Elijah Woods was the Virginian. He was probably not nominated by the Corresponding societies. See Chillicothe, Ohio, *Scioto Gazette*, Oct. 9, 1802, and J. A. Caldwell, *History of Belmont and Jefferson Counties, Ohio* (Wheeling, W. Va., 1880), 283. James Caldwell was a native of Baltimore. See Chillicothe, Ohio, *Scioto Gazette*, June 12, Aug. 7, Sept. 11, and Oct. 9, 1802; and Galbreath, *History of Ohio*, II, 19.

62. The Republicans were John Milligan, George Humphrey, and Rudolph Bair, and the Federalists were Bezaleel Wells and Nathan Updegraff. The latter was a native of York, Pennsylvania, and a Quaker. See marriage certificate, and History and Partial Genealogy of the Updegraff Family, by Milton Updegraff. Both were (1935) in the possession of Miss Emma Luanna Kinsey of Mt. Pleasant, Ohio. See also Caldwell, *History of Belmont and Jefferson Counties, Ohio*, 530. Wells was born in Baltimore. He came to the Ohio Valley in extreme northwestern Virginia, where he and James Ross, a close friend of St. Clair, founded Steubenville, Ohio. See Caldwell, *History of Belmont and Jefferson Counties, Ohio*, 463, *et passim*, and Joseph B. Doyle, *20th Century History of Steubenville and Jefferson County, Ohio* (Chicago, 1910), 134, 329–331. Bair was a native of Pennsylvania according to John Danner, *Old Landmarks of Canton and Stark County, Ohio* (Logansport, Ind., 1904), 65, 97–98, 122. The origin of Milligan and Humphrey was not learned.

63. Henry Abrams. Howe, *Historical Collections of Ohio*, II, 492, 496; and A. A. Graham (comp.), *History of Fairfield and Perry Counties, Ohio* (Chicago, 1883), 218; Lyle S. Evans, *A Standard History of Ross County, Ohio* (2 vols., Chicago, 1917), I, 245, 439.

64. Emanuel Carpenter. C. M. L. Wiseman, *Centennial History of Lancaster, Ohio* (Lancaster, Ohio, 1898), 60–64; and *The Official Roster of the Soldiers of the American Revolution Buried in the State of Ohio* (Columbus, 1929), 68.

65. These were David Abbot, who was a native of Massachusetts, before making his way through New York state to the Western Reserve; and Samuel Huntington, who came from Connecticut. See Howe, *Historical Collections of Ohio*, I, 578; and William T. Utter, "Samuel Huntington," in *Dictionary of American Biography*, I, 419–420.

66. Cutler, *Life and Times of Ephraim Cutler*; Buell, *The Memoirs of Rufus Putnam*; Hildreth, *Memoirs of the Early Settlers of Ohio*, 305–320. Cutler's statement in the *Life and Times of Ephraim Cutler* still betrays his prejudices. It is also contradictory. See 69–70.

67. C. M. L. Wiseman, *Pioneer Period and Pioneer People of Fairfield County, Ohio* (Columbus, 1901), 23–29; and Thomas W. Lewis, *History of Southeastern Ohio* (3 vols., Chicago, 1928), I, 71–73, 387–389, 415–416.

68. Howe, *Historical Collections of Ohio*, II, 517.

69. Evans, *A Standard History of Ross County, Ohio*, I, 356; Osman C. Hooper, *History of Ohio Journalism, 1793–1933* (Columbus, 1933), 18–20.

The "Journal of the Convention" was printed in the *Ohio Archaeological and Historical Quarterly*, V (1897), 80–132. For the election of officers see 83–84, 93–94. Willis was said to have been involved in the Boston Tea Party.

70. Cincinnati, *Western Spy*, Nov. 17, 1802. This issue contains St. Clair's speech in which he refers to his effort to help organize the convention. See also "John Smith to the President, Chillicothe *Nov* 9th 1802," in Carter, *The Territorial Papers of the United States*, III, 255, and footnote.

71. "Journal of the Convention," in *Ohio Archaeological and Historical Quarterly*, V, 88.

72. *Ibid.*, 90–91.

73. *Ibid.*, 97–98.

74. *Ibid.*, 105–109.

75. *Ibid.*, 113.

76. *Ibid.*, 114, 122.

77. *Ibid.*, 122.

78. *Ibid.*, 115–116, 124–125

79. Cutler, *Life and Times of Ephraim Cutler*, 70–73. Cutler erred in stating that the article contained fourteen sections. The "Journal of the Convention" indicates that amendments were made, but it is impossible to find in it either confirmation or contradiction of Cutler's story. The journal does not clearly indicate that the changes were made on third reading as stated by Cutler. See "Journal of the Convention," in *Ohio Archaeological and Historical Quarterly*, V, 116, 120, 123, 127–128.

80. Since the constitutions of Kentucky, Tennessee, and Delaware were very similar to the Pennsylvania document, it is often difficult to determine which of them was followed by the persons who drafted a particular section of the Ohio Constitution. Thorpe, *Federal and State Constitutions*, contains the various constitutions arranged alphabetically and chronologically. The original manuscript copies of the constitutions of Tennessee and Kentucky have been photostated and used. Isaac F. Patterson, *The Constitutions of Ohio* (Cleveland, 1912), contains the constitution of 1802 and other pertinent documents.

CHAPTER 11. THE DEMOCRATIZATION OF TERRITORIAL GOVERNMENT: INDIANA

1. Natalia M. Belting, "Kaskaskia, 'The Versailles of the West,'" in the *Indiana Magazine of History*, XLI (1945), 1–18; Clarence W. Alvord (ed.), *Cahokia Records, 1778–1790*, in the Illinois State Historical Library

Collections, II (1907), xiii–clvi; and Clarence W. Alvord, *The Illinois Country, 1673–1818 (Centennial History of Illinois,* I, Springfield, Ill., 1920), 329–378, *et passim.*

2. Francis S. Philbrick (ed.), *The Laws of Indiana Territory, 1801–1809,* in the Illinois State Historical Library *Collections,* XXI (1930), ccxii–ccxiii, xiii, ccxx–ccxxii, *et passim.* See also Leonard Lux, "The Vincennes Donation Lands," in Indiana Historical Society *Publications,* XV (1949), 418–497.

3. Philbrick, *The Laws of Indiana Territory, 1801–1809,* xxi.

4. "Petition of the Inhabitants of Post Vincennes [*July* 26, 1787]," in Carter, *The Territorial Papers of the United States,* II, 58–61; "Address to Colonel Josiah Harmar," in *ibid.,* II, 65–66; and "Petition to Congress from Post Vincennes," in *ibid.,* II, 66–67; "John Cleves Symmes to Robert Morris," in Bond, *The Correspondence of John Cleves Symmes,* 287–292.

5. *United States Statutes at Large,* I, 221–222.

6. "Report of the Secretary of State to the President [*Dec.* 14, 1790]," in Carter, *The Territorial Papers of the United States,* II, 315–316. See also the petition of thirty Americans who had received no grants or small ones in *ibid.,* II, 634–636.

7. "Lt-Col. Josiah Harmar to General Knox, Camp at Vincennes, August 7, 1787," in the *Military Journal of Major Ebenezer Denny,* 218.

8. *Return of the Whole Number of Persons . . . according to the second census,* 86. The census is also reprinted in Carter, *The Territorial Papers of the United States,* VII, 24–25.

9. *Aggregate amount of each description of Persons within the United States of America, and the Territories thereof, agreeably to actual enumeration made according to law, in the year 1810* [Washington, 1811], 86.

10. *Return of the Whole Number of Persons . . . according to the second census,* 86; Carter, *The Territorial Papers of the United States,* VII, 24–25.

11. John Woods, *Two Years' Residence in the settlement on the English Prairie in the Illinois Country* (London, 1822), 109–114.

12. "Petition to the President and Senate by Citizens of Clark County [1809]," in Carter, *The Territorial Papers of the United States,* VII, 705–707; and note large vote for Jennings reported in Vincennes, Ind., *Western Sun,* July 1, 1809.

13. "Governor St. Clair to the Secretary of State [January, 1796]," in Carter, *The Territorial Papers of the United States,* II, 548–549.

14. "Acting Governor Sargent to the Secretary of State, Cincinnati 20th of January 1797," in *ibid.,* II, 587.

15. The settlement of the Miami Valley is described by "Dr. Daniel Drake's Memoir of the Miami Country, 1779–1794," edited by Bond in the *Quarterly Publication* of the Historical and Philosophical Society of Ohio,

XVIII; the "Memoirs of Benjamin Van Cleve," edited by Bond in *ibid.*, XVII; and Dr. Ezra Ferris, "The Early Settlement of the Miami Country," in Indiana Historical Society *Publications* (Indianapolis, 1895–   ), I, 245–364. See also Lawrence H. Gipson (ed.), *The Moravian Indian Mission on White River,* in the Indiana Historical *Collections,* XXIII (1939), 83.

16. John L. Heineman, *The Indian Trail Down the Whitewater Valley* (n.p., 1912), 19. Bernhard Knollenberg, "Pioneer Sketches of the Upper Whitewater Valley, Quaker Stronghold of the West," in Indiana Historical Society *Publications,* XV (1945), 21–22, 32–33, 42, *et passim;* and Chelsea L. Lawlis, "Settlement of the Whitewater Valley, 1790–1810," in *Indiana Magazine of History,* XLIII (1947), 23–40.

17. "Autobiography" of Elijah Coffin in *The Life of Elijah Coffin with a Reminiscence By his son Charles F. Coffin,* edited by Mary C. Johnson (n.p., 1863), 17–18; and *Reminiscences of Levi Coffin* (Cincinnati, 1876), 76, 100, 106. See also Stephen B. Weeks, *Southern Quakers and Slavery, A Study in Institutional History,* in John Hopkins University *Studies in Historical and Political Science* (Baltimore, 1883–   ), Extra Vol. XV (1896), 246–247.

18. *Eighteenth Annual Report of the Bureau of American Ethnology* (Washington, 1899), map 55; *Treaties Between the United States . . . and . . . Indian Tribes, from 1778 to 1837,* pp. 8–17, 34–40.

19. See the letters of John Gibson to Captain William Hargrove in William M. Cockrum, *Pioneer History of Indiana* (Oakland City, Ind., 1907), 203–229, and George R. Wilson, "Early Indiana Trails and Surveys," in Indiana Historical Society *Publications,* VI (1919), 349–457. Roads extended toward Vincennes from Clarksville, the mouth of Blue River (Fredonia), Yellow Banks (Rockport), and from opposite Red Banks (Henderson, Kentucky). The latter somewhat paralleled the Wabash. Running east and west were trails connecting the roads between the Ohio and Vincennes; one ran a few miles north of the Ohio, another was marked a little to the south of the Patoka River. See also George R. Wilson and Gayle Thornbrough, "The Buffalo Trace," in Indiana Historical Society *Publications,* XV (1946), 172–279.

20. *History of Dearborn and Ohio Counties, Indiana* (Chicago, 1885), 148–149; Oliver H. Smith, *Early Indiana Trials and Sketches* (Cincinnati, 1858), 172–173; sketches of James Dill, English Collection, Biographical Sketches, D; Jacob P. Dunn, *Indiana and Indianians* (5 vols., Chicago, 1919), I, 287; William Wesley Woollen, *et al.* (eds.), "Executive Journal of Indiana Territory, 1800–1816," Indiana Historical Society *Publications,* III (1900), 117, 154, 167, 174, 180, 201, 205, 209, and 217.

21. "The Memorial of the Legislature of the Indiana Territory, 31st August, 1814," in *American State Papers, Public Lands,* II, 888; *ibid.,* IV,

793–795; *ibid.*, VI, 456; C. F. Emerick, *The Credit System and the Public Domain* (Nashville, Tenn., 1899).

22. *Annals of Congress*, 6 Cong., 1 Sess., 1498–1500.

23. Goebel, *William Henry Harrison*, 53–88; Homer G. Webster, "William Henry Harrison's Administration of Indiana Territory," in Indiana Historical Society *Publications*, IV (1907), 179–297; Bond, *Civilization of the Old Northwest*, 173–174, *et passim*.

24. Vincennes *Indiana Gazette*, 1804–1806, and the Vincennes *Western Sun*, 1807 f., are the chief sources of this criticism. Some of the writers took the trouble to trace the controversy as they saw it from the beginning. Numerous references to these newspapers will be made in the following pages.

25. Petition of John Edgar, *et al.*, of Jan. 12, 1796, in *American State Papers, Public Lands*, I, 69–70; Memorial of Thomas Posey, Nov. 18, 1799, in Smith, *St. Clair Papers*, II, 451 note; *ibid.*, 447–448 note; and Jacob P. Dunn, "Slavery Petitions and Papers," in Indiana Historical Society *Publications*, II (1895), 455–461. See also *Letters of Decius . . .* (Louisville, Ky., 1805), 7.

26. The proclamation calling the convention, the resolution respecting Article VI of the Northwest Ordinance, and the petition of the convention are printed in Esarey, *Messages and Letters of William Henry Harrison*, I, 60–67. Harrison was charged with undue influence in bringing this convention into existence, *Letters of Decius*, 27; and "A Freeholder of Knox County" (William McIntosh), in Vincennes *Indiana Gazette*, Aug. 7, 1804.

27. Philbrick, *The Laws of Indiana Territory, 1801–1809*, 42–45.

28. Carter, *The Territorial Papers of the United States*, VII, 243–247, 140–145, 99–106, and 118–123.

29. Vincennes *Indiana Gazette*, Aug. 7, 1804; Esarey, *Messages and Letters of Harrison*, I, 106–107, 112–113; Woollen, *et al.*, "Executive Journal," Indiana Historical Society *Publications*, III, 124, 125–126.

30. Vincennes *Indiana Gazette*, Aug. 7, 1804.

31. *Ibid.*, Aug. 7, 1804.

32. *Ibid.*, Aug. 14, 1804.

33. *Ibid.*, Aug. 21 and 28, Sept. 11 and 18, 1804.

34. "Jefferson to Harrison, Washington Apr. 28, 1805," in Esarey, *Messages and Letters of Harrison*, I, 126–128; Cincinnati *Liberty Hall*, Sept. 17, 1805.

35. Philbrick, *Laws of Indiana Territory, 1801–1809*, pp. 115–118, 153.

36. Dunn, "Slavery Petitions and Papers," in Indiana Historical Society *Publications*, II, 476–483.

37. Philbrick, *Laws of Indiana Territory, 1801–1809*, pp. 136–139.

38. Dunn, in his "Slavery Petitions and Papers," did not print all of the petitions concerning slavery, and omitted other petitions probably of

equal or greater significance. Esarey printed some of those which Dunn omitted in his *Messages and Letters of William Henry Harrison,* but the larger number are found in Carter, *The Territorial Papers of the United States,* VII, *et passim.* The issues of the Vincennes *Western Sun* contain a large amount of political news during the years 1807–1809.

39. Carter, *The Territorial Papers of the United States,* VII, 600–602; "Gen. W. Johnston [to] Fellow Citizens, Nov. 2, 1808," in Vincennes *Western Sun,* Nov. 12, 1808; and Gayle Thornbrough and Dorothy Riker (eds.), *Journals of the General Assembly of Indiana Territory, 1805–1815* (Indianapolis, 1950), 213–15, and 286.

40. *Ibid.,* 190, 191, 195–96, 202, 210–13, and 246.

41. *Ibid.,* 183, 187–90, 192–93, 198, 220–25, 232–38. See also Vincennes *Western Sun,* Dec. 17, 1808.

42. Thornbrough and Riker, *Journals of the General Assembly,* 214.

43. *Ibid.,* 248, and note 64.

44. Solon J. Buck, *Illinois in 1818* (Springfield, Ill., 1917), 181–193, gives a brief but excellent account of the territorial period previous to separation.

45. *Annals of Congress,* 10 Cong., 2 Sess., 1808–1810, 1821–1822.

46. Thornbrough and Riker, *Journals of the General Assembly,* 315–44.

47. Randolph, the defeated candidate for Congress, challenged M'Namee to a duel, but was refused. Vincennes *Western Sun,* June 10, 1809. Waller Taylor, one of the leading Harrisonites, tried to pick a quarrel with Jennings, the successful candidate. William W. Woollen, *Biographical and Historical Sketches of Early Indiana* (Indianapolis, 1883), 391–399.

48. Vincennes *Western Sun,* Jan. 28, 1809. See also other communications in *ibid.,* Feb. 11, 1809; Feb. 18, 1809; and two handbills by "A Citizen of Vincennes" to "The Citizens of Indiana" and "A Detector Detected" to "Fellow Citizens of Indiana," both of which were written during the election campaign.

49. Vincennes *Western Sun,* Jan. 28, 1809.

50. *Ibid.,* Feb. 4 and 11, 1809.

51. *Ibid.,* Feb. 11 and 18, 1809.

52. *Ibid.,* Feb. 18, 1809. See also "A Citizen of Vincennes" in the same issue.

53. *Ibid.,* March 4 and 18, and April 15, 1809.

54. *Ibid.,* March 11, 1809.

55. *Ibid.,* April 22, and May 6, 1809.

56. *Ibid.,* Aug. 26, 1809.

57. *Ibid.,* Extra, May 15, 1809.

58. Thornbrough and Riker, *Journals of the General Assembly,* 338–39.

59. Louis B. Ewbank and Dorothy Riker (eds.), *The Laws of Indiana Territory, 1809–1816,* in Indiana Historical *Collections,* XX (1934), 104–105, 108–111, 138–139, 171–172.

60. Jonathan Jennings to Samuel Manwarring, Washington, Jan. 22, 1811, Esarey, *Messages and Letters of William Henry Harrison*, I, 501–503; *Annals of Congress*, 11 Cong., 3 Sess., 453, 508, 787; *ibid.*, 12 Cong., 1 Sess., 846, 1248; and Goebel, *William Henry Harrison*, 61–65, 85–88.

61. Carter, *The Territorial Papers of the United States*, VIII, *The Territory of Indiana, 1810–1816* (1939), 142–147.

62. "Address to Congress by Citizens of Jefferson County [*December* 27, 1811]," in *ibid.*, VIII, 154–156.

63. *Annals of Congress*, 11 Cong., 3 Sess., 1347–1348; *United States Statutes at Large*, II, 659–660.

64. Ewbank and Riker, *The Laws of Indiana Territory, 1809–1816*, 225–236.

CHAPTER 12. INDIANA'S IDEAL: A DEMOCRATIC STATE

1. Thornbrough and Riker, *Journals of the General Assembly*, 370.

2. *Ibid.*, 493.

3. Ewbank and Riker, *The Laws of Indiana Territory, 1809–1816*, p. 793.

4. Thornbrough and Riker, *Journals of the General Assembly*, 520.

5. *Ibid.*, 596.

6. *Ibid.*, 688, 711, 727, *et passim.*

7. *Annals of Congress*, 13 Cong., 2 Sess., 2798.

8. Thornbrough and Riker, *Journals of the General Assembly*, 745–53, and Vincennes *Western Sun*, July 2, 1814.

9. Thornbrough and Riker, *Journals of the General Assembly*, 812–14, *et passim.* A session of the General Court was adjourned; a new circuit court system was established; changes were made in the procedure for the collection of debts, for small causes, and in chancery; and the time of meeting of the various courts were regulated by other acts. Ewbank and Riker, *Laws of Indiana Territory, 1809–1816*, pp. 517, 517–522, 523–525, 533–538, 548–557, 557–559, 562–565, 567–585.

10. Thornbrough and Riker, *Journals of the General Assembly*, 769, 771, 777, 783, 784.

11. *Ibid.*, 846, 850–53, 855–56, 858, 863–64; and Vincennes *Western Sun*, Jan. 27, 1816.

12. Lexington, Indiana, *Western Eagle*, Jan. 13, 1816.

13. Vincennes *Western Sun*, Jan. 20, 27, Feb. 3, 10, and 17, 1816.

14. *Ibid.*, Feb. 10 and 24, 1816.

15. *Ibid.*, Feb. 3, 1816.

16. *Ibid.*, March 2, 1816.

17. *Ibid.*, March 30, 1816.

18. *Ibid.*, April 20, 1816.

19. *Ibid.*, April 20, 1816.

20. *Ibid.*, May 4, 1816.

21. *Ibid.*, May 11, 1816.

22. *Ibid.*, June 1, 1816, an extra issue. The financial objections to statehood were described by Donald F. Carmony, "Fiscal Objection to Statehood in Indiana," in *Indiana Magazine of History*, XLII (1946), 311–321.

23. Timothy Flint, *Recollections of the Last Ten Years* . . . (Boston, 1826), 57.

24. Vincennes *Western Sun*, June 22, 1816.

25. Compare Logan Esarey in *Messages and Papers of Jonathan Jennings* . . . , Indiana Historical *Collections*, XII (1924), 5–12, and his *History of Indiana* (2 vols., Indianapolis, 1915–1918), I, 213–221, with Jacob P. Dunn, *Indiana, A Redemption from Slavery* (Boston, 1890), 417–418, *et passim*.

26. "Governor Posey to the Secretary of State, Jeffersonville Indiana Territory 26th *Jany* 1816," in Carter, *The Territorial Papers of the United States*, VIII, 380.

27. *Journal of the Convention of the Indiana Territory* . . . (Louisville, Ky., 1816), 4–12. The *Journal* was also published in the State Bar Association of Indiana *Report of the Sixteenth Annual Meeting* (n.p., 1912), 137–231. For Hendricks, see *A Biographical History of Eminent and Self-Made Men of the State of Indiana* (2 vols., Cincinnati, 1880), I, 4th Dist., 32–33; and Dunn, *Indiana and Indianans*, I, 302.

28. The Virginians included James Noble, William Cotton, Dennis Pennington, Enoch McCarty, Samuel Smock, Davis Floyd, John Bennefield, Alexander Devin, James Smith, William Polke, Patrick Shields, and Daniel C. Lane. The Pennsylvanians were Jeremiah Cox, James Brownlee, John K. Graham, John Johnson, Robert McIntire, Samuel Milroy, and James Scott. John DePauw, Daniel Grass, Joseph Holman, James Lemon, Dann Lynn, and Dr. David H. Maxwell were the natives of Kentucky. The evidence is not too convincing in the case of Grass and Lemon. The natives of Maryland were John Boone, Hugh Cull, Thomas Carr, William H. Eads, and Charles Polke. President Jonathan Jennings and Benjamin Parke were the natives of New Jersey. The two New Englanders were Ezra Ferris and Nathaniel Hunt. William Lowe was the North Carolinian. The native of Delaware was Solomon Manwaring. Robert Hanna was the South Carolinian. The Irish delegates were Patrick Beard, James Dill, William Graham, and David Robb. John Badollet came from Switzerland and Frederick Rapp from Germany.

29. See *ante*, 170–81.

30. Jennings was elected governor, Hendricks congressman, and Noble one of the United States senators.

31. *The Journal of the Convention* gives thirty-eight recorded votes from which the partisan alignment can be reconstructed.

32. "Governor Harrison to the Secretary of the Treasury, Vincennes 29th *August* 1809," in Carter, *The Territorial Papers of the United States,* VII, 665–670; Journal of the House of Representatives, Oct. 14, 1808; Henry Adams, *The Life of Albert Gallatin* (Philadelphia, 1880), 404–406, 645–649; and sketches in English Collection, University of Chicago Library, Biographical Sketches, B.

33. Undated obituary notice in the William H. English Collection, University of Chicago Library, Biographical Sketches, P; George S. Cottman, "Benjamin Parke," in *Dictionary of American Biography,* XIV (1934), 209–210; Woollen, *Biographical and Historical Sketches of Early Indiana,* 373–383, 384–390; and "Executive Journal of Indiana Territory," in Indiana Historical Society *Publications,* III, 109, 146, and 196.

34. Will of John Johnson, a commission signed by William Henry Harrison, and a sketch of Johnson, in English Collection, University of Chicago Library, Biographical Sketches, I–J; Dunn, *Indiana, A Redemption from Slavery,* 239, 322, 327–328, *et passim;* and "Executive Journal of Indiana Territory," in Indiana Historical Society *Publications,* III, 146, 169, and 192. He served also as attorney general, being one of the ablest lawyers in the territory.

35. Sketches by his son and daughter in English Collection, University of Chicago, Biographical Sketches, R; and "Executive Journal of Indiana Territory," in Indiana Historical Society *Publications,* III, 105, 129, 160, 194, and 204.

36. References for the biographical information about the less important members of the convention, which are here omitted, may be found in the footnotes of the following article: John D. Barnhart, "The Southern Influence in the Formation of Indiana," in *Indiana Magazine of History,* XXXIII (1937), 261–276. Elected with Robb from Gibson County were Frederick Rapp, of the New Harmony society; Alexander Devin, a Baptist minister from Virginia and Kentucky; and James Smith, likewise a native of Virginia and a former resident of Kentucky, who had worked with Harrison's friends in the territorial legislature. Rapp voted with the opposition more regularly than his colleagues, but all the delegates from Gibson were opposed to the Jennings group. Robb and Rapp voted against proceeding to form a state constitution. Dann Lynn, a native Kentuckian and a slaveowner, was a member of the opposition and the only delegate from Posey County. The case of Charles Polke, the delegate from Perry County on the Ohio River, is not so clear but he voted with the opposition more than against it. From Harrison County in the extreme southern part of the territory came two members of the oppo-

sition, John Boone and Daniel C. Lane, both of whom had formerly resided in Kentucky. The first was born probably in Maryland, and the second in Virginia. The three other delegates from this county worked with the Jennings group. The delegation from Clark County was also divided, James Scott and James Lemon adhering to the opposition and the latter voting against statehood. One of the territorial judges at the time of the convention, Scott was a Pennsylvanian by birth and a Kentuckian by former residence. Lemon was born probably in Kentucky and like Scott was an officeholder.

37. Sketch of Maxwell by James D. Maxwell, a son, another sketch by "W.H.J.," and a clipping from the Bloomington, Ind., *News Letter,* June 24, 1854, in the Albert Gallatin Porter Collection, Indiana State Library, Indianapolis. See also the sketch of Maxwell in English Collection, University of Chicago Library, Biographical Sketches, M, and Louise Maxwell, "Sketch of Dr. David H. Maxwell," in *Indiana Magazine of History,* VIII (1912), 101–108.

38. *History of Dearborn and Ohio Counties,* 148.

39. *Ibid.,* 148.

40. Dunn, *Indiana, A Redemption from Slavery,* 389; Dorothy Riker, "Jonathan Jennings," in *Indiana Magazine of History,* XXVIII (1932), 223–239; Esarey, *Messages and Papers of Jonathan Jennings,* 6–12, 27–28.

41. Journal of the House of Representatives of the Indiana Territory, December 6, 1813; Woollen, *Biographical and Historical Sketches of Early Indiana,* 178–184; and Joe L. Norris, "James Noble," in *Dictionary of American Biography,* XIII, 538–539.

42. John H. B. Nowland, *Early Reminiscences of Indianapolis* (Indianapolis, 1870), 193–195; Indianapolis *Daily Journal,* Nov. 22, 1858; sketch of Robert Hanna, English Collection, University of Chicago, Biographical Sketches, H.

43. *Journal of the Convention,* 13–14, 39–40.

44. *Ibid.,* 7–9.

45. *Ibid.,* 38–39.

46. *Ibid.,* 54, 55–56.

47. *Ibid.,* 63–64.

48. *Ibid.,* 10–11.

49. *Ibid.,* 64–66.

50. The Indiana Constitution of 1816, Article XI, section 7. A manuscript copy prepared by the secretary of the constitutional convention is in the Indiana History Division, Indiana State Library, and a second copy similarly prepared is in the William Henry Smith Memorial Library of the Indiana Historical Society, both in Indianapolis. A suitable printed copy is in Charles Kettleborough, *Constitution Making in Indiana* (3 vols., Indiana Historical Collections, I, II, XVII, 1916, 1930), I, 83–125.

51. The Indiana Constitution of 1816, Article XI, section 7; Article VII, section 1; Article VI, section 1; and Article III, section 2.

52. John D. Barnhart, "Sources of Indiana's First Constitution," in *Indiana Magazine of History*, XXXIX (1943), 55–94.

CHAPTER 13. A BLAZED TRAIL: ILLINOIS

1. Alvord, *Illinois Country*, 428.

2. This has been described *ante,* chapter XI.

3. "Elijah Backus to the Secretary of the Treasury, Kaska Septr 24th 1809," and "John Edgar to [the Secretary of the Treasury], Kaskaskia 6th September 1810," in Carter, *Territorial Papers of the United States,* XVI, *The Territory of Illinois, 1809–1814* (1948), 58–59, 120–129.

4. *United States Statutes at Large,* II, 514–516.

5. Magaret C. Norton (ed.), *Illinois Census Returns, 1810, 1818,* in Illinois State Historical Library *Collections,* XXIV (1935), xxx and 53.

6. *Census for 1820* (Washington, 1821), 40 and reverse side; Norton, *Illinois Census Returns, 1810, 1818,* chart opposite p. xxxii. The state census listed 469 free Negroes, 668 servants or slaves, and 375 unclassified blacks, a total of 1,512. See *ibid.,* xxxii. See also Margaret C. Norton (ed.), *Illinois Census Returns, 1820,* in Illinois State Historical Library *Collections,* XXVI (1934).

7. The information about Negroes is scattered through the pages of Miss Norton's two volumes which were cited in the two preceding notes. See also N. Dwight Harris, *The History of Negro Servitude in Illinois* (Chicago, 1904).

8. This point has been developed more fully in John D. Barnhart, "Southern Contributions to the Social Order of the Old Northwest," in *The North Carolina Historical Review* (Raleigh, N. C., 1924–   ), XVII (1940), 237–248, especially 246–247.

9. Ferdinand Ernst, "Travels in Illinois in 1819," in Illinois Historical Society *Transactions, 1903* (Springfield, Ill., 1904), 150–165, see 152.

10. Albert J. Beveridge, *Abraham Lincoln, 1809–1858* (4 vols., Boston, 1928), II, 9–12; and John Reynolds, *The Pioneer History of Illinois . . . to the Year 1818* (Chicago, 1887), 165–166.

11. Buck, *Illinois in 1818,* pp. 36–55, especially 46–49.

12. *Ibid.,* 45–46.

13. Ninian W. Edwards, *History of Illinois from 1778 to 1833; and Life and Times of Ninian Edwards* (Springfield, Ill., 1870), 12–26; E. B. Wash-

burne (ed.), *The Edwards Papers,* in Chicago Historical Society *Collections* (12 vols., Chicago, 1882–1928), III (1884), 17–36; and "John Pope to the President [April 19, 1809]," and "William Wirt to the President, Richmond April 26th 1809," in Carter, *Territorial Papers of the United States,* XVI, 23–24, 29–30.

14. Edwards, *History of Illinois,* 35.

15. *Ibid.,* 27–35.

16. Buck, *Illinois in 1818,* p. 195.

17. "Proclamation of Public Land Sales," April 25, 1814, in Carter, *Territorial Papers of the United States,* XVI, 416–417. The sales were to begin in October.

18. "Governor Edwards to Richard M. Johnson, Elvirade Randolph County Illinois Territory March 14, 1812," in *ibid.,* XVI, 199–202, and Edwards, *History of Illinois,* 306–309.

19. *United States Statutes at Large,* II, 741–752. See *ante,* chapter XI, 176; and Ewbank and Riker, *Laws of Indiana Territory, 1809–1816,* pp. 225–236. Buck, in *Illinois in 1818,* p. 196, stated that Illinois Territory had the most democratic territorial government.

20. O. Turner, *Pioneer History of the Holland Purchase of Western New York . . .* (Buffalo, N. Y., 1849), 506–507. Tilly Buttrick, Jr., in *Voyages, Travels and Discoveries* (Boston, 1831, reprinted in Thwaites, *Early Western Travels,* VIII, 1904), 56–57, gives the number in 1815 as 1200. See also Edwin James, *Account of an Expedition from Pittsburgh to the Rocky Mountains, performed in the years 1819, 1820, . . . under the command of Maj. S. H. Long . . .* (London, 1823, reprinted in Thwaites, *Early Western Travels,* XIV and XV, 1905), XIV, 59.

21. Alvord, *Illinois Country,* 454.

22. Norton, *Illinois Census Returns, 1810, 1818,* xxx.

23. *Census for 1820,* p. 40 and reverse side.

24. See *ante,* chapter X.

25. Paul M. Angle, "Nathaniel Pope, 1784–1850," in Illinois State Historical Society *Transactions for the Year 1936* (Springfield, Ill., n.d.), 111–181, see 114–115, 143. See also William H. Brown, "Memoir of the Late Hon. Daniel P. Cook," in Edwards, *History of Illinois,* 253–268.

26. Kaskaskia, Ill., *Western Intelligencer,* Nov. 27, 1817.

27. *Ibid.,* Dec. 4 and 11, 1817.

28. *Ibid.,* Dec. 11, 1817.

29. *Ibid.,* Dec. 11, 1817.

30. *Ibid.,* Dec. 18, 1817, and Jan. 13, 1818.

31. *Ibid.,* Nov. 27, 1817.

32. *Ibid.,* April 1, 1818.

33. *Ibid.,* April 15, 1818.

34. *Ibid.,* May 6, 1818.

35. Kaskaskia *Illinois Intelligencer,* June 17, 1818. When the news of

the passage of the enabling act arrived, the editors changed the name of the *Western Intelligencer* to the *Illinois Intelligencer*. It became effective May 27, 1818.

36. *Ibid.*, July 1, 1818.

37. *Ibid.*, June 22, 1818.

38. *Ibid.*, Aug. 12, 1818.

39. *Ibid.*, July 29, 1818.

40. *Ibid.*, Aug. 19, 1818.

41. *Ibid.*, Aug. 5, 1818.

42. *Ibid.*, Aug. 5, 1818; and Buck, *Illinois in 1818*, pp. 256–261.

43. John Messinger married the daughter of Matthew Lyon. The latter was the Jeffersonian Congressman in Vermont who was prosecuted under the Sedition Act. Newton Bateman and Paul Selby, *Biographical and Memorial Edition of the Historical Encyclopedia of Illinois* (2 vols., Chicago, 1905), I, 371–372; Reynolds, *Pioneer History of Illinois*, 328–332; and Philbrick, *Laws of Indiana Territory, 1801–1809*, ccl–ccli.

44. Elias K. Kane. Reynolds, *Pioneer History of Illinois*, 410; Thomas Ford, *History of Illinois, from its Commencement as a State in 1818 to 1847* (Chicago, 1854), 24–25; and Bateman and Selby, *Historical Encyclopedia of Illinois*, I, 312–313.

45. Benjamin Stephenson was one of the leaders of the Edwards party. Edwardsville, Ill., *Spectator*, Oct. 12, 1822; and Reynolds, *Pioneer History of Illinois*, 411.

46. Conrad Will and Dr. Caldwell Cairns were the other Pennsylvanians. John F. Snyder, "Forgotten Statesmen of Illinois: Hon. Conrad Will," in Illinois State Historical Society *Transactions, 1905* (Springfield, Ill., 1906), 349–377; Reynolds, *Pioneer History of Illinois*, 360; *Combined History of Randolph, Monroe and Perry Counties, Illinois* (published by J. L. McDonough and Co., Philadelphia, 1883), 412–413. Joseph Kitchell was probably a native of New Jersey.

47. "Caution" in Kaskaskia *Western Intelligencer*, April 15, 1818, stated: "Does not the influx begin to flow from a different channel than it did formerly? I mean from the northern states. . . ." "A Republican," probably Daniel P. Cook, wrote: "We all know that emigration from the Eastern and Northern states has been far greater to every part of the western country, than from the Southern. We know that those states are possessed of a greater population, and will therefore admit of greater emigration; and our emigration has been mostly from the former." *Ibid.*, April 1, 1818. These statements sound more like arguments than facts. Perhaps the editor in his reply to "Caution" indicated considerable doubt on the subject: "Friend Caution would beseech us to wait five years till his brothers of the north could come in with their notions and make a constitution for us. We like the northern emigration, but we don't

think it proper to wait for them exclusively to frame our constitution." *Ibid.*, April 15, 1818.

48. Levi Compton. *Combined History of Edwards, Lawrence and Wabash Counties, Illinois* (Philadelphia, 1883), 298.

49. Dr. George Fisher and Judge Jesse B. Thomas. Reynolds, *Pioneer History of Illinois*, 358; and Elizabeth B. Ellis, "Jesse Burgess Thomas," in *Dictionary of American Biography*, XVIII, 436–437. The other two Virginians were Isham Harrison and Joseph Borough. The evidence about each is not very satisfactory. H. M. Aiken, *Franklin County History* (Centennial ed., n.p., n.d.), 5, 21, 27, 58, 78; and *History of Macoupin County, Illinois* (Philadelphia, 1879), 27.

50. Hezekiah West. Mrs. P. T. Chapman, *A History of Johnson County, Illinois* (Herrin, Ill., 1925), 458–459; *Heads of Families at the First Census of the United States, 1790: South Carolina* (Washington, 1908), 14.

51. For Michael Jones see Frances H. Relf, "The Two Michael Joneses," in *Illinois State Historical Society Journal* (Springfield, Ill., 1908–   ), IX (1916–1917), 146–151; Norton, *Illinois Census Returns, 1810, 1818*, p. 98.

52. Thomas Kirkpatrick, according to his obituary notice in the Edwardsville, Ill., *Spectator*, January 8, 1822, was born and educated in aristocratic surroundings and was a former resident of Georgia. That he was a native of one of the Carolinas is stated in W. T. Norton (ed.), *Centennial History of Madison County and Its People, 1812–1912* (2 vols., Chicago, 1912), I, 497; and *History of Madison County, Illinois* (Edwardsville, Ill., 1882), 333.

53. Samuel Omelvany seems to have lived in South Carolina and perhaps Kentucky before coming to Illinois. Reynolds, *Pioneer History of Illinois*, 385–386, 389–390; and Bateman and Selby, *Historical Encyclopedia of Illinois*, I, 409. William McFatridge came by way of North Carolina and Tennessee. Elihu B. Washburne, *Sketch of Edward Coles* (Chicago, 1882), 84–85; *The Biographical Review of Johnson, Massac, Pope, and Hardin Counties* (Chicago, 1893), 380; *Journal of the House of Representatives, Illinois, 3 general assembly, 1 sess., 1822* (Vandalia, Ill., 1823), 268–269; and Chapman, *Johnson County, Illinois*, 151.

54. James Hall, Jr., should not be confused with Judge James Hall, the author, who did not come to Illinois until 1820. Little is known about the member of the convention. *History of Jackson County, Illinois* (Philadelphia, 1878), 33–36; Norton, *Illinois Census Returns, 1810, 1818*, p. 106; Norton, *Illinois Census Returns, 1820*, p. 100. The other Tennessean was Andrew Bankson. See Bateman and Selby, *Historical Encyclopedia of Illinois*, I, 35.

55. The Kentuckians were Willis Hargrave, William McHenry, Edward N. Cullom, Abraham Prickett, and Thomas Roberts. Hargrave was identified with the salt industry in which slaves were used and in 1823 was very active in the proslavery cause. See Washburne, *Edward Coles*,

165–166; Evarts B. Greene and Clarence W. Alvord (eds.), *The Governors' Letter Books, 1818–1834*, Illinois State Historical Library *Collections*, IV (1909), 13, note 2. For McHenry see Bateman and Selby, *Historical Encyclopedia of Illinois*, I, 364; and *History of White County, Illinois* (Chicago, 1883), 221–222. For Cullom see William H. Perrin (ed.), *History of Crawford and Clark Counties, Illinois* (Chicago, 1883), 32 *et passim*. For Prickett see Bateman and Selby, *Historical Encyclopedia of Illinois*, I, 433, and Norton, *History of Madison County*, I, 163, 442. For Roberts see *An Illustrated Historical Atlas Map of Randolph County, Illinois* (Philadelphia, 1875), 54, and *Combined History of Randolph, Monroe and Perry Counties*, 69.

56. Edwardsville, Ill., *Spectator*, March 9, 1824; Reynolds, *Pioneer History of Illinois*, 411–413; Bateman and Selby, *Historical Encyclopedia of Illinois*, I, 332–333, for James Lemen, Jr., whose father was born of Irish parents near Harper's Ferry. Enoch Moore was the son of one of Clark's soldiers who was born in Maryland and who led a company of immigrants from Virginia to Illinois. See Reynolds, *Pioneer History of Illinois*, 113–114; Bateman and Selby, *Historical Encyclopedia of Illinois*, I, 382–383.

57. They were William Echols, Hamlet Ferguson, Seth Gard, Adolphus Hubbard, John K. Mangham, Samuel G. Morse, Leonard White, and John Whiteaker. Seth Gard may have come from Hamilton County, Ohio. See *History of Edwards, Lawrence and Wabash Counties, Illinois*, 82.

58. See *ante*, note 49.

59. Letter of Ninian Edwards, Jan. 18, 1818, and another without date but written about the same time, in Chicago Historical Society Manuscripts, 49: 235 and 51: 484. See also Buck, *Illinois in 1818*, p. 263.

60. The "Journal of the Convention" is printed in the Illinois State Historical Society *Journal*, VI (1913), 355–424. It contains the names of the members, the officials, the committees, their reports, the motions made, the actions taken and the recorded roll calls. It does not contain the speeches or debates.

61. This group probably included White, Ferguson, Hargrave, Stephenson, Messinger, Will, Omelvany, Prickett, McHenry, Roberts, Kitchell, Morse, and Hubbard. The appointments were recorded in Edmund J. James (ed.), *The Territorial Records of Illinois*, in Illinois State Historical Library *Publications* (43 vols., Springfield, Ill., 1899–1937), III (1901), and in Carter, *Territorial Papers of the United States*, XVII, *The Territory of Illinois, 1814–1818* (1950), 617–672.

62. This group included Thomas, Kane, Jones, Cairns, Kirkpatrick, McFatridge, Whiteaker, West, Compton, Cullom, Gard, Lemen, Hall, and Echols.

63. The middle group included Moore, Bankson, Harrison, Borough, and Fisher.

64. "Journal of the Convention," in Illinois State Historical Society *Journal*, VI, 359–360.

65. *Ibid.*, VI, 380. The ages were added by the convention, see 392. This draft was taken from the Ohio constitution.

66. *Ibid.*, VI, 400–401.

67. *Ibid.*, VI, 406–407, and 411.

The location of the capital caused considerable difference of opinion in the convention, although the subject might have been omitted altogether. Several proposals were made and rejected on August 20. Among these were schemes of land speculators and other proposals meant to avoid the tendency toward speculation. On the succeeding day one of the non-speculative proposals was renewed and adopted by a recorded roll call, the Edwards group generally voting against it and their opponents almost unanimously favoring it. On third reading a motion to refer the subject to the state legislature was supported by the Edwards group but was defeated by their opponents. With a further change in the previously adopted provision which seemed to satisfy a few of the Edwards men, it was approved by the last recorded vote in the convention. The record seems to indicate that some of the Edwards delegates attempted to establish a speculative venture, which was defeated by their opponents. *Ibid.*, VI, 407–409, 416–417, 423–424; and Buck, *Illinois in 1818*, pp. 286–292.

68. A photostat copy of the Illinois Constitution of 1818 was secured from the Department of Archives, Springfield, Illinois.

CHAPTER 14. THE DEMOCRACY OF THE VALLEY

1. *Ninth Census of the United States, 1870, Statistics of Population*, 31–33.

2. *Ibid.*, 61–63.

3. Turner, *Frontier in American History*, 1–38. See also Frederick J. Turner, "Problems in American History," as reprinted in *The Early Writings of Frederick Jackson Turner* (Madison, Wis., 1938), 71–83, see 83.

4. Turner, *Frontier in American History*, 2–4.

5. Turner, "The Old West," in *ibid.*, 67–125; see 98 ff.

6. Ambler, *Sectionalism in Virginia from 1776 to 1861;* Orin G. Libby, "Geographical Distribution of the Vote of the Thirteen States on the Federal Constitution, 1787–8," in *Bulletin* of the University of Wisconsin, Economics, Political Science, and History Series (2 vols., Madison, Wis.,

1894–1899), I, 1–116; and Schaper, "Sectionalism and Representation in South Carolina," in the American Historical Association *Annual Report for the Year 1900*, I, 237–463. The works of John S. Bassett and others which were cited *ante,* chapter I, are in general agreement with Turner. Ambler was studying with Turner when he was writing "The Old West."

7. Abernethy, *Three Virginia Frontiers*, 58–60.

8. Wertenbaker, *The Old South*, 6, 123, 164–219.

9. Frederick J. Turner, "Western State-making in the Revolutionary Era," in *The Significance of Sections in American History*, 86–138. Note particularly 88 and 135. This article originally appeared in the *American Historical Review*, I, 70–87, 251–269.

10. Abernethy's views are found in *From Frontier to Plantation*, 64–90, *et passim; Western Lands and the American Revolution*, 175–179, 244–246.

11. Turner, *Frontier in American History*, 183.

12. Turner, "The Ohio Valley in American History," in *Frontier in American History*, 157–176. See 165 for the quotation.

13. Ulrich B. Phillips (ed.), *Plantation and Frontier, 1649–1863* (2 vols., Cleveland, 1909), I, 70–71.

14. *Ibid.*, 73.

15. Avery O. Craven, "The 'Turner Theories' and the South," in the *Journal of Southern History*, V (1939), 291–314.

16. See note 11 *ante* and his presidential address before the Southern Historical Association, "Democracy and the Southern Frontier," in *Journal of Southern History*, IV, 3–13.

17. Turner, "The Problem of the West," in *Frontier in American History*, 205–221. See 205–206, and 216 for the quotations.

18. Turner, "Contributions of the West to American Democracy," in *Frontier in American History*, 243–268. See 243 and 266 for the quotations.

19. Turner, "The West and American Ideals," in *ibid.*, 290–310. See 293 for the quotation.

20. Benjamin F. Wright, "American Democracy and the Frontier," in the *Yale Review* (N.S., New Haven, Conn., 1911–   ), XX (1930), 349–365; "Political Institutions and the Frontier," in *Sources of Culture in the Middle West* (ed. by Dixon R. Fox, New York, c. 1934), 15–38; and his review of *The Significance of Sections in American History* in the *New England Quarterly* (Portland, Me., 1928–   ), VI (1933), 630–634.

21. George W. Pierson, "The Frontier and Frontiersmen of Turner's Essays," in the *Pennsylvania Magazine of History and Biography* (Philadelphia, 1877–   ), LXIV (1940), 449–478.

22. Frederic L. Paxson, "A Generation of the Frontier Hypothesis, 1893–1932," in the *Pacific Historical Review* (Glendale, Calif., 1932–   ), II (1933), 34–51, see 51.

23. Carl Becker, "Frederick Jackson Turner," in Howard W. Odum

(ed.), *American Masters of Social Science* (New York, c. 1927), 273–318; Merle E. Curti, "The Section and the Frontier in American History: The Methodological Concepts of Frederick Jackson Turner," in Stuart A. Rice (ed.), *Methods in Social Science* (Chicago, c. 1931), 353–367; John D. Hicks, "The Development of Civilization in the Middle West, 1860–1900," in Fox (ed.), *Sources of Culture in the Middle West*, 73–101; and Joseph Schafer, "Turner's Frontier Philosophy," in *Wisconsin Magazine of History* (Madison, Wis., 1917–   ), XVI (1933), 451–469, and "Turner's America," in *ibid.*, XVII (1934), 447–465. Schafer's writings on the "Safety Valve Theory" are omitted.

24. Thomas J. Wertenbaker, "The Molding of the Middle West," in *American Historical Review*, LIII (1947–1948), 223–234, see 228.

Index

Abernethy, Thomas, P. 46, 226–30;
  Three Virginia Frontiers, 226
Adams County, Ohio, 147, 148, 153
Allegheny Front, 5, 20, 26, 27, 48
Allegheny Mountains, *see* Appalachian
  Mountains
Allegheny River, 202
Ambler, Charles H., 226
American Revolution, 7, 9, 10, 14, 28,
  34, 35, 37–38, 42, 48–49, 52, 58, 65,
  88, 92, 95, 106, 113, 124, 128, 143,
  163, 213, 216, 219
Anderson, Joseph, 113–16
Anglican or Episcopal Church, Angli-
  cans, 5, 7, 11, 14, 95, 217
anti-Edwards group, 208–11
anti-slavery, 104, 189, 204, 207, 211;
  see also slavery
Appalachian Mountains and region,
  4–9, 20, 32, 34, 48, 55–56, 64–65, 67–
  68, 83, 159, 219, 228; *see also* Piedmont, Appalachian Valley, Appalachian Plateau, and Blue Ridge
  Mountains
Appalachian Plateau, 5, 20
Appalachian Valley, or Great Valley,
  5, 7, 20, 22, 26, 32, 43, 77, 120, 141,
  185, 207, 217, 225, 227; *see also*
  Hagerstown Valley, Shenandoah Valley, and Valley of Virginia
aristocracy, aristocrats, 4–5, 9, 10–11,
  14–15, 19, 63–67, 81–82, 84, 86–87,
  90, 137, 166–68, 174, 200, 202, 204,
  217, 219, 220, 226–28, 233–34
Armstrong, John, 130

Article VI, Northwest Ordinance, 106,
  135–36, 133, 169–71, 194, 200, 204–05;
  see also Northwest Ordinance
Asbury, Francis, 22–24
Avery's Trace, 42

back country, 10, 104, 217, 219; *see
  also* Upland South and Piedmont
Badollet, John, 186
Baldwin, Michael, 149–51, 153
ballot, voting by, 84, 88, 117–18, 149,
  193
Baptist Church, or Baptists, 8, 93
Beard, John, 109
Becker, Carl, 232
Belmont County, Ohio, 150–51
Bennehed, John, 186, 188
bicameral legislature, 89, 96, 98, 118
bill of rights, 11, 13, 62, 82–84, 86–
  89, 95–96, 99, 100, 117–18, 133, 155,
  159, 191, 212; *see also* civil rights
Blount group, 112–18
Blount, William, 106–11, 113–14
Blue Ridge Mountains, 5–7, 20, 22–25,
  33, 61, 228, 234
Bond, Shadrach, 198–99
Boone, Daniel, 22, 27, 37, 51; *see also*
  Wilderness Trace
Boonesboro, Kentucky, 29, 35, 41, 94
Braddock, Edward, 25–26, 202
Braddock's Road, 25–28, 33–34, 43, 165
Bradford, John, *Notes on Kentucky*, 70
Breckinridge, Robert, 95
Bright's Trace, 22–23
Brodhead, Daniel, 30, 38

329

D&T 10.508